CONTENTS

beginner puzzles
#1 - #59
Page 1

intermediate puzzles
#60 - #120
Page 61

advanced puzzles
#121 - #178
Page 123

answers
Page 182

state capitals

animals

JUMBLE®

BrainBusters Junior II

Smart Entertainment for Smart Kids!

outer space

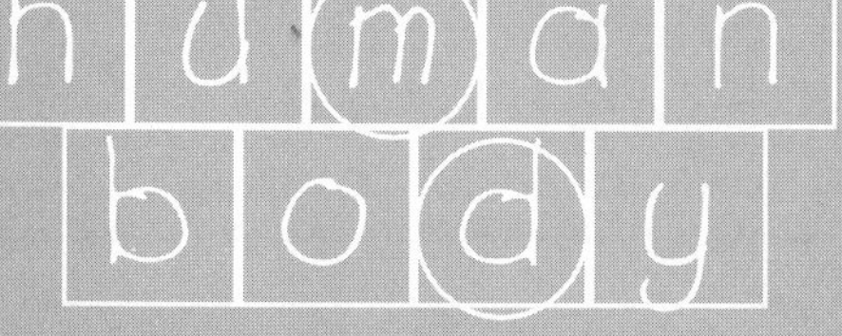

David L. Hoyt
and
Russell L. Hoyt

money

This book is available in quantity at special discounts
for your group or organization.

For further information, contact:

Triumph Books
601 South LaSalle Street
Suite 500
Chicago, Illinois 60605
(312) 939-3330
FAX (312) 663-3557

ISBN 1-57243-425-2

Printed in the United States of America

state capitals

animals

JUMBLE® BrainBusters Junior II

BEGINNER PUZZLES

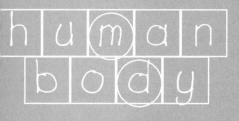

human body

outer space

sports

money

PUZZLE

1

ANIMALS

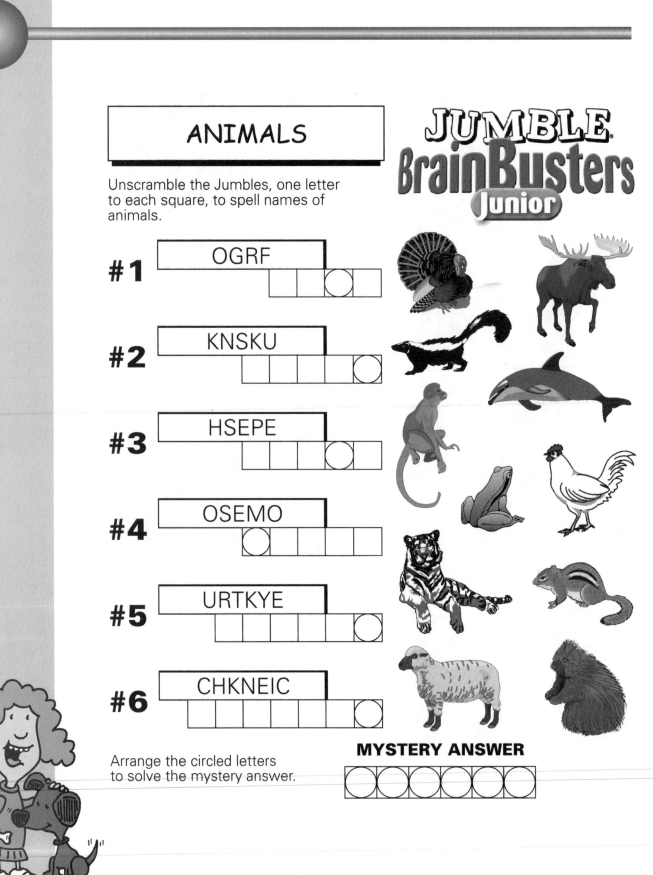

JUMBLE® BrainBusters Junior

Unscramble the Jumbles, one letter to each square, to spell names of animals.

#1 OGRF

#2 KNSKU

#3 HSEPE

#4 OSEMO

#5 URTKYE

#6 CHKNEIC

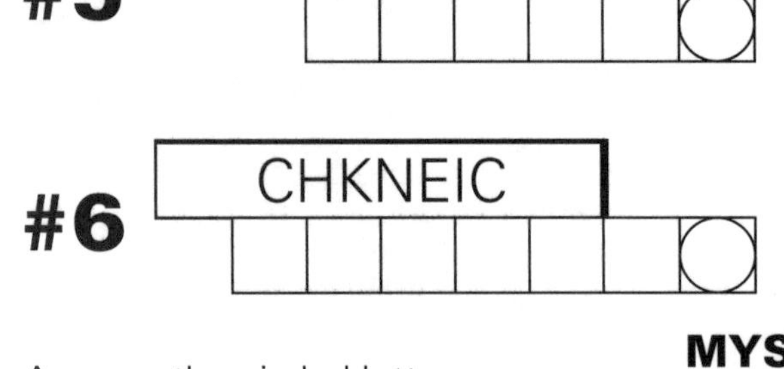

MYSTERY ANSWER

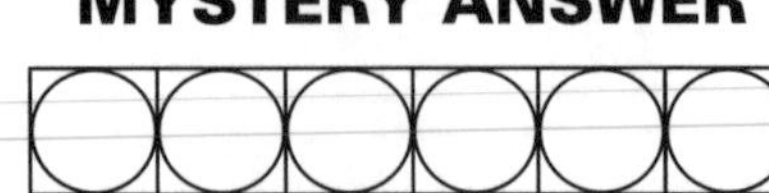

Arrange the circled letters to solve the mystery answer.

U.S. STATE CAPITALS

Unscramble the Jumbles, one letter to each square, to spell names of U.S. state capitals.

#1

#2

#3
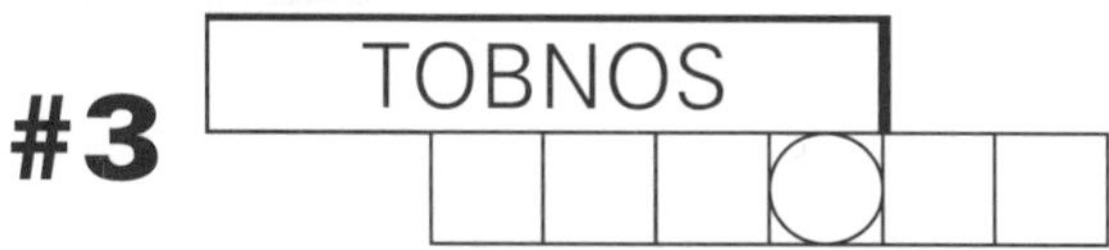

#4

#5

#6

Montgomery
Juneau
Phoenix
Little Rock
Sacramento
Denver
Hartford
Dover
Tallahassee
Atlanta
Honolulu
Boise
Springfield
Indianapolis
Des Moines
Topeka
Frankfort

Baton Rouge
Augusta
Annapolis
Boston
Lansing
St. Paul
Jackson
Jefferson City
Helena
Lincoln
Carson City
Concord
Trenton
Santa Fe
Albany
Raleigh
Bismarck

Columbus
Oklahoma City
Salem
Harrisburg
Providence
Columbia
Pierre
Nashville
Austin
Salt Lake City
Montpelier
Richmond
Olympia
Charleston
Madison
Cheyenne

Arrange the circled letters to solve the mystery answer.

MYSTERY ANSWER

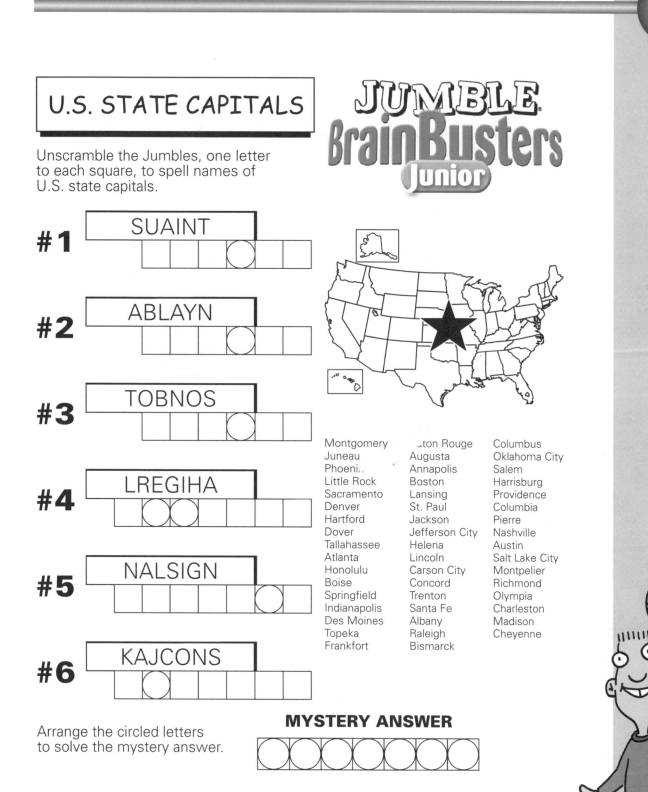

PUZZLE 3

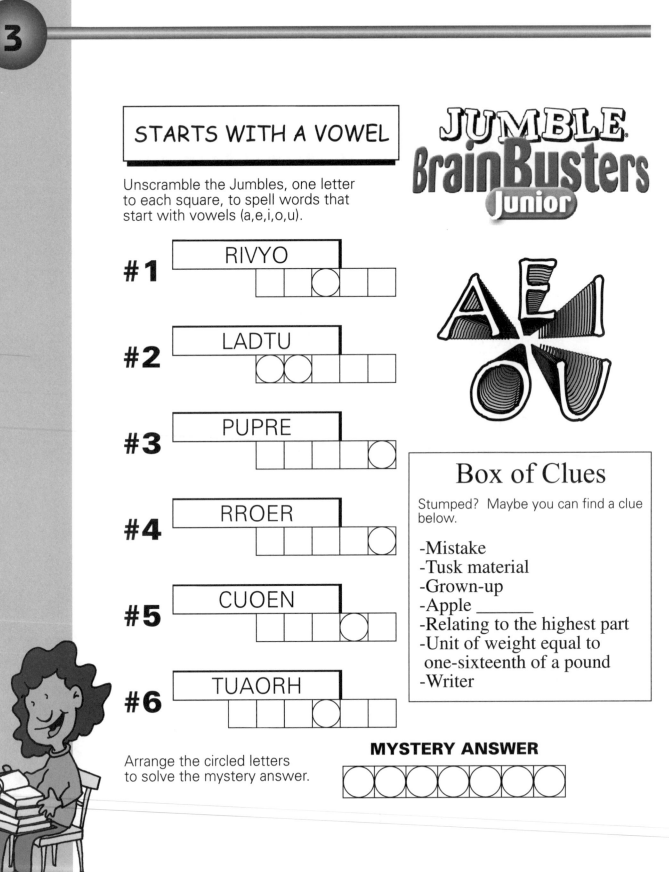

STARTS WITH A VOWEL

Unscramble the Jumbles, one letter to each square, to spell words that start with vowels (a,e,i,o,u).

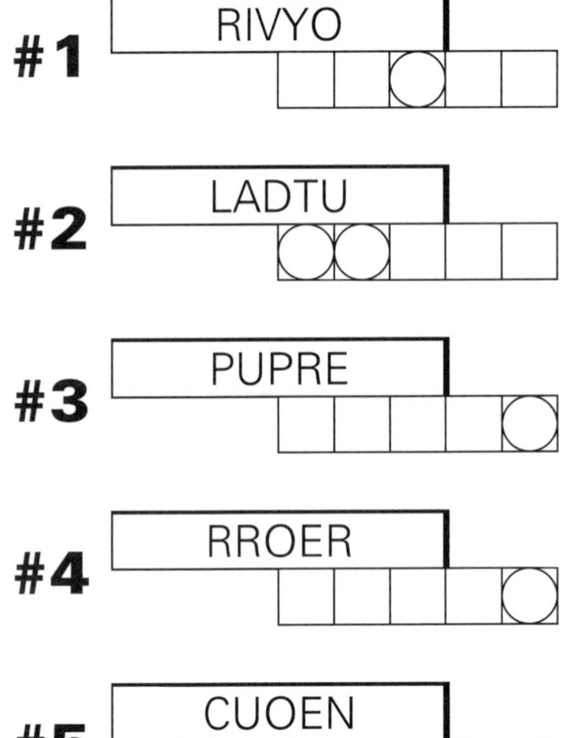

Box of Clues

Stumped? Maybe you can find a clue below.

-Mistake
-Tusk material
-Grown-up
-Apple _______
-Relating to the highest part
-Unit of weight equal to one-sixteenth of a pound
-Writer

Arrange the circled letters to solve the mystery answer.

MYSTERY ANSWER

U.S. PRESIDENTS

JUMBLE® BrainBusters Junior

Unscramble the Jumbles, one letter to each square, to spell last names of U.S. presidents.

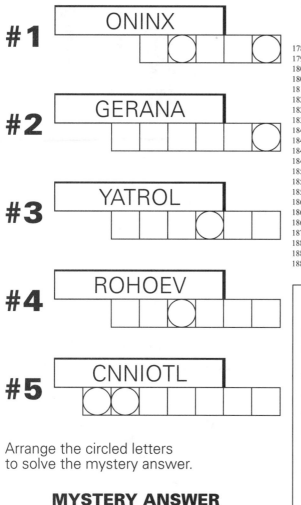

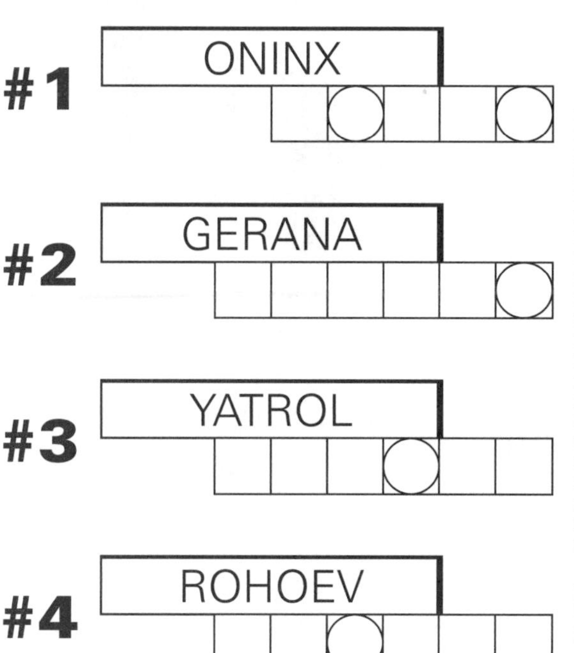

#5 CNNIOTL

Arrange the circled letters to solve the mystery answer.

MYSTERY ANSWER

PRESIDENTS OF THE
UNITED STATES OF AMERICA

1789-1797 George Washington
1797-1801 John Adams
1801-1809 Thomas Jefferson
1809-1817 James Madison
1817-1825 James Monroe
1825-1829 John Quincy Adams
1829-1837 Andrew Jackson
1837-1841 Martin Van Buren
1841 William Henry Harrison
1841-1845 John Tyler
1845-1849 James Polk
1849-1850 Zachary Taylor
1850-1853 Millard Fillmore
1853-1857 Franklin Pierce
1857-1861 James Buchanan
1861-1865 Abraham Lincoln
1865-1869 Andrew Johnson
1869-1877 Ulysses S. Grant
1877-1881 Rutherford B. Hayes
1881 James A. Garfield
1881-1885 Chester A. Arthur
1885-1889 Stephen Grover Cleveland
1889-1893 Benjamin Harrison
1893-1897 Grover Cleveland
1897-1901 William McKinley
1901-1909 Theodore (Teddy) Roosevelt
1909-1913 William Howard Taft
1913-1921 Thomas Woodrow Wilson
1921-1923 Warren G. Harding
1923-1929 John Calvin Coolidge
1929-1933 Herbert Hoover
1933-1945 Franklin D. Roosevelt
1945-1953 Harry S. Truman
1953-1961 Dwight David Eisenhower
1961-1963 John Fitzgerald Kennedy
1963-1969 Lyndon B. Johnson
1969-1974 Richard M. Nixon
1974-1977 Gerald R. Ford
1977-1981 James (Jimmy) Carter
1981-1989 Ronald Reagan
1989-1993 George W. Bush
1993-2001 William Jefferson Clinton
2001- George Walker Bush

Box of Clues

Stumped? Maybe you can find a clue below.

#1- 37th U.S. president
#2- Ronald ______
#3- 12th U.S. president
#4- President with a large dam named after him
#5- 42nd U.S. president

Mystery Answer:
Very tall U.S. president

PUZZLE

5

MAMMALS

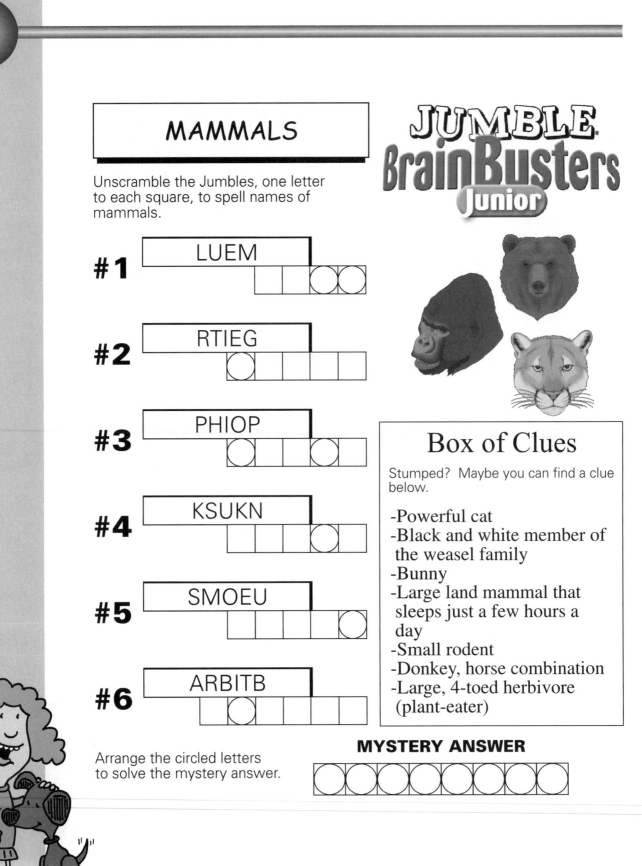

JUMBLE BrainBusters Junior

Unscramble the Jumbles, one letter to each square, to spell names of mammals.

#1
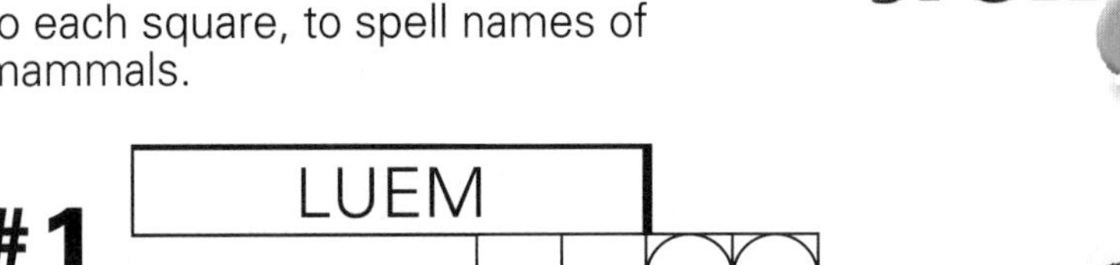

#2

#3

#4
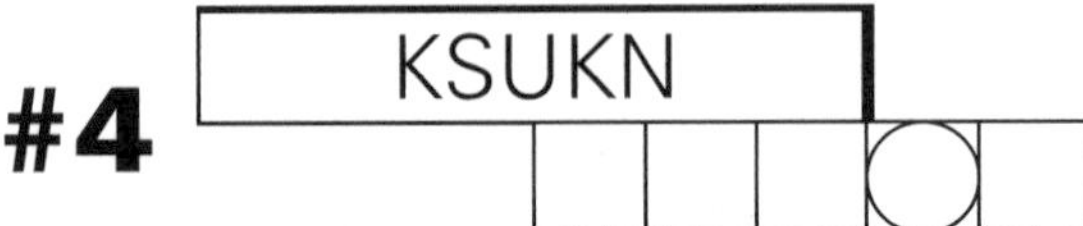

#5

#6
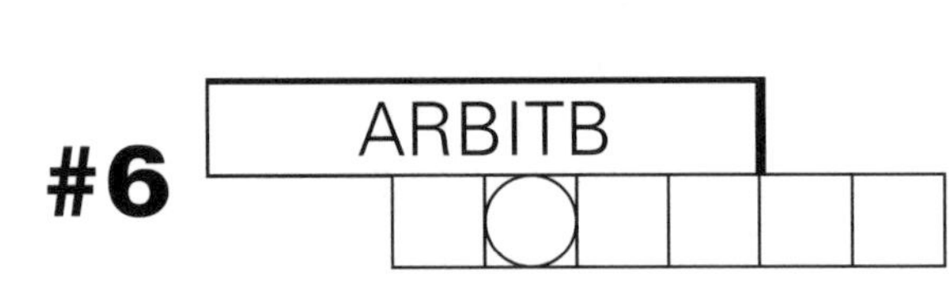

Box of Clues

Stumped? Maybe you can find a clue below.

-Powerful cat
-Black and white member of the weasel family
-Bunny
-Large land mammal that sleeps just a few hours a day
-Small rodent
-Donkey, horse combination
-Large, 4-toed herbivore (plant-eater)

Arrange the circled letters to solve the mystery answer.

MYSTERY ANSWER

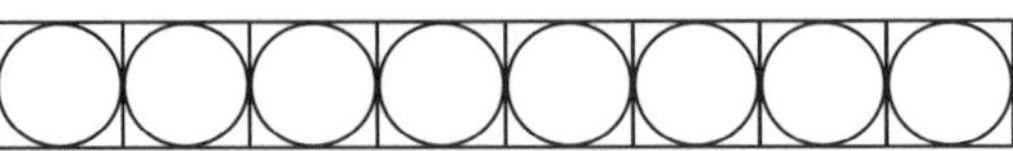

ADJECTIVES

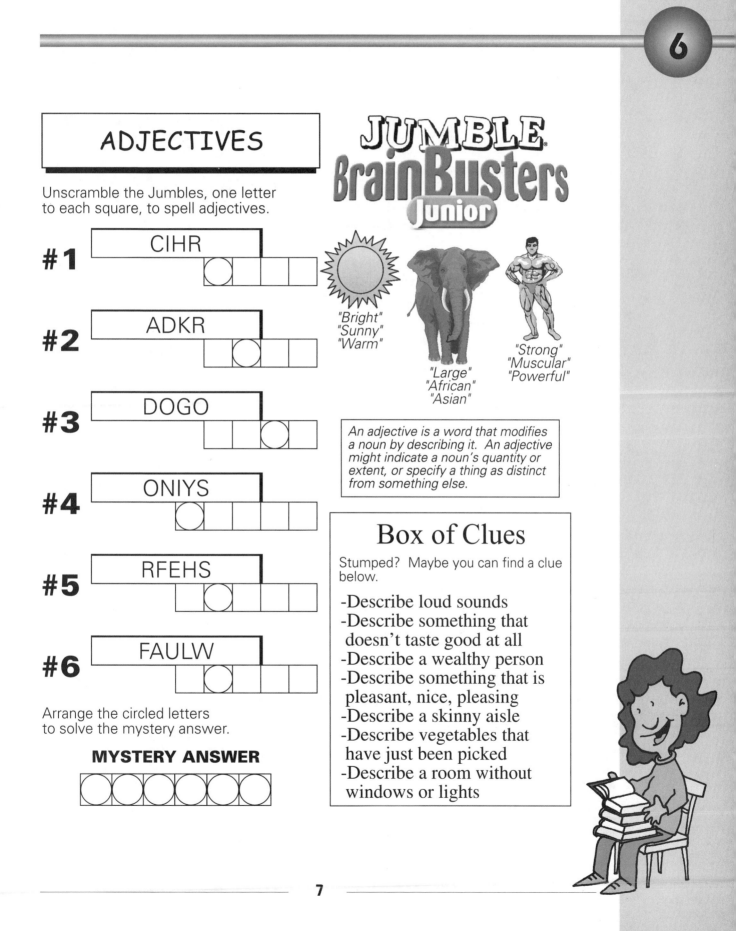

Unscramble the Jumbles, one letter to each square, to spell adjectives.

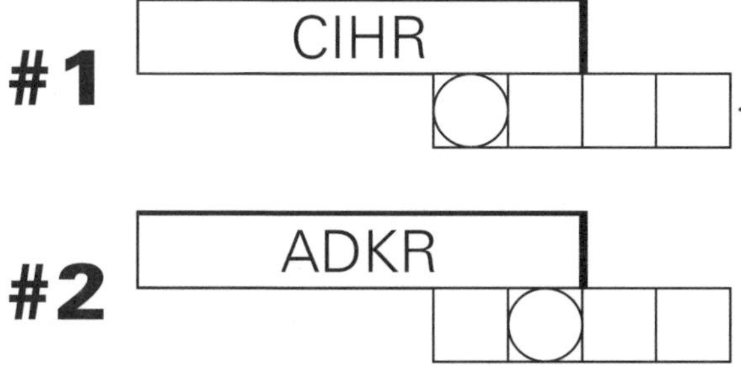

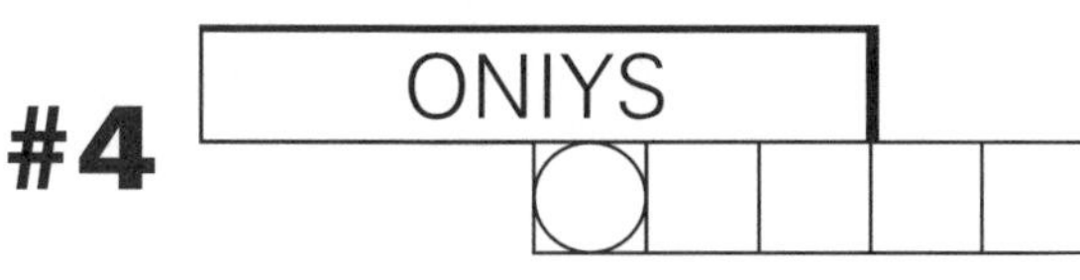

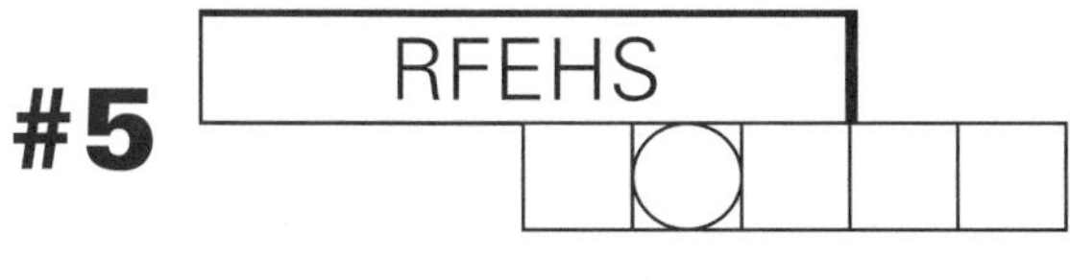

Arrange the circled letters to solve the mystery answer.

MYSTERY ANSWER

JUMBLE BrainBusters Junior

"Bright"
"Sunny"
"Warm"

"Large"
"African"
"Asian"

"Strong"
"Muscular"
"Powerful"

An adjective is a word that modifies a noun by describing it. An adjective might indicate a noun's quantity or extent, or specify a thing as distinct from something else.

Box of Clues

Stumped? Maybe you can find a clue below.

- -Describe loud sounds
- -Describe something that doesn't taste good at all
- -Describe a wealthy person
- -Describe something that is pleasant, nice, pleasing
- -Describe a skinny aisle
- -Describe vegetables that have just been picked
- -Describe a room without windows or lights

PUZZLE 7

MATH

JUMBLE BrainBusters Junior

Unscramble the Jumbled letters, one letter to each square, so that each equation is correct.

For example: NONTEOEOW
ONE + ONE = TWO

#1 EVFVIEIF

☐☐☐◯ + ◯☐☐☐ = TEN

#2 NEETNT

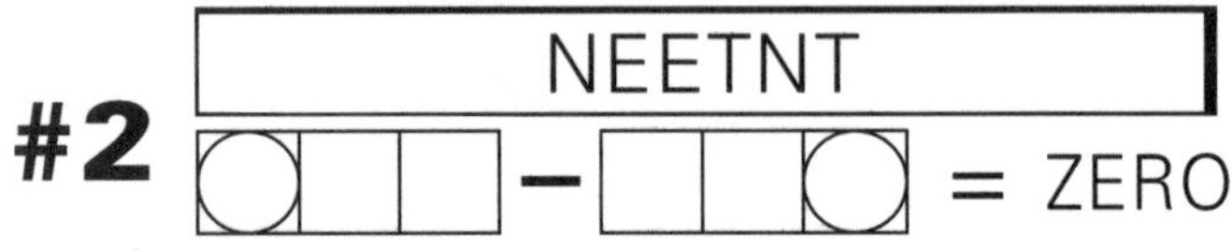

◯☐☐ − ☐☐◯ = ZERO

#3 TFUOORW

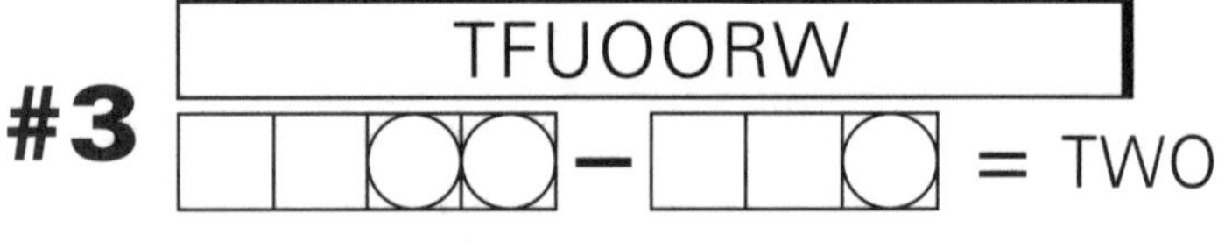

☐☐◯◯ − ☐☐◯ = TWO

#4 EEENNVOS

◯☐☐ + SIX = ☐◯☐◯☐

#5 TXREIEHS

☐◯◯☐☐ + THREE = ☐☐☐

Interesting Math Fact

In 1843, mathematician Ada Byron published the first computer programs, based on punch-cards.

Arrange the circled letters to solve the mystery equation.

MYSTERY EQUATION

◯◯◯ + ◯◯◯◯◯ = ◯◯◯◯

9×7=63

PUZZLE 8

COUNTRIES

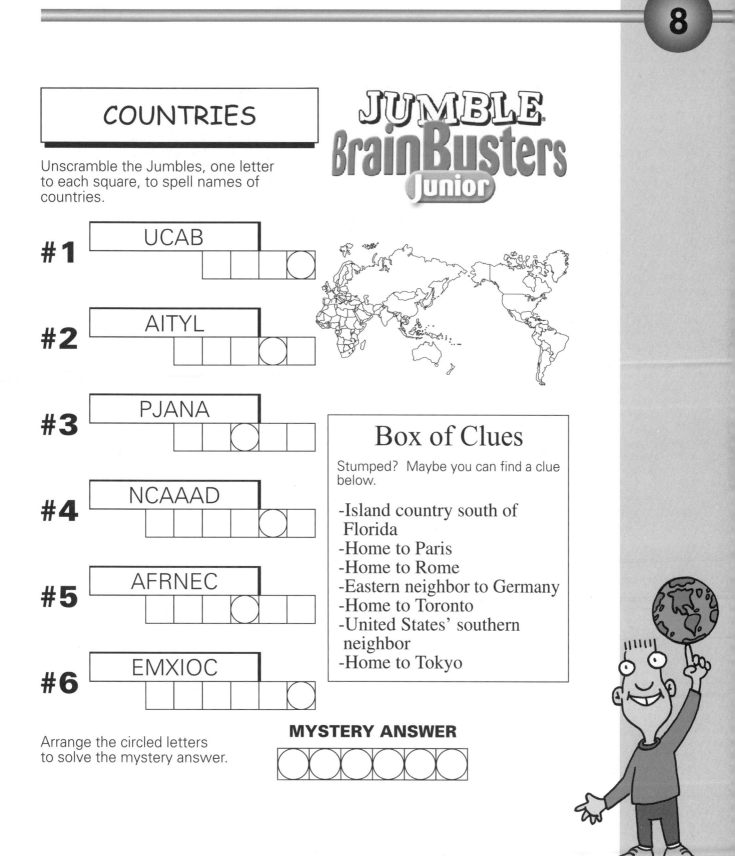

Unscramble the Jumbles, one letter to each square, to spell names of countries.

#1 UCAB

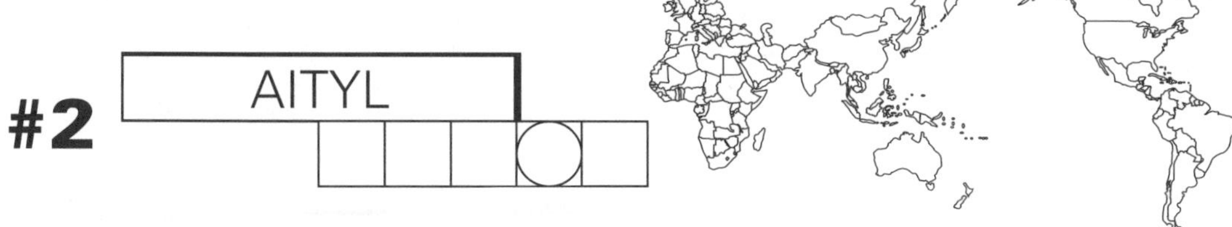

#2 AITYL

#3 PJANA

#4 NCAAAD

#5 AFRNEC

#6 EMXIOC

Box of Clues

Stumped? Maybe you can find a clue below.

- Island country south of Florida
- Home to Paris
- Home to Rome
- Eastern neighbor to Germany
- Home to Toronto
- United States' southern neighbor
- Home to Tokyo

Arrange the circled letters to solve the mystery answer.

MYSTERY ANSWER

PUZZLE 9

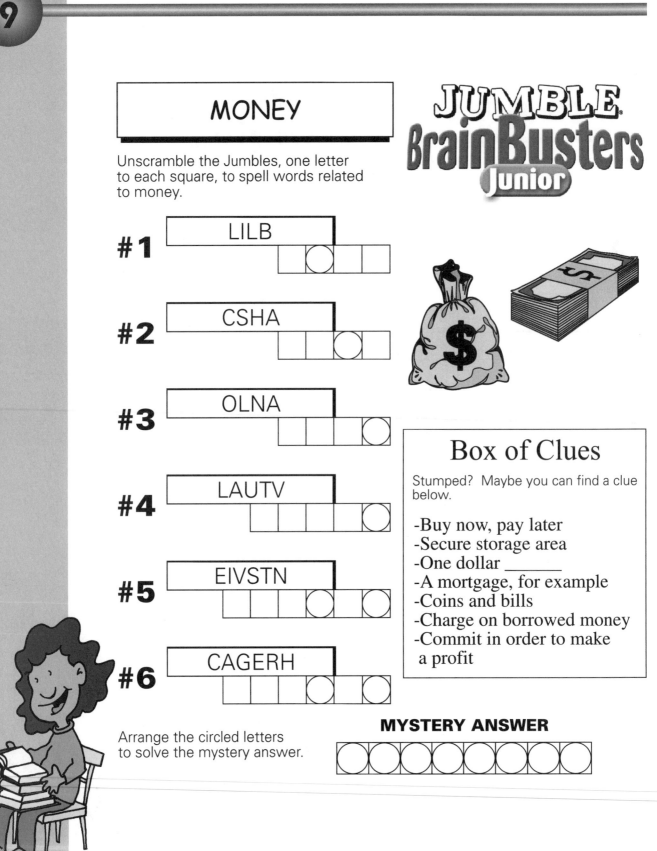

MONEY

Unscramble the Jumbles, one letter to each square, to spell words related to money.

#1

#2

#3
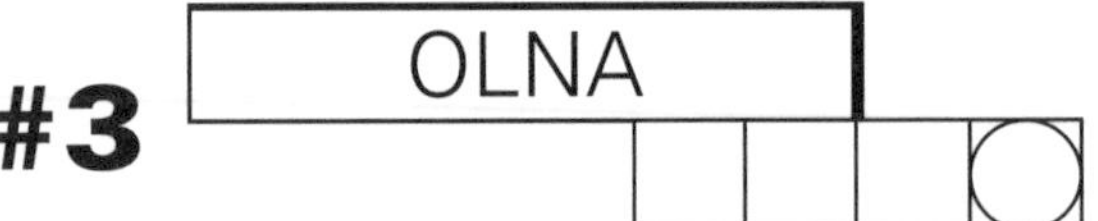

#4

#5

#6
CAGERH

Box of Clues

Stumped? Maybe you can find a clue below.

- -Buy now, pay later
- -Secure storage area
- -One dollar ______
- -A mortgage, for example
- -Coins and bills
- -Charge on borrowed money
- -Commit in order to make a profit

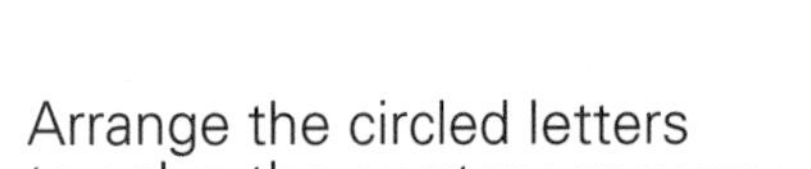

MYSTERY ANSWER

Arrange the circled letters to solve the mystery answer.

OUTER SPACE

Unscramble the Jumbles, one letter to each square, to spell words related to outer space.

#1 PUOTL

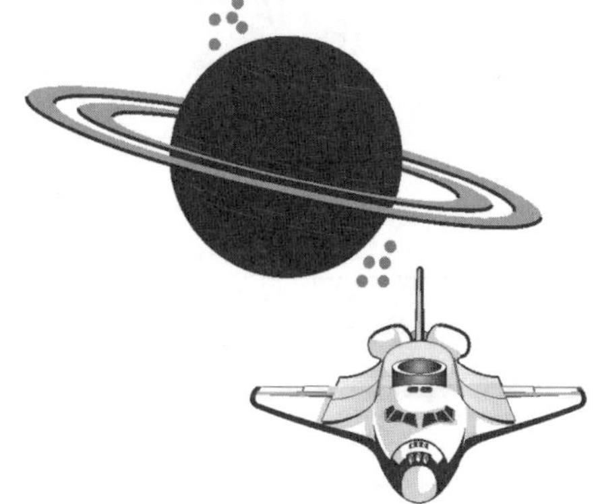

#2 TAUSRN

#3 SSYETM

#4 JEUPIRT

#5 REMCRUY

Box of Clues

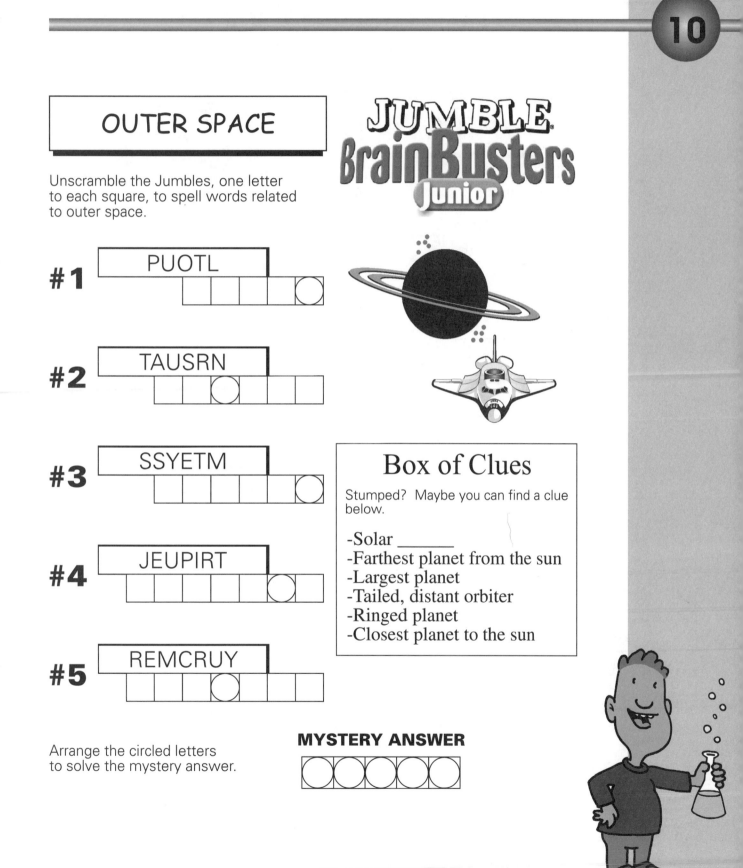

Stumped? Maybe you can find a clue below.

- -Solar ______
- -Farthest planet from the sun
- -Largest planet
- -Tailed, distant orbiter
- -Ringed planet
- -Closest planet to the sun

Arrange the circled letters to solve the mystery answer.

MYSTERY ANSWER

PUZZLE

11

RHYMING WORDS

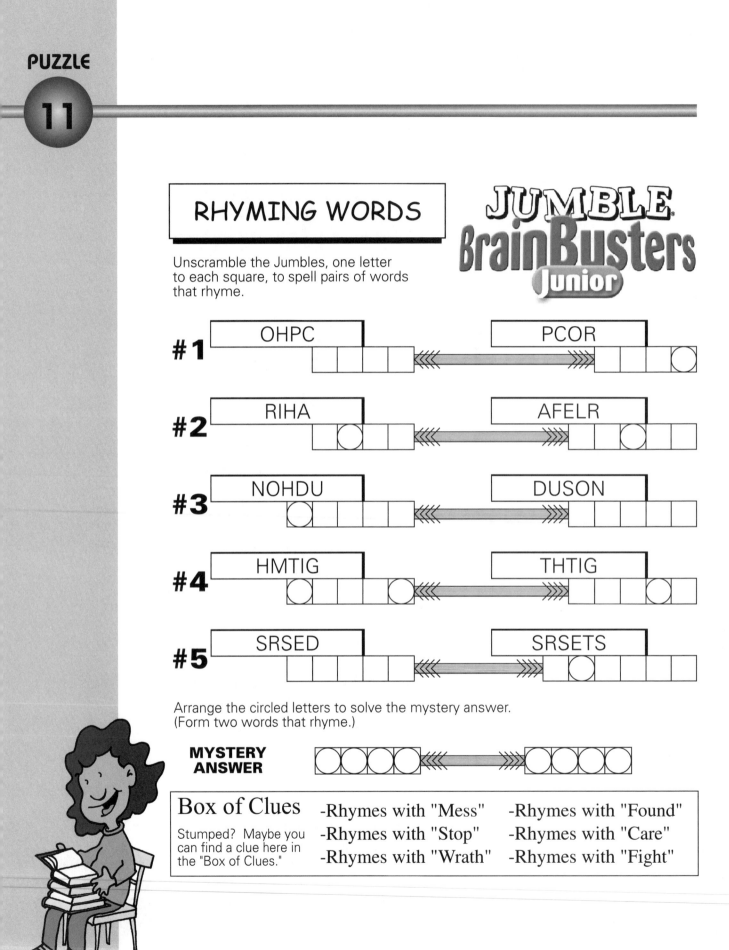

JUMBLE BrainBusters Junior

Unscramble the Jumbles, one letter to each square, to spell pairs of words that rhyme.

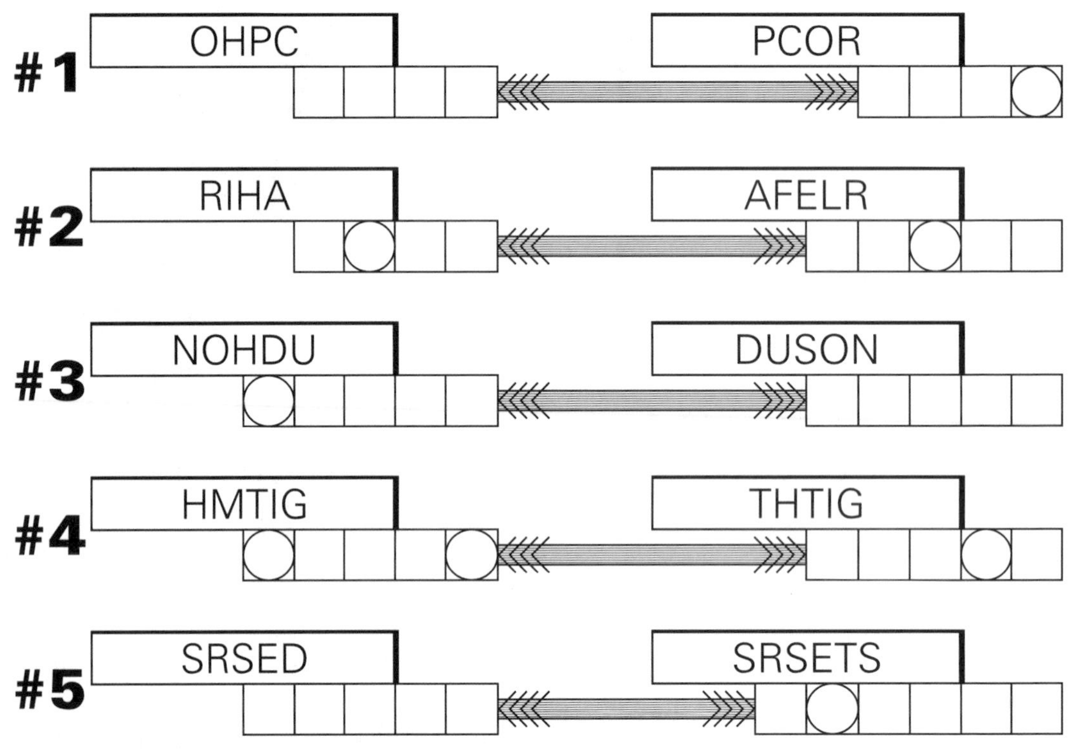

Arrange the circled letters to solve the mystery answer. (Form two words that rhyme.)

MYSTERY ANSWER

Box of Clues

Stumped? Maybe you can find a clue here in the "Box of Clues."

-Rhymes with "Mess"
-Rhymes with "Stop"
-Rhymes with "Wrath"
-Rhymes with "Found"
-Rhymes with "Care"
-Rhymes with "Fight"

U.S. STATE CAPITALS

Unscramble the Jumbles, one letter to each square, to spell names of U.S. state capitals.

#1 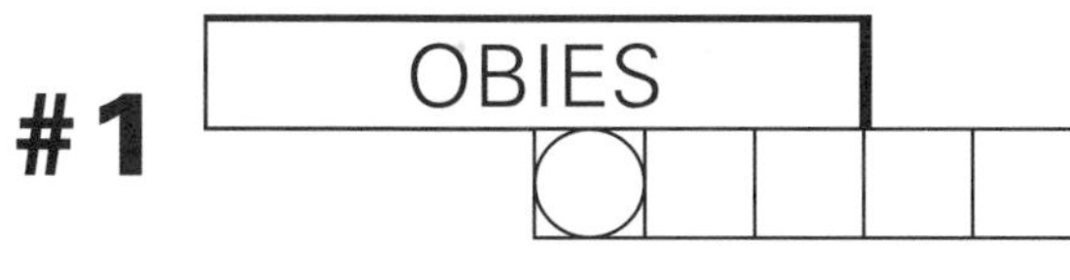

#2 

#3 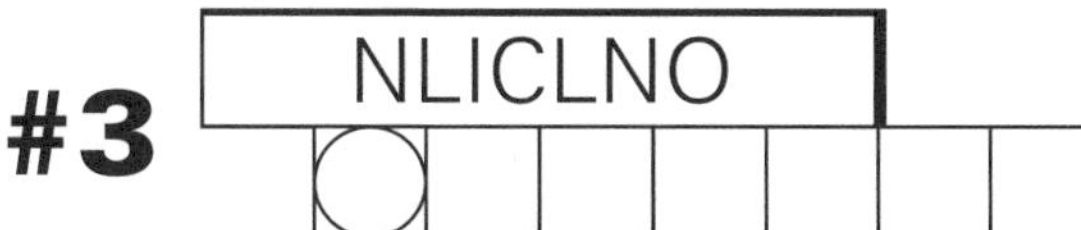

#4 

#5 

#6 

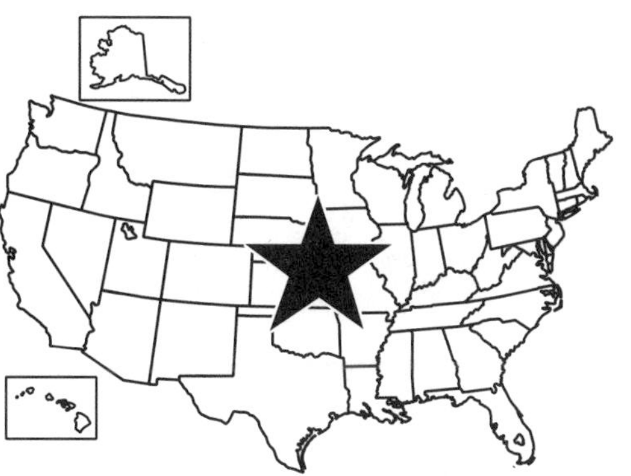

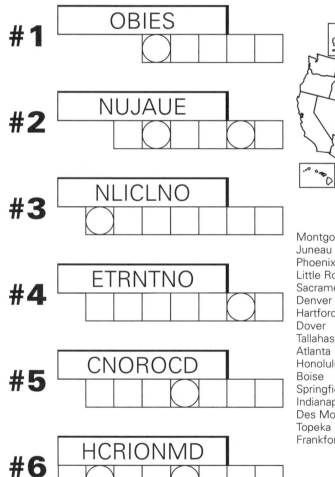

Montgomery
Juneau
Phoenix
Little Rock
Sacramento
Denver
Hartford
Dover
Tallahassee
Atlanta
Honolulu
Boise
Springfield
Indianapolis
Des Moines
Topeka
Frankfort
Baton Rouge
Augusta
Annapolis
Boston
Lansing
St. Paul
Jackson
Jefferson City
Helena
Lincoln
Carson City
Concord
Trenton
Santa Fe
Albany
Raleigh
Bismarck
Columbus
Oklahoma City
Salem
Harrisburg
Providence
Columbia
Pierre
Nashville
Austin
Salt Lake City
Montpelier
Richmond
Olympia
Charleston
Madison
Cheyenne

Arrange the circled letters to solve the mystery answer.

MYSTERY ANSWER

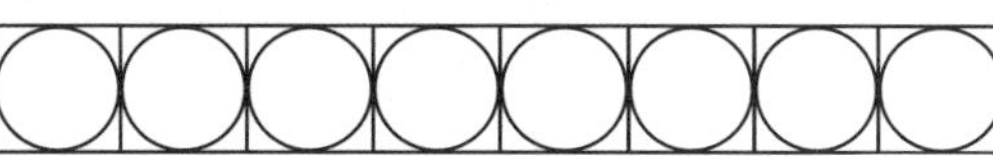

PUZZLE 13

TIME LINE

Unscramble the Jumbles, one letter to each square, to spell words as suggested by the time line.

#1 **1898** U.S. annexes ______

#1 HIWAIA

#2 **1920** ______ broadcasting begins

#2 ARIOD

#3 **1922** Formation of the ______ Union

#3 OSIEVT

#4 **1947** First supersonic ______

#4 HFITGL

#5 **1962** Missile crisis in ______

#5 UCAB

#6 **1990** Mandela released from prison in South ______

#6 FAICRA

Arrange the circled letters to solve the mystery answer.

1861 U.S. ______ ______ begins

MYSTERY ANSWER

COOKING

Unscramble the Jumbles, one letter to each square, to spell words related to cooking.

#1 

#2 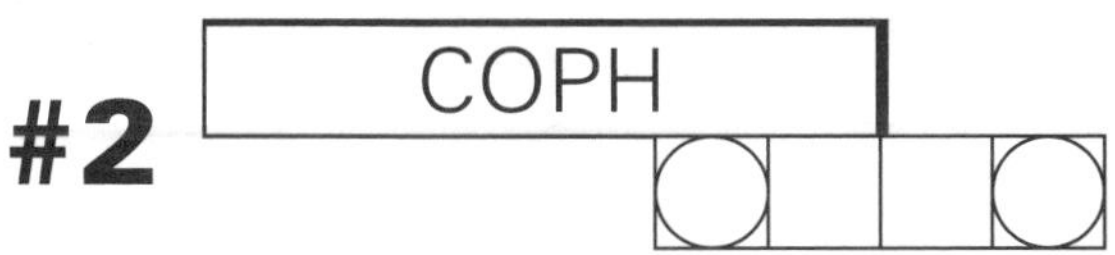

#3 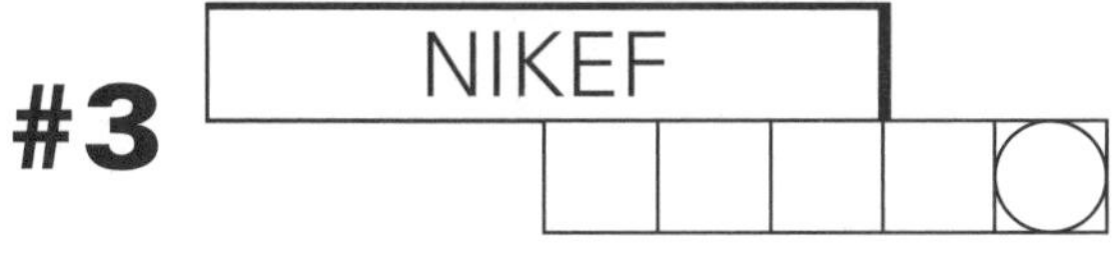

#4 

#5 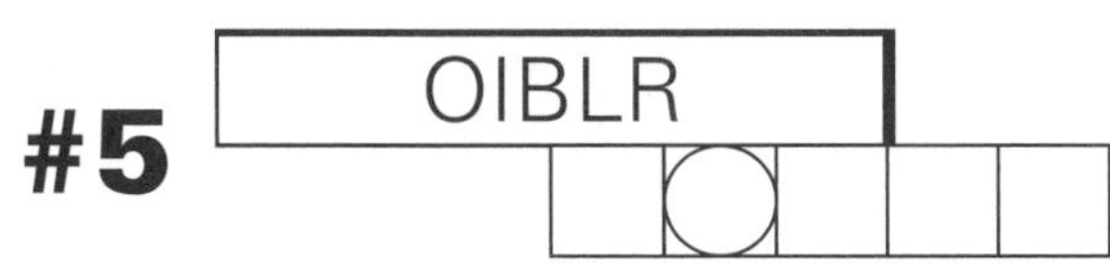

Box of Clues

Stumped? Maybe you can find a clue below.

-Cook over an open flame
-Cutting instrument
-Cook by direct heat
-Instructions
-Cut into small pieces, dice
-Cook, food preparer

Arrange the circled letters to solve the mystery answer.

MYSTERY ANSWER

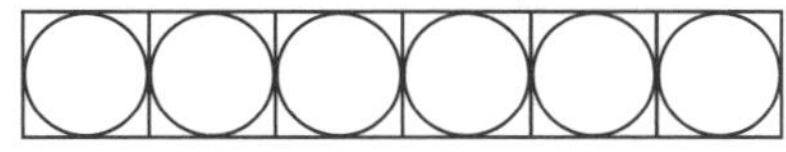

PUZZLE 15

ELEMENTS

JUMBLE BrainBusters Junior

Unscramble the Jumbles, one letter to each square, to spell names of elements.

#1 RINO

#2 OBONR

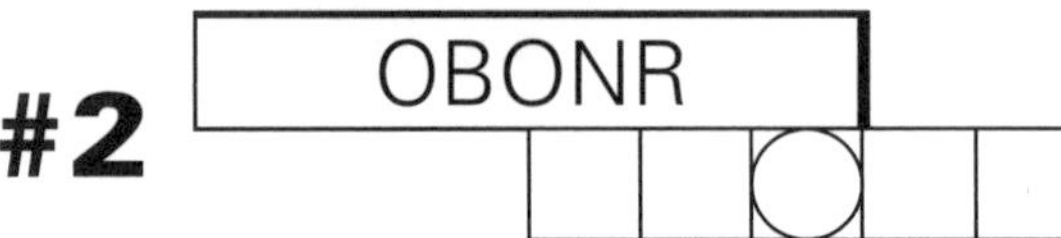

#3 LSUURF

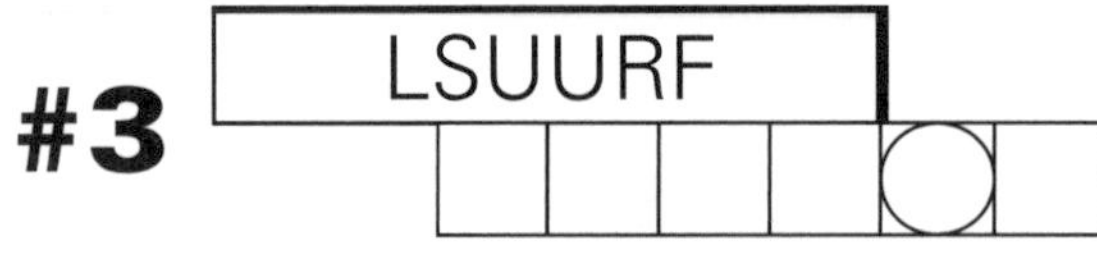

#4 CAICUML

#5 GYHDRENO

Arrange the circled letters to solve the mystery answer.

MYSTERY ANSWER

THE PERIODIC TABLE

Name
Actinium
Aluminum
Americium
Antimony
Argon
Arsenic
Astatine
Barium
Berkelium
Beryllium
Bismuth
Bohrium
Boron
Bromine
Cadmium
Calcium
Californium
Carbon
Cerium
Cesium
Chlorine
Chromium
Cobalt
Copper
Curium
Dubnium
Dysprosium
Einsteinium
Erbium
Europium
Fermium
Fluorine
Francium
Gadolinium
Gallium
Germanium
Gold
Hafnium
Hassium
Helium
Holmium
Hydrogen
Indium
Iodine
Iridium
Iron
Krypton
Lanthanum
Lawrencium
Lead
Lithium
Lutetium
Magnesium
Manganese
Meitnerium
Mendelevium
Mercury
Molybdenum
Neodymium
Neon
Neptunium
Nickel
Niobium
Nitrogen
Nobelium
Osmium
Oxygen
Palladium
Phosphorus
Platinum
Plutonium
Polonium
Potassium
Potassium
Praseodymium
Promethium
Protactinium
Radium
Radon
Rhenium
Rhodium
Rubidium
Ruthenium
Rutherfordium
Samarium
Scandium
Seaborgium
Selenium
Silicon
Silver
Sodium
Strontium
Sulfur
Tantalum
Technetium
Tellurium
Terbium
Thallium
Thorium
Thulium
Tin
Titanium
Tungsten
Uranium
Vanadium
Xenon
Ytterbium
Yttrium
Zinc
Zirconium

PUZZLE 16

SPORTS TEAMS

JUMBLE BrainBusters Junior

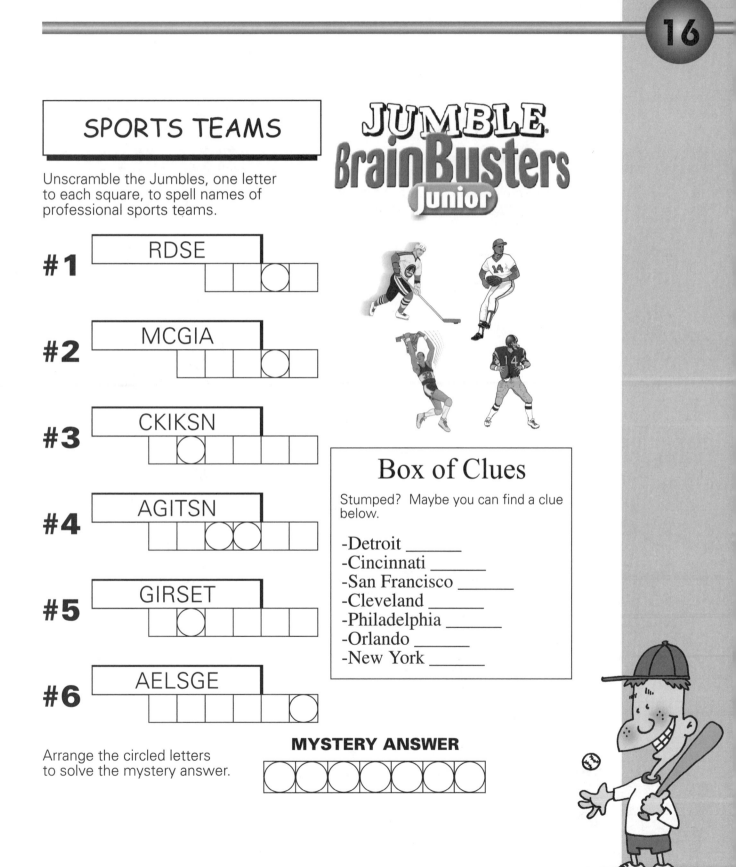

Unscramble the Jumbles, one letter to each square, to spell names of professional sports teams.

#1 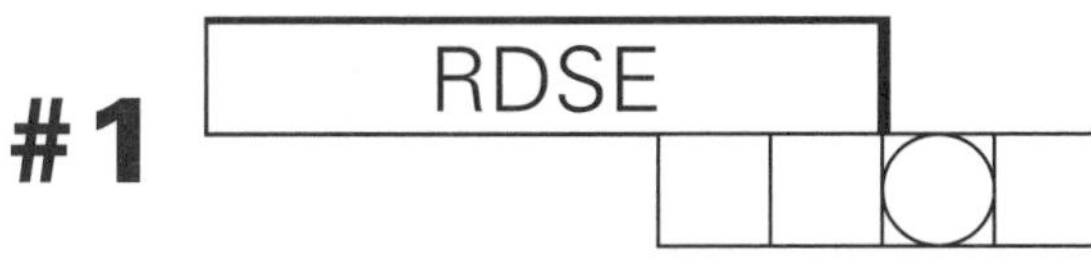

#2 

#3 

#4 

#5 

#6 

Box of Clues

Stumped? Maybe you can find a clue below.

-Detroit ______
-Cincinnati ______
-San Francisco ______
-Cleveland ______
-Philadelphia ______
-Orlando ______
-New York ______

Arrange the circled letters to solve the mystery answer.

MYSTERY ANSWER

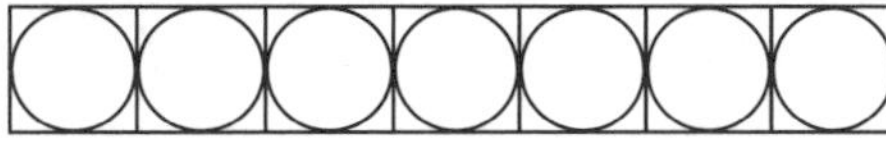

PUZZLE

17

PLANTS

Unscramble the Jumbles, one letter to each square, to spell words related to plants.

#1
#2

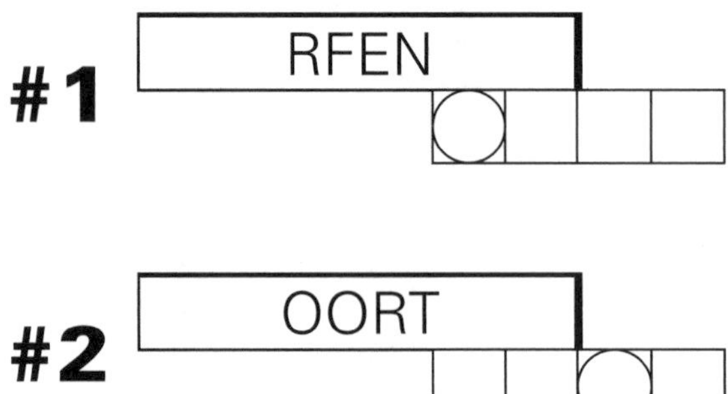

#3

#4

#5

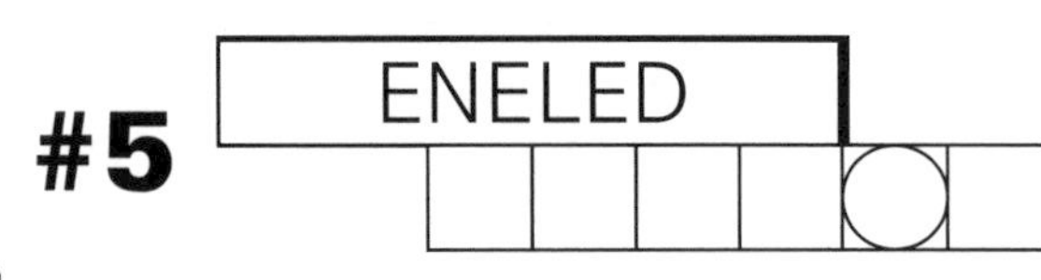

Box of Clues

Stumped? Maybe you can find a clue below.

-Important liquid for plants
-Main stem of a tree
-Vascular plant that reproduces with spores
-Colorful bloom
-Pine ______
-Underground plant support

Arrange the circled letters to solve the mystery answer.

MYSTERY ANSWER

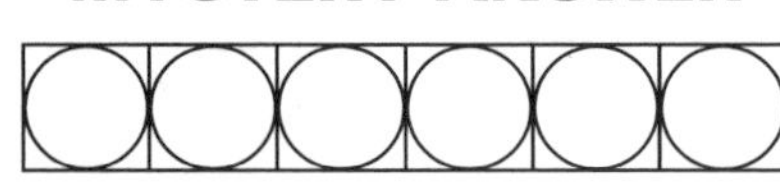

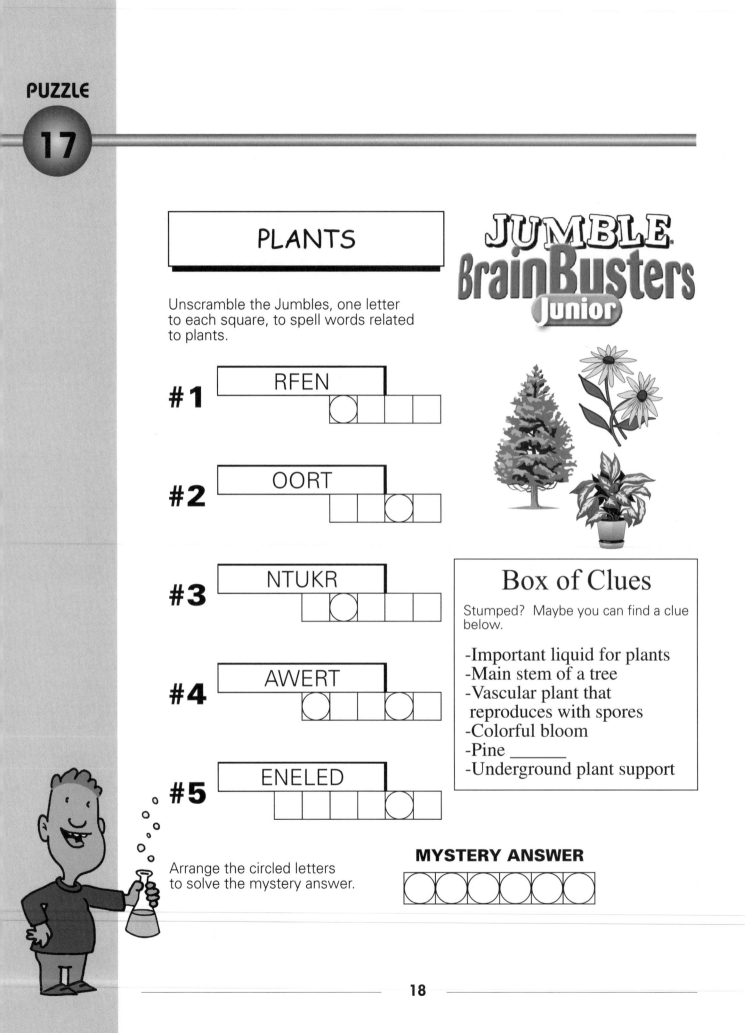

PUZZLE
18

COUNTRIES

JUMBLE BrainBusters Junior

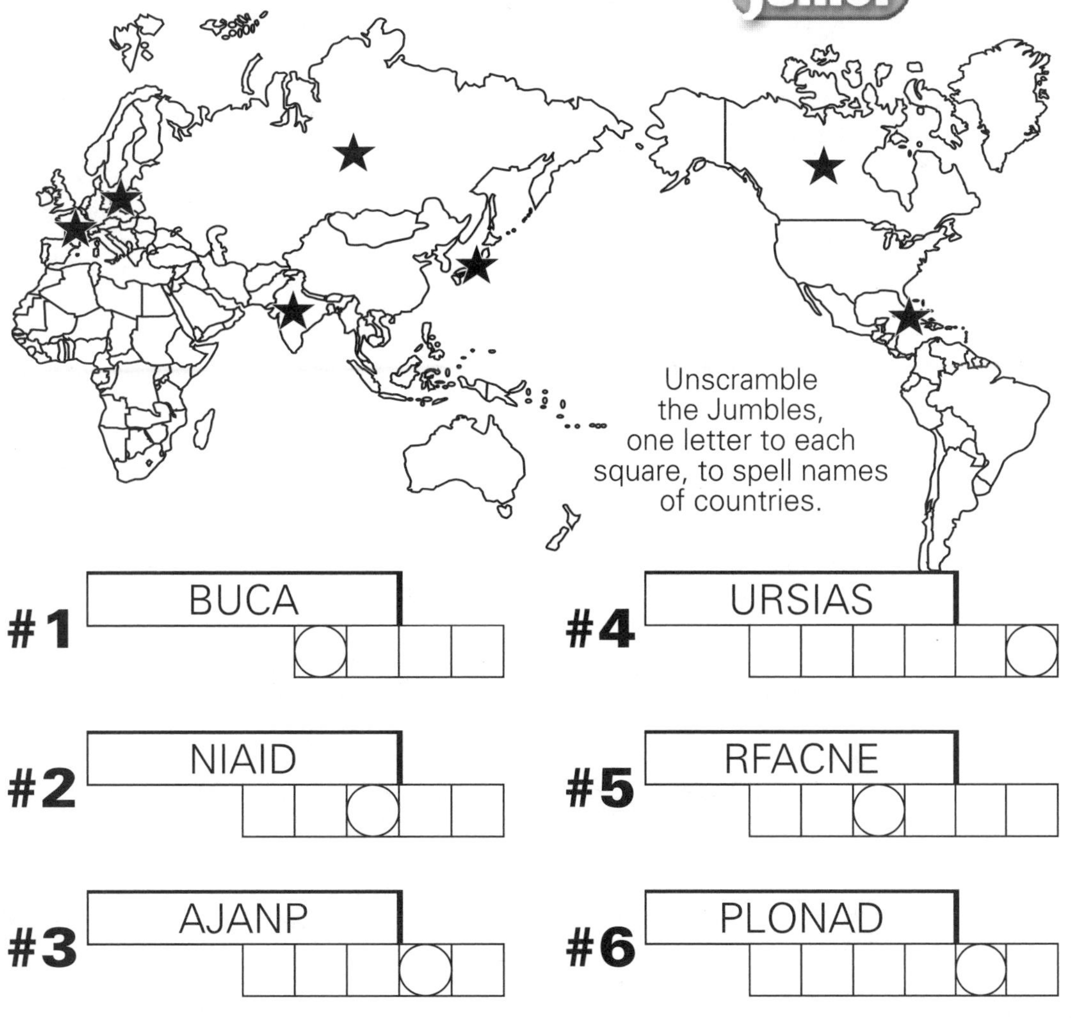

Unscramble the Jumbles, one letter to each square, to spell names of countries.

#1 BUCA

#2 NIAID

#3 AJANP

#4 URSIAS

#5 RFACNE

#6 PLONAD

Arrange the circled letters to solve the mystery answer.

MYSTERY ANSWER

PUZZLE

19

ALL ABOUT MUSIC

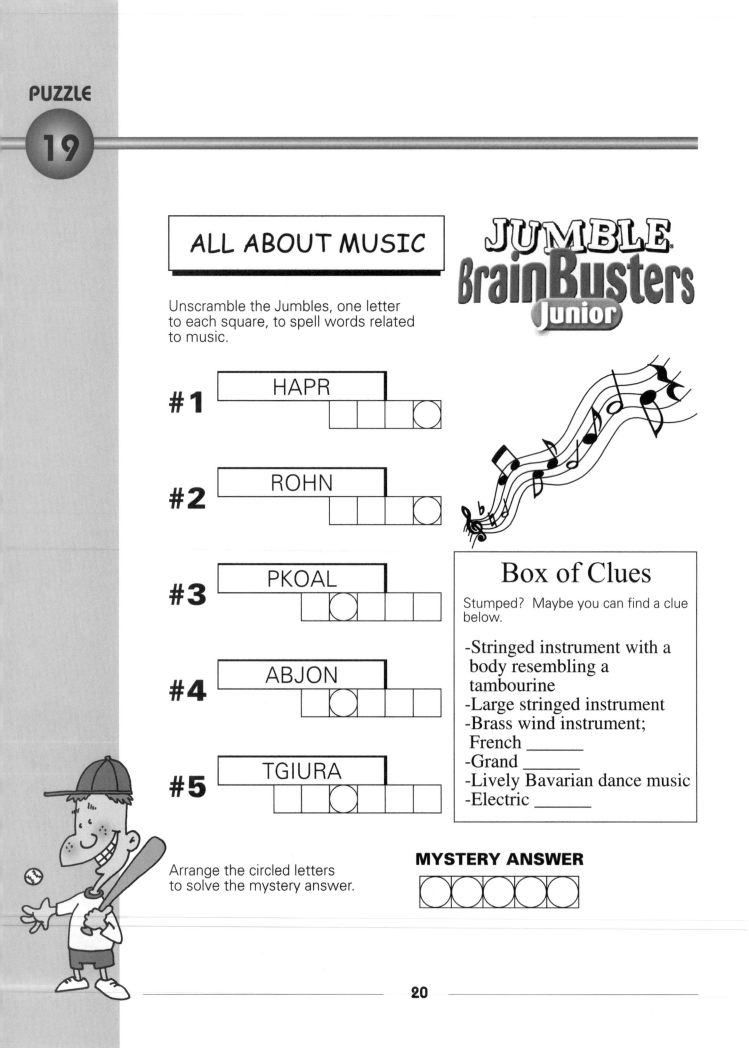

Unscramble the Jumbles, one letter to each square, to spell words related to music.

#1

#2

#3

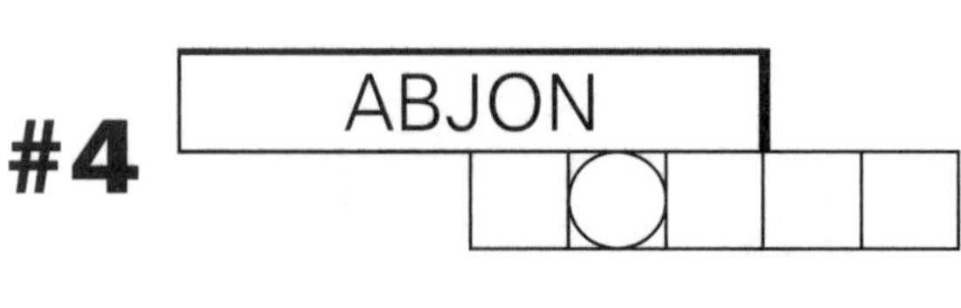

#4

#5

TGIURA

Box of Clues

Stumped? Maybe you can find a clue below.

-Stringed instrument with a body resembling a tambourine
-Large stringed instrument
-Brass wind instrument; French ______
-Grand ______
-Lively Bavarian dance music
-Electric ______

Arrange the circled letters to solve the mystery answer.

MYSTERY ANSWER

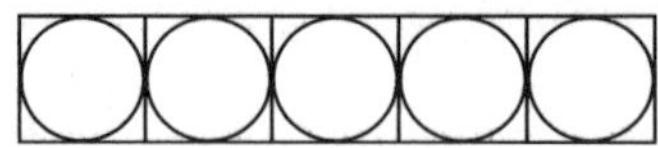

U.S. STATES

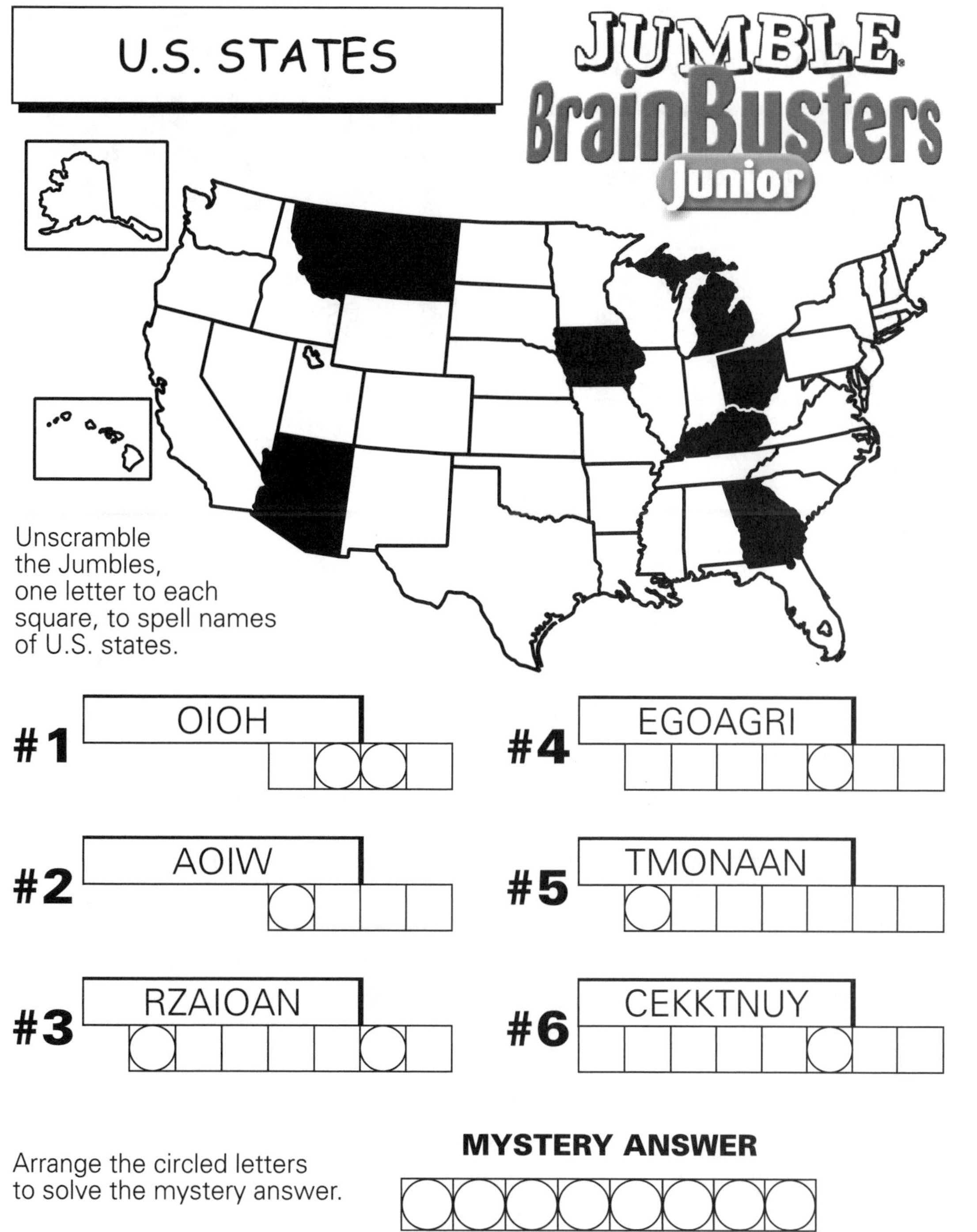

Unscramble the Jumbles, one letter to each square, to spell names of U.S. states.

#1 OIOH

#2 AOIW

#3 RZAIOAN

#4 EGOAGRI

#5 TMONAAN

#6 CEKKTNUY

MYSTERY ANSWER

Arrange the circled letters to solve the mystery answer.

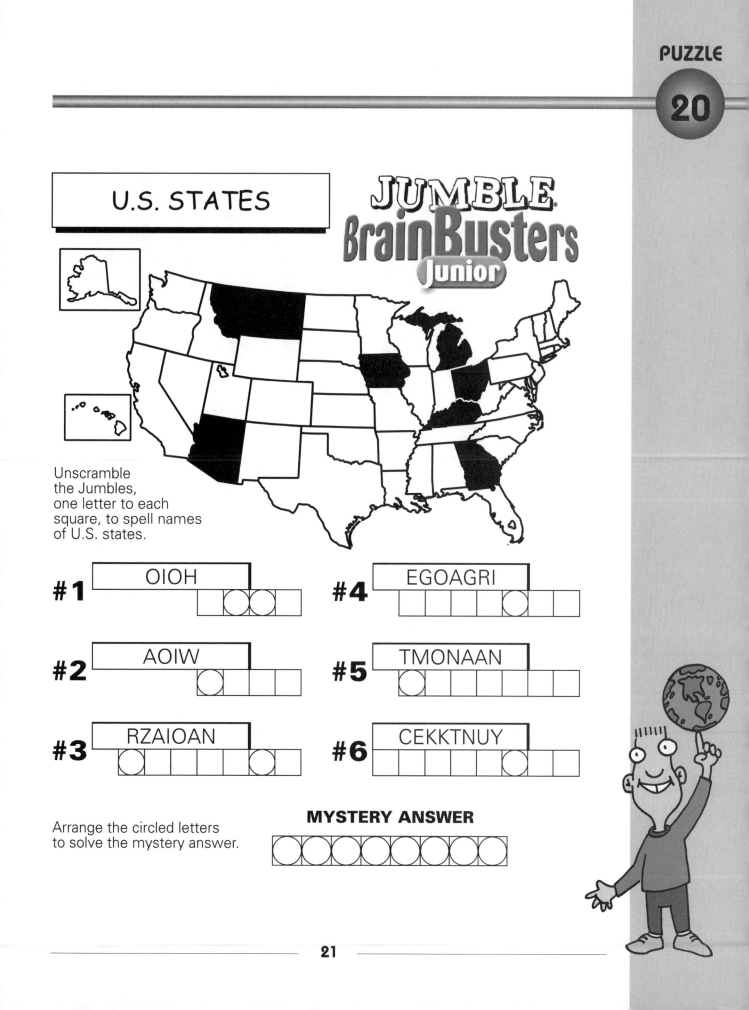

PUZZLE

21

STARTS WITH "B"

Unscramble the Jumbles, one letter to each square, to spell words that start with "B."

#1 LELB

#2 ABDN

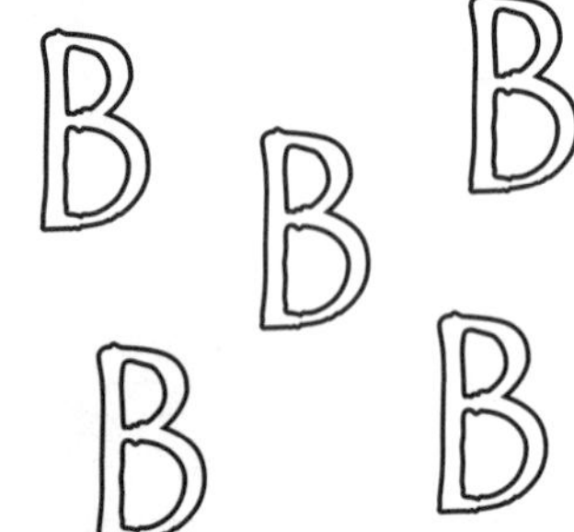

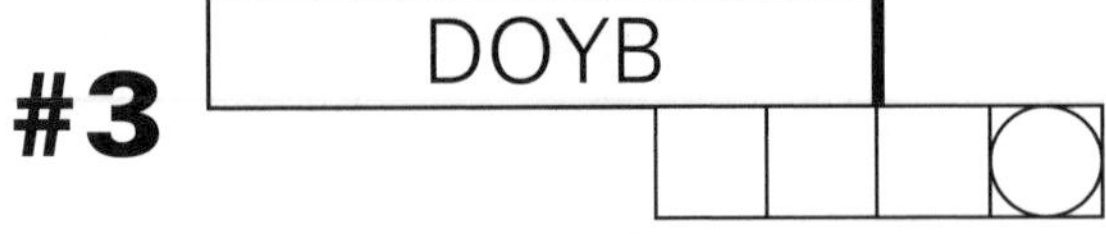

#3 DOYB

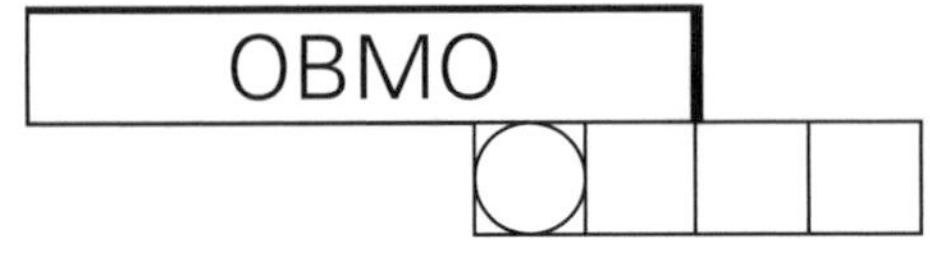

#4 OBMO

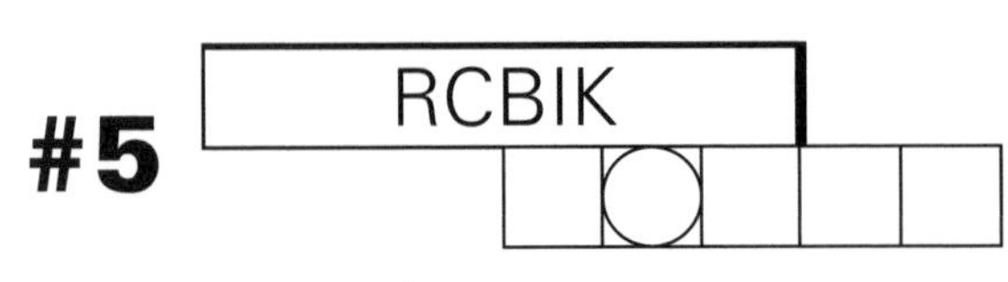

#5 RCBIK

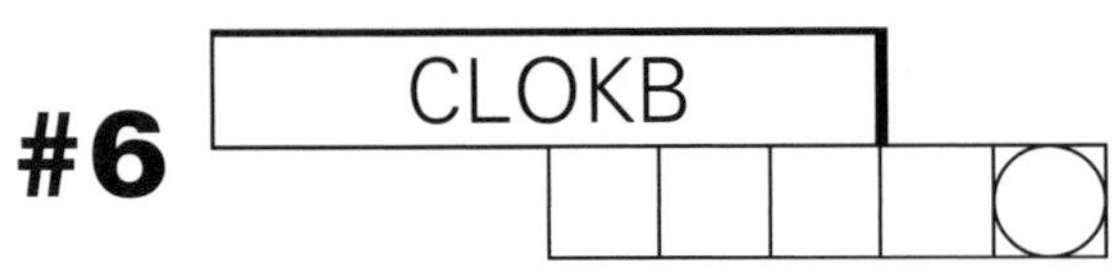

#6 CLOKB

Box of Clues

Stumped? Maybe you can find a clue below.

- -Musical group
- -Writer's or butcher ______
- -Hollow metallic device
- -Bread factory
- -Main part of an animal
- -Deep, hollow sound
- -Rectangular building block

Arrange the circled letters to solve the mystery answer.

MYSTERY ANSWER

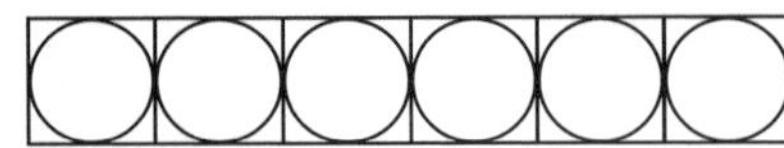

ANIMALS

JUMBLE BrainBusters Junior

Unscramble the Jumbles, one letter to each square, to spell names of animals.

#1 CUDK

#2 HRION

#3 RZEAB

#4 OGSEO

#5 ACELM

#6 FUBFLOA

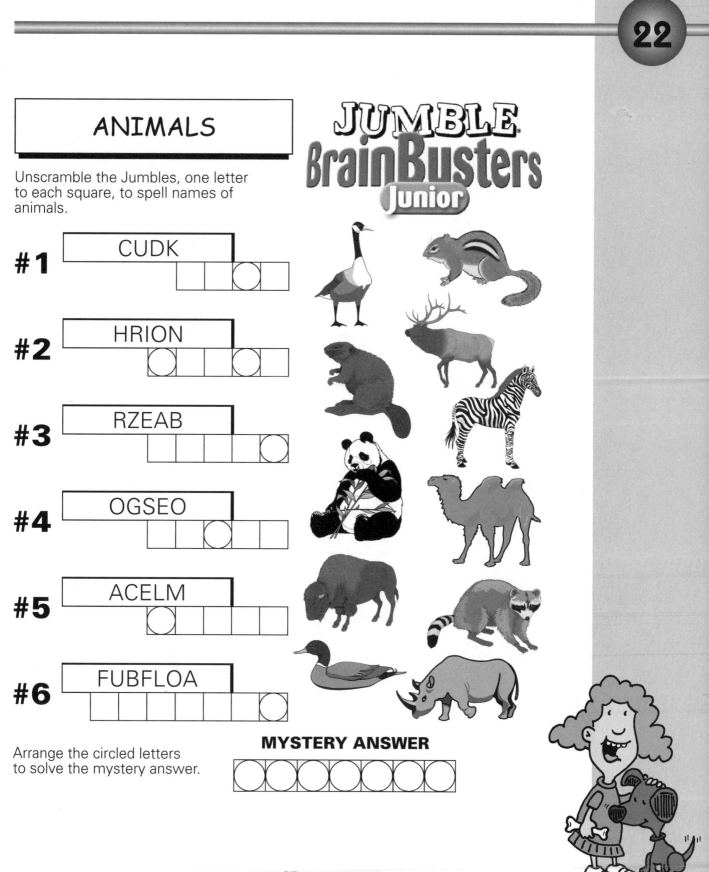

Arrange the circled letters to solve the mystery answer.

MYSTERY ANSWER

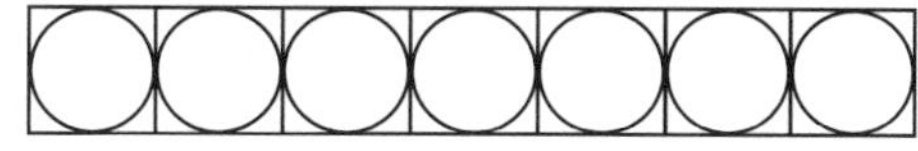

PUZZLE

23

U.S. STATES

Unscramble the Jumbles, one letter to each square, to spell names of U.S. states.

#1 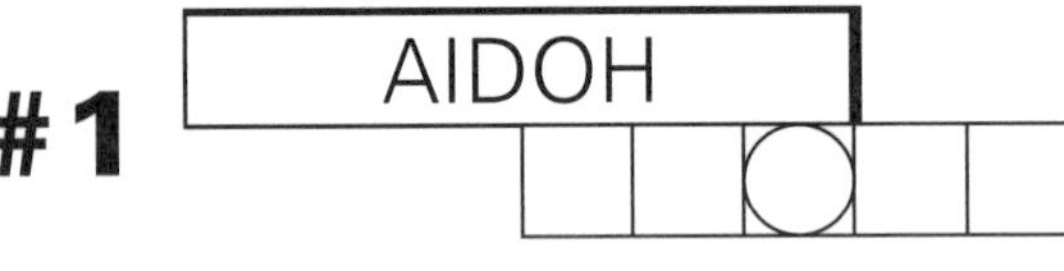

#2 

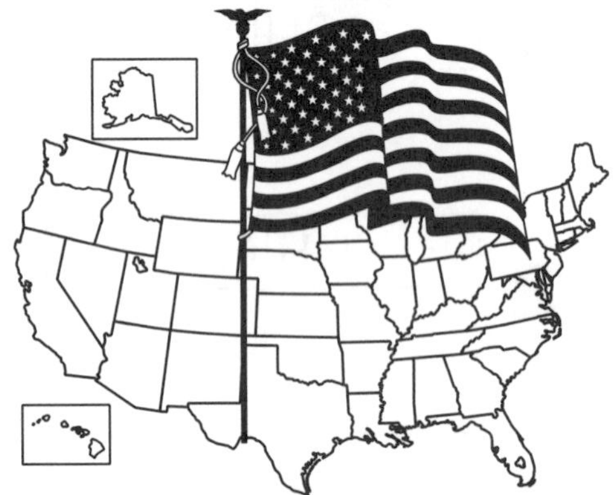

#3 

#4 

#5 

Box of Clues

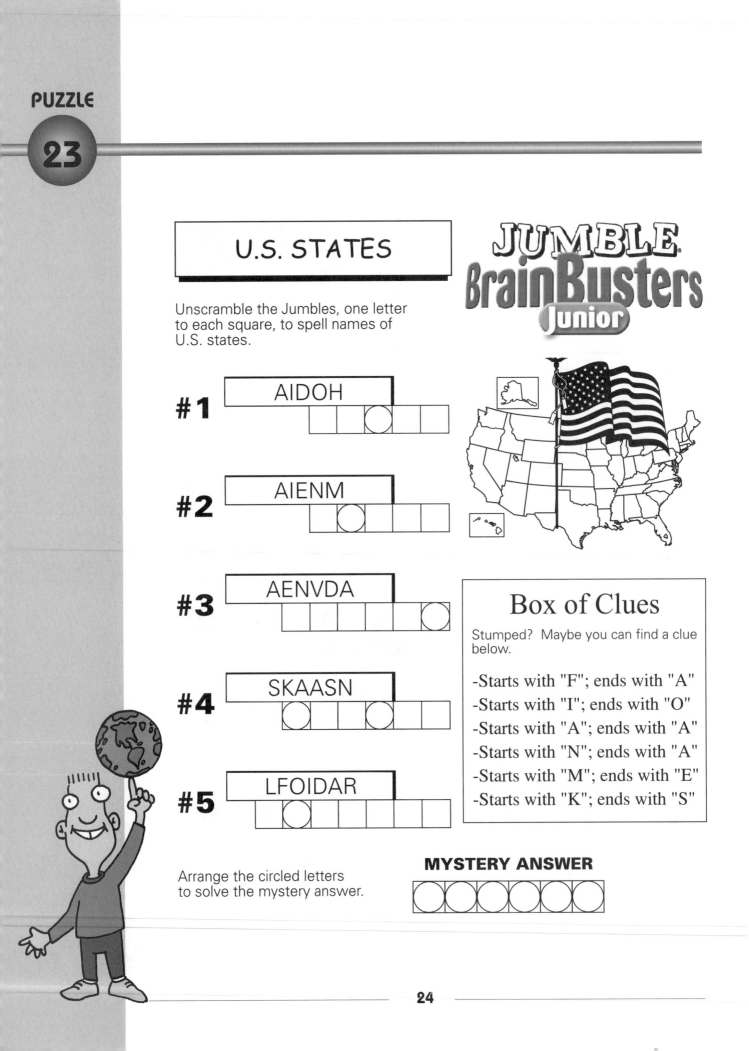

Stumped? Maybe you can find a clue below.

- -Starts with "F"; ends with "A"
- -Starts with "I"; ends with "O"
- -Starts with "A"; ends with "A"
- -Starts with "N"; ends with "A"
- -Starts with "M"; ends with "E"
- -Starts with "K"; ends with "S"

MYSTERY ANSWER

Arrange the circled letters to solve the mystery answer.

TIME LINE

JUMBLE BrainBusters Junior

Unscramble the Jumbles, one letter to each square, to spell words as suggested by the time line.

#1 1666 "Great Fire" destroys much of ______

#2 1682 ______ discovers "his" comet

#3 1922 Benito Mussolini gains power in ______

#4 1945 Atomic bomb dropped on ______

#5 1950 ______ War begins

#6 1974 President ______ resigns

#1 NLNOOD

#2 LAHEYL

#3 TILYA

#4 AJPNA

#5 OKEANR

#6 ONINX

Arrange the circled letters to solve the mystery answer.

1963 ______ ______ assassinated

MYSTERY ANSWER

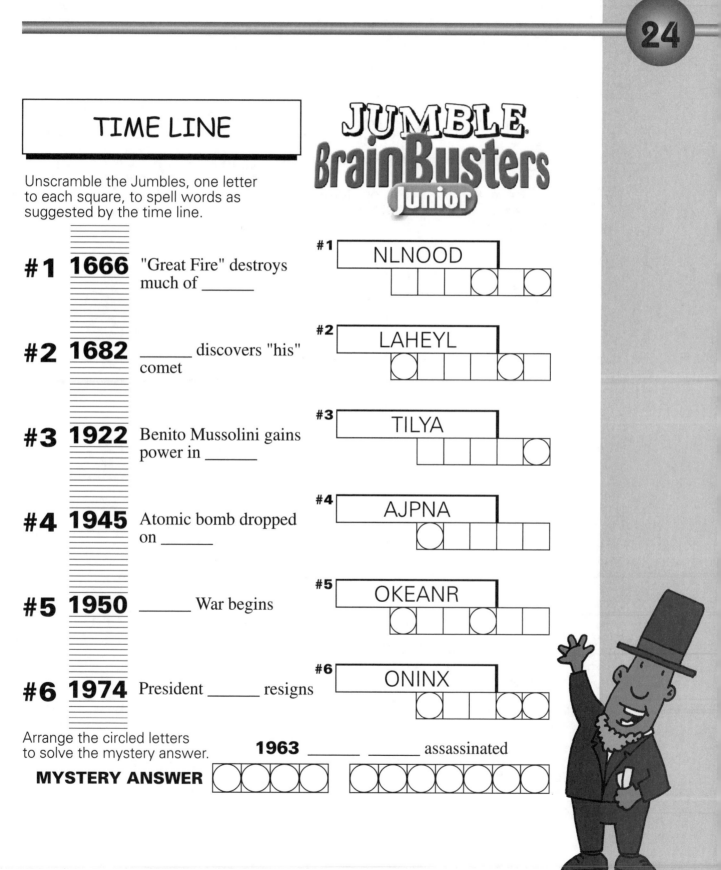

PUZZLE 25

WEATHER

Unscramble the Jumbles, one letter to each square, to spell words related to weather.

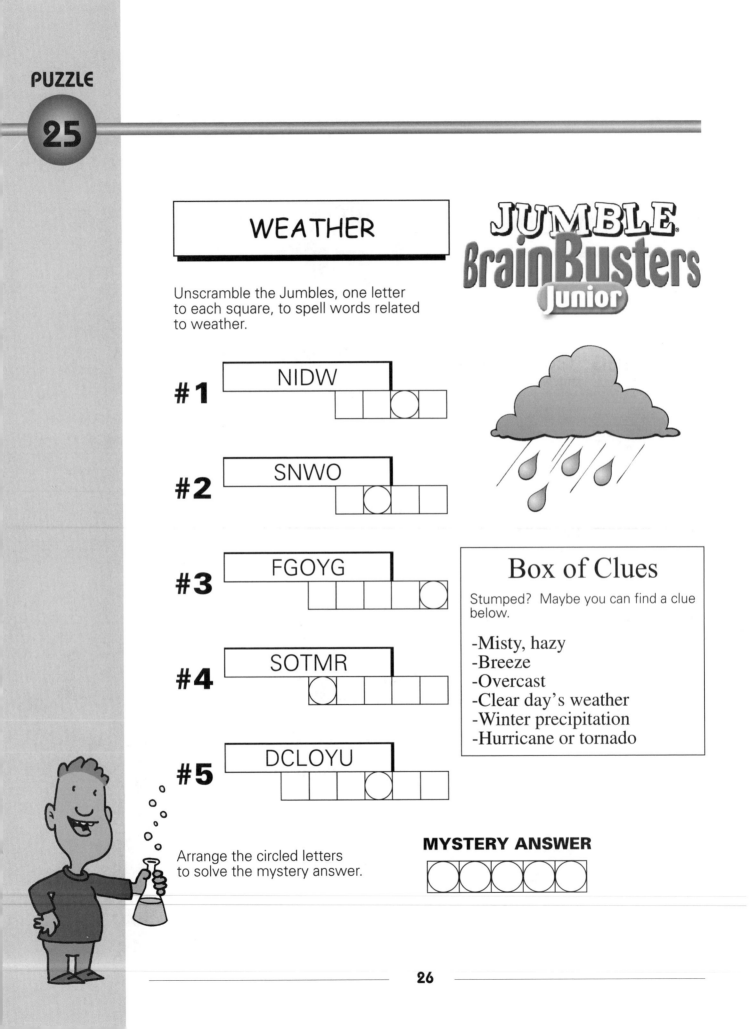

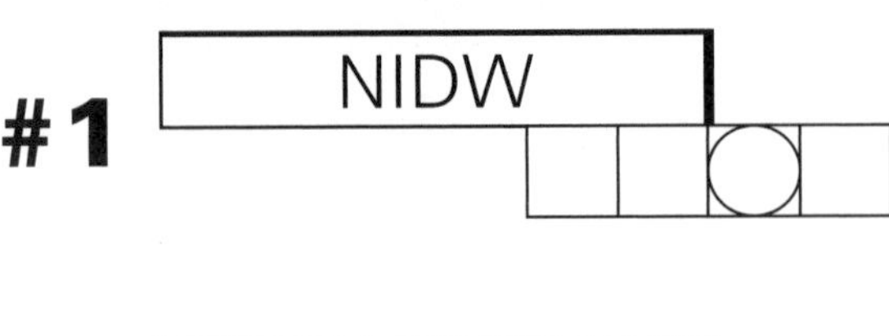

#1 NIDW

#2 SNWO

#3 FGOYG

#4 SOTMR

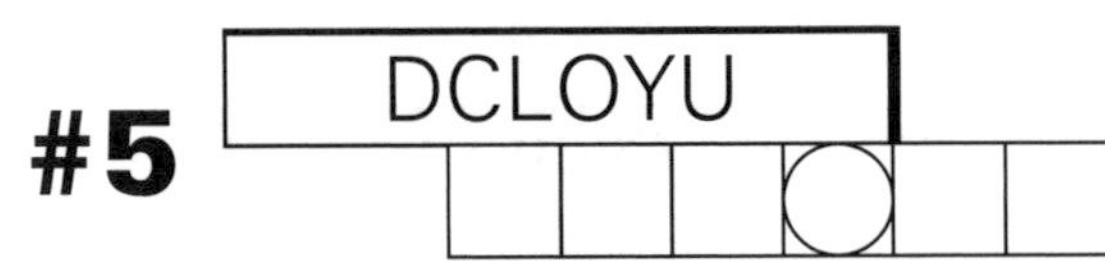

#5 DCLOYU

Box of Clues

Stumped? Maybe you can find a clue below.

-Misty, hazy
-Breeze
-Overcast
-Clear day's weather
-Winter precipitation
-Hurricane or tornado

Arrange the circled letters to solve the mystery answer.

MYSTERY ANSWER

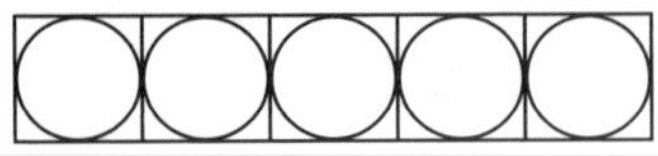

RHYMING WORDS

JUMBLE BrainBusters Junior

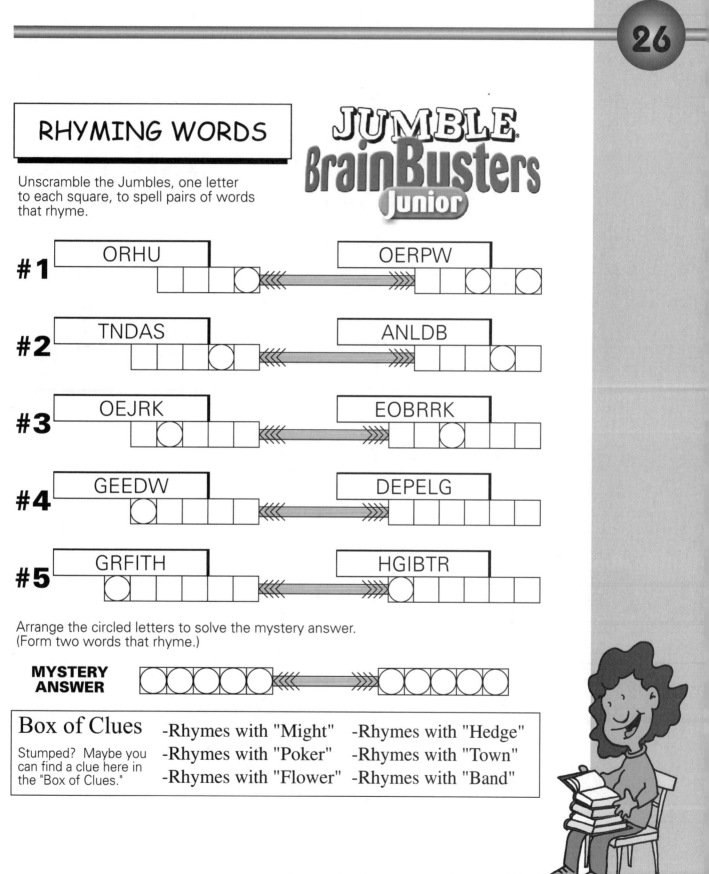

Unscramble the Jumbles, one letter to each square, to spell pairs of words that rhyme.

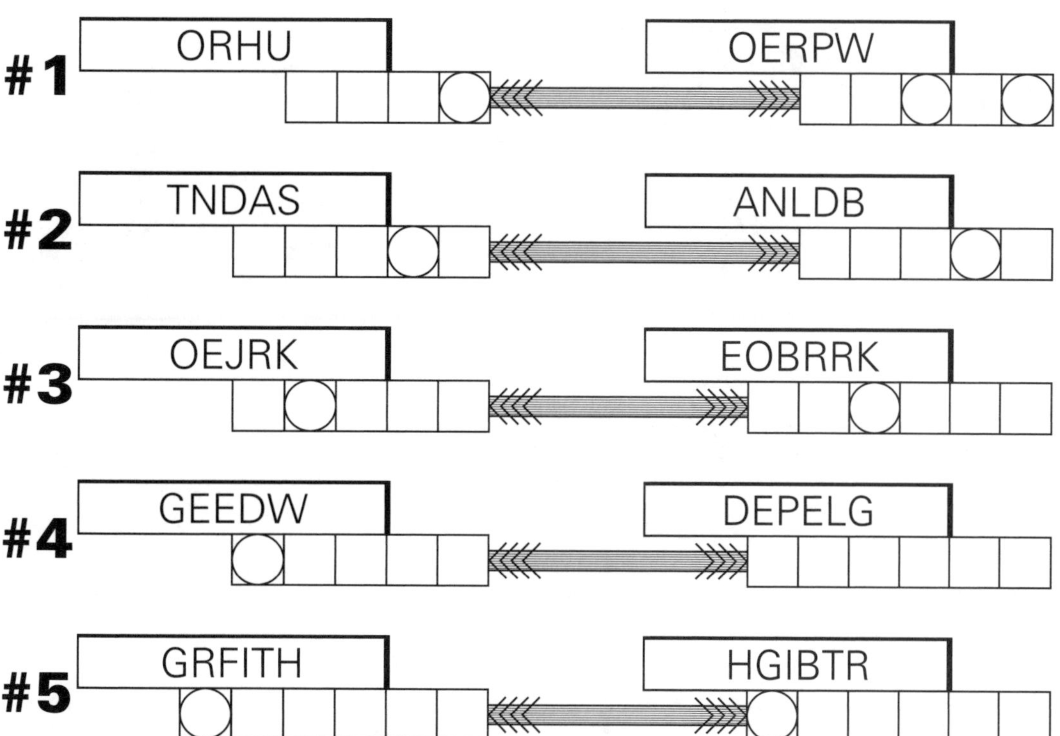

Arrange the circled letters to solve the mystery answer. (Form two words that rhyme.)

Box of Clues

Stumped? Maybe you can find a clue here in the "Box of Clues."

-Rhymes with "Might"
-Rhymes with "Poker"
-Rhymes with "Flower"
-Rhymes with "Hedge"
-Rhymes with "Town"
-Rhymes with "Band"

PUZZLE

27

COMPUTERS

JUMBLE BrainBusters Junior

Unscramble the Jumbles, one letter to each square, to spell words related to computers.

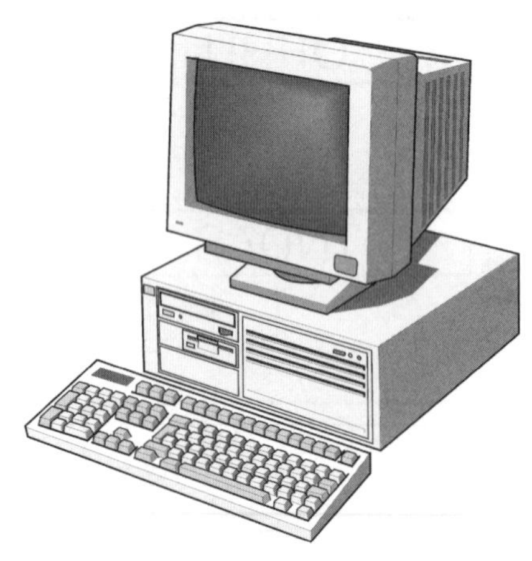

#1

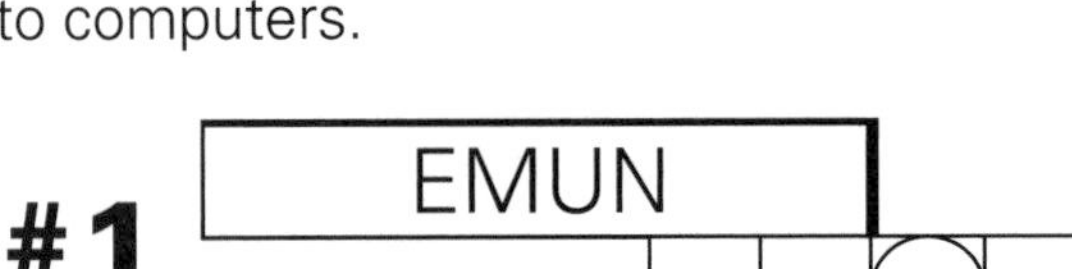

#2

#3

#4

#5

#6

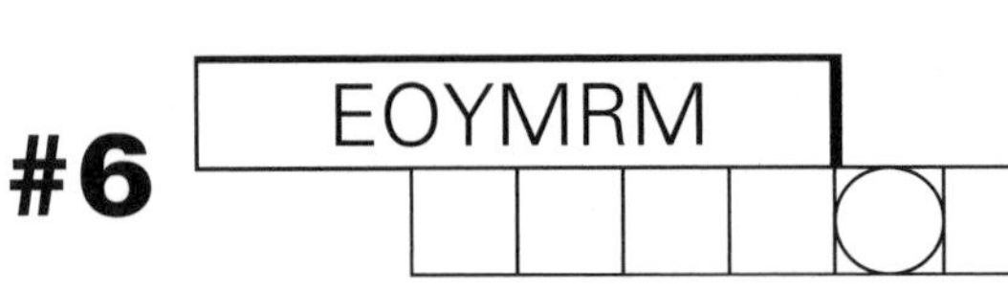

Box of Clues

Stumped? Maybe you can find a clue below.

-Pointer
-Mouse sound
-Screen
-Remove, eliminate
-List of choices on screen
-The "M" in RAM or ROM
-Phone connection device

Arrange the circled letters to solve the mystery answer.

MYSTERY ANSWER

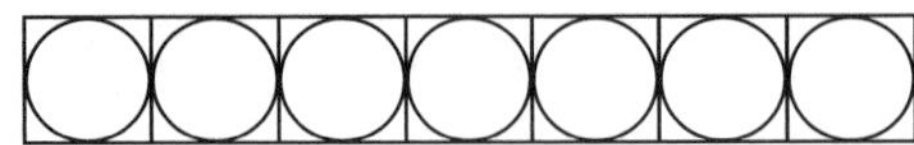

PUZZLE 28

THE HUMAN BODY

Unscramble the Jumbles, one letter to each square, to spell words related to the human body.

#1 

#2 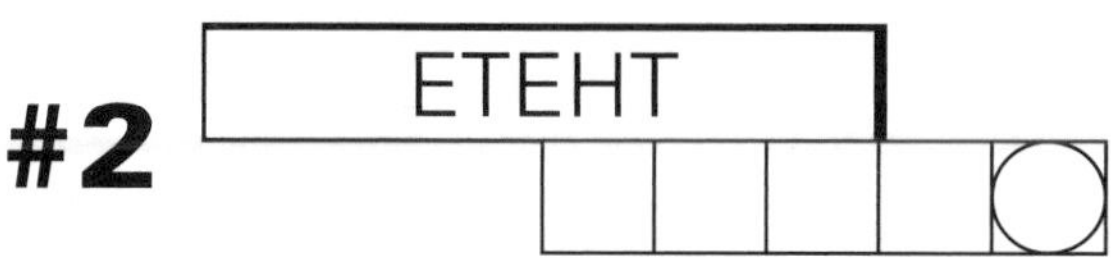

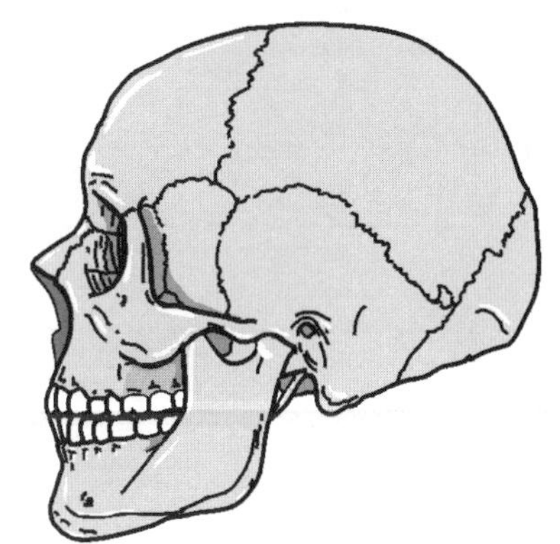

#3 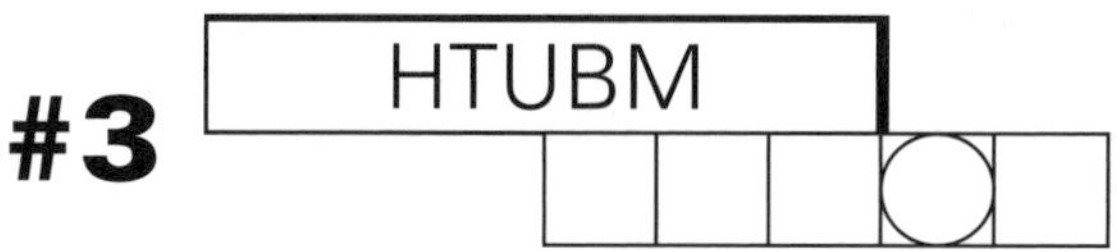

#4 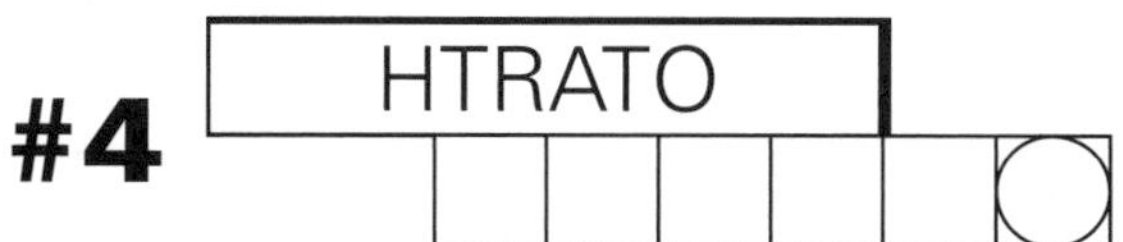

#5 

Box of Clues

Stumped? Maybe you can find a clue below.

-Starts with "T"; ends with "T"
-Starts with "M"; ends with "E"
-Starts with "F"; ends with "T"
-Starts with "M"; ends with "H"
-Starts with "T"; ends with "H"
-Starts with "T"; ends with "B"

Arrange the circled letters to solve the mystery answer.

MYSTERY ANSWER

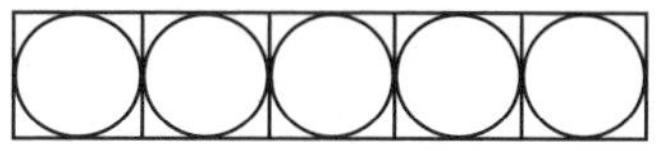

PUZZLE 29

MATH

JUMBLE BrainBusters Junior

Unscramble the Jumbled letters, one letter to each square, so that each equation is correct.

For example: NONTEOEOW
ONE + ONE = TWO

#1 ETIETNGH
☐◯◯◯☐ + TWO = ☐◯☐

#2 ROROFUUF
☐☐☐☐ + ☐◯☐☐ = EIGHT

#3 EWHTEVRELET
NINE + ☐☐☐☐☐ = ☐☐☐☐☐◯

#4 UONOFENORE
☐◯☐ + TWO + ☐☐◯ = ☐◯☐☐

#5 OTZETNERNE
☐☐◯ – ☐☐☐☐ + ◯☐☐ = TWENTY

Arrange the circled letters to solve the mystery equation.

MYSTERY EQUATION

◯◯◯ + ◯◯◯ + ◯◯◯◯◯ = TEN

NOUNS

JUMBLE® BrainBusters Junior

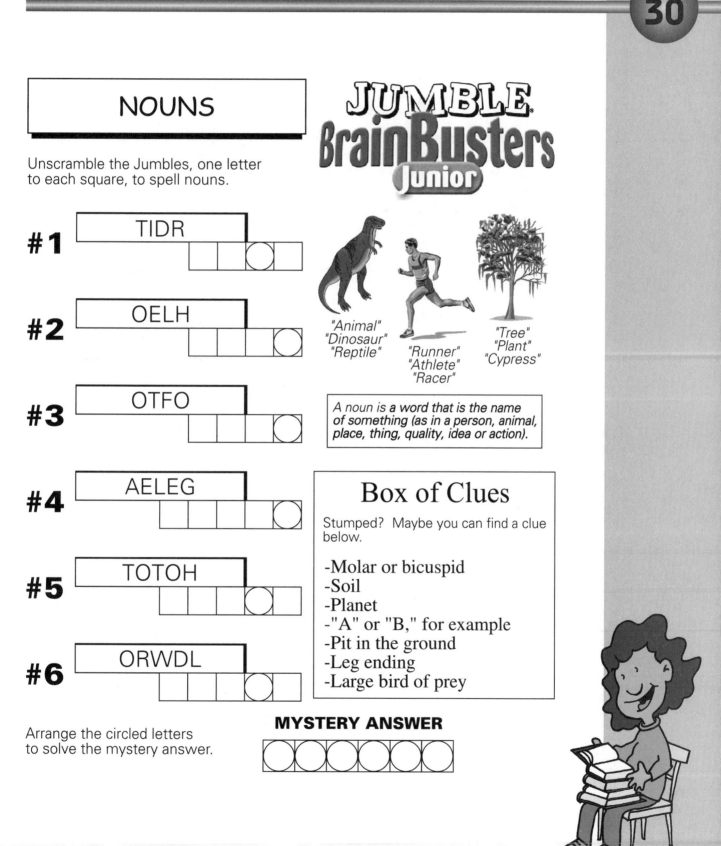

Unscramble the Jumbles, one letter to each square, to spell nouns.

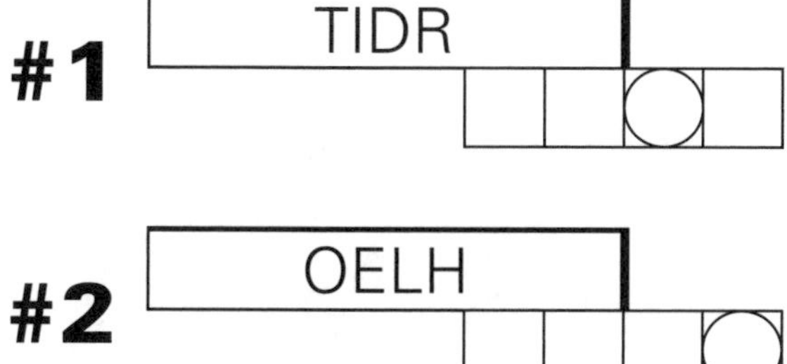

#1 TIDR

#2 OELH

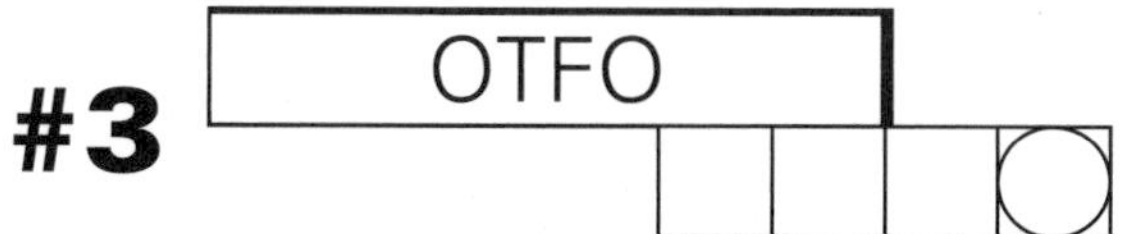

#3 OTFO

A noun is a word that is the name of something (as in a person, animal, place, thing, quality, idea or action).

#4 AELEG

#5 TOTOH

#6 ORWDL

Box of Clues

Stumped? Maybe you can find a clue below.

- Molar or bicuspid
- Soil
- Planet
- "A" or "B," for example
- Pit in the ground
- Leg ending
- Large bird of prey

Arrange the circled letters to solve the mystery answer.

MYSTERY ANSWER

PUZZLE

31

AUTOMOBILES

Unscramble the Jumbles, one letter to each square, to spell words related to automobiles.

#1
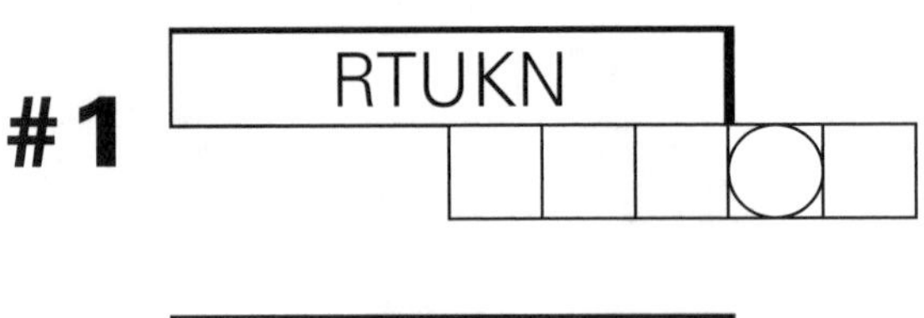

#2

#3

#4

#5

#6

Box of Clues

Stumped? Maybe you can find a clue below.

-Part of a car's body around the wheel
-Gas ______
-Circular frame
-Power provider
-Front or rear shock absorber
-Storage area
-Truck style

Arrange the circled letters to solve the mystery answer.

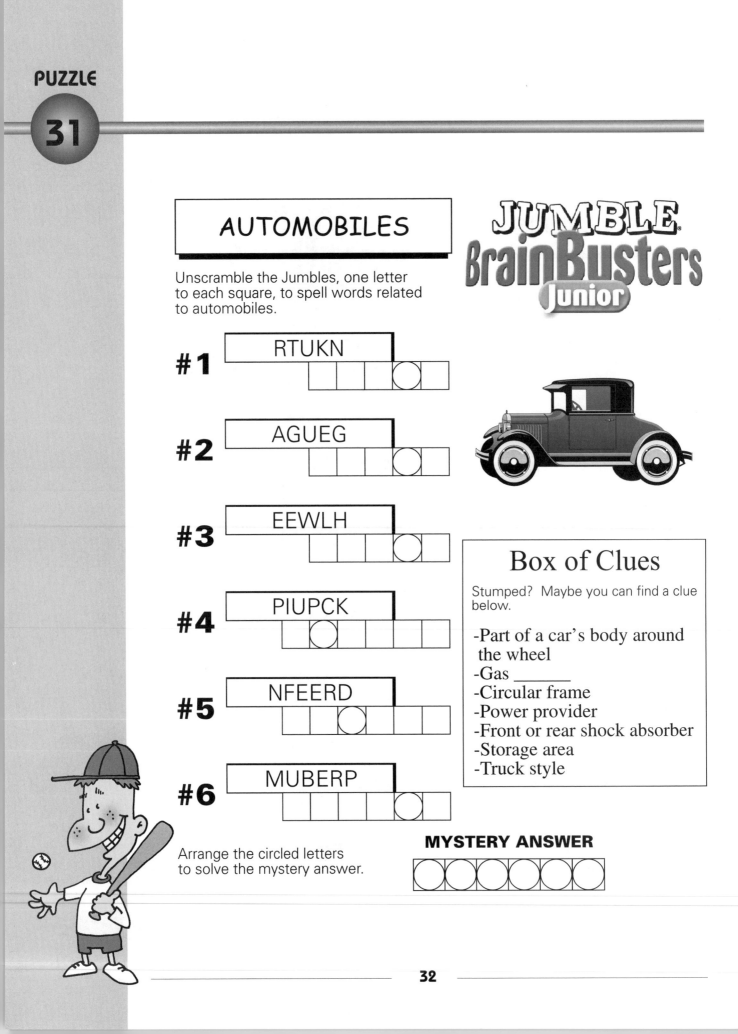

U.S. PRESIDENTS

JUMBLE BrainBusters Junior

Unscramble the Jumbles, one letter to each square, to spell last names of U.S. presidents.

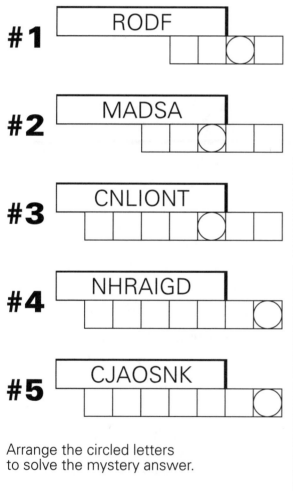

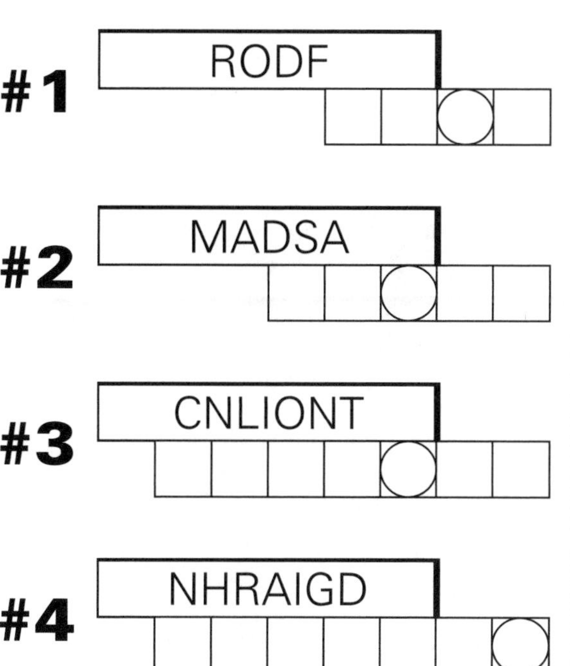

#5 CJAOSNK

Arrange the circled letters to solve the mystery answer.

MYSTERY ANSWER

1789-1797 George Washington
1797-1801 John Adams
1801-1809 Thomas Jefferson
1809-1817 James Madison
1817-1825 James Monroe
1825-1829 John Quincy Adams
1829-1837 Andrew Jackson
1837-1841 Martin Van Buren
1841 William Henry Harrison
1841-1845 John Tyler
1845-1849 James Polk
1849-1850 Zachary Taylor
1850-1853 Millard Fillmore
1853-1857 Franklin Pierce
1857-1861 James Buchanan
1861-1865 Abraham Lincoln
1865-1869 Andrew Johnson
1869-1877 Ulysses S. Grant
1877-1881 Rutherford B. Hayes
1881 James A. Garfield
1881-1885 Chester A. Arthur
1885-1889 Stephen Grover Cleveland
1889-1893 Benjamin Harrison
1893-1897 Grover Cleveland
1897-1901 William McKinley
1901-1909 Theodore (Teddy) Roosevelt
1909-1913 William Howard Taft
1913-1921 Thomas Woodrow Wilson
1921-1923 Warren G. Harding
1923-1929 John Calvin Coolidge
1929-1933 Herbert Hoover
1933-1945 Franklin D. Roosevelt
1945-1953 Harry S. Truman
1953-1961 Dwight David Eisenhower
1961-1963 John Fitzgerald Kennedy
1963-1969 Lyndon B. Johnson
1969-1974 Richard M. Nixon
1974-1977 Gerald R. Ford
1977-1981 James (Jimmy) Carter
1981-1989 Ronald Reagan
1989-1993 George W. Bush
1993-2001 William Jefferson Clinton
2001- George Walker Bush

Box of Clues

Stumped? Maybe you can find a clue below.

#1- 38th U.S. president
#2- 2nd or 6th U.S. president
#3- Bill ______
#4- 29th U.S. president
#5- A commander in the War of 1812

Mystery Answer:
President with “Simpson” for a middle name

PUZZLE

33

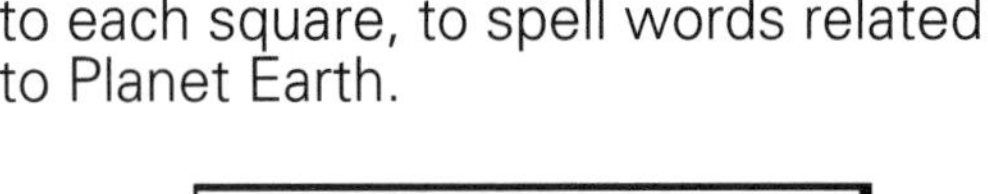

Unscramble the Jumbles, one letter to each square, to spell words related to Planet Earth.

#1 

#2 

#3 

#4 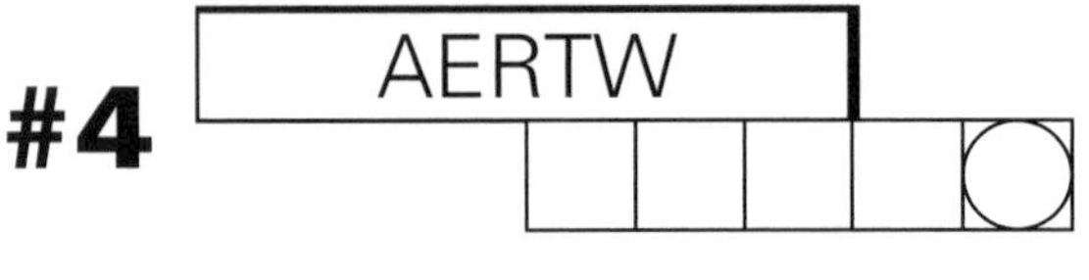

#5 

Box of Clues

Stumped? Maybe you can find a clue below.

-Starts with "B"; ends with "H"
-Starts with "V"; ends with "Y"
-Starts with "H"; ends with "L"
-Starts with "R"; ends with "R"
-Starts with "G"; ends with "S"
-Starts with "W"; ends with "R"

Arrange the circled letters to solve the mystery answer.

MYSTERY ANSWER

WEATHER

Unscramble the Jumbles, one letter to each square, to spell words related to weather.

#1 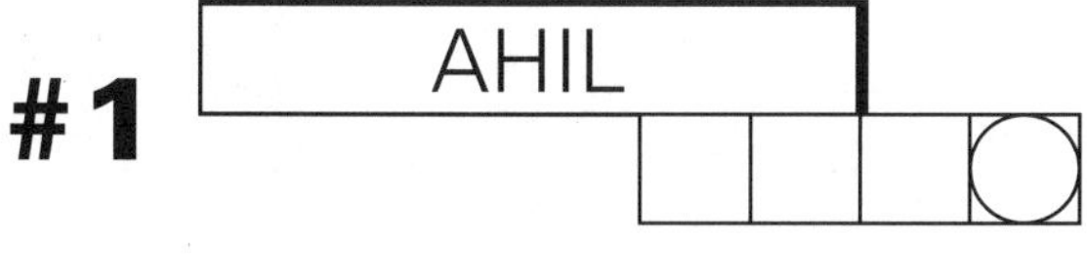

#2 

#3 ODFOL

#4 UHIDM

Box of Clues

Stumped? Maybe you can find a clue below.

- -Hot and moist
- -Frozen pellets
- -A result of too much rain
- -Cool
- -Partly ______
- -Moist

#5 

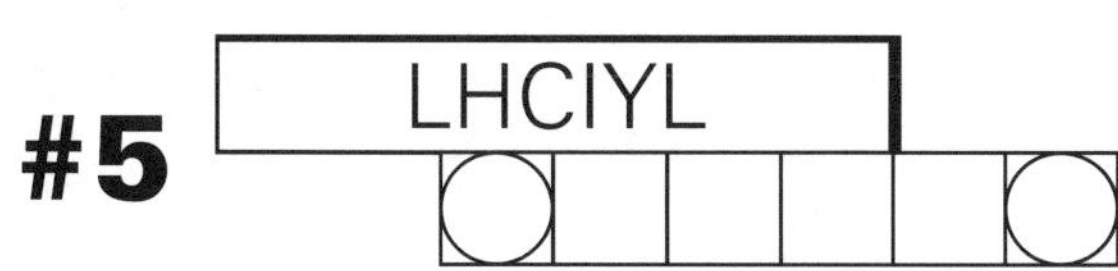

MYSTERY ANSWER

Arrange the circled letters to solve the mystery answer.

PUZZLE

35

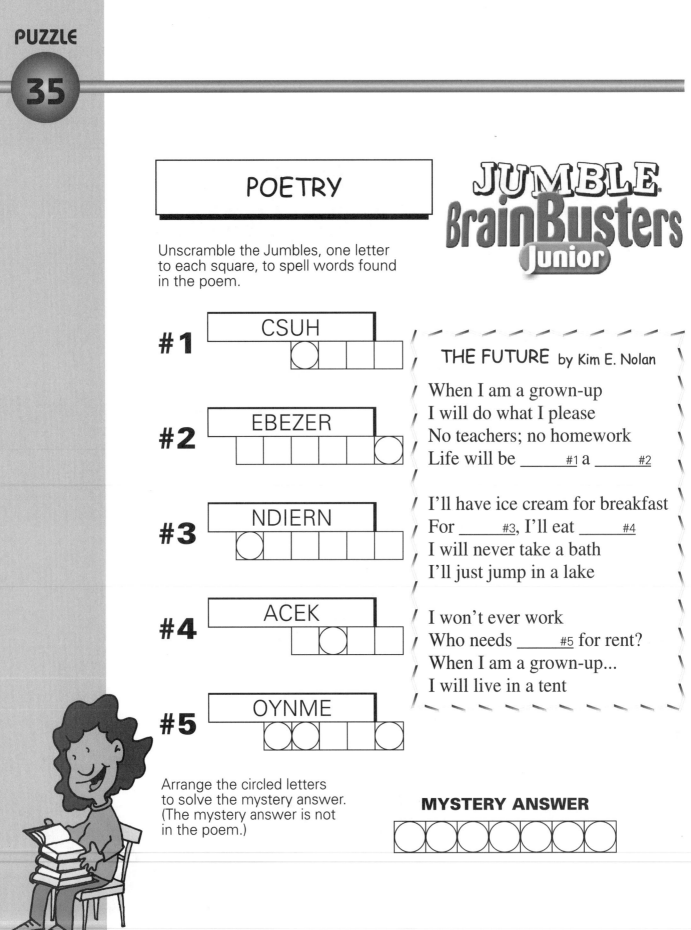

Jumble BrainBusters Junior

POETRY

Unscramble the Jumbles, one letter to each square, to spell words found in the poem.

#1 CSUH

#2 EBEZER

#3 NDIERN

#4 ACEK

#5 OYNME

THE FUTURE by Kim E. Nolan

When I am a grown-up
I will do what I please
No teachers; no homework
Life will be ______#1 a ______#2

I'll have ice cream for breakfast
For ______#3, I'll eat ______#4
I will never take a bath
I'll just jump in a lake

I won't ever work
Who needs ______#5 for rent?
When I am a grown-up...
I will live in a tent

Arrange the circled letters to solve the mystery answer. (The mystery answer is not in the poem.)

MYSTERY ANSWER

OCCUPATIONS

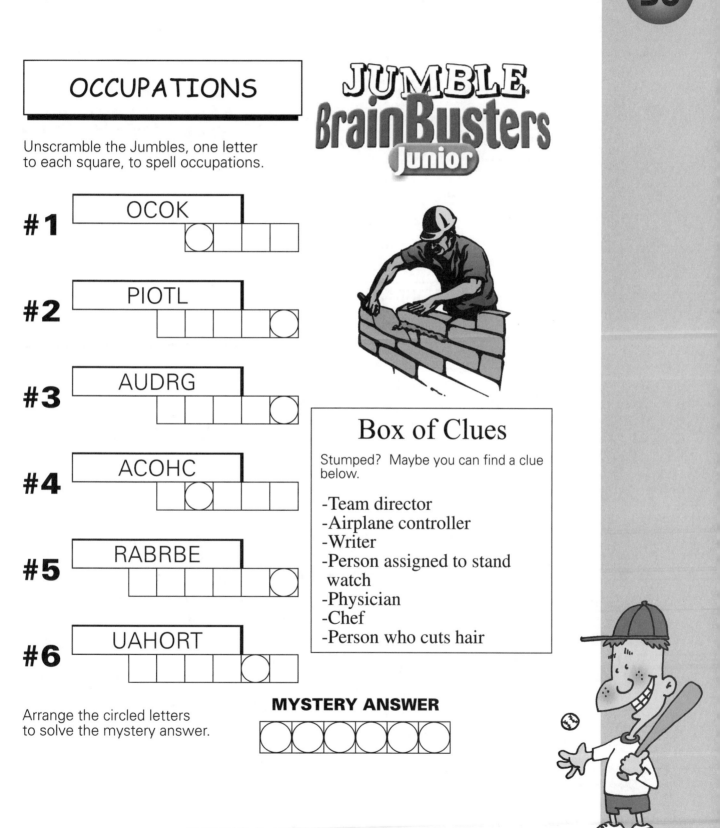

Unscramble the Jumbles, one letter to each square, to spell occupations.

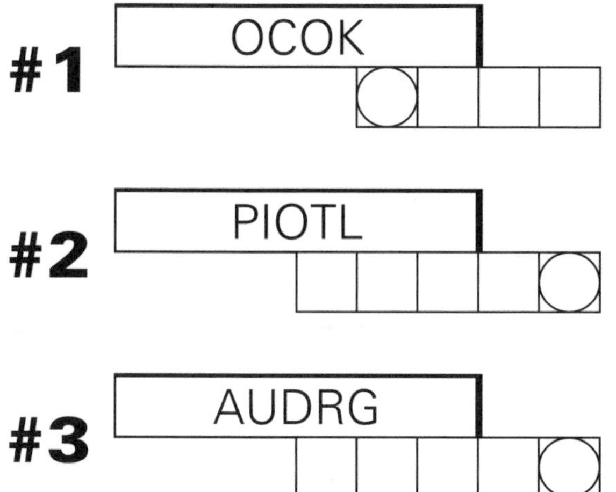

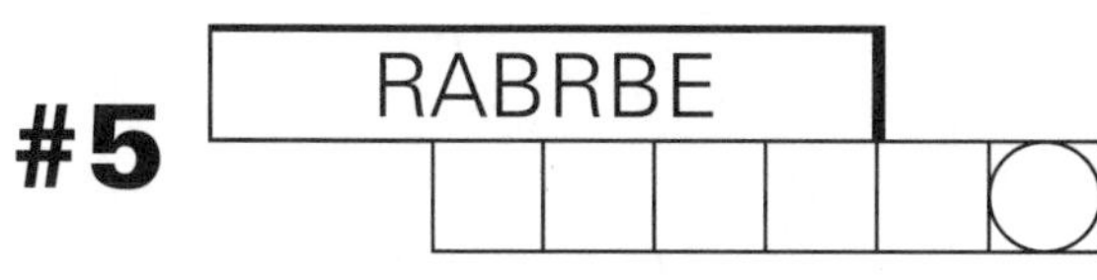

Box of Clues

Stumped? Maybe you can find a clue below.

- -Team director
- -Airplane controller
- -Writer
- -Person assigned to stand watch
- -Physician
- -Chef
- -Person who cuts hair

Arrange the circled letters to solve the mystery answer.

MYSTERY ANSWER

PUZZLE

37

STARTS WITH "D"

Unscramble the Jumbles, one letter to each square, to spell words that start with "D."

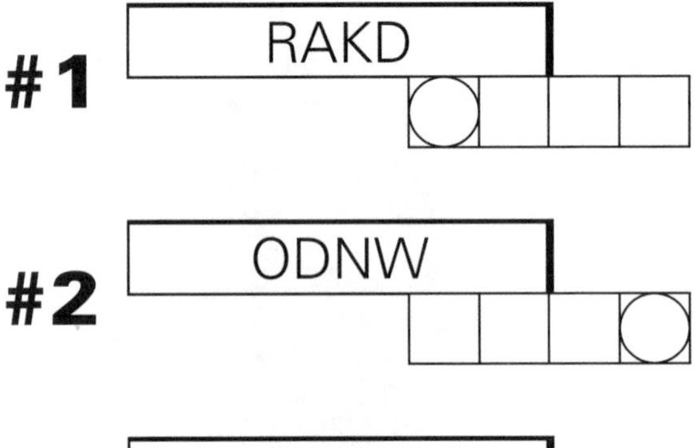

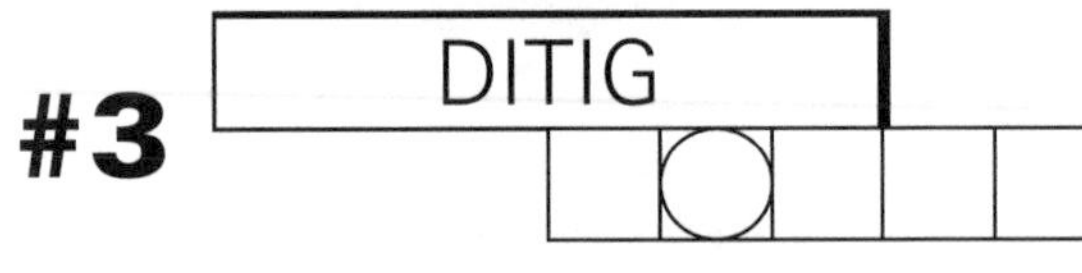

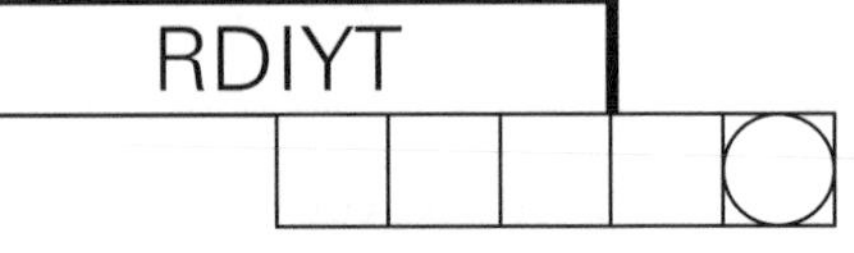

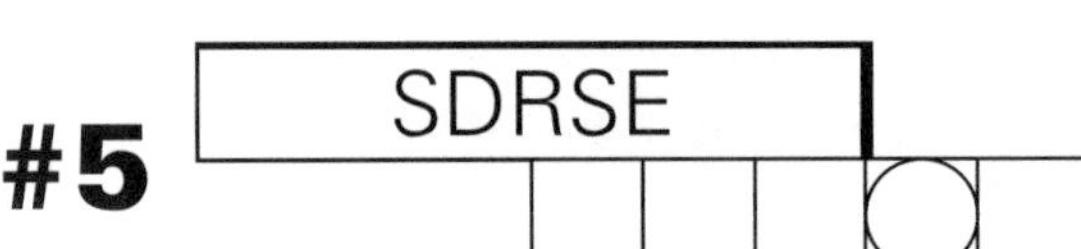

Box of Clues

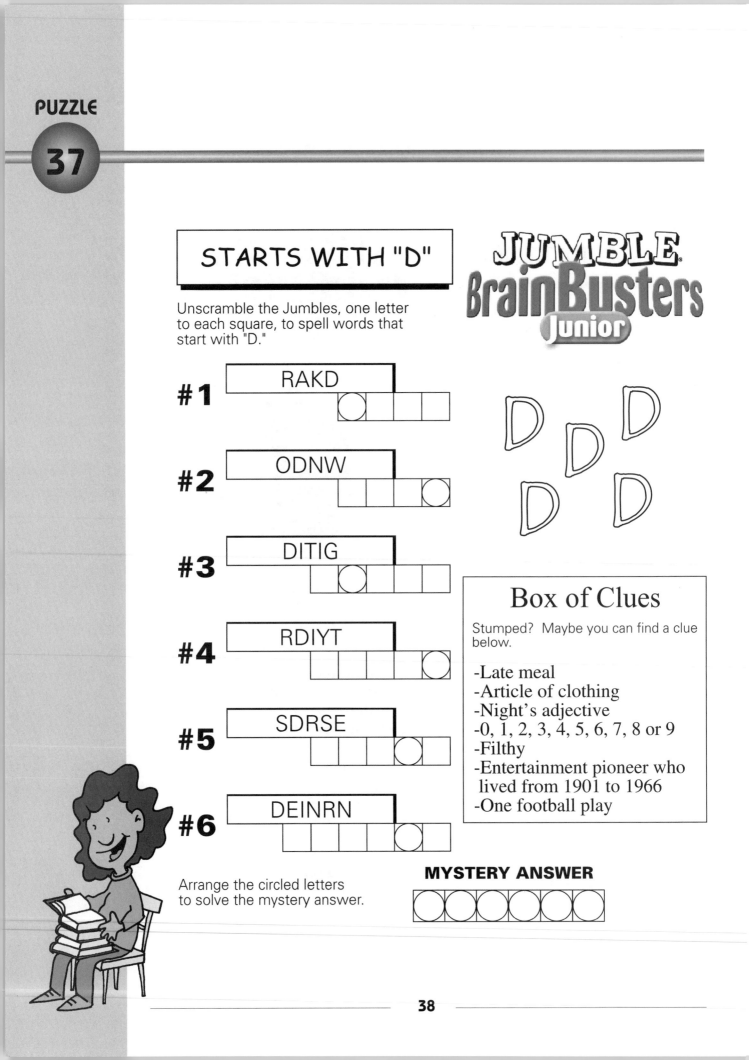

Stumped? Maybe you can find a clue below.

- -Late meal
- -Article of clothing
- -Night's adjective
- -0, 1, 2, 3, 4, 5, 6, 7, 8 or 9
- -Filthy
- -Entertainment pioneer who lived from 1901 to 1966
- -One football play

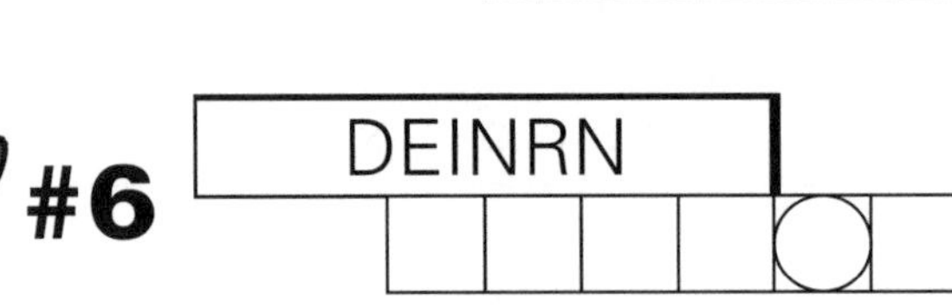

Arrange the circled letters to solve the mystery answer.

MYSTERY ANSWER

PUZZLE 38

ANIMALS

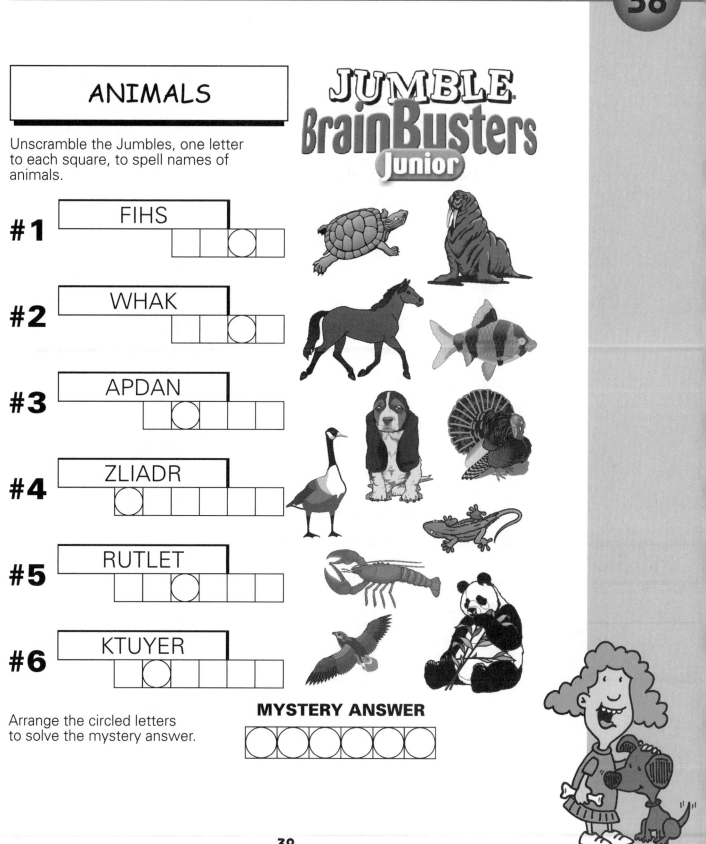

JUMBLE BrainBusters Junior

Unscramble the Jumbles, one letter to each square, to spell names of animals.

#1 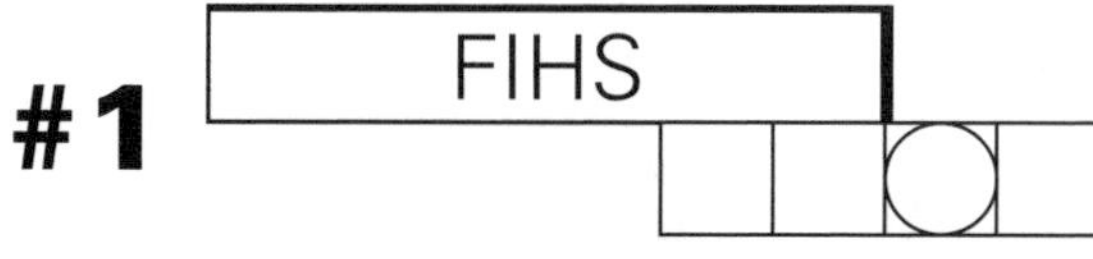

#2 

#3 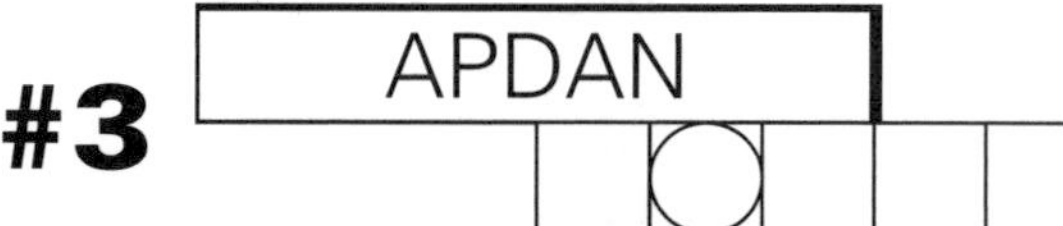

#4 

#5 

#6 

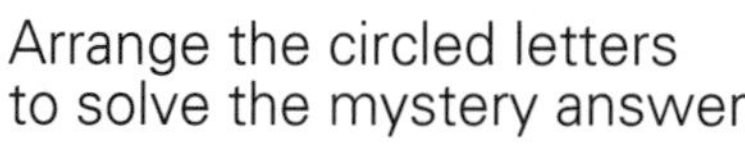

Arrange the circled letters to solve the mystery answer.

MYSTERY ANSWER

PUZZLE

39

FOOD

Unscramble the Jumbles, one letter to each square, to spell words related to food.

#1
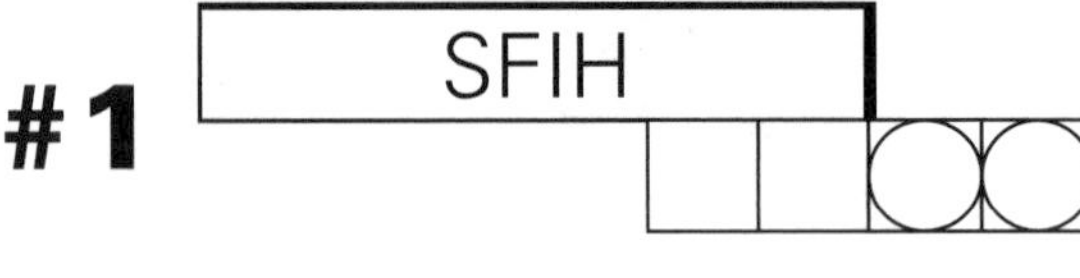

#2
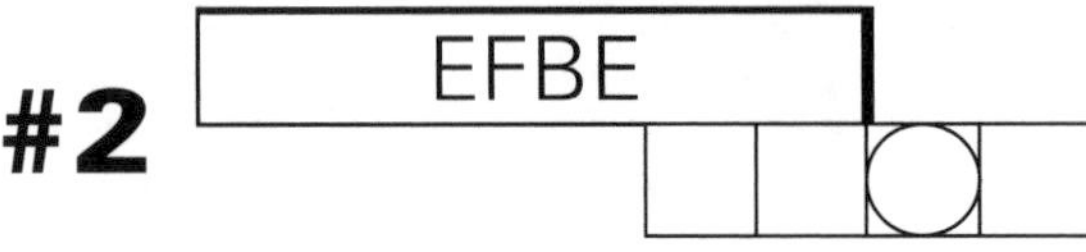

#3 ACEK

Box of Clues

Stumped? Maybe you can find a clue below.

-Peanut butter's partner
-Hamburger, for example
-Type of fruit
-American ______
-Grouper or trout
-Pound or birthday ______

#4
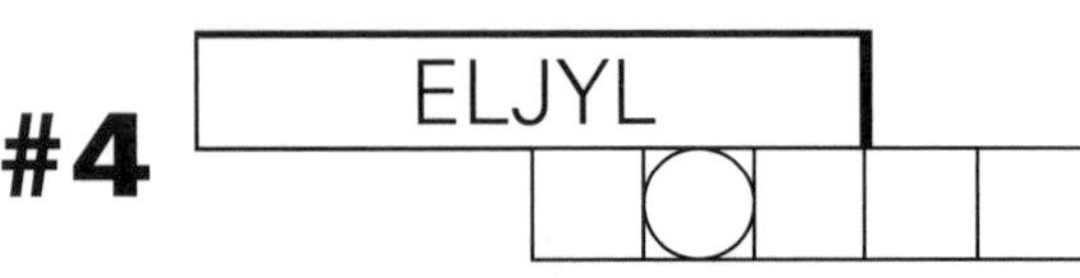

#5

Arrange the circled letters to solve the mystery answer.

MYSTERY ANSWER

THE HUMAN BODY

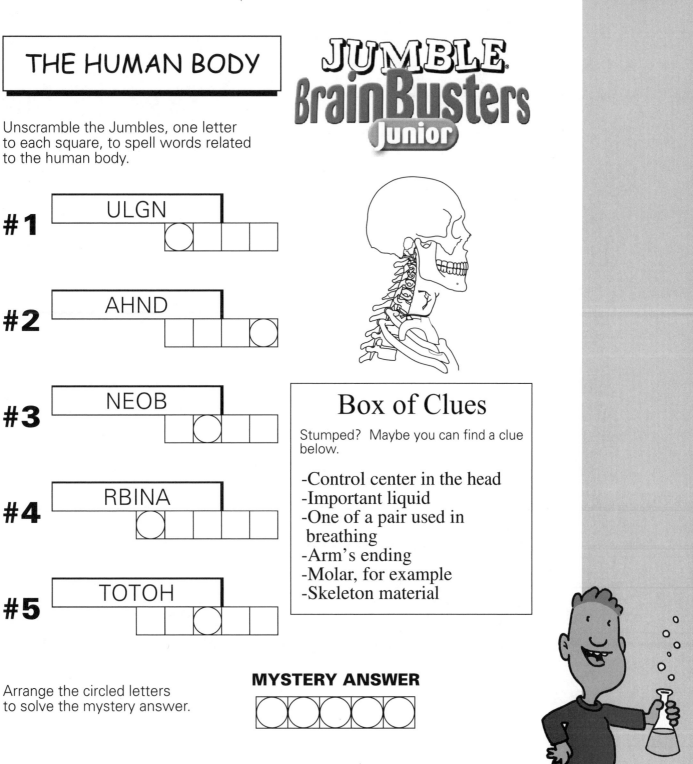

Unscramble the Jumbles, one letter to each square, to spell words related to the human body.

#1

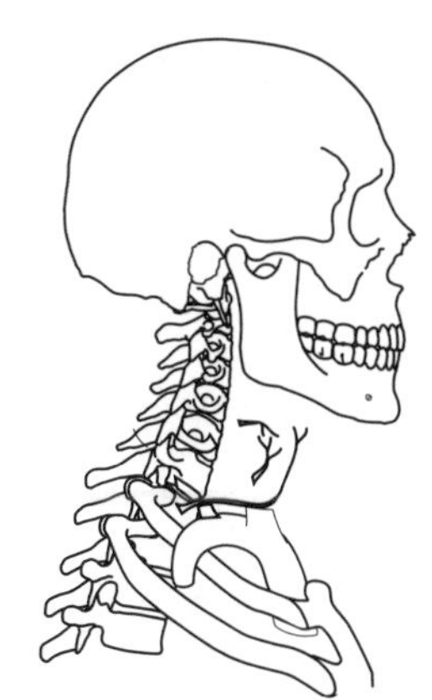

#2

#3

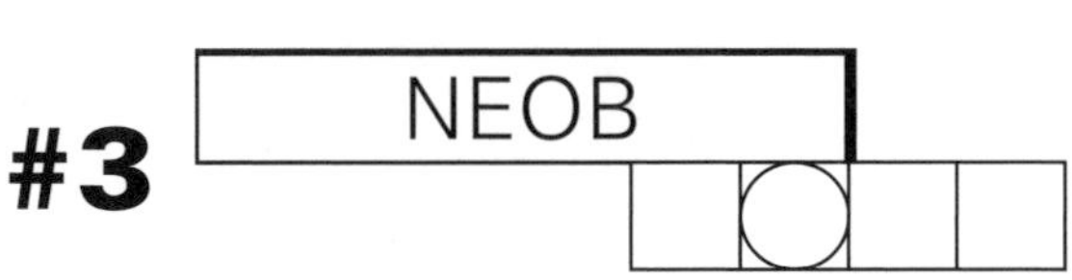

Box of Clues

Stumped? Maybe you can find a clue below.

- -Control center in the head
- -Important liquid
- -One of a pair used in breathing
- -Arm's ending
- -Molar, for example
- -Skeleton material

#4

#5

Arrange the circled letters to solve the mystery answer.

MYSTERY ANSWER

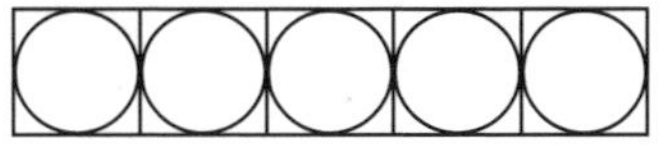

PUZZLE

41

SPORTS TEAMS

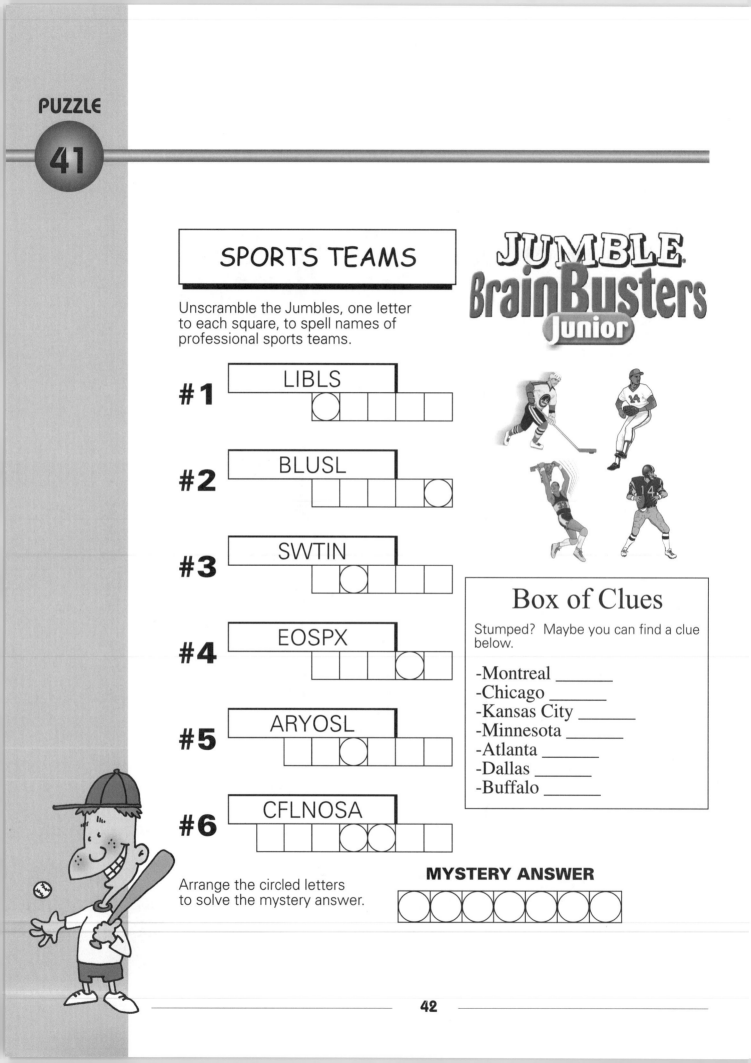

JUMBLE BrainBusters Junior

Unscramble the Jumbles, one letter to each square, to spell names of professional sports teams.

#1 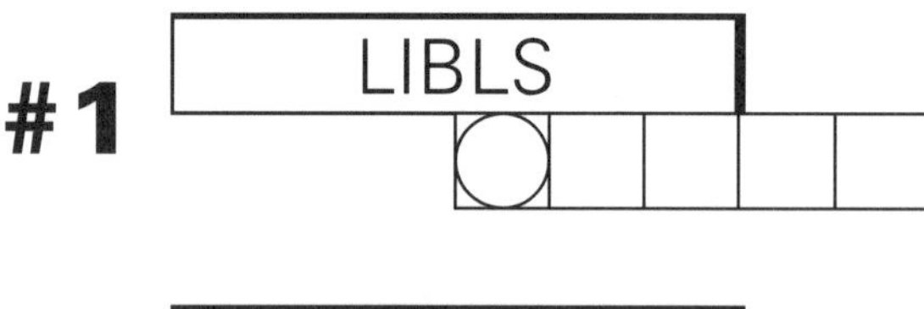

#2 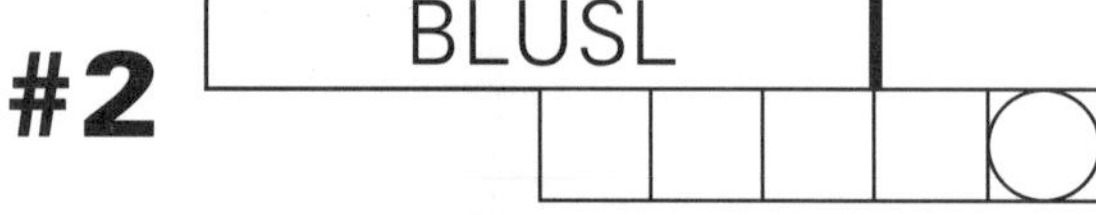

#3 

#4 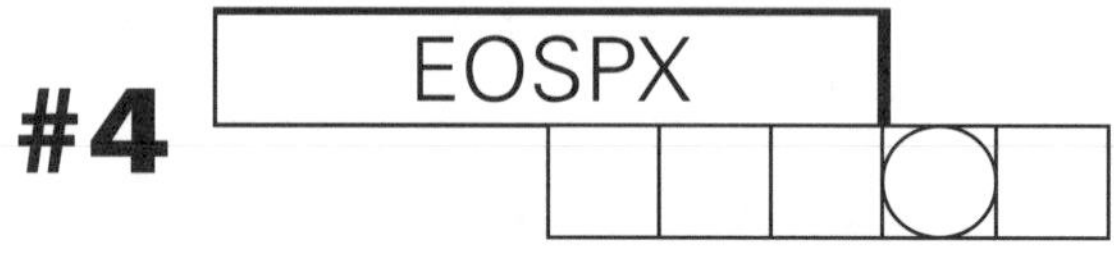

#5 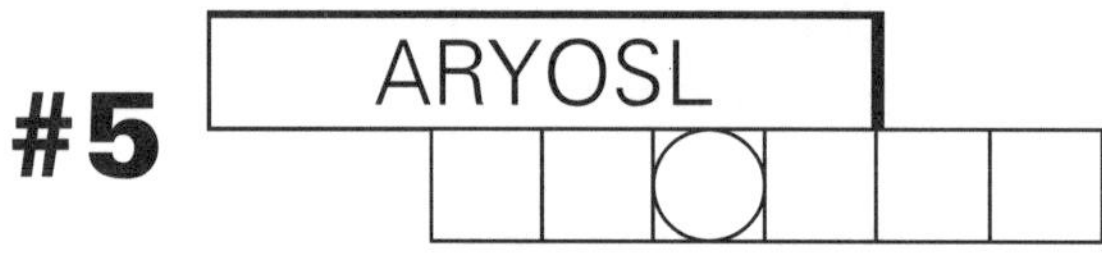

#6 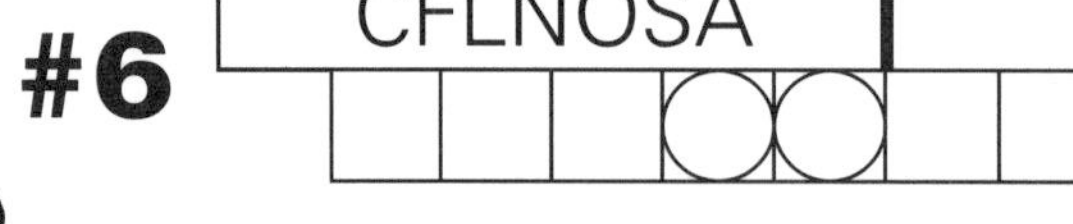

Box of Clues

Stumped? Maybe you can find a clue below.

- -Montreal _______
- -Chicago _______
- -Kansas City _______
- -Minnesota _______
- -Atlanta _______
- -Dallas _______
- -Buffalo _______

Arrange the circled letters to solve the mystery answer.

MYSTERY ANSWER

MATH

JUMBLE BrainBusters Junior

Unscramble the Jumbled letters, one letter to each square, so that each equation is correct.

For example: NONTEOEOW
ONE + ONE = TWO

#1 ZOENOEERON

☐☐◯ – ☐☐◯ = ☐☐☐☐

#2 FTOEREEONURH

☐☐◯ + ◯☐☐☐☐ = ☐☐☐◯

#3 ESRTXIHETHEER

☐☐☐ – ◯☐☐☐☐ = ☐◯☐☐☐

#4 URFZOUEORORF

◯☐☐☐ + ☐☐☐☐ = ☐◯☐☐

#5 WSIFEVOEENVT

☐◯☐☐ + ☐◯☐ = ☐☐◯☐☐

Arrange the circled letters to solve the mystery equation.

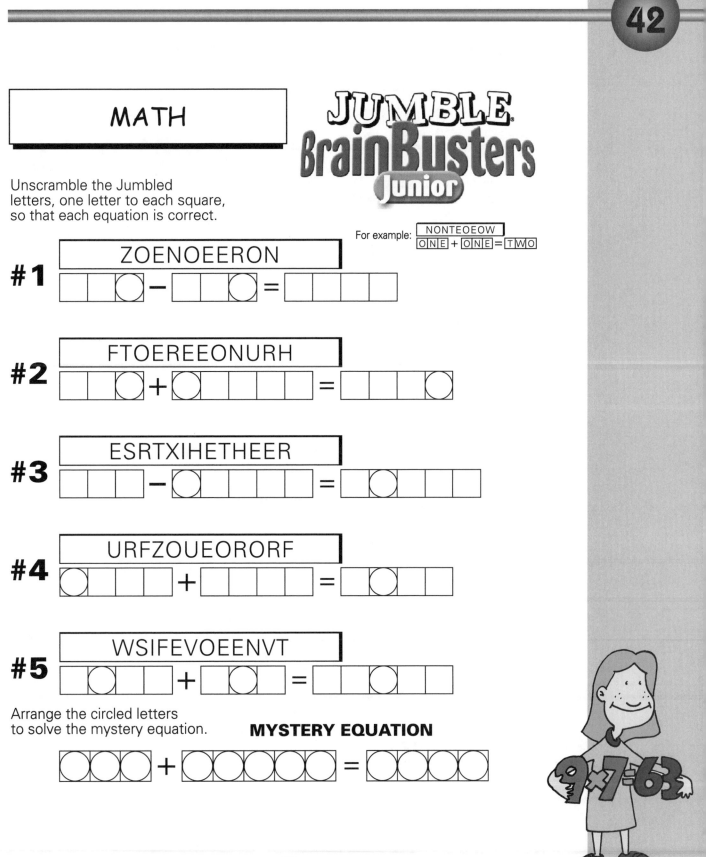

MYSTERY EQUATION

◯◯◯ + ◯◯◯◯◯ = ◯◯◯◯

PUZZLE

43

PLANTS

Unscramble the Jumbles, one letter to each square, to spell words related to plants.

#1 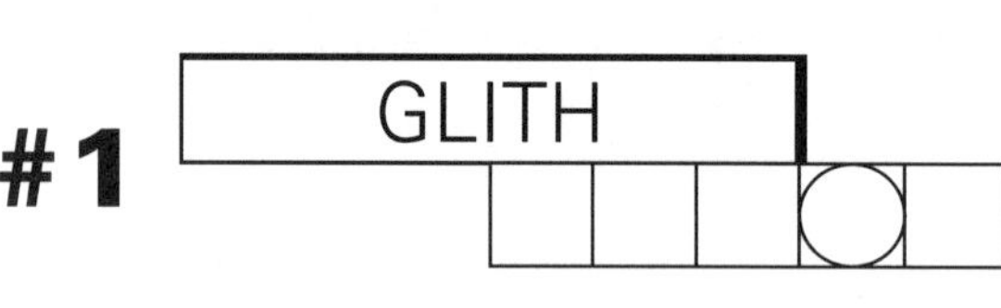

#2 

#3 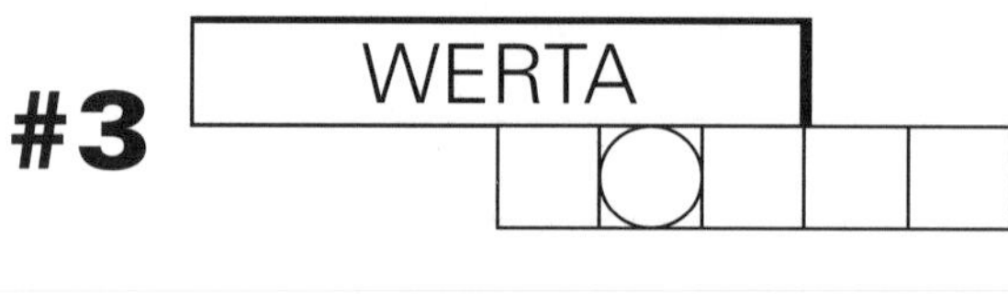

#4 

#5 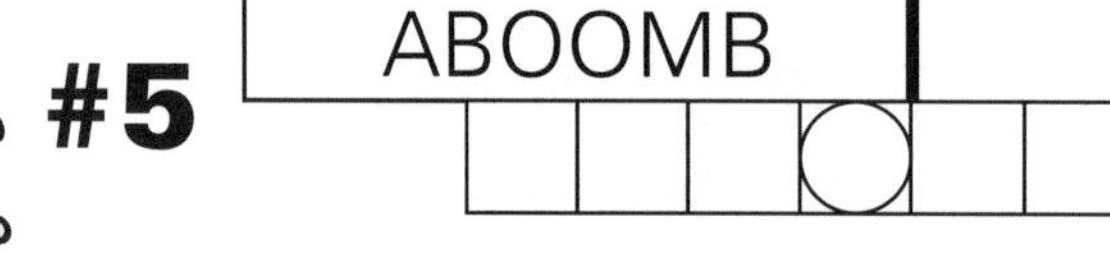

Box of Clues

Stumped? Maybe you can find a clue below.

- -Bright component in photosynthesis
- -Tall, woody grass
- -Natural division of a plant
- -Important liquid for plants
- -Desert plant
- -Main stem of a tree

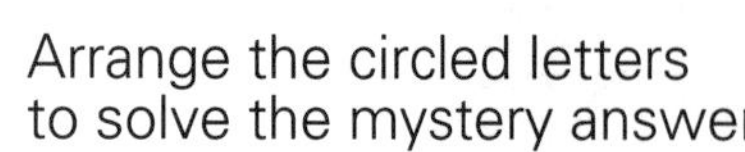

Arrange the circled letters to solve the mystery answer.

MYSTERY ANSWER

PUZZLE 44

COUNTRIES

Unscramble the Jumbles, one letter to each square, to spell names of countries.

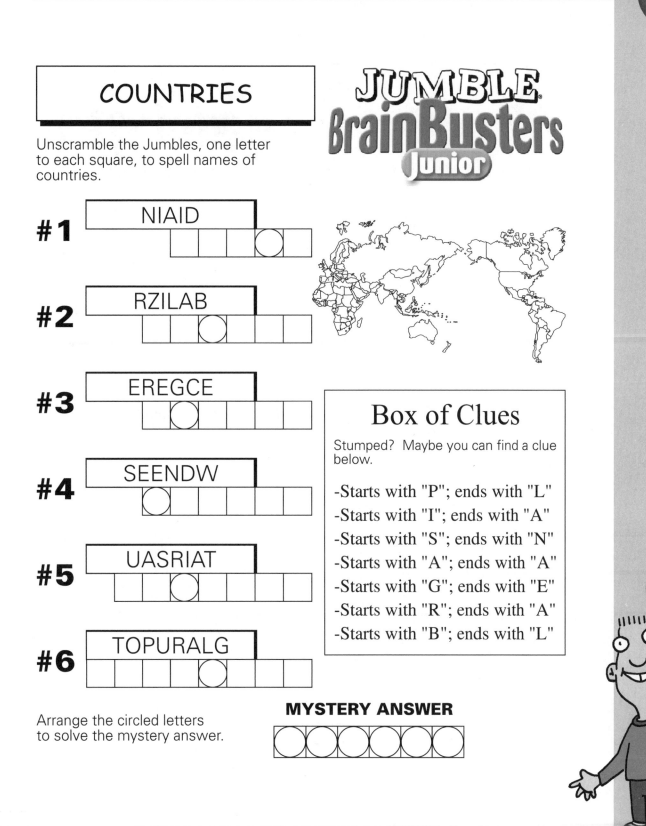

#1 

#2 

#3 

#4 

#5 

#6 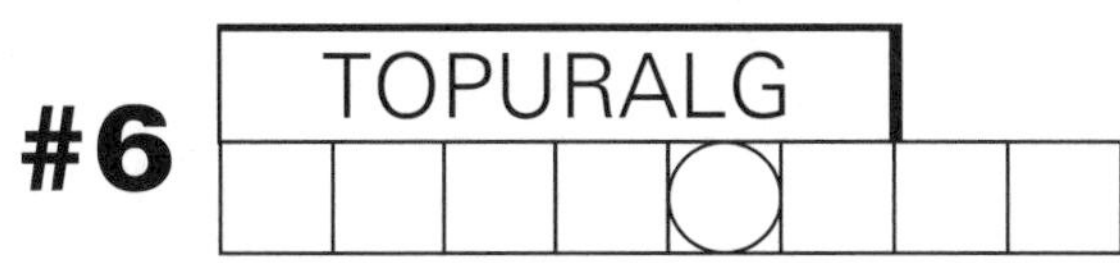

Box of Clues

Stumped? Maybe you can find a clue below.

-Starts with "P"; ends with "L"
-Starts with "I"; ends with "A"
-Starts with "S"; ends with "N"
-Starts with "A"; ends with "A"
-Starts with "G"; ends with "E"
-Starts with "R"; ends with "A"
-Starts with "B"; ends with "L"

Arrange the circled letters to solve the mystery answer.

MYSTERY ANSWER

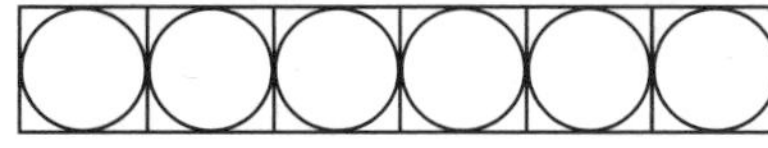

PUZZLE

45

ALL ABOUT MUSIC

Unscramble the Jumbles, one letter to each square, to spell words related to music.

#1 

#2 

#3 

#4 

#5 

Box of Clues

Stumped? Maybe you can find a clue below.

-Starts with "T"; ends with "O"
-Starts with "P"; ends with "O"
-Starts with "G"; ends with "R"
-Starts with "T"; ends with "T"
-Starts with "F"; ends with "E"
-Starts with "D"; ends with "M"

Arrange the circled letters to solve the mystery answer.

MYSTERY ANSWER

U.S. STATES

JUMBLE BrainBusters Junior

Unscramble the Jumbles, one letter to each square, to spell names of U.S. states.

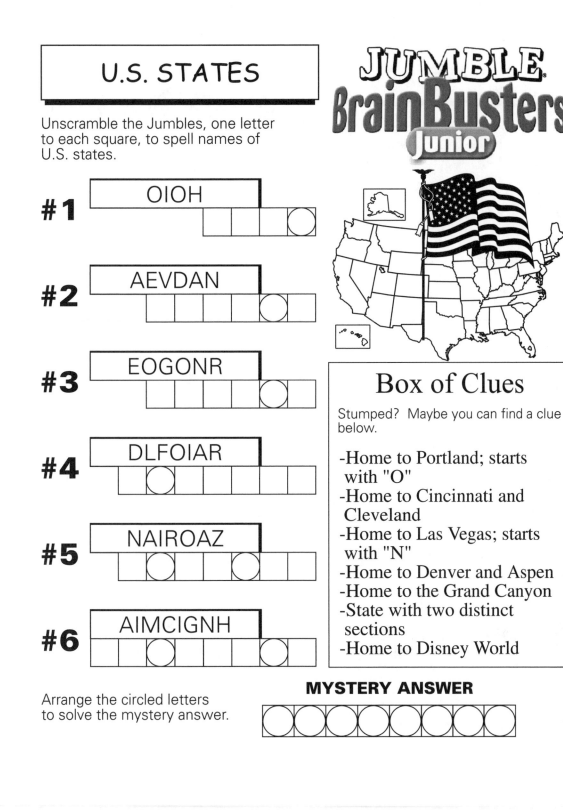

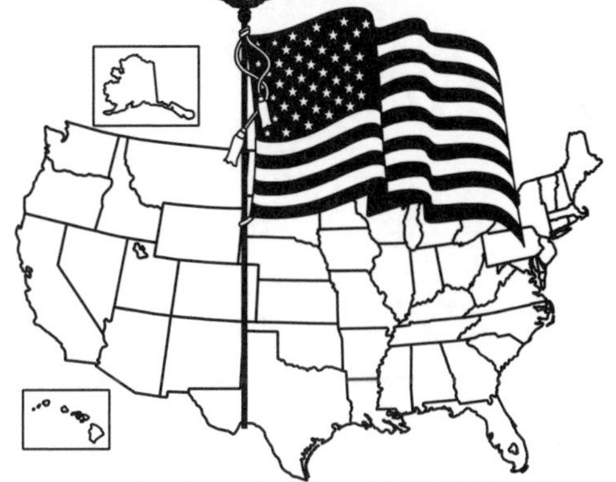

#1 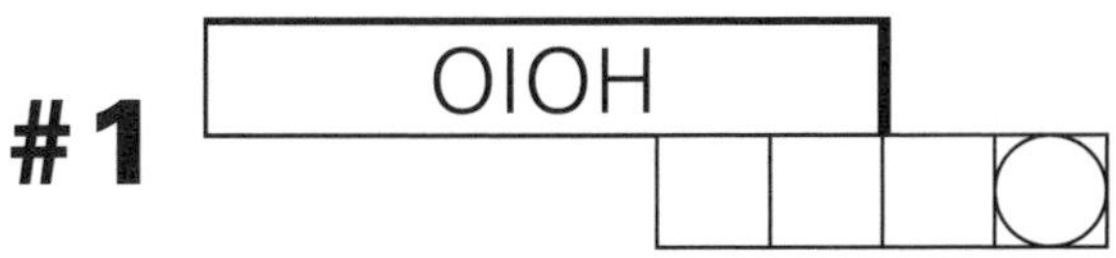

#2 

#3 

#4 

#5 

#6 

Box of Clues

Stumped? Maybe you can find a clue below.

-Home to Portland; starts with "O"
-Home to Cincinnati and Cleveland
-Home to Las Vegas; starts with "N"
-Home to Denver and Aspen
-Home to the Grand Canyon
-State with two distinct sections
-Home to Disney World

Arrange the circled letters to solve the mystery answer.

MYSTERY ANSWER

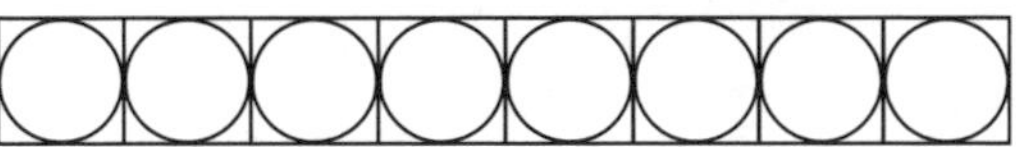

PUZZLE

47

TIME LINE

Unscramble the Jumbles, one letter to each square, to spell words as suggested by the time line.

#1 **1769** ______ of Napoleon Bonaparte

#1 TBIHR

#2 **1819** U.S. purchases ______

#2 DFOLIAR

#3 **1914** First ______ War begins

#3 OWLDR

#4 **1981** Martial law declared in ______

#4 LOPADN

#5 **1986** U.S. space ______ explodes after takeoff

#5 UHTLETS

#6 **1991** Boris Yeltsin becomes president of ______

#6 SRISAU

Arrange the circled letters to solve the mystery answer. **1961** ______ ______ constructed in Germany

MYSTERY ANSWER

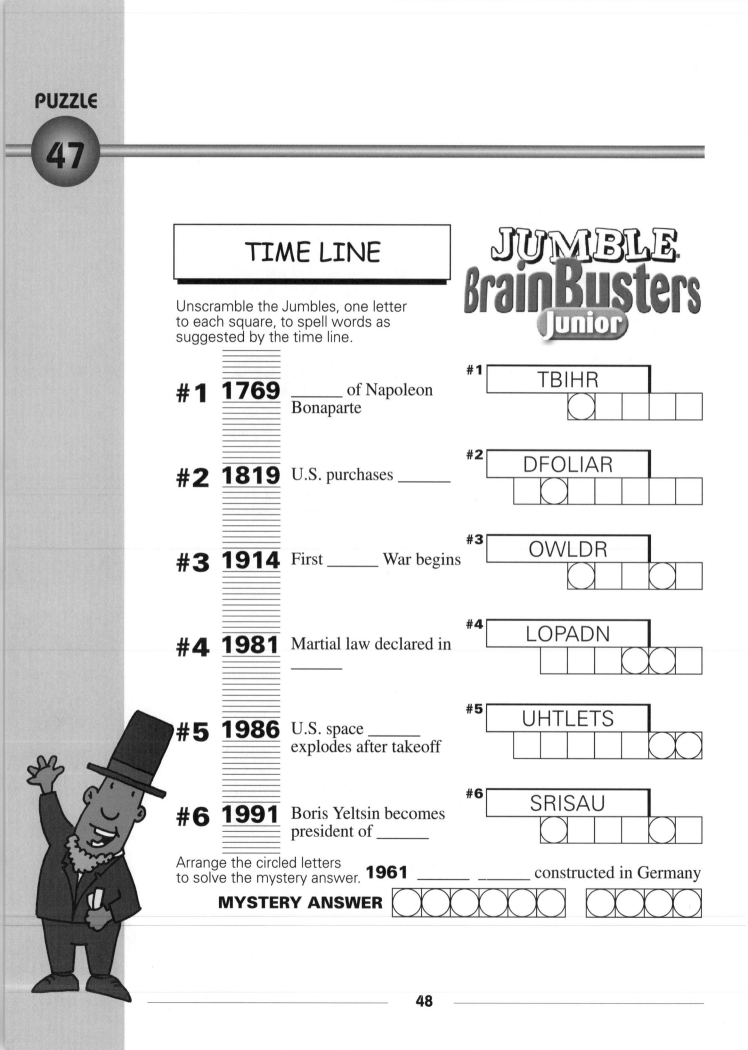

FOOD

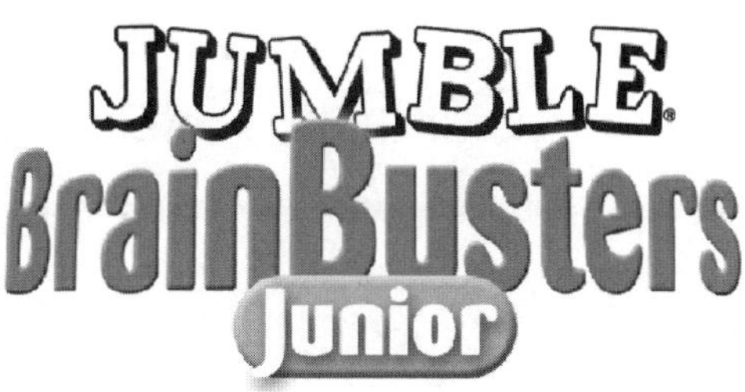

Unscramble the Jumbles, one letter to each square, to spell words related to food.

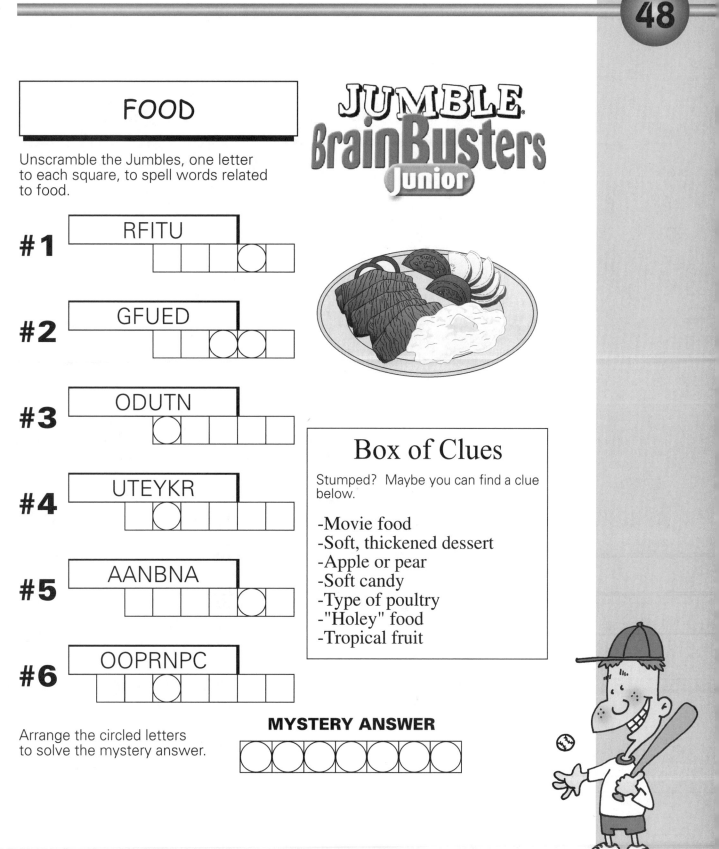

#1

#2

#3

#4

#5

#6

Box of Clues

Stumped? Maybe you can find a clue below.

-Movie food
-Soft, thickened dessert
-Apple or pear
-Soft candy
-Type of poultry
-"Holey" food
-Tropical fruit

Arrange the circled letters to solve the mystery answer.

MYSTERY ANSWER

PUZZLE

49

FAMOUS ATHLETES

JUMBLE® BrainBusters Junior

Unscramble the Jumbles, one letter to each square, to spell last names of famous athletes.

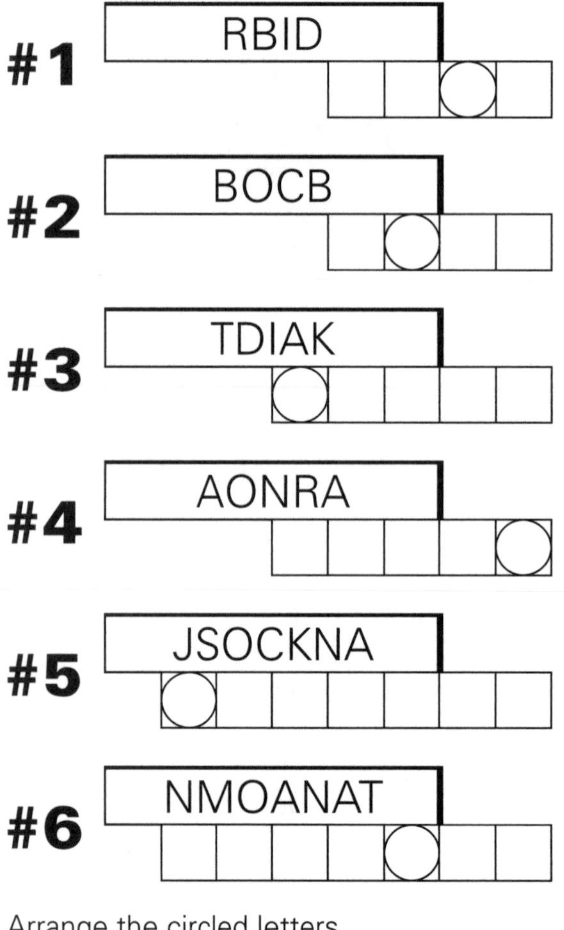

Arrange the circled letters to solve the mystery answer.

MYSTERY ANSWER

Box of Clues

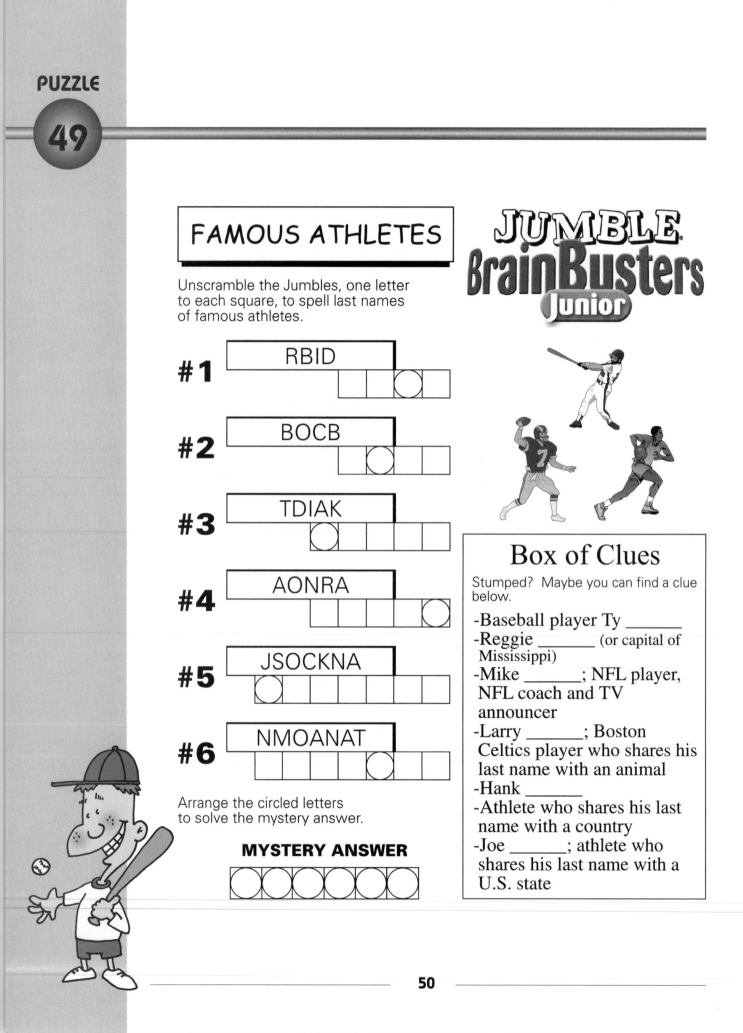

Stumped? Maybe you can find a clue below.

- -Baseball player Ty ______
- -Reggie ______ (or capital of Mississippi)
- -Mike ______; NFL player, NFL coach and TV announcer
- -Larry ______; Boston Celtics player who shares his last name with an animal
- -Hank ______
- -Athlete who shares his last name with a country
- -Joe ______; athlete who shares his last name with a U.S. state

THE HUMAN BODY

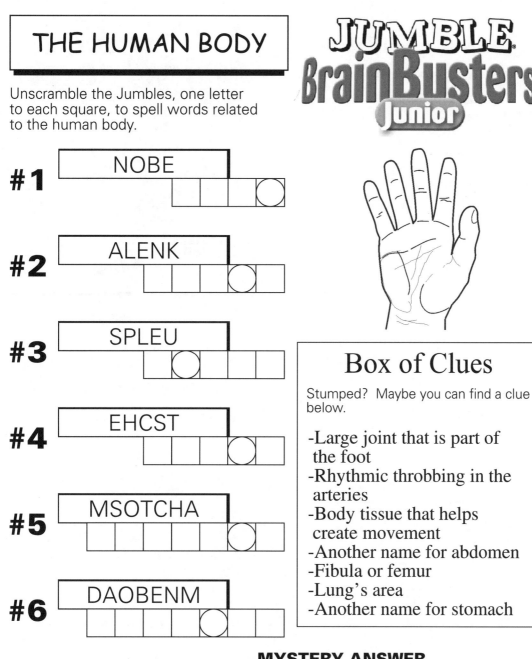

JUMBLE BrainBusters Junior

Unscramble the Jumbles, one letter to each square, to spell words related to the human body.

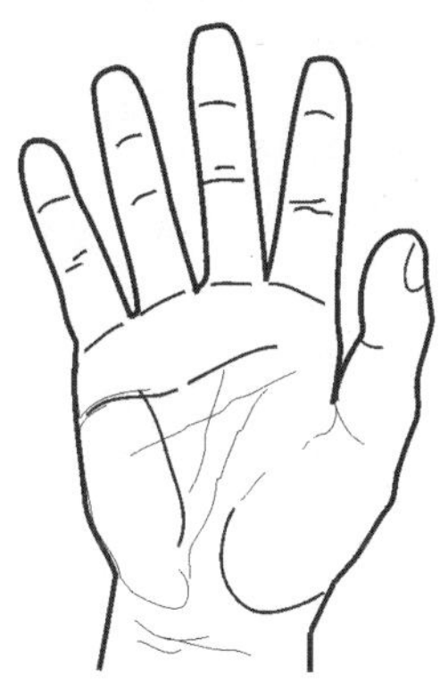

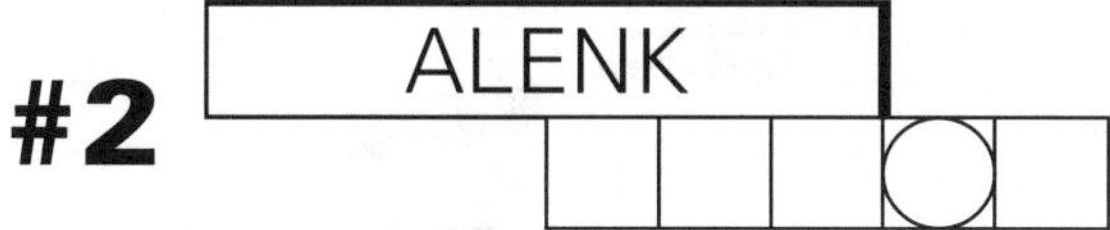

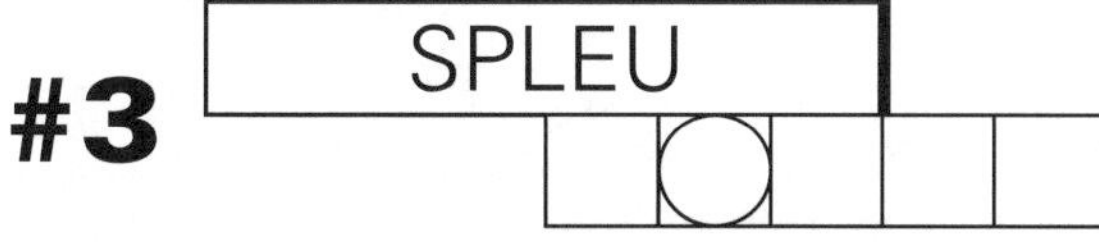

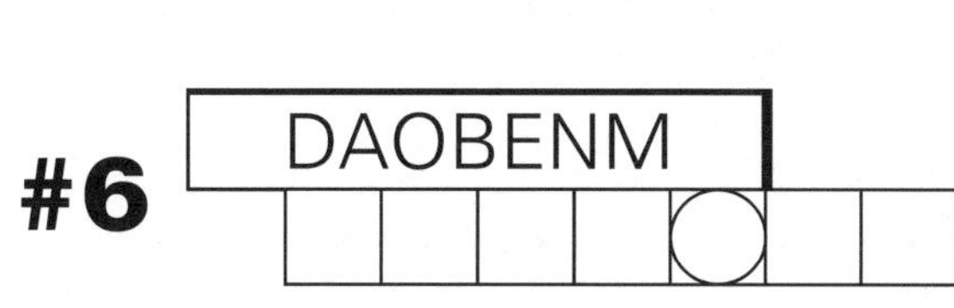

Box of Clues

Stumped? Maybe you can find a clue below.

- -Large joint that is part of the foot
- -Rhythmic throbbing in the arteries
- -Body tissue that helps create movement
- -Another name for abdomen
- -Fibula or femur
- -Lung's area
- -Another name for stomach

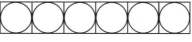

Arrange the circled letters to solve the mystery answer.

MYSTERY ANSWER

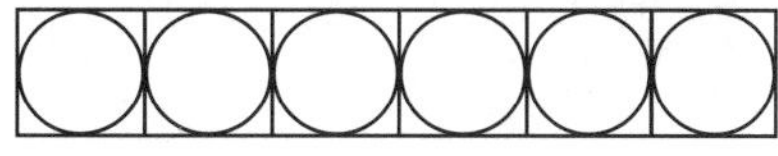

PUZZLE

51

DOUBLE CONSONANTS

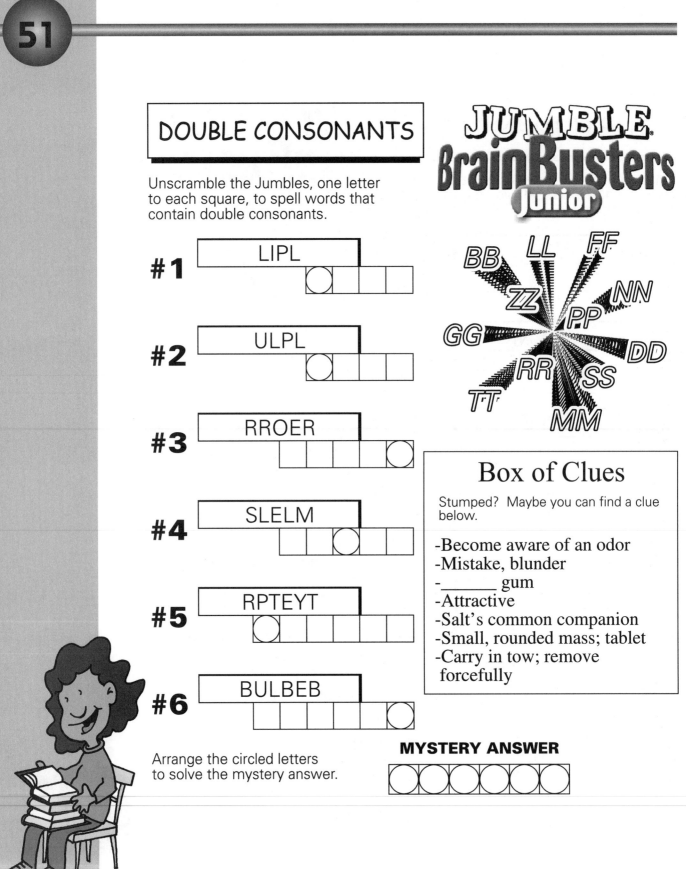

Unscramble the Jumbles, one letter to each square, to spell words that contain double consonants.

#1 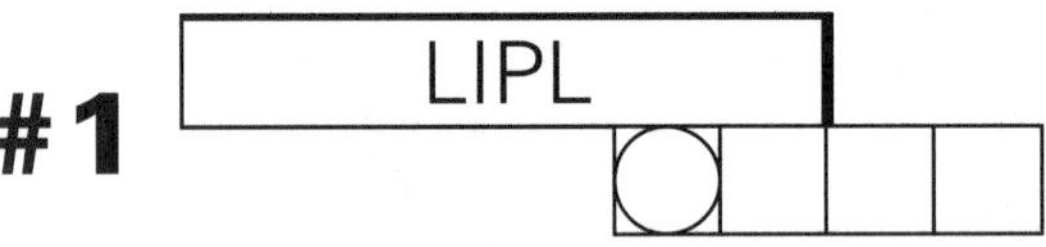

#2 

#3 

#4 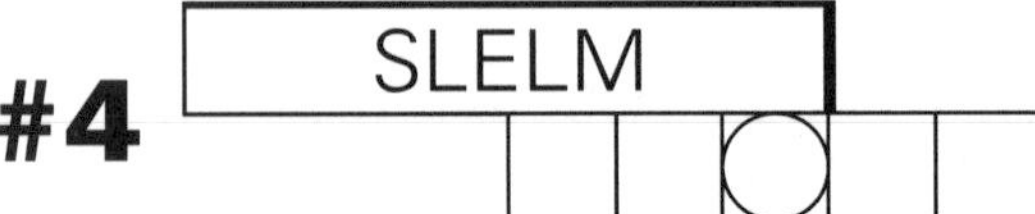

#5 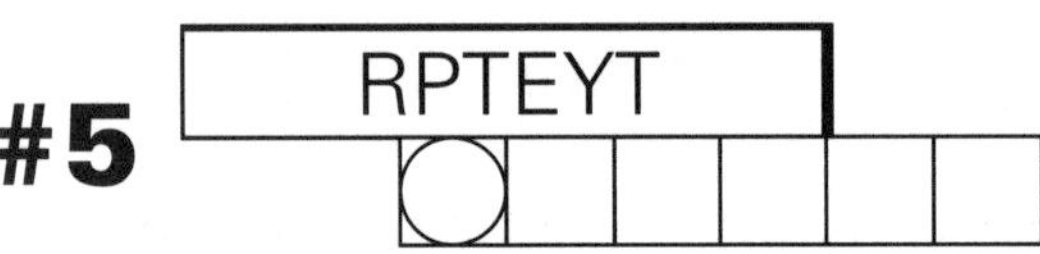

#6 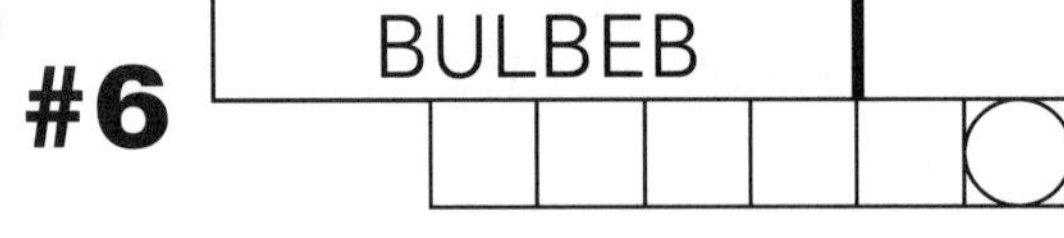

JUMBLE BrainBusters Junior

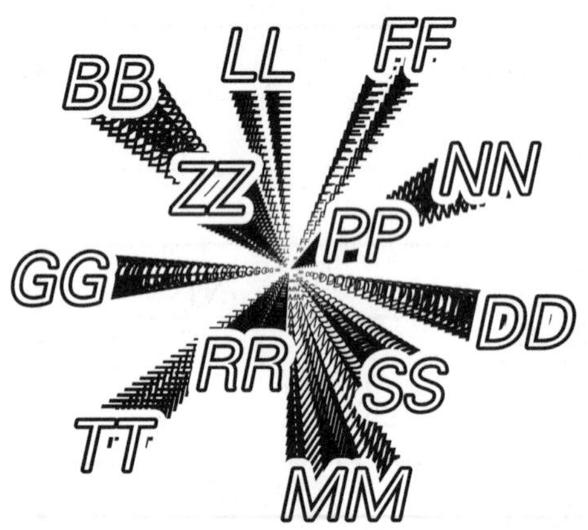

Box of Clues

Stumped? Maybe you can find a clue below.

-Become aware of an odor
-Mistake, blunder
-______ gum
-Attractive
-Salt's common companion
-Small, rounded mass; tablet
-Carry in tow; remove forcefully

Arrange the circled letters to solve the mystery answer.

MYSTERY ANSWER

CLOTHING

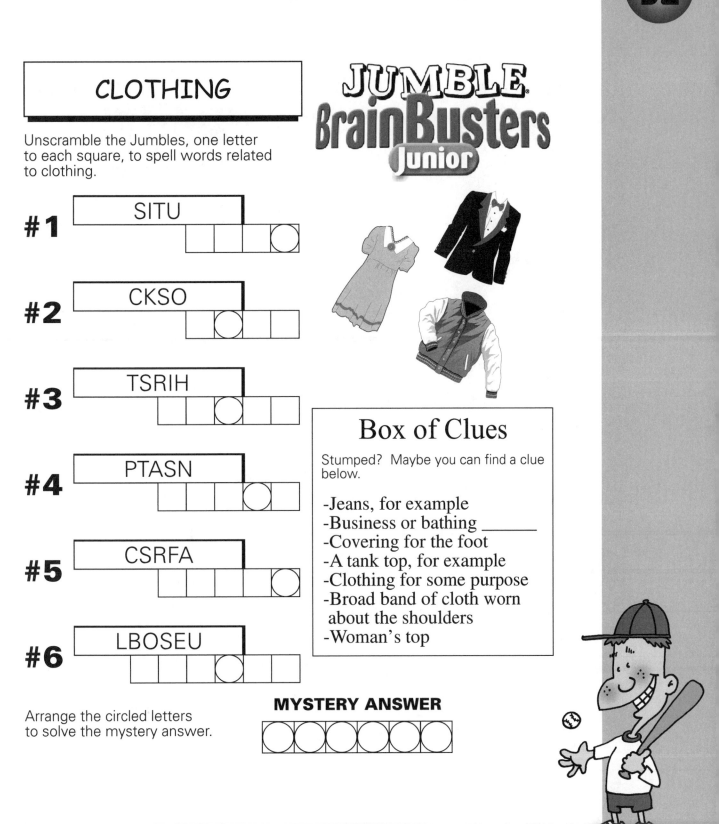

Unscramble the Jumbles, one letter to each square, to spell words related to clothing.

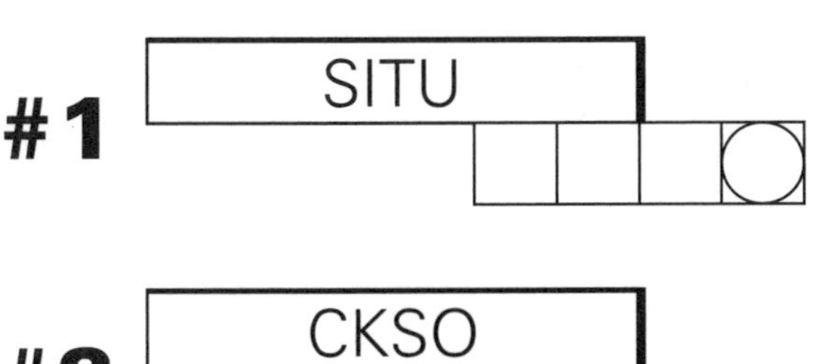

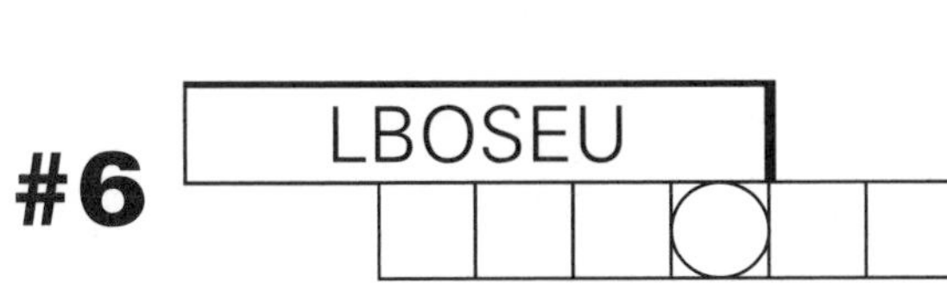

JUMBLE® BrainBusters Junior

Box of Clues

Stumped? Maybe you can find a clue below.

- -Jeans, for example
- -Business or bathing ______
- -Covering for the foot
- -A tank top, for example
- -Clothing for some purpose
- -Broad band of cloth worn about the shoulders
- -Woman's top

Arrange the circled letters to solve the mystery answer.

MYSTERY ANSWER

PUZZLE

53

COUNTRIES

JUMBLE BrainBusters Junior

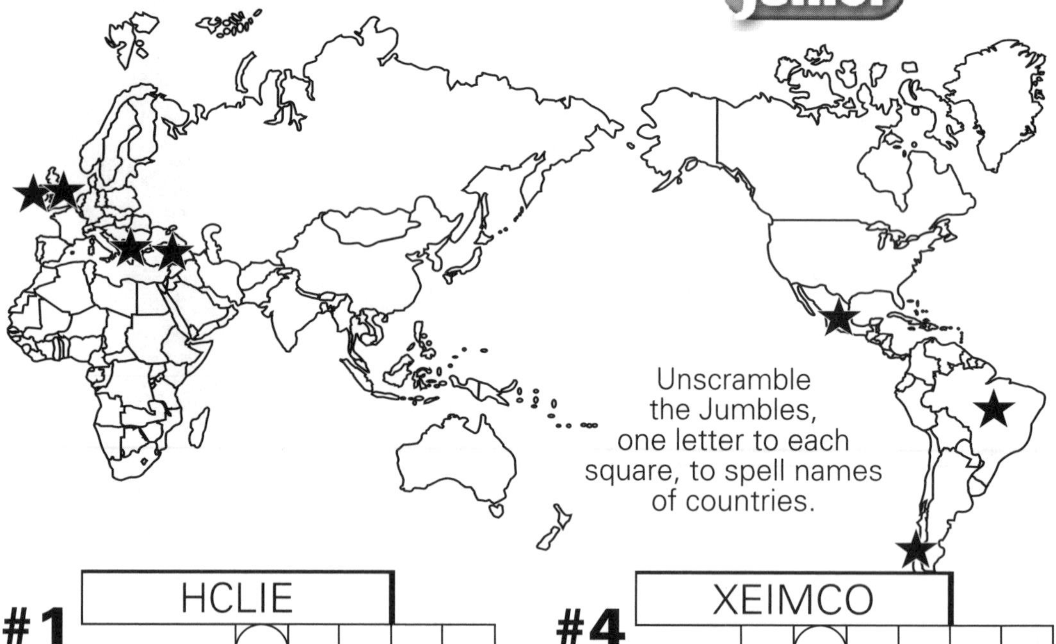

Unscramble the Jumbles, one letter to each square, to spell names of countries.

#2 RBZILA

#5 NIRLEAD

Arrange the circled letters to solve the mystery answer.

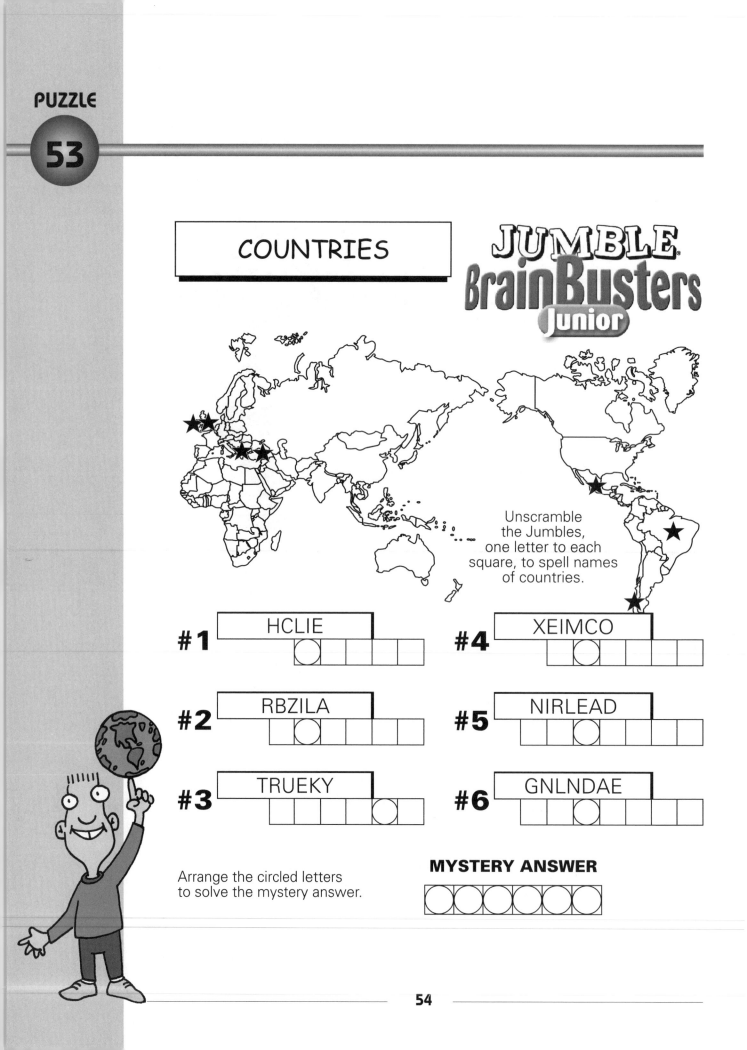

MYSTERY ANSWER

PLANET EARTH

JUMBLE BrainBusters Junior

Unscramble the Jumbles, one letter to each square, to spell words related to Planet Earth.

#1
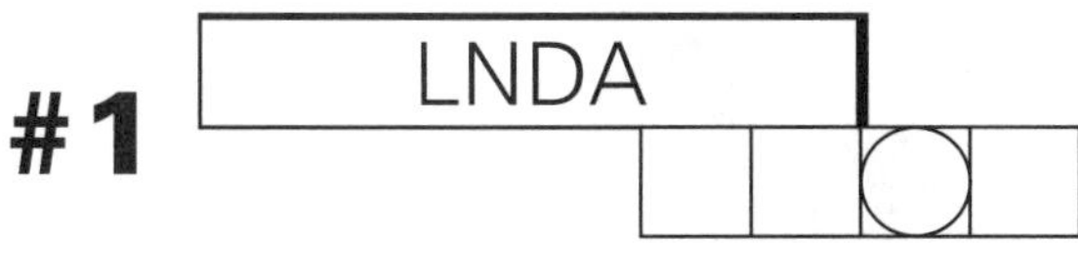

#2

#3

#4
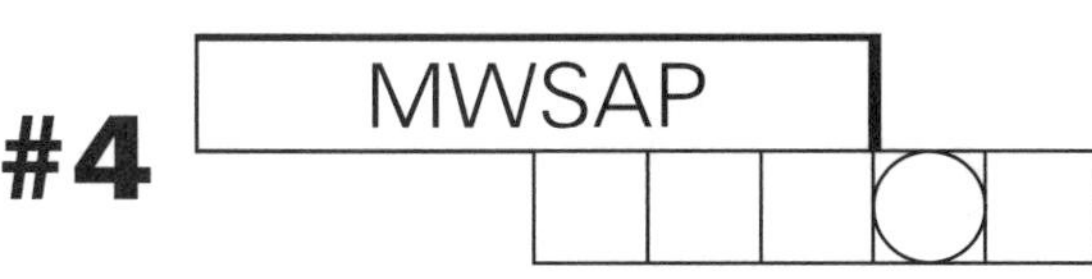

#5

#6

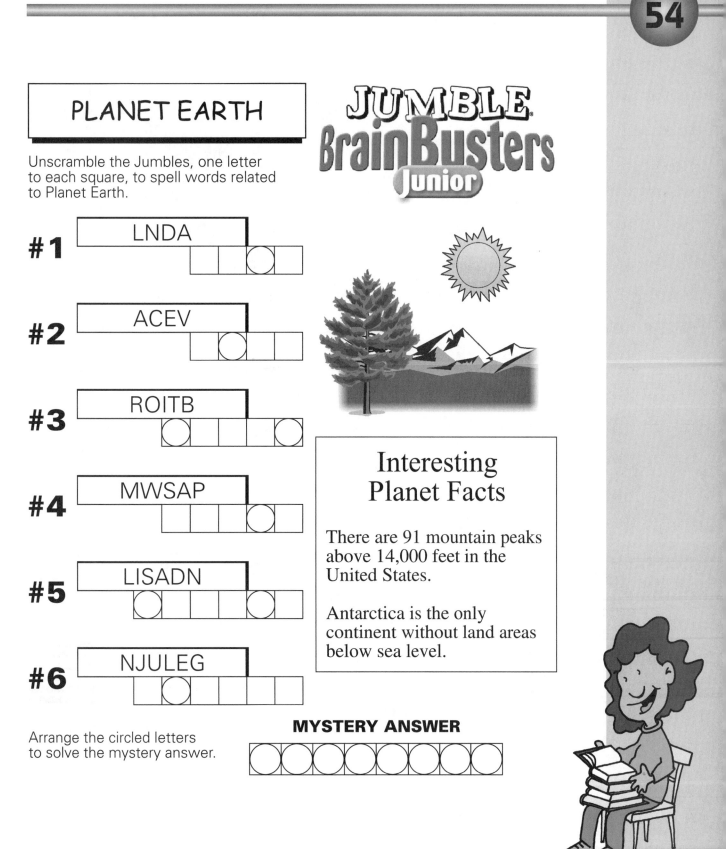

Interesting Planet Facts

There are 91 mountain peaks above 14,000 feet in the United States.

Antarctica is the only continent without land areas below sea level.

Arrange the circled letters to solve the mystery answer.

MYSTERY ANSWER

PUZZLE 55

COUNTRY FLAGS

Unscramble the Jumbles, one letter to each square, to spell names of countries, as suggested by the flags.

#1 DIAIN

#4 MAAANP

#2 GETPY

#5 LBIOIAV

#3 REECGE

#6 GEIMBUL

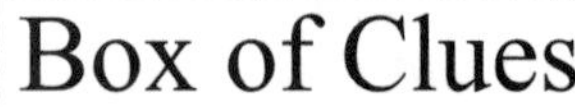

Box of Clues Stumped? Maybe you can find a clue below.

- -Starts with "E"; ends with "T"
- -Starts with "B"; ends with "M"
- -Starts with "L"; ends with "A"
- -Starts with "I"; ends with "A"
- -Starts with "P"; ends with "A"
- -Starts with "B"; ends with "A"
- -Starts with "G"; ends with "E"

Arrange the circled letters to solve the mystery answer.

MYSTERY ANSWER

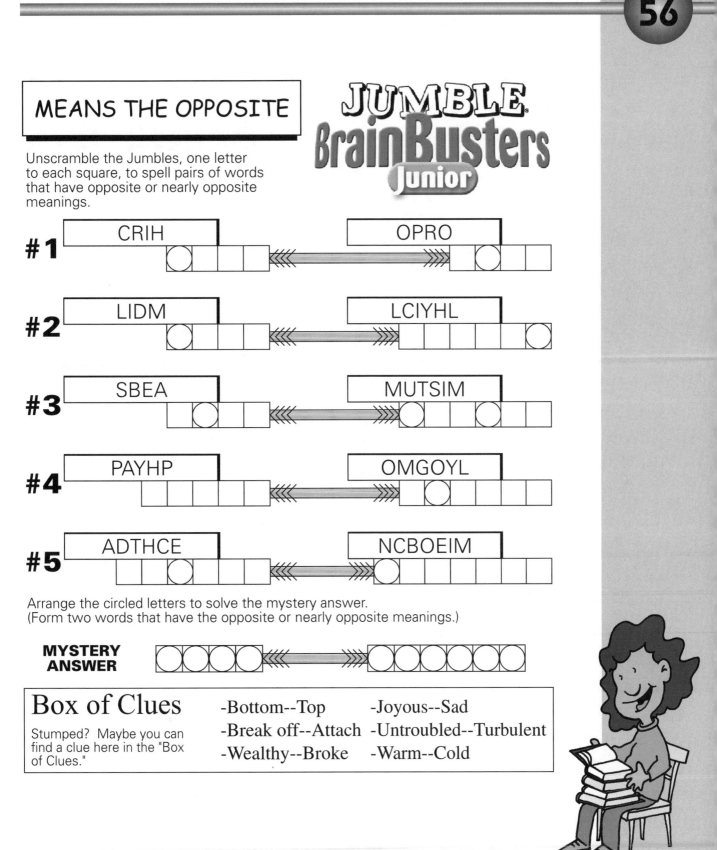

MEANS THE OPPOSITE

JUMBLE BrainBusters Junior

Unscramble the Jumbles, one letter to each square, to spell pairs of words that have opposite or nearly opposite meanings.

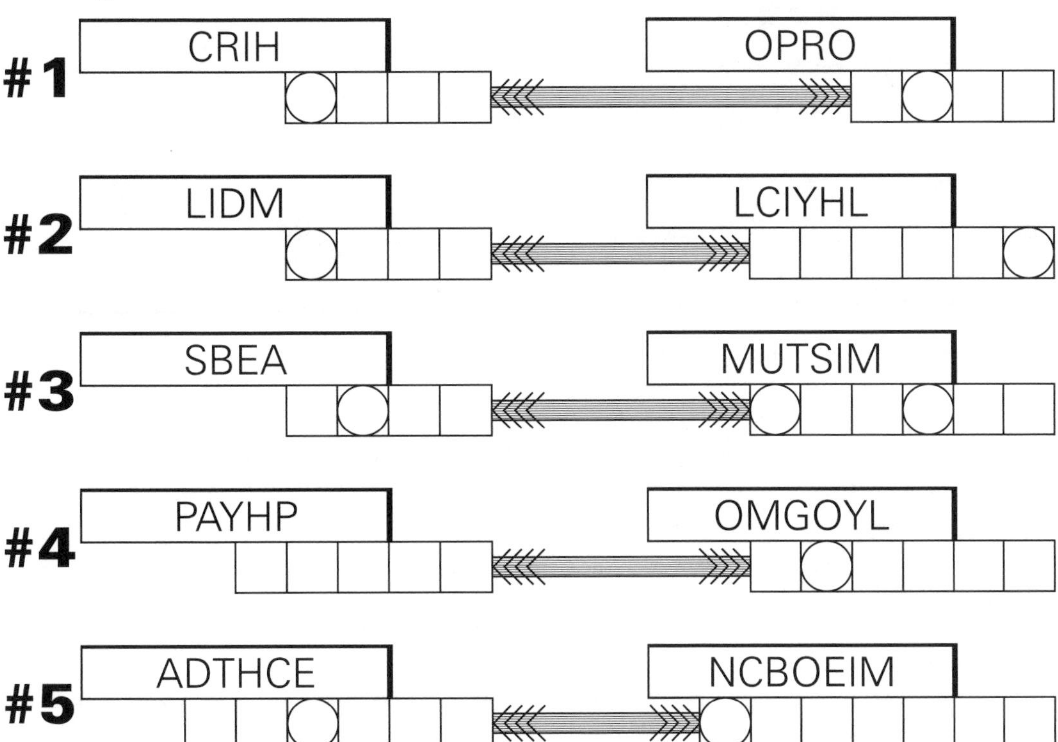

Arrange the circled letters to solve the mystery answer.
(Form two words that have the opposite or nearly opposite meanings.)

MYSTERY ANSWER

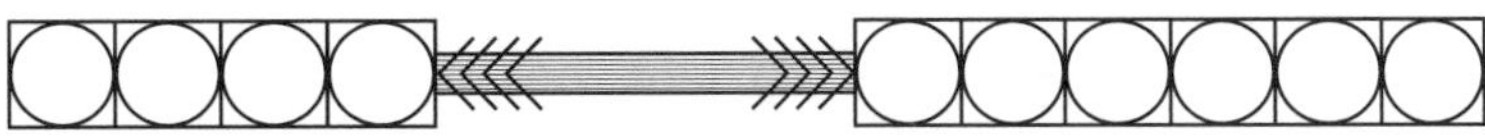

Box of Clues

Stumped? Maybe you can find a clue here in the "Box of Clues."

-Bottom--Top
-Break off--Attach
-Wealthy--Broke
-Joyous--Sad
-Untroubled--Turbulent
-Warm--Cold

PUZZLE

57

SPORTS

Unscramble the Jumbles, one letter to each square, to spell words related to sports.

#1

#2

#3

#4

#5

#6

Box of Clues

Stumped? Maybe you can find a clue below.

- Sprinter
- Boxing bout
- New player, young player
- Judge
- Group of games
- British sport
- Offense's opponent

Arrange the circled letters to solve the mystery answer.

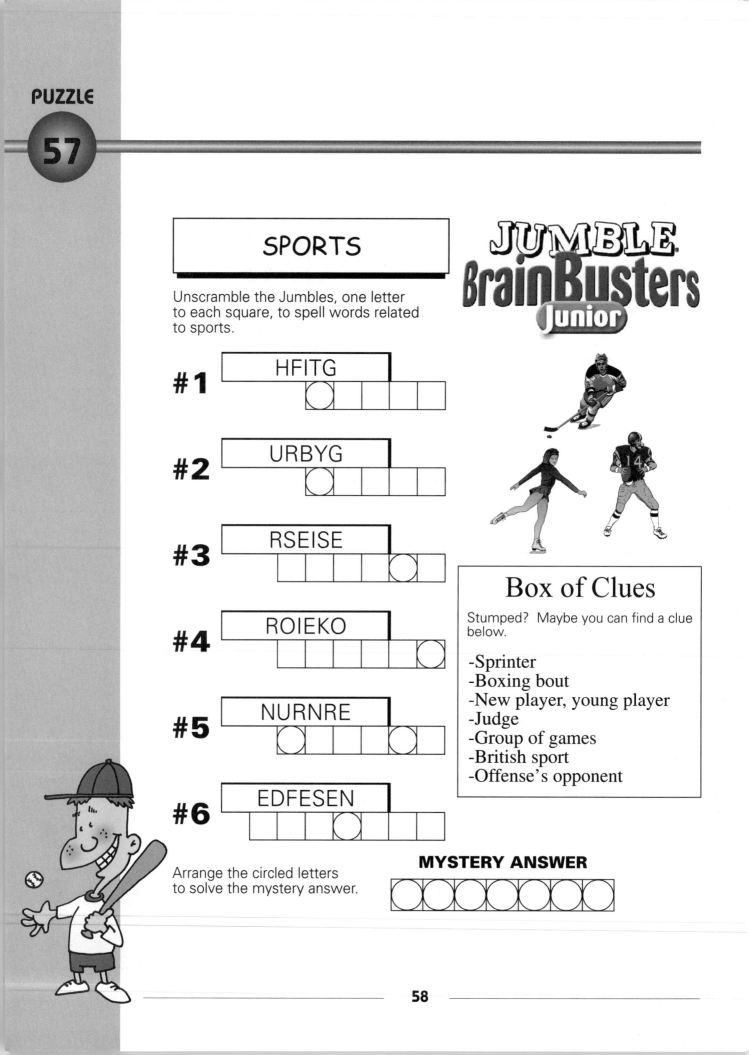

MYSTERY ANSWER

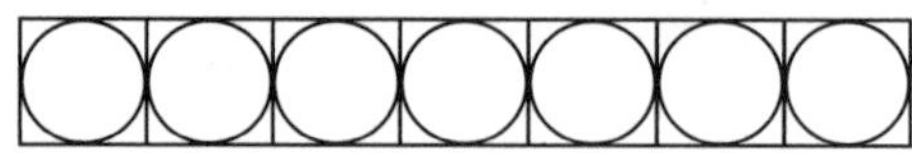

NOUNS

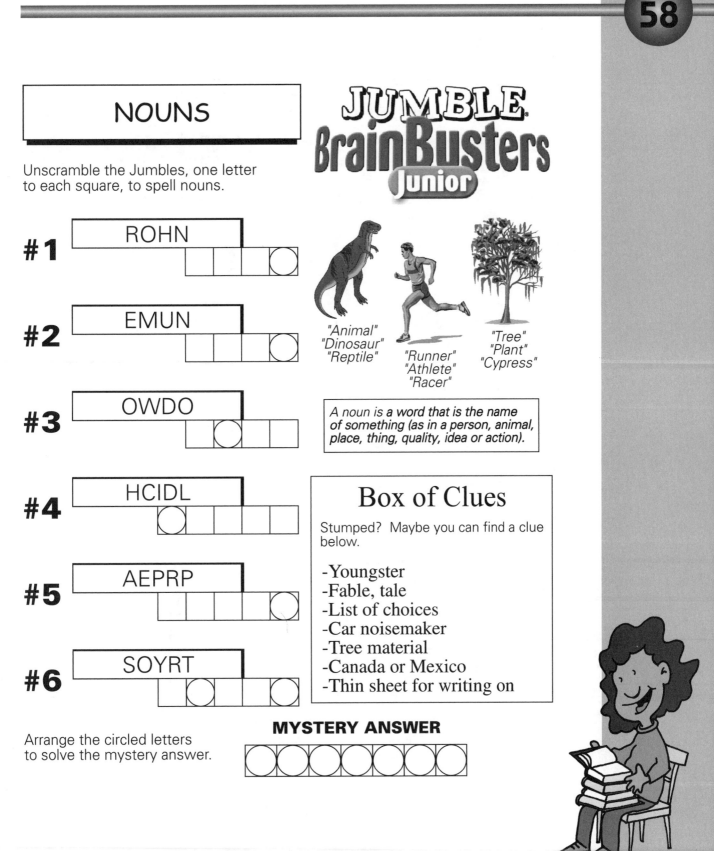

JUMBLE BrainBusters Junior

Unscramble the Jumbles, one letter to each square, to spell nouns.

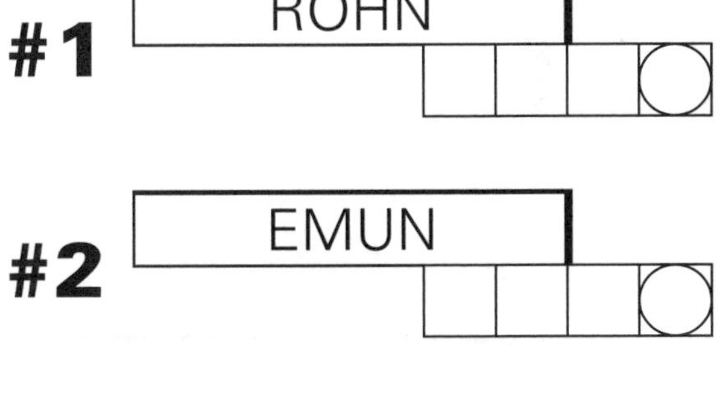

"Animal"
"Dinosaur"
"Reptile"

"Runner"
"Athlete"
"Racer"

"Tree"
"Plant"
"Cypress"

#3 OWDO

A noun is a word that is the name of something (as in a person, animal, place, thing, quality, idea or action).

#4 HCIDL

Box of Clues

Stumped? Maybe you can find a clue below.

- Youngster
- Fable, tale
- List of choices
- Car noisemaker
- Tree material
- Canada or Mexico
- Thin sheet for writing on

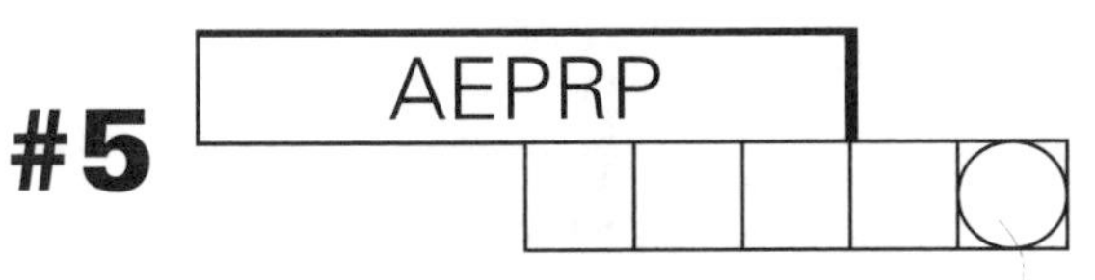

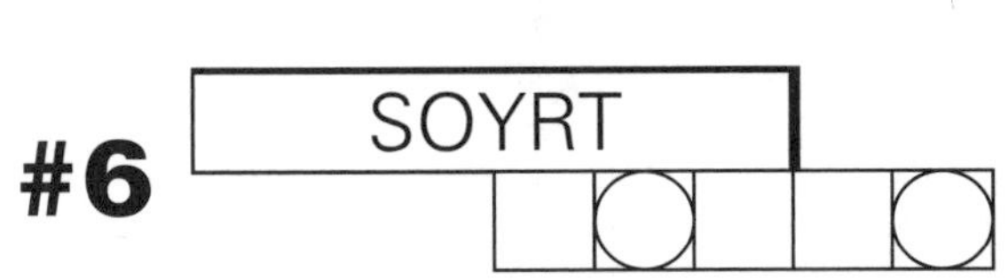

MYSTERY ANSWER

Arrange the circled letters to solve the mystery answer.

PUZZLE

59

U.S. STATE CAPITALS

Unscramble the Jumbles, one letter to each square, to spell names of U.S. state capitals.

#1 

#2 

#3 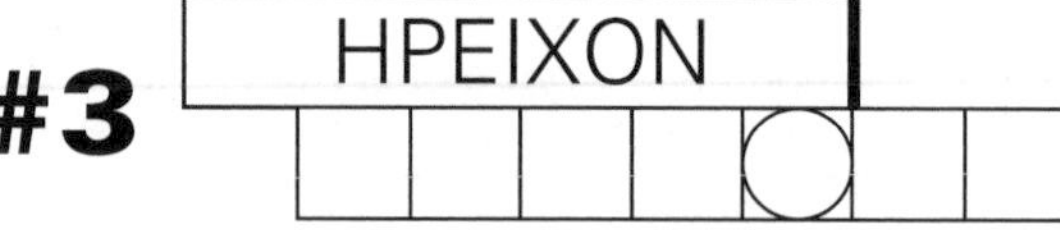

#4 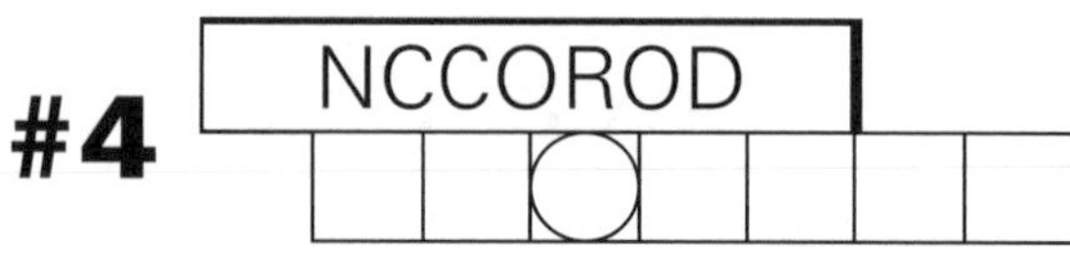

#5 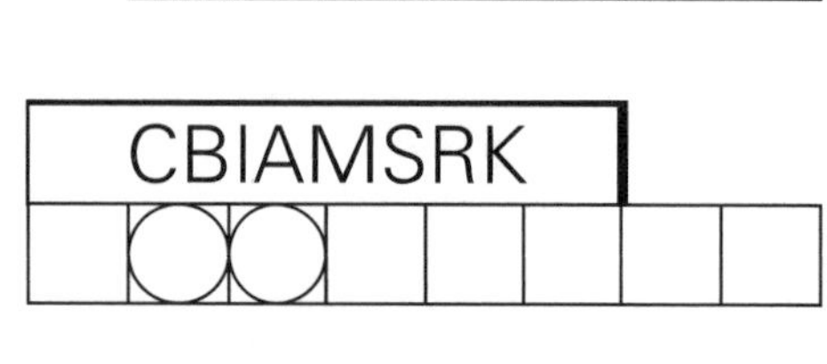

#6 LHNOUUOL

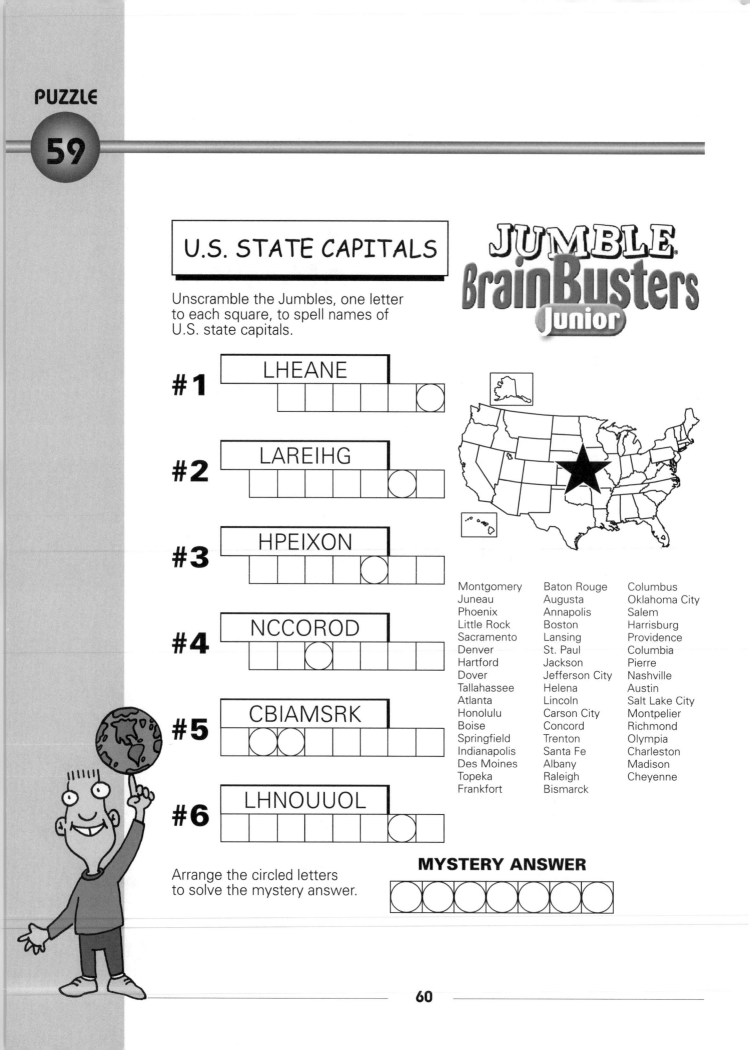

Montgomery
Juneau
Phoenix
Little Rock
Sacramento
Denver
Hartford
Dover
Tallahassee
Atlanta
Honolulu
Boise
Springfield
Indianapolis
Des Moines
Topeka
Frankfort
Baton Rouge
Augusta
Annapolis
Boston
Lansing
St. Paul
Jackson
Jefferson City
Helena
Lincoln
Carson City
Concord
Trenton
Santa Fe
Albany
Raleigh
Bismarck
Columbus
Oklahoma City
Salem
Harrisburg
Providence
Columbia
Pierre
Nashville
Austin
Salt Lake City
Montpelier
Richmond
Olympia
Charleston
Madison
Cheyenne

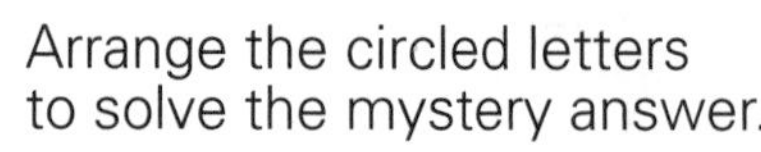

Arrange the circled letters to solve the mystery answer.

MYSTERY ANSWER

state capitals

animals

JUMBLE®

BrainBusters Junior II

INTERMEDIATE PUZZLES

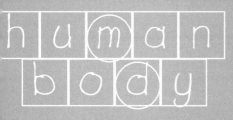

human body

outer space

sports

money

PUZZLE

60

STARTS WITH A VOWEL

JUMBLE BrainBusters Junior

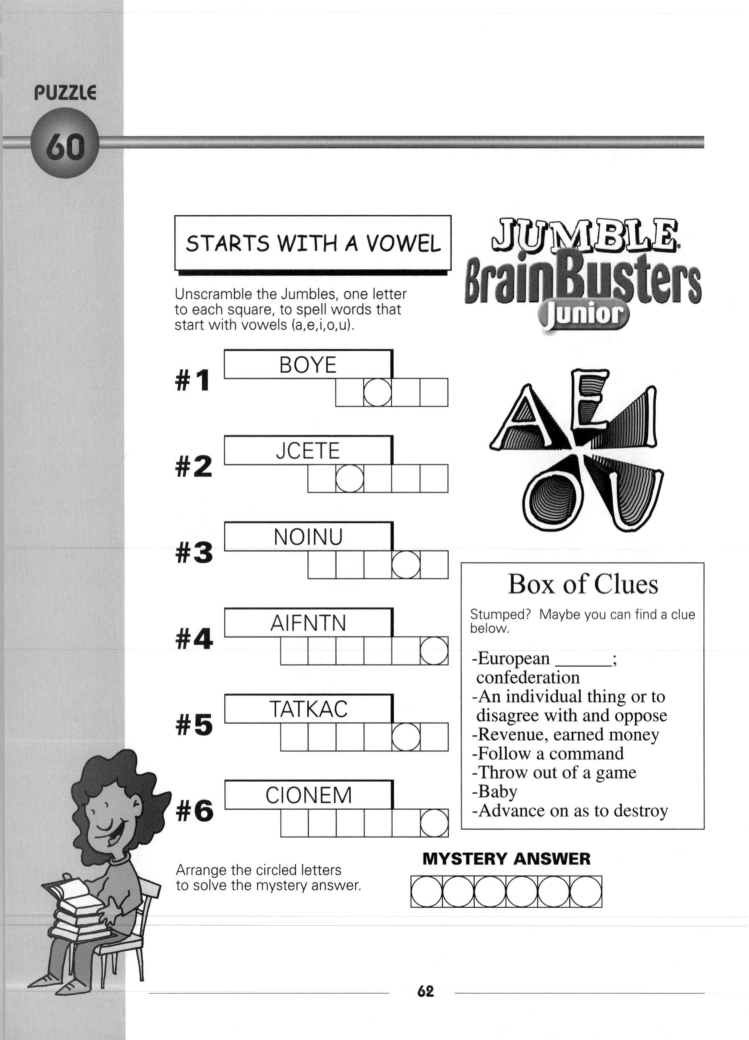

Unscramble the Jumbles, one letter to each square, to spell words that start with vowels (a,e,i,o,u).

#1

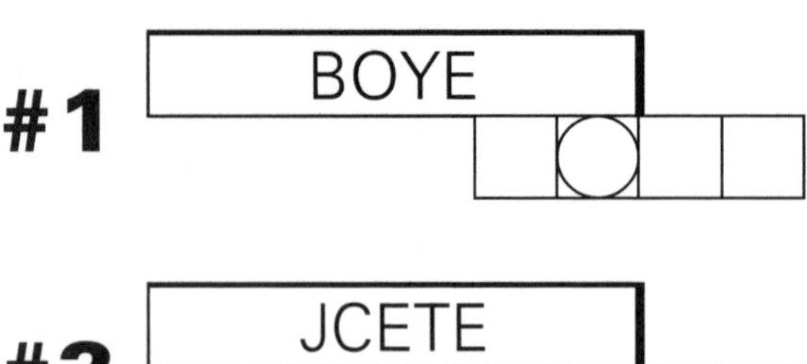

#2

#3

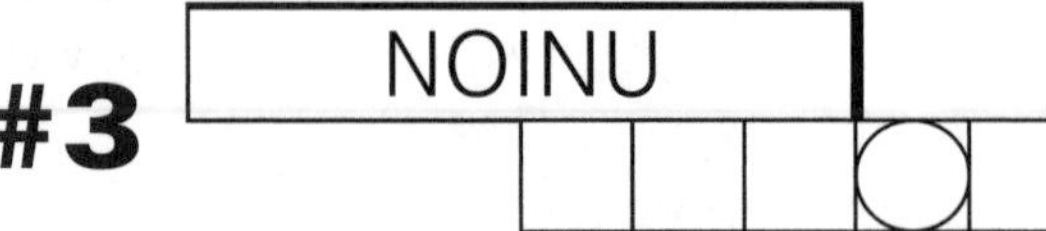

#4

#5

#6

Box of Clues

Stumped? Maybe you can find a clue below.

- -European ______; confederation
- -An individual thing or to disagree with and oppose
- -Revenue, earned money
- -Follow a command
- -Throw out of a game
- -Baby
- -Advance on as to destroy

Arrange the circled letters to solve the mystery answer.

MYSTERY ANSWER

JUMBLE® BrainBusters Junior

FOOTBALL

Unscramble the Jumbles, one letter to each square, to spell words related to football.

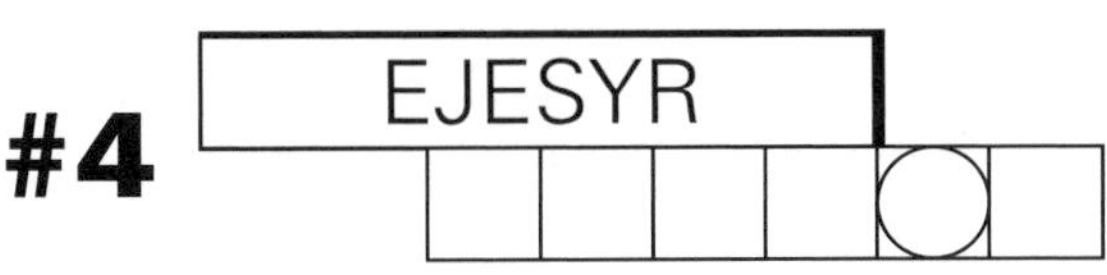

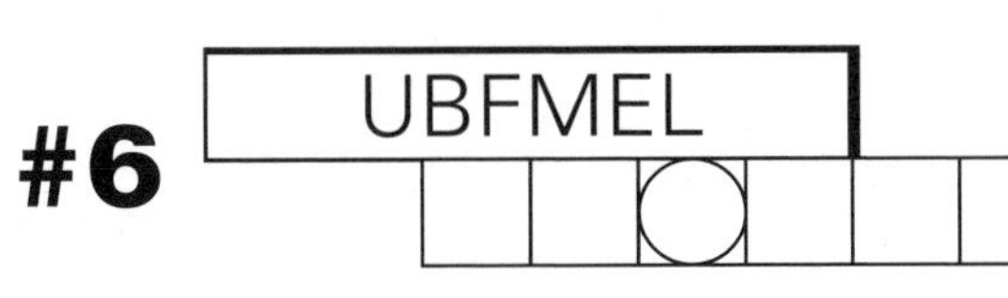

Box of Clues

Stumped? Maybe you can find a clue below.

-Starts with "J"; ends with "Y"
-Starts with "H"; ends with "F"
-Starts with "P"; ends with "T"
-Starts with "H"; ends with "E"
-Starts with "K"; ends with "R"
-Starts with "H"; ends with "T"
-Starts with "F"; ends with "E"

Arrange the circled letters to solve the mystery answer.

MYSTERY ANSWER

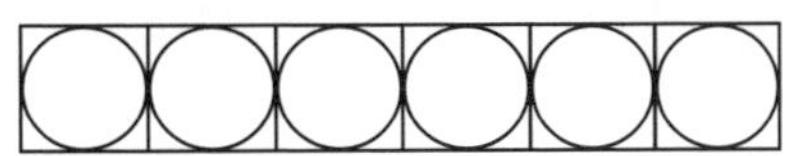

PUZZLE 62

STARTS WITH "F"

Unscramble the Jumbles, one letter to each square, to spell words that start with "F."

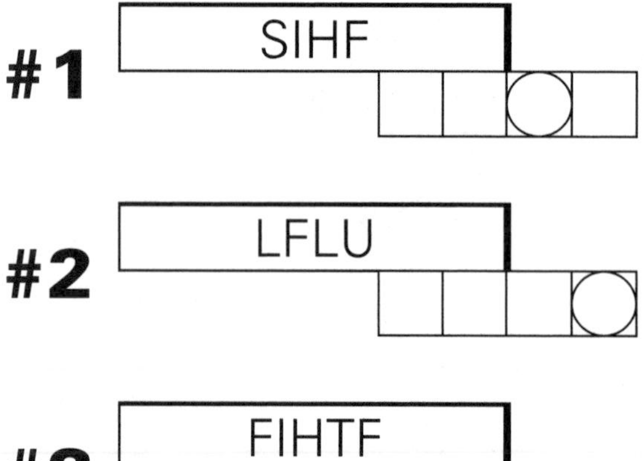

Box of Clues

Stumped? Maybe you can find a clue below.

- -Fail
- -Stuffed
- -Preserved trace of past animal
- -Jupiter's position from the sun
- -A bass or grouper
- -Smile's opposite
- -Picky

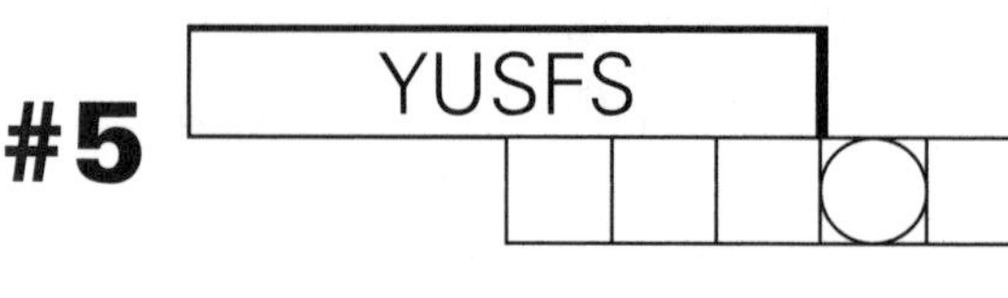

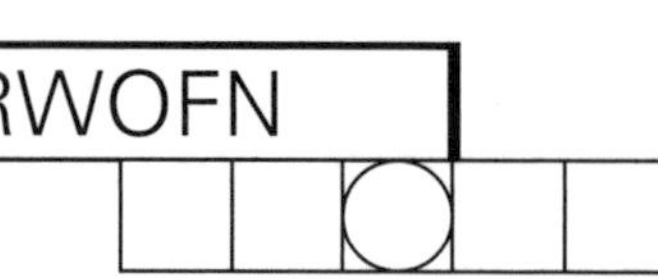

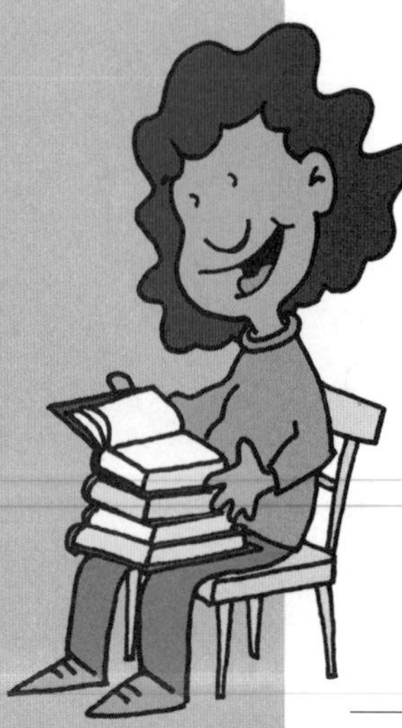

Arrange the circled letters to solve the mystery answer.

MYSTERY ANSWER

BIRDS

JUMBLE BrainBusters Junior

Unscramble the Jumbles, one letter to each square, to spell names of birds.

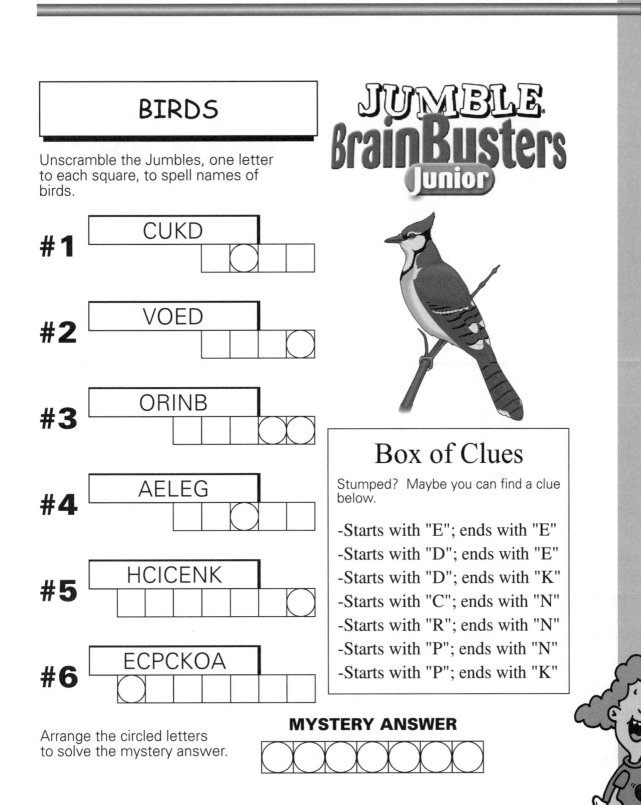

#1 

#2 

#3 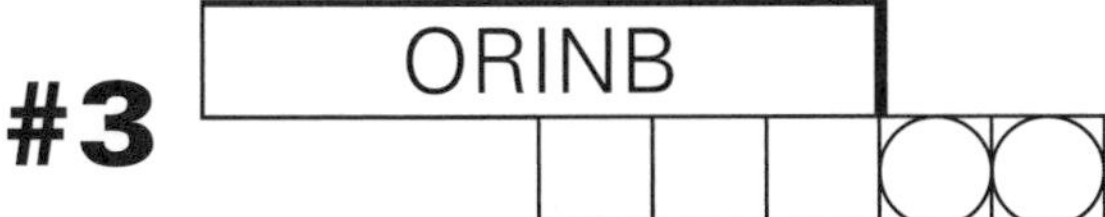

#4 

#5 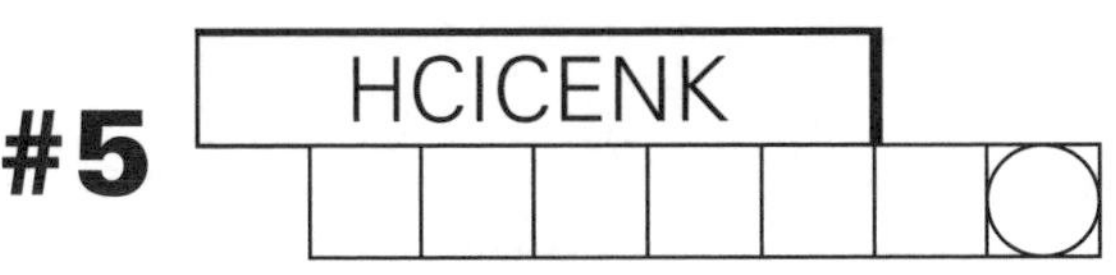

#6 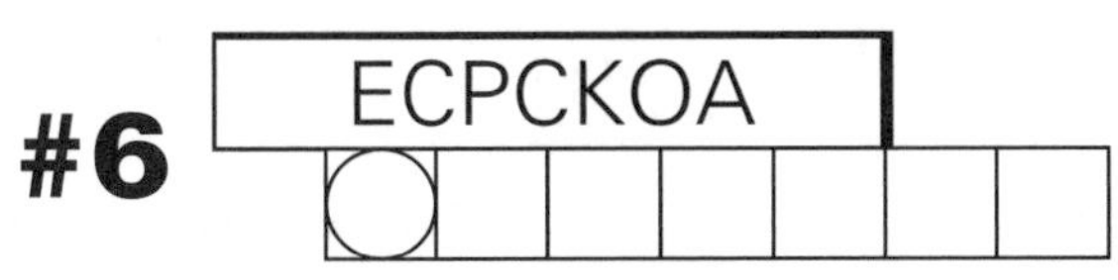

Box of Clues

Stumped? Maybe you can find a clue below.

- -Starts with "E"; ends with "E"
- -Starts with "D"; ends with "E"
- -Starts with "D"; ends with "K"
- -Starts with "C"; ends with "N"
- -Starts with "R"; ends with "N"
- -Starts with "P"; ends with "N"
- -Starts with "P"; ends with "K"

Arrange the circled letters to solve the mystery answer.

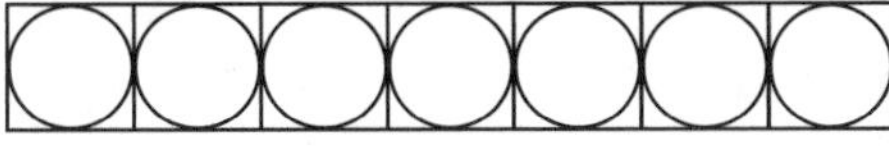

PUZZLE

64

TIME LINE

Unscramble the Jumbles, one letter to each square, to spell words as suggested by the time line.

#1 1743 ______ explorers reach the Rocky Mountains

#1 EFCRHN

#2 1798 Napoleon Bonaparte invades ______

#2 PGETY

#3 1949 Creation of East and West ______

#3 AEGNRYM

#4 1957 ______ of first artificial satellite (Sputnik)

#4 ULCAHN

#5 1972 ______ calculators introduced

#5 PCETKO

#6 1979 Thatcher becomes ______ prime minister

#6 RIBTIHS

Arrange the circled letters to solve the mystery answer.

1774 First commercial ______ ______ produced

MYSTERY ANSWER

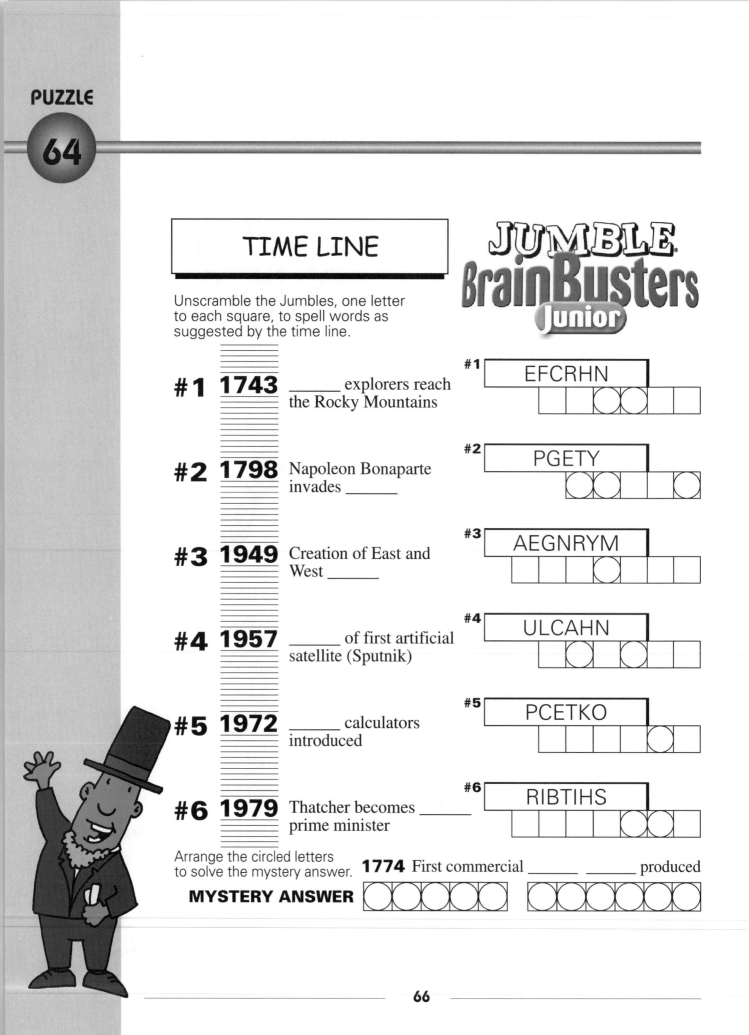

ANIMALS

JUMBLE BrainBusters Junior

Unscramble the Jumbles, one letter to each square, to spell names of animals.

#1 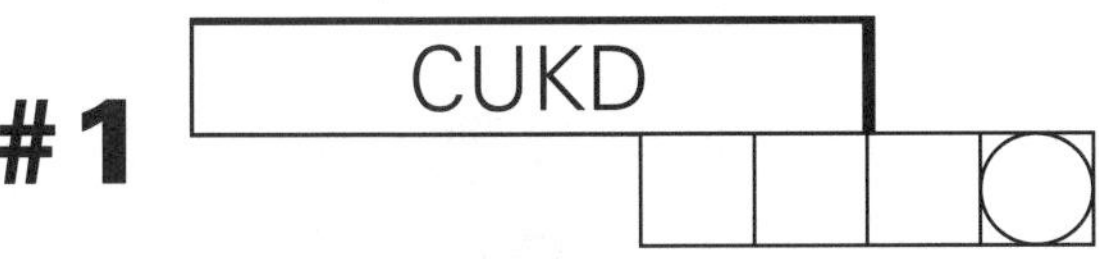

#2 

#3 

#4 

#5 

#6 

Box of Clues

Stumped? Maybe you can find a clue below.

-Starts with "H"; ends with "O"
-Starts with "D"; ends with "K"
-Starts with "M"; ends with "E"
-Starts with "E"; ends with "E"
-Starts with "M"; ends with "Y"
-Starts with "P"; ends with "R"
-Starts with "G"; ends with "Y"

Arrange the circled letters to solve the mystery answer.

MYSTERY ANSWER

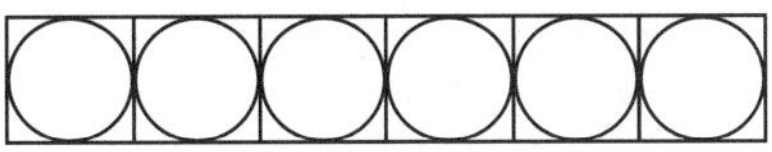

PUZZLE

66

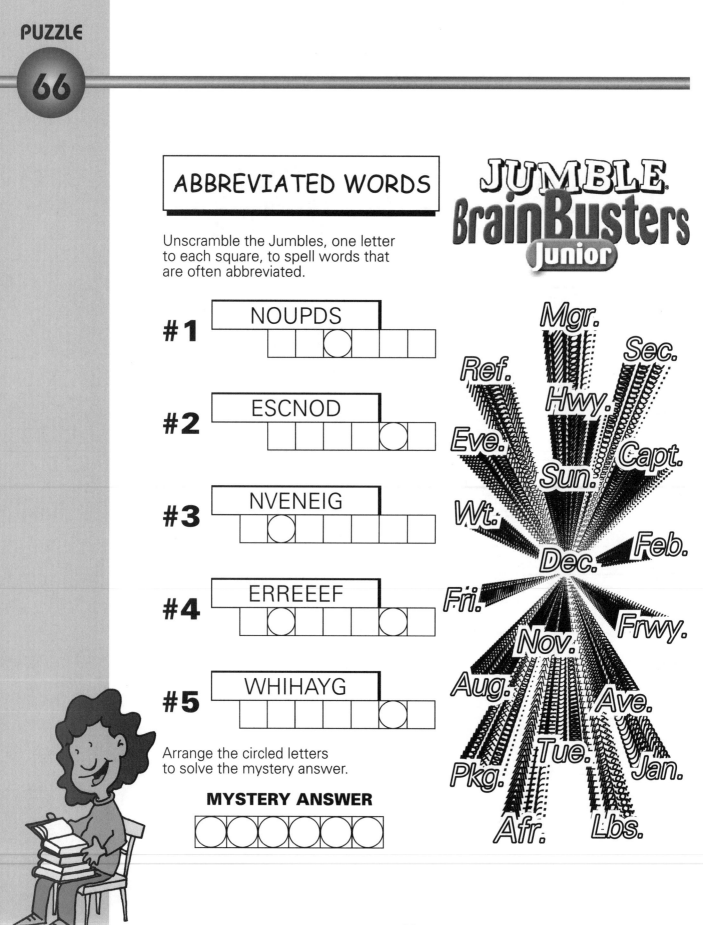

ABBREVIATED WORDS

Unscramble the Jumbles, one letter to each square, to spell words that are often abbreviated.

#1

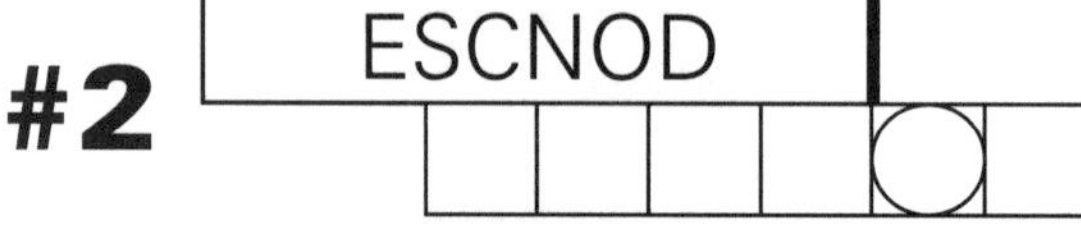

#2

#3

#4

ERREEEF

#5

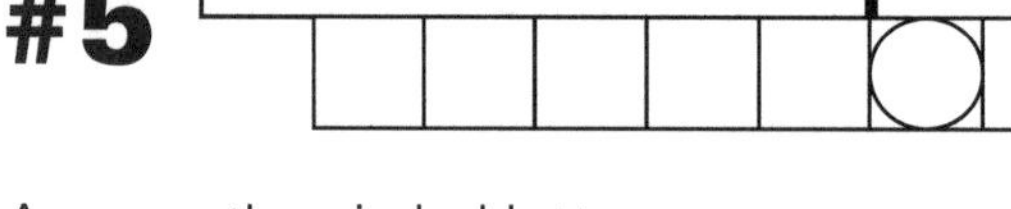

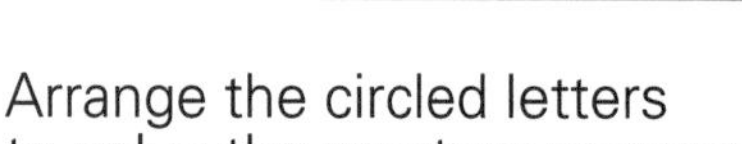

Arrange the circled letters to solve the mystery answer.

MYSTERY ANSWER

MATH

JUMBLE BrainBusters Junior

Unscramble the Jumbled letters, one letter to each square, so that each equation is correct.

For example: NONTEOEOW
ONE + ONE = TWO

#1 FOWOUTR

☐◯◯ × TWO = ☐◯☐☐

#2 TOROUWF

☐◯☐ × ☐☐◯☐ = EIGHT

#3 ENOVESNE

◯☐☐ × SEVEN = ☐☐☐☐☐

#4 HRETEEERTH

◯☐☐☐☐ × ◯☐☐☐☐ = NINE

#5 RFUOHERET

◯☐☐☐ × ☐☐◯☐☐ = TWELVE

Arrange the circled letters to solve the mystery equation.

MYSTERY EQUATION

◯◯◯ × ◯◯◯ = ◯◯◯◯ × ONE

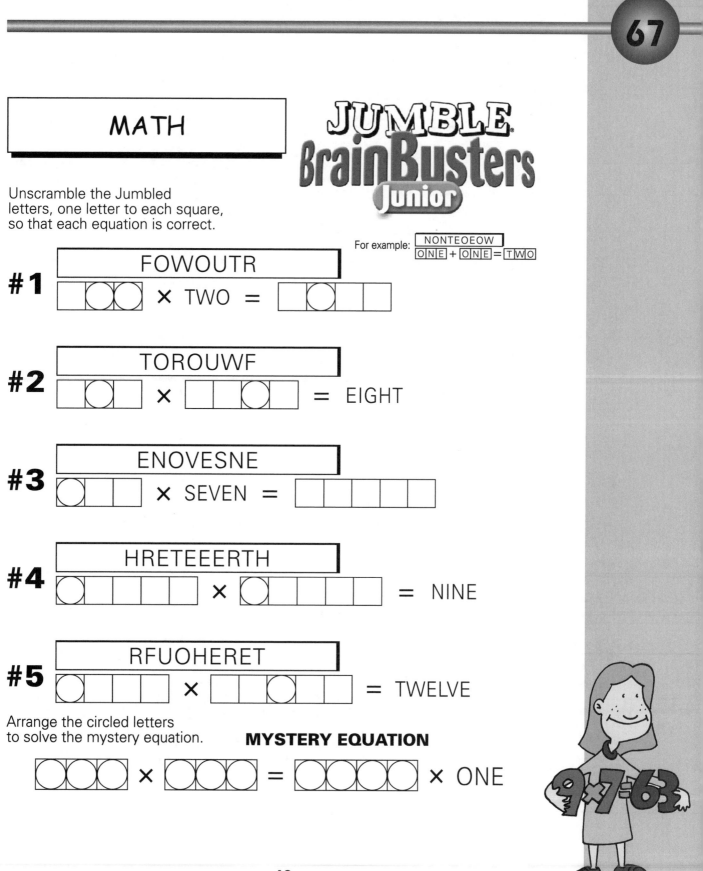

PUZZLE

68

U.S. PRESIDENTS

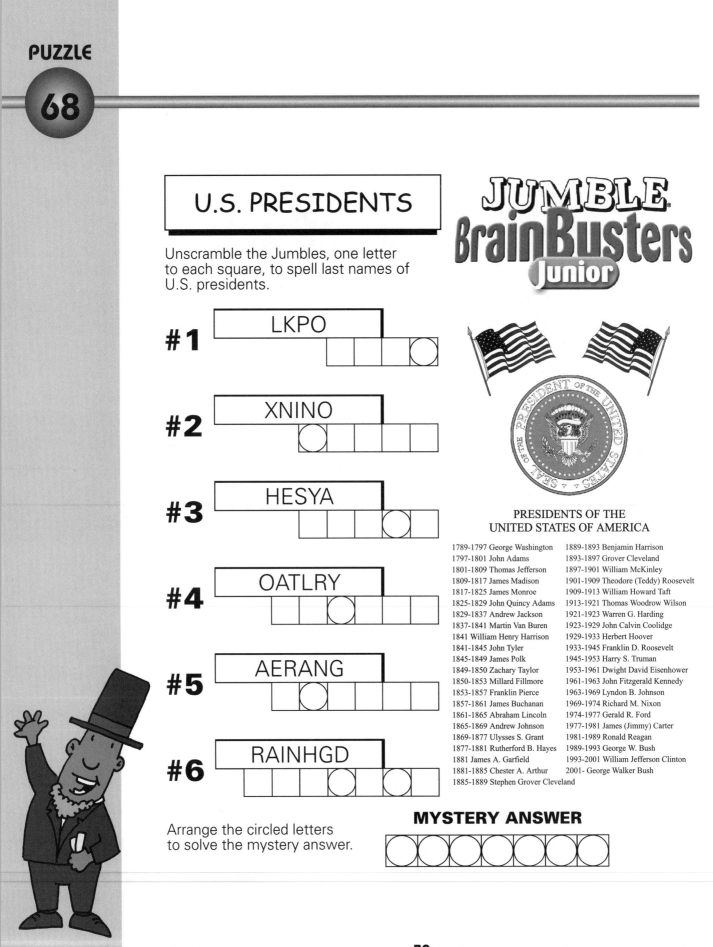

JUMBLE BrainBusters Junior

Unscramble the Jumbles, one letter to each square, to spell last names of U.S. presidents.

#1
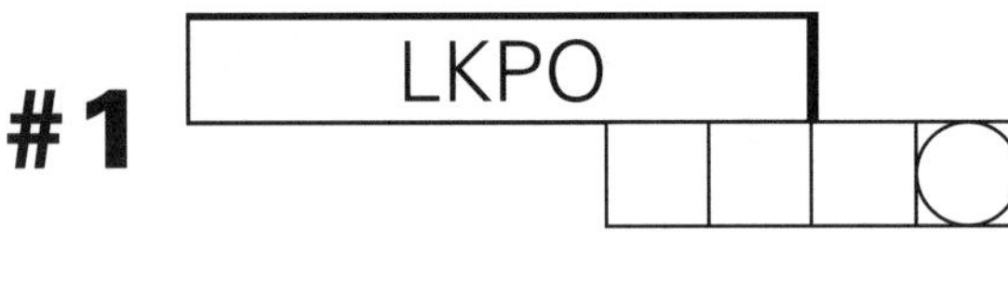

#2

#3
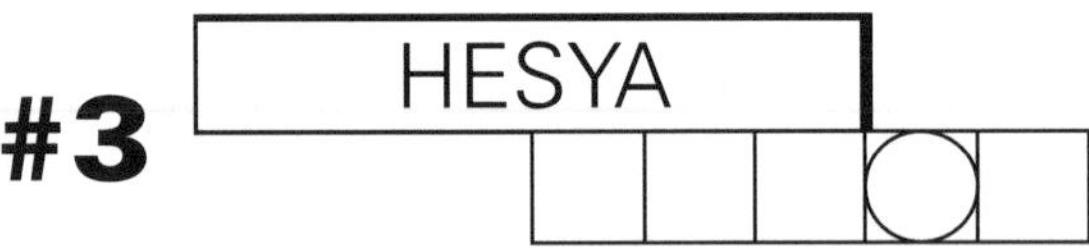

#4
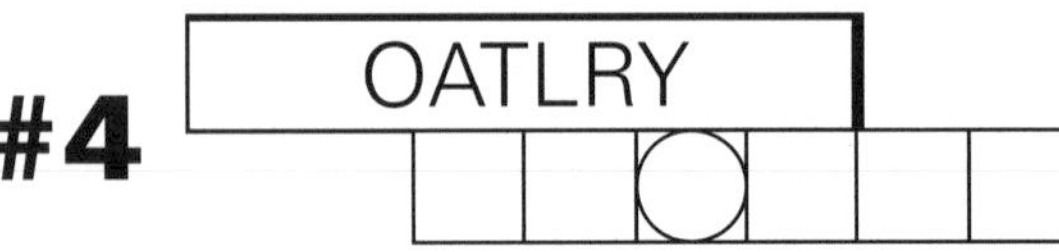

#5

#6

PRESIDENTS OF THE
UNITED STATES OF AMERICA

1789-1797 George Washington
1797-1801 John Adams
1801-1809 Thomas Jefferson
1809-1817 James Madison
1817-1825 James Monroe
1825-1829 John Quincy Adams
1829-1837 Andrew Jackson
1837-1841 Martin Van Buren
1841 William Henry Harrison
1841-1845 John Tyler
1845-1849 James Polk
1849-1850 Zachary Taylor
1850-1853 Millard Fillmore
1853-1857 Franklin Pierce
1857-1861 James Buchanan
1861-1865 Abraham Lincoln
1865-1869 Andrew Johnson
1869-1877 Ulysses S. Grant
1877-1881 Rutherford B. Hayes
1881 James A. Garfield
1881-1885 Chester A. Arthur
1885-1889 Stephen Grover Cleveland
1889-1893 Benjamin Harrison
1893-1897 Grover Cleveland
1897-1901 William McKinley
1901-1909 Theodore (Teddy) Roosevelt
1909-1913 William Howard Taft
1913-1921 Thomas Woodrow Wilson
1921-1923 Warren G. Harding
1923-1929 John Calvin Coolidge
1929-1933 Herbert Hoover
1933-1945 Franklin D. Roosevelt
1945-1953 Harry S. Truman
1953-1961 Dwight David Eisenhower
1961-1963 John Fitzgerald Kennedy
1963-1969 Lyndon B. Johnson
1969-1974 Richard M. Nixon
1974-1977 Gerald R. Ford
1977-1981 James (Jimmy) Carter
1981-1989 Ronald Reagan
1989-1993 George W. Bush
1993-2001 William Jefferson Clinton
2001- George Walker Bush

Arrange the circled letters to solve the mystery answer.

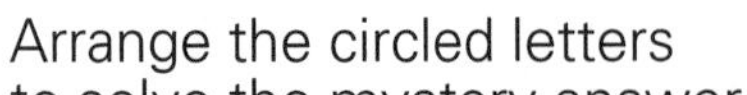

MYSTERY ANSWER

JUMBLE® BrainBusters Junior

ADJECTIVES

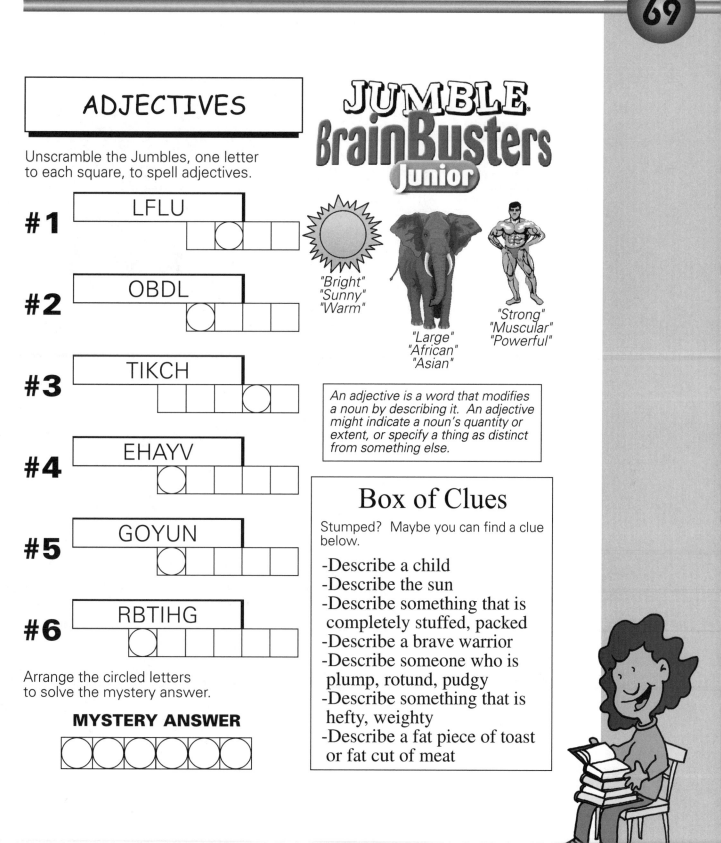

Unscramble the Jumbles, one letter to each square, to spell adjectives.

#1 LFLU

#2 OBDL

#3 TIKCH

#4 EHAYV

#5 GOYUN

#6 RBTIHG

Arrange the circled letters to solve the mystery answer.

MYSTERY ANSWER

"Bright"
"Sunny"
"Warm"

"Large"
"African"
"Asian"

"Strong"
"Muscular"
"Powerful"

An adjective is a word that modifies a noun by describing it. An adjective might indicate a noun's quantity or extent, or specify a thing as distinct from something else.

Box of Clues

Stumped? Maybe you can find a clue below.

- -Describe a child
- -Describe the sun
- -Describe something that is completely stuffed, packed
- -Describe a brave warrior
- -Describe someone who is plump, rotund, pudgy
- -Describe something that is hefty, weighty
- -Describe a fat piece of toast or fat cut of meat

PUZZLE

70

MAMMALS

Unscramble the Jumbles, one letter to each square, to spell names of mammals.

JUMBLE BrainBusters Junior

#1
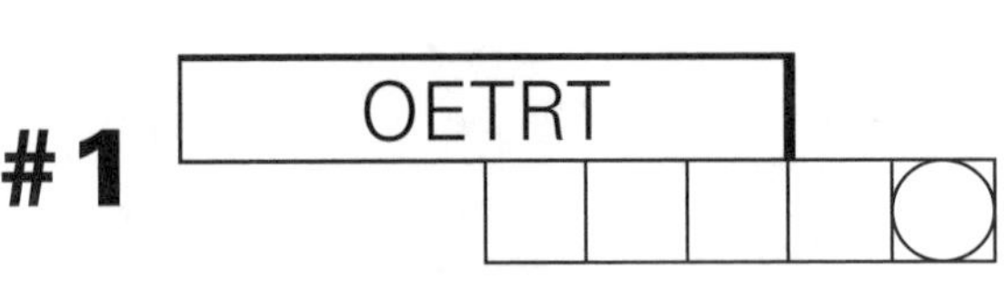

#2
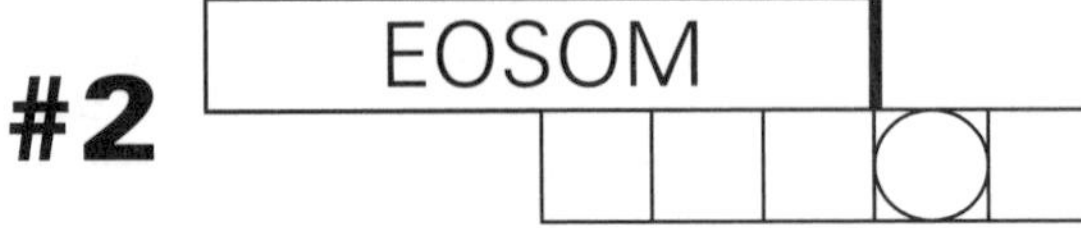

#3

#4

#5

#6

Box of Clues

Stumped? Maybe you can find a clue below.

- -Largest member of the deer family
- -Large, powerful, ground-living monkey
- -Large, tusked mammal
- -Puma
- -Water-loving member of the weasel family
- -Powerful ape
- -Skunk, badger or ferret

Arrange the circled letters to solve the mystery answer.

MYSTERY ANSWER

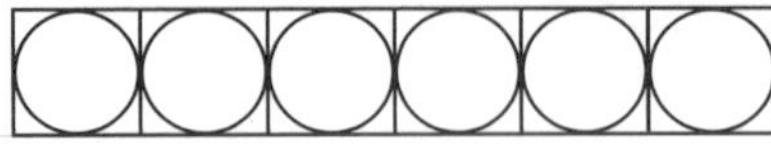

PUZZLE 71

MONEY

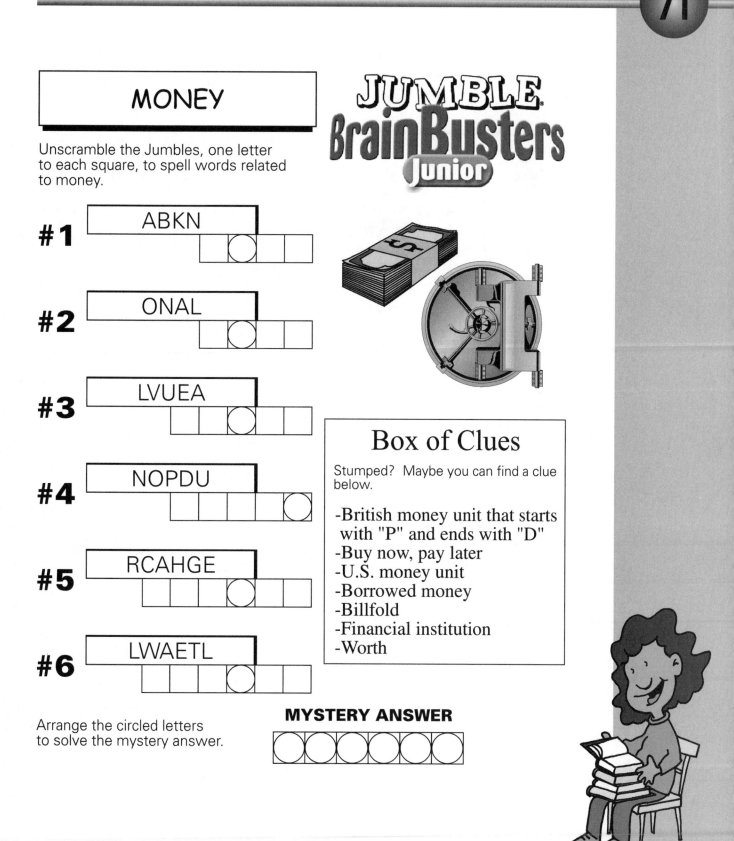

Unscramble the Jumbles, one letter to each square, to spell words related to money.

#1
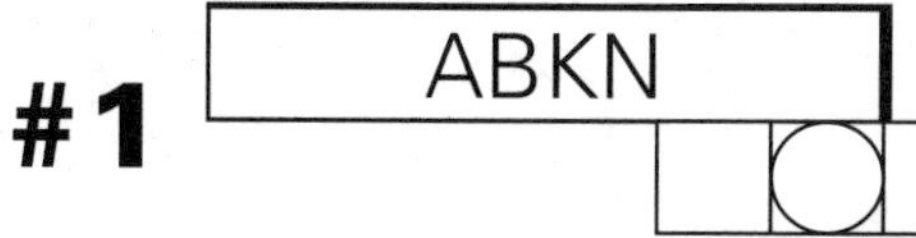

#2

#3
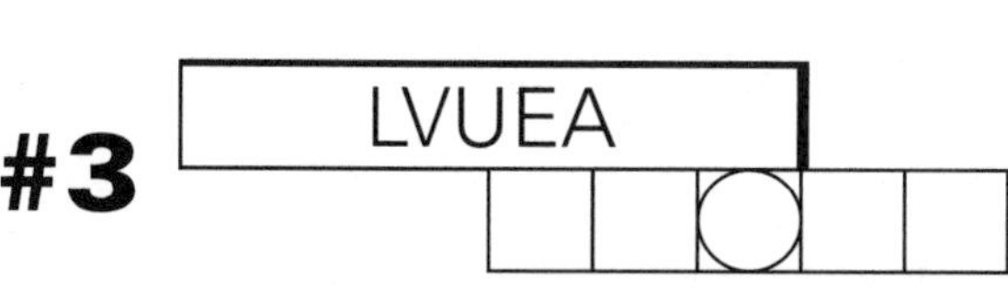

#4
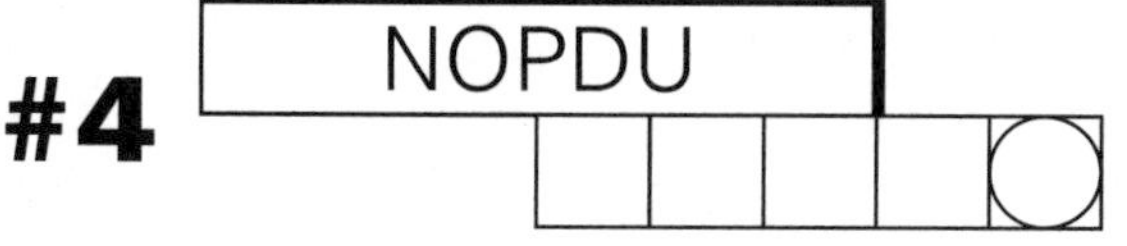

#5
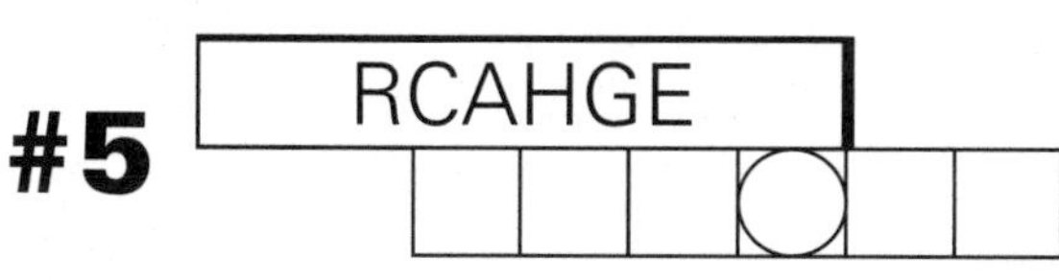

#6

Box of Clues

Stumped? Maybe you can find a clue below.

-British money unit that starts with "P" and ends with "D"
-Buy now, pay later
-U.S. money unit
-Borrowed money
-Billfold
-Financial institution
-Worth

MYSTERY ANSWER

Arrange the circled letters to solve the mystery answer.

PUZZLE

72

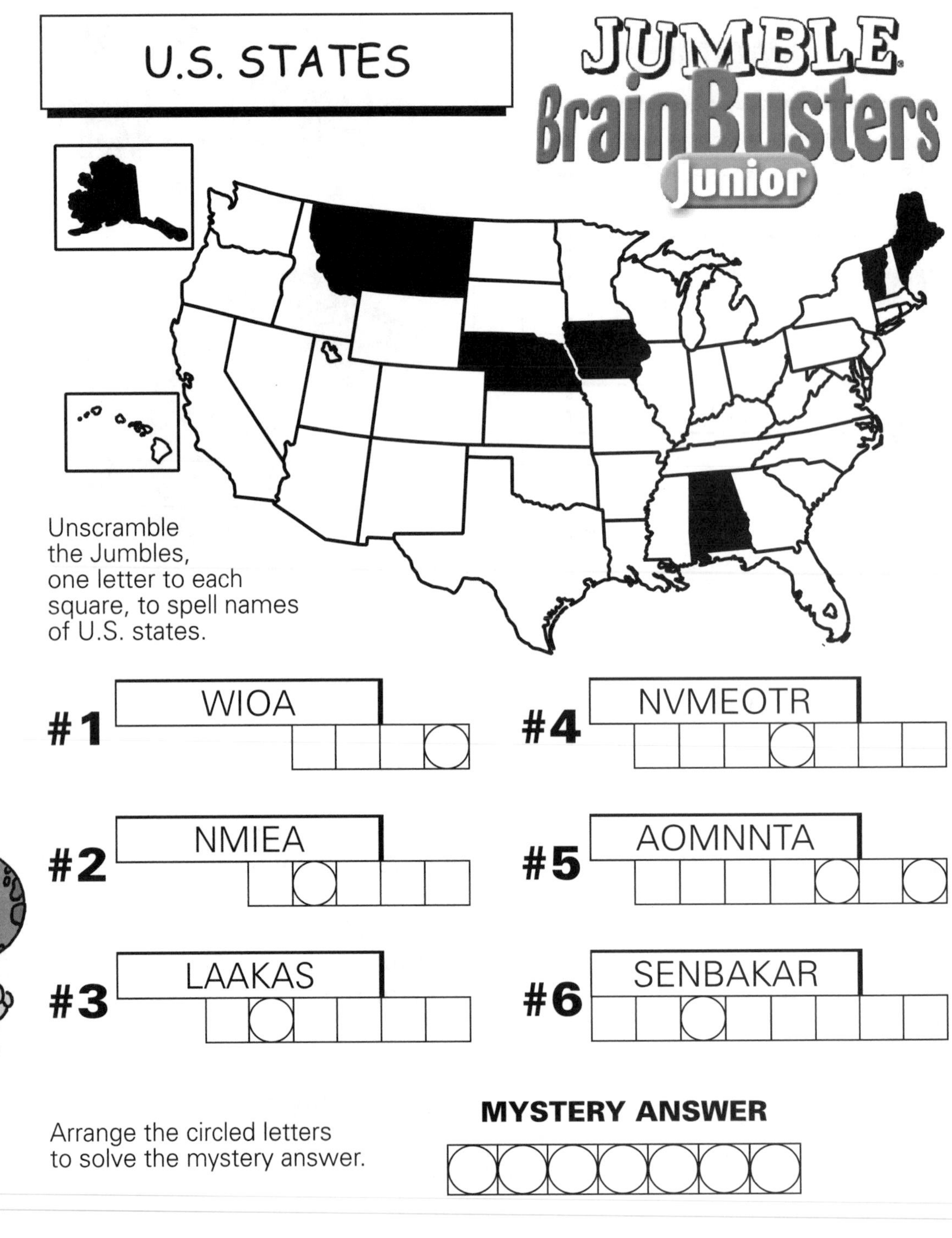

U.S. STATES

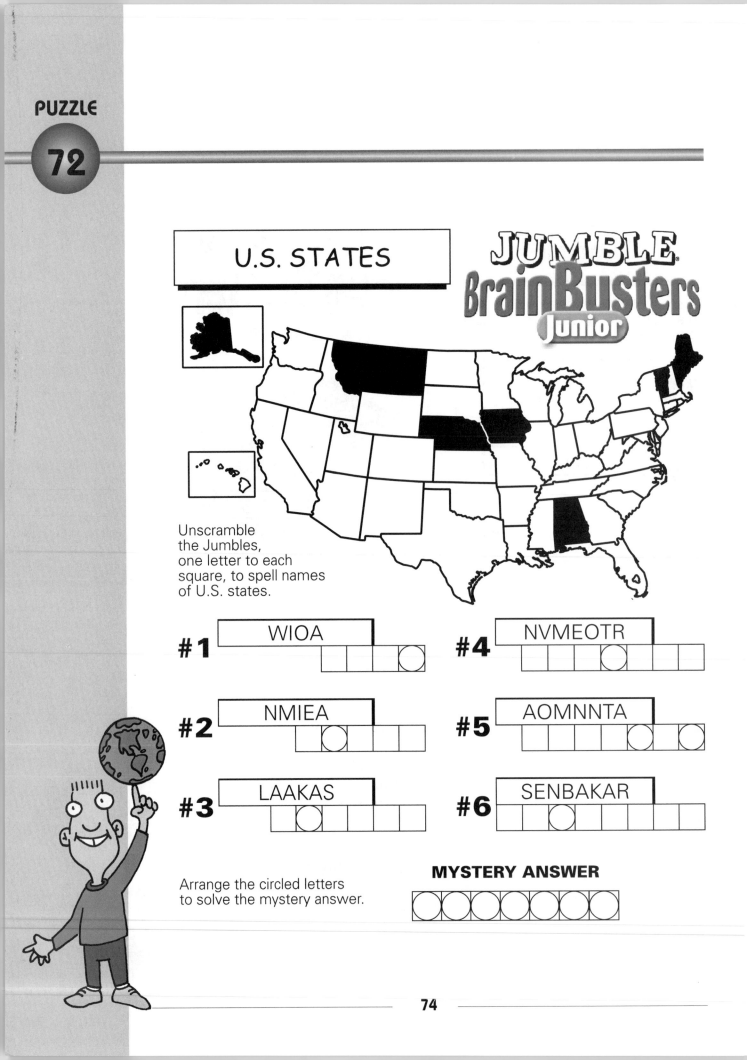

Unscramble the Jumbles, one letter to each square, to spell names of U.S. states.

#1 WIOA

#2 NMIEA

#3 LAAKAS

#4 NVMEOTR

#5 AOMNNTA

#6 SENBAKAR

Arrange the circled letters to solve the mystery answer.

MYSTERY ANSWER

ELEMENTS

JUMBLE® BrainBusters Junior

Unscramble the Jumbles, one letter to each square, to spell names of elements.

#1

#2
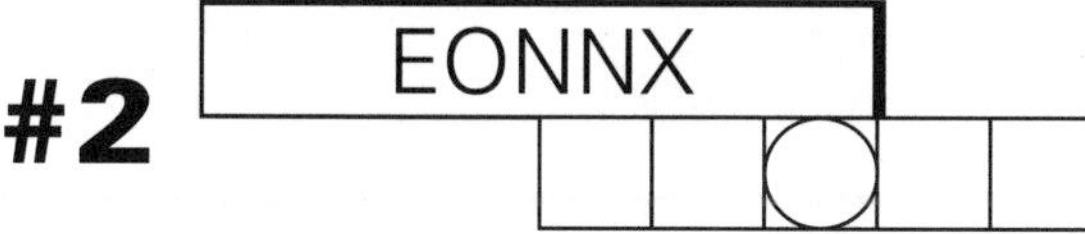

#3
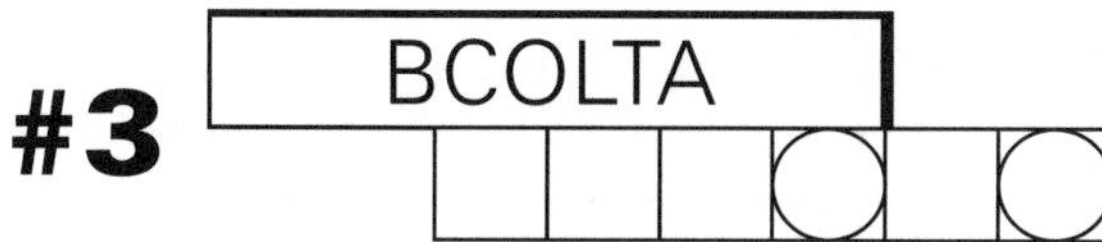

#4
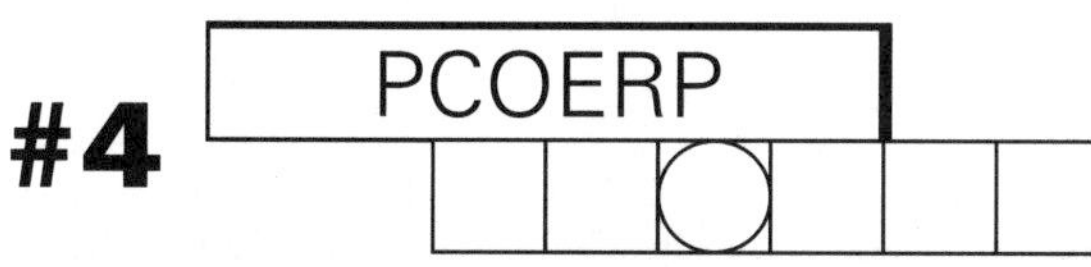

#5

Arrange the circled letters to solve the mystery answer.

MYSTERY ANSWER

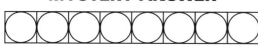

THE PERIODIC TABLE

Atomic #
Atomic Symbol

H																	He
Li	Be											B	C	N	O	F	Ne
Na	Mg											Al	Si	P	S	Cl	Ar
K	Ca	Sc	Ti	V	Cr	Mn	Fe	Co	Ni	Cu	Zn	Ga	Ge	As	Se	Br	Kr
Rb	Sr	Y	Zr	Nb	Mo	Tc	Ru	Rh	Pd	Ag	Cd	In	Sn	Sb	Te	I	Xe
Cs	Ba		Hf	Ta	W	Re	Os	Ir	Pt	Au	Hg	Tl	Pb	Bi	Po	At	Rn
Fr	Ra		Unq	Unp	Unh	Uns		Une									

Name
Actinium
Aluminum
Americium
Antimony
Argon
Arsenic
Astatine
Barium
Berkelium
Beryllium
Bismuth
Bohrium
Boron
Bromine
Cadmium
Calcium
Californium
Carbon
Cerium
Cesium
Chlorine
Chromium
Cobalt
Copper
Curium
Dubnium
Dysprosium
Einsteinium
Erbium
Europium
Fermium
Fluorine
Francium
Gadolinium
Gallium
Germanium
Gold
Hafnium
Hassium
Helium
Holmium
Hydrogen
Indium
Iodine
Iridium
Iron
Krypton
Lanthanum
Lawrencium
Lead
Lithium
Lutetium
Magnesium
Manganese
Meitnerium
Mendelevium
Mercury
Molybdenum
Neodymium
Neon
Neptunium
Nickel
Niobium
Nitrogen
Nobelium
Osmium
Oxygen
Palladium
Phosphorus
Platinum
Plutonium
Polonium
Potassium
Potassium
Praseodymium
Promethium
Protactinium
Radium
Radon
Rhenium
Rhodium
Rubidium
Ruthenium
Rutherfordium
Samarium
Scandium
Seaborgium
Selenium
Silicon
Silver
Sodium
Strontium
Sulfur
Tantalum
Technetium
Tellurium
Terbium
Thallium
Thorium
Thulium
Tin
Titanium
Tungsten
Uranium
Vanadium
Xenon
Ytterbium
Yttrium
Zinc
Zirconium

PUZZLE 74

MEANS THE SAME

Unscramble the Jumbles, one letter to each square, to spell pairs of words that have the same or similar meanings.

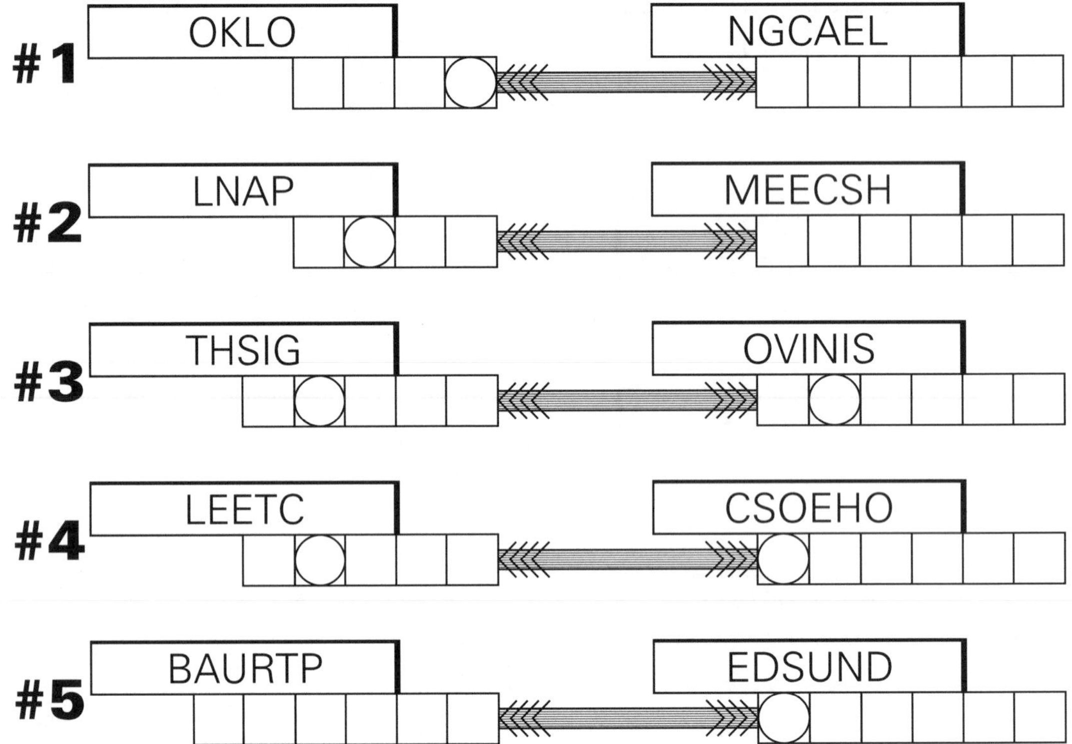

Arrange the circled letters to solve the mystery answer. (Form two words that have the same or similar meanings.)

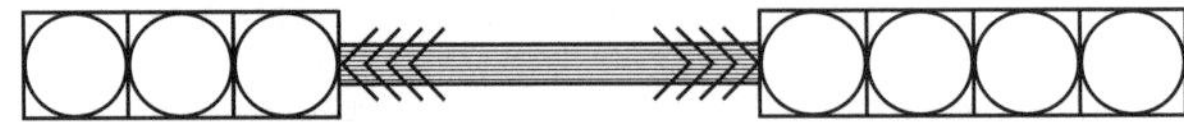

Box of Clues

Stumped? Maybe you can find a clue here in the "Box of Clues."

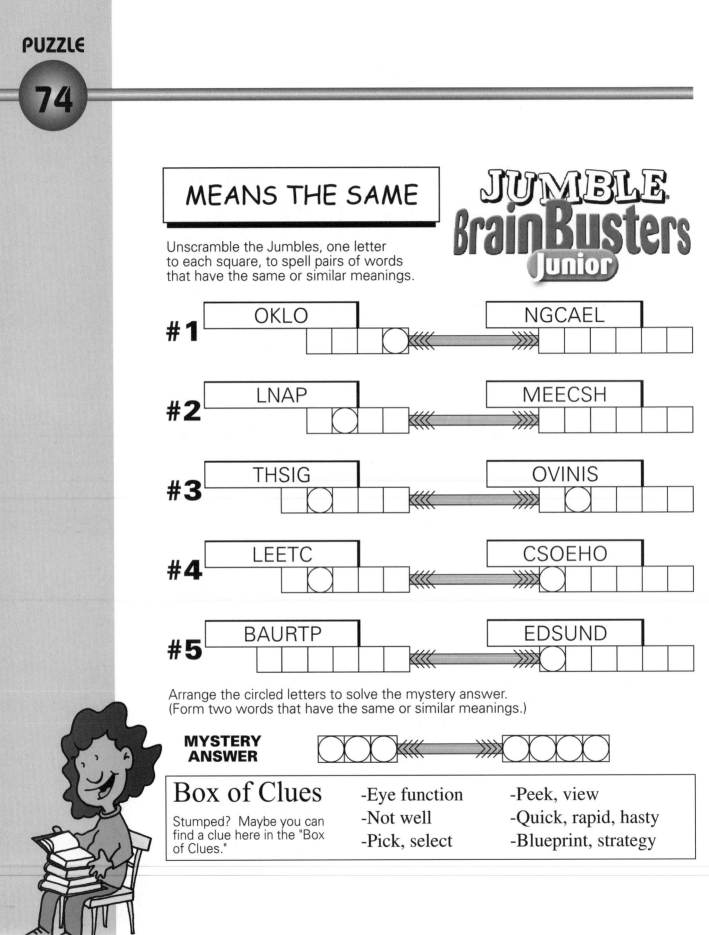

-Eye function
-Not well
-Pick, select
-Peek, view
-Quick, rapid, hasty
-Blueprint, strategy

JUMBLE® BrainBusters Junior

SPORTS

Unscramble the Jumbles, one letter to each square, to spell words related to sports.

#1 SABE

#2 OLFU

#3 ACCHT

#4 BOKCL

#5 OHERM

#6 CTALEK

Box of Clues

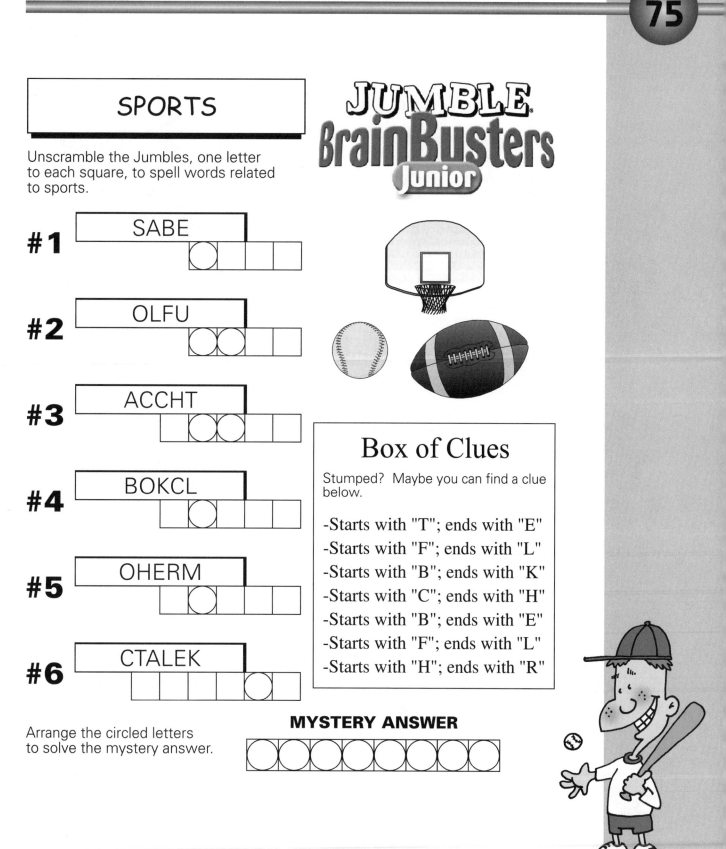

Stumped? Maybe you can find a clue below.

-Starts with "T"; ends with "E"
-Starts with "F"; ends with "L"
-Starts with "B"; ends with "K"
-Starts with "C"; ends with "H"
-Starts with "B"; ends with "E"
-Starts with "F"; ends with "L"
-Starts with "H"; ends with "R"

Arrange the circled letters to solve the mystery answer.

MYSTERY ANSWER

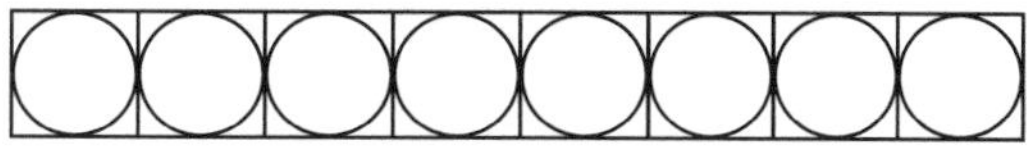

PUZZLE

76

MATH

JUMBLE BrainBusters Junior

Unscramble the Jumbled letters, one letter to each square, so that each equation is correct.

For example: NONTEOEOW
ONE + ONE = TWO

#1 WTOFUOOTRW

☐☐☐ + ☐☐☐ = ◯☐☐☐

#2 RZEEOREZOROZ

☐◯☐☐ + ☐☐☐☐ = ☐☐☐◯

#3 EISRETIENHXN

◯☐◯ + ☐☐☐☐☐ = ☐◯☐☐

#4 TETEWNTNNETY

☐☐☐◯☐☐ − ☐◯☐ = ☐☐☐

#5 LNIENOWEEVNTE

☐◯☐☐ + ☐☐☐ = ☐☐☐◯☐☐

Arrange the circled letters to solve the mystery equation.

MYSTERY EQUATION

◯◯◯◯ + ◯◯◯ = ◯◯◯

9×7=63

JUMBLE® BrainBusters Junior

WEATHER

Unscramble the Jumbles, one letter to each square, to spell words related to weather.

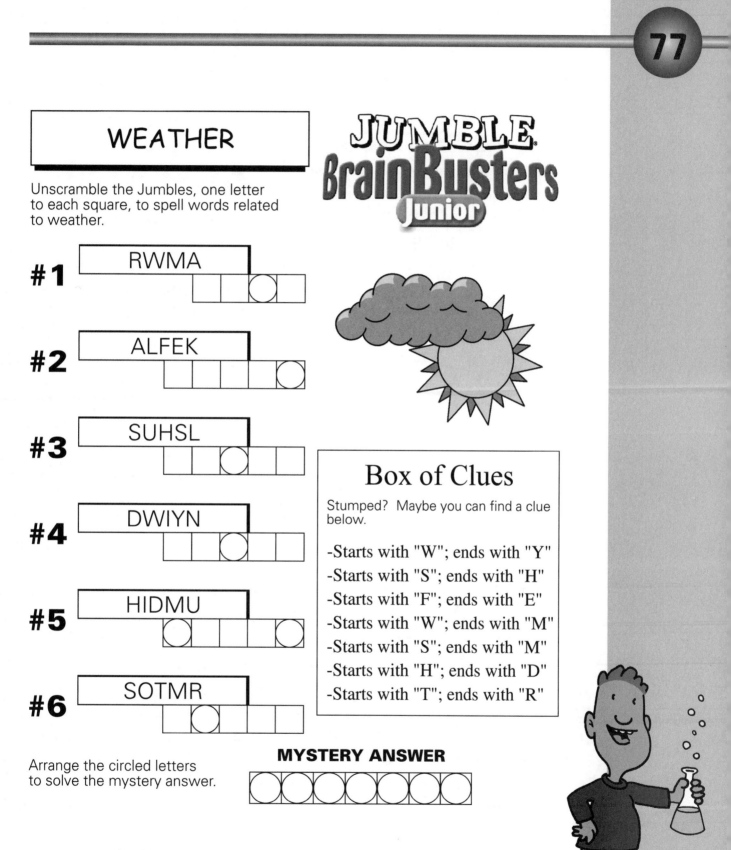

#1
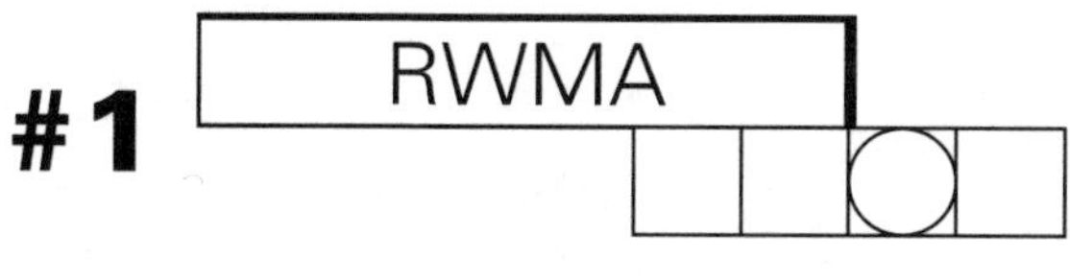

#2

#3
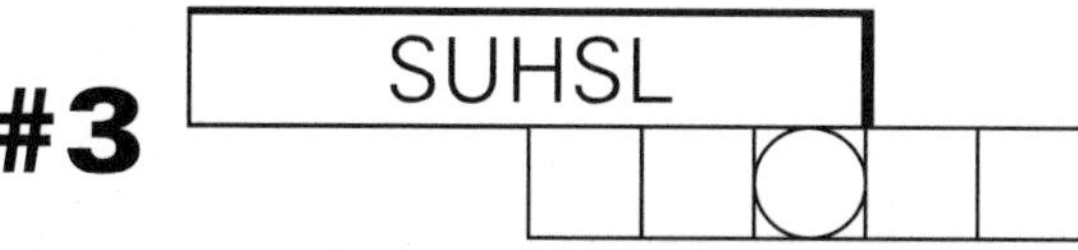

#4
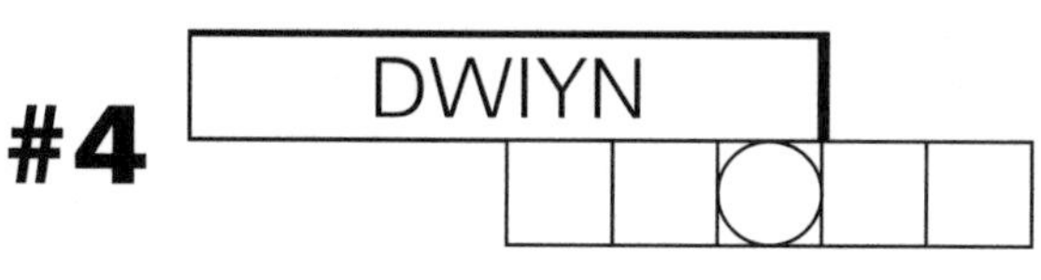

#5

#6
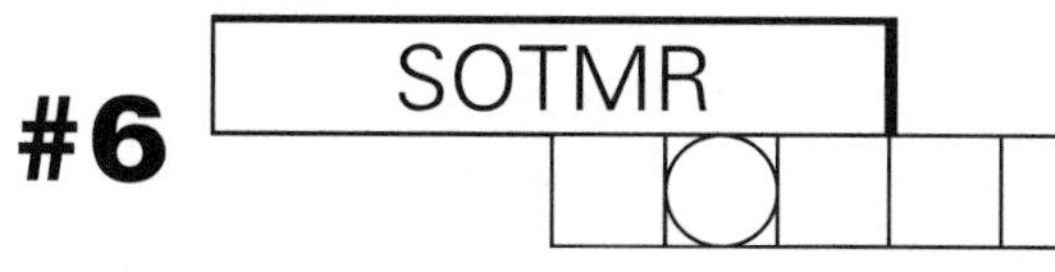

Box of Clues

Stumped? Maybe you can find a clue below.

-Starts with "W"; ends with "Y"
-Starts with "S"; ends with "H"
-Starts with "F"; ends with "E"
-Starts with "W"; ends with "M"
-Starts with "S"; ends with "M"
-Starts with "H"; ends with "D"
-Starts with "T"; ends with "R"

Arrange the circled letters to solve the mystery answer.

MYSTERY ANSWER

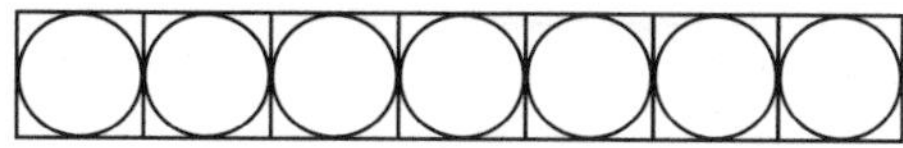

PUZZLE

78

ADJECTIVES

Unscramble the Jumbles, one letter to each square, to spell adjectives.

#1

#2

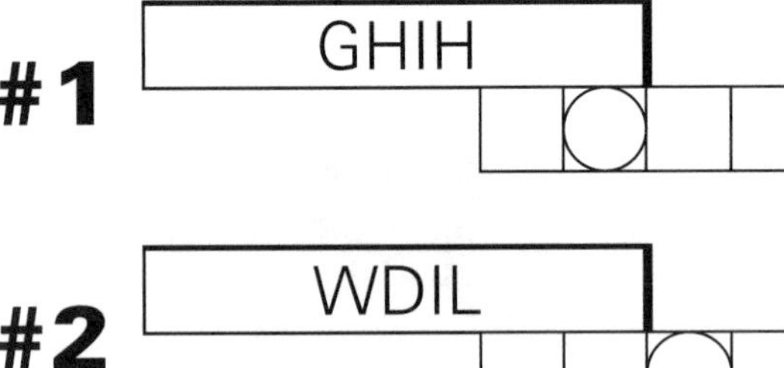

#3

#4

#5

#6

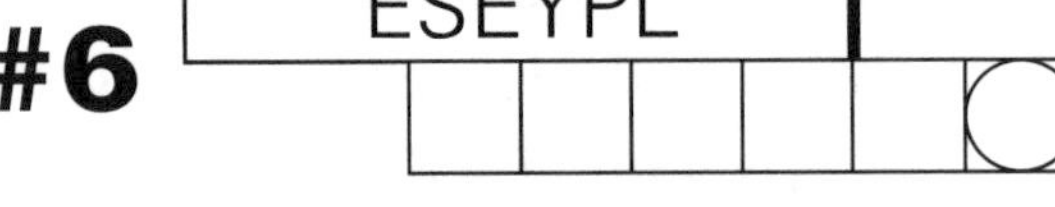

Arrange the circled letters to solve the mystery answer.

MYSTERY ANSWER

JUMBLE® BrainBusters Junior

"Bright"
"Sunny"
"Warm"

"Large"
"African"
"Asian"

"Strong"
"Muscular"
"Powerful"

An adjective is a word that modifies a noun by describing it. An adjective might indicate a noun's quantity or extent, or specify a thing as distinct from something else.

Box of Clues

Stumped? Maybe you can find a clue below.

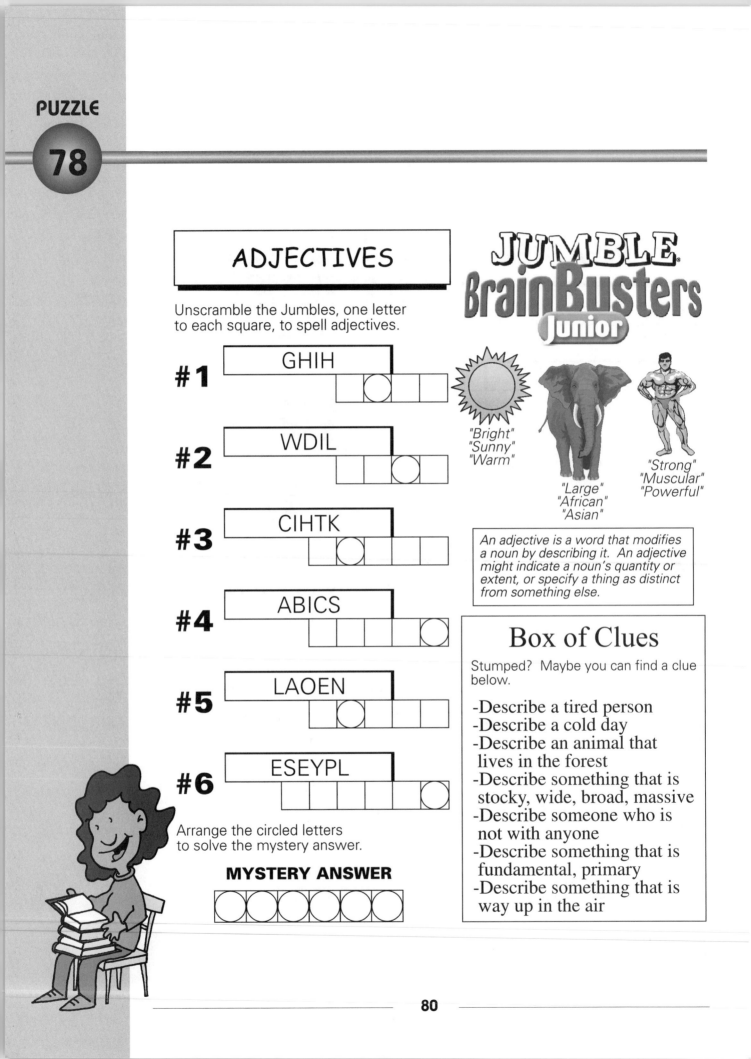

-Describe a tired person
-Describe a cold day
-Describe an animal that lives in the forest
-Describe something that is stocky, wide, broad, massive
-Describe someone who is not with anyone
-Describe something that is fundamental, primary
-Describe something that is way up in the air

PUZZLE

79

OUTER SPACE

Unscramble the Jumbles, one letter to each square, to spell words related to outer space.

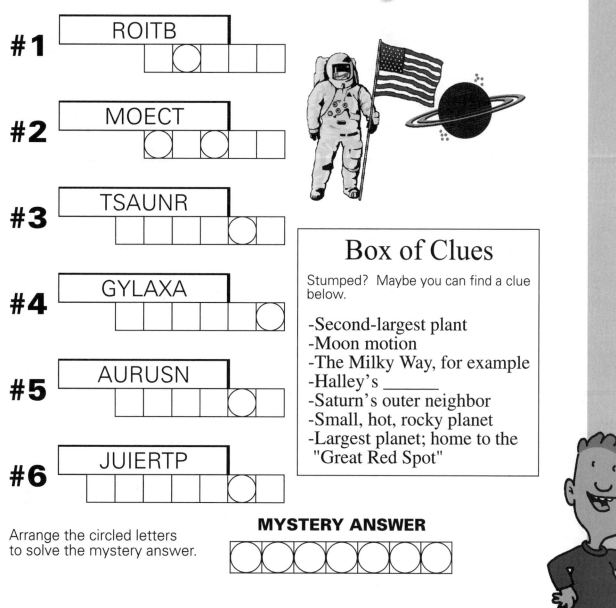

#1
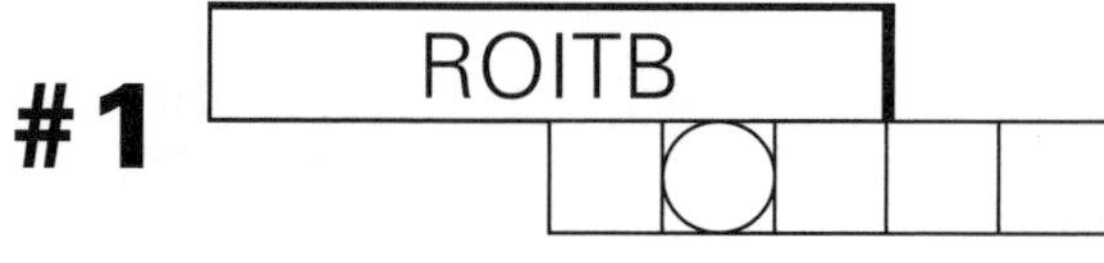
ROITB

#2

MOECT

#3

TSAUNR

#4
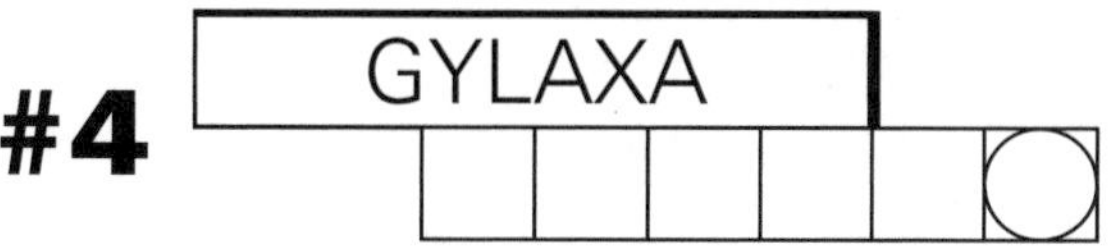
GYLAXA

#5
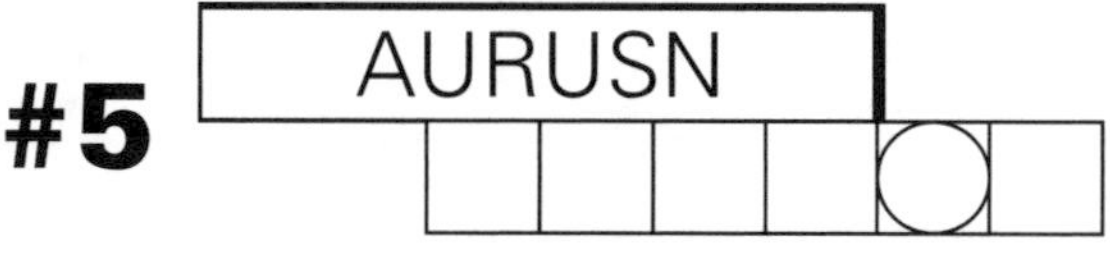
AURUSN

#6
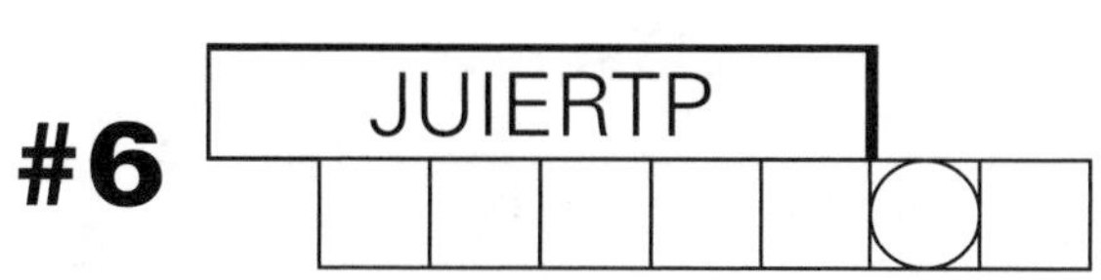
JUIERTP

Box of Clues

Stumped? Maybe you can find a clue below.

-Second-largest plant
-Moon motion
-The Milky Way, for example
-Halley's ______
-Saturn's outer neighbor
-Small, hot, rocky planet
-Largest planet; home to the "Great Red Spot"

MYSTERY ANSWER

Arrange the circled letters to solve the mystery answer.

PUZZLE 80

U.S. PRESIDENTS

JUMBLE® BrainBusters Junior

Unscramble the Jumbles, one letter to each square, to spell last names of U.S. presidents.

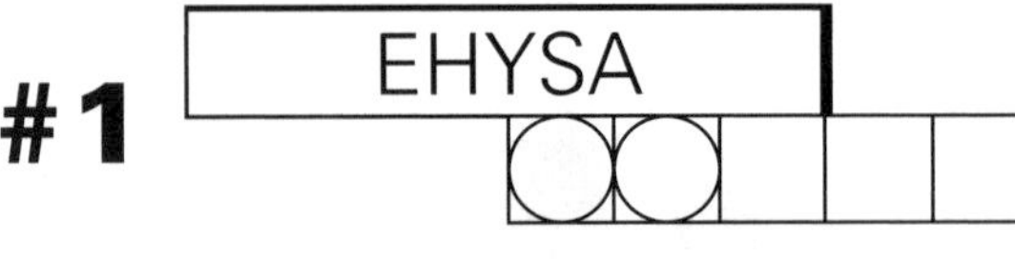

PRESIDENTS OF THE UNITED STATES OF AMERICA

1789-1797 George Washington
1797-1801 John Adams
1801-1809 Thomas Jefferson
1809-1817 James Madison
1817-1825 James Monroe
1825-1829 John Quincy Adams
1829-1837 Andrew Jackson
1837-1841 Martin Van Buren
1841 William Henry Harrison
1841-1845.John Tyler
1845-1849 James Polk
1849-1850 Zachary Taylor
1850-1853 Millard Fillmore
1853-1857 Franklin Pierce
1857-1861 James Buchanan
1861-1865 Abraham Lincoln
1865-1869 Andrew Johnson
1869-1877 Ulysses S. Grant
1877-1881 Rutherford B. Hayes
1881 James A. Garfield
1881-1885 Chester A. Arthur
1885-1889 Stephen Grover Cleveland
1889-1893 Benjamin Harrison
1893-1897 Grover Cleveland
1897-1901 William McKinley
1901-1909 Theodore (Teddy) Roosevelt
1909-1913 William Howard Taft
1913-1921 Thomas Woodrow Wilson
1921-1923 Warren G. Harding
1923-1929 John Calvin Coolidge
1929-1933 Herbert Hoover
1933-1945 Franklin D. Roosevelt
1945-1953 Harry S. Truman
1953-1961 Dwight David Eisenhower
1961-1963 John Fitzgerald Kennedy
1963-1969 Lyndon B. Johnson
1969-1974 Richard M. Nixon
1974-1977 Gerald R. Ford
1977-1981 James (Jimmy) Carter
1981-1989 Ronald Reagan
1989-1993 George W. Bush
1993-2001 William Jefferson Clinton
2001- George Walker Bush

Arrange the circled letters to solve the mystery answer.

MYSTERY ANSWER

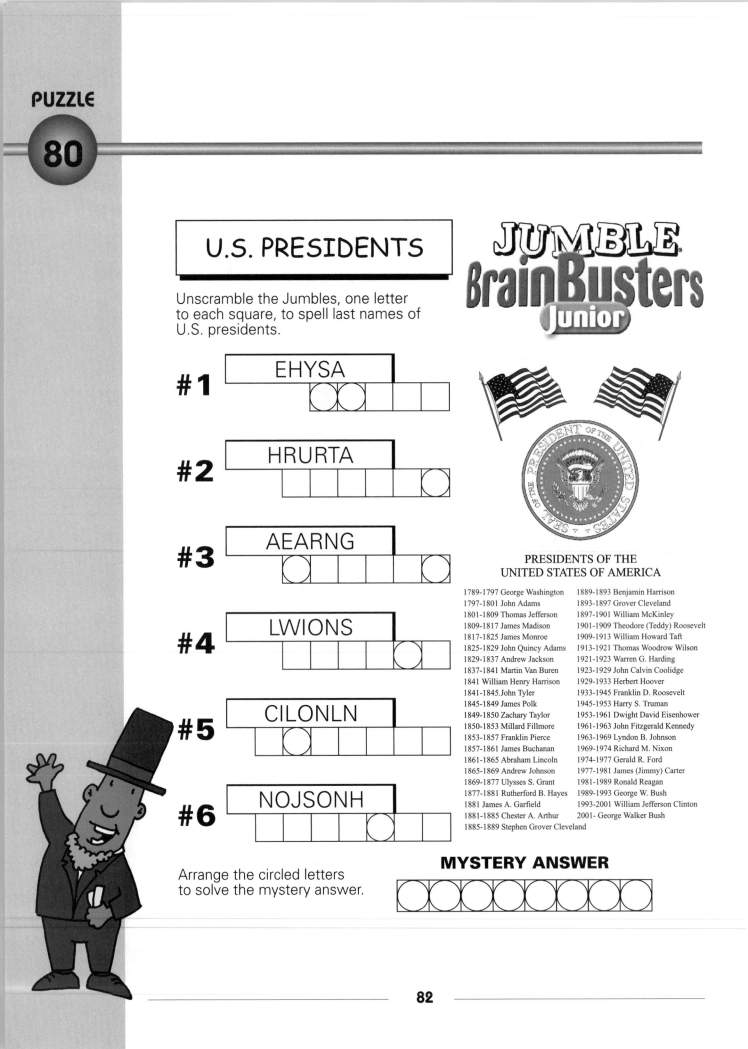

PUZZLE

81

STARTS WITH "J"

Unscramble the Jumbles, one letter to each square, to spell words that start with "J."

#1 JILA

#2

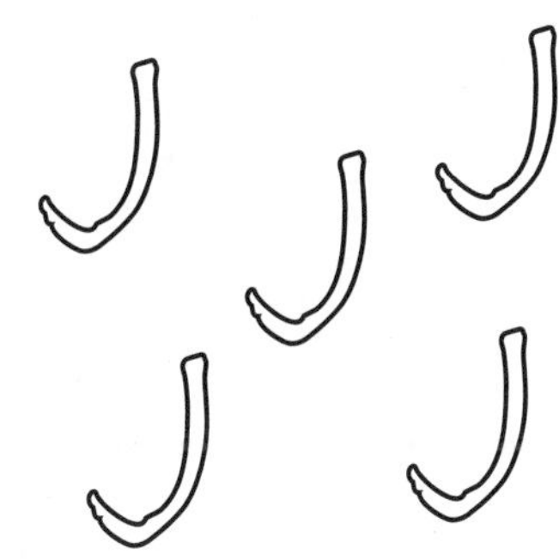

#3

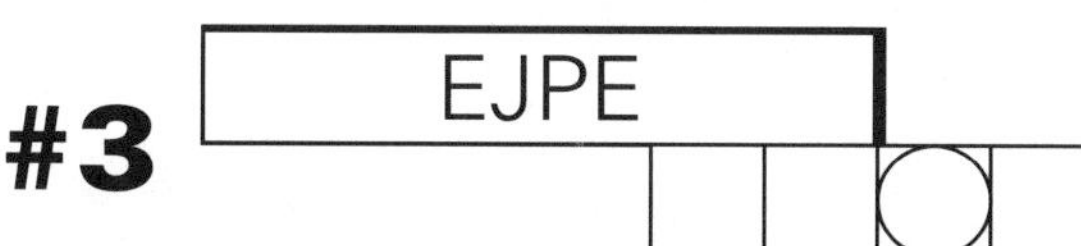

Box of Clues

Stumped? Maybe you can find a clue below.

-Style of pants; blue ______
-Type of vehicle
-Courtroom referee
-Warm, dense forest
-Peanut butter's companion
-Worthless material
-Police lockup

#4

#5

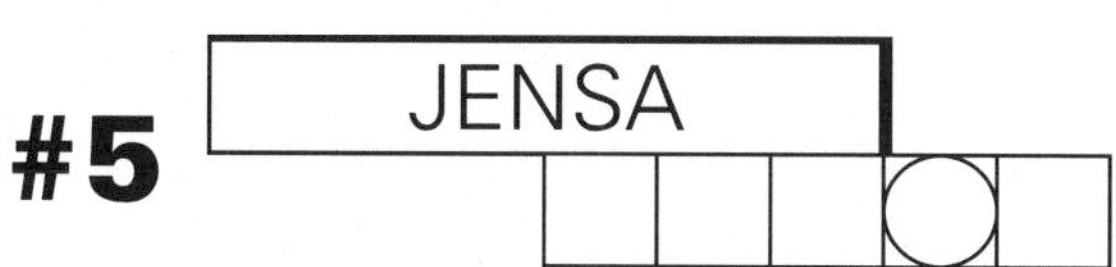

#6

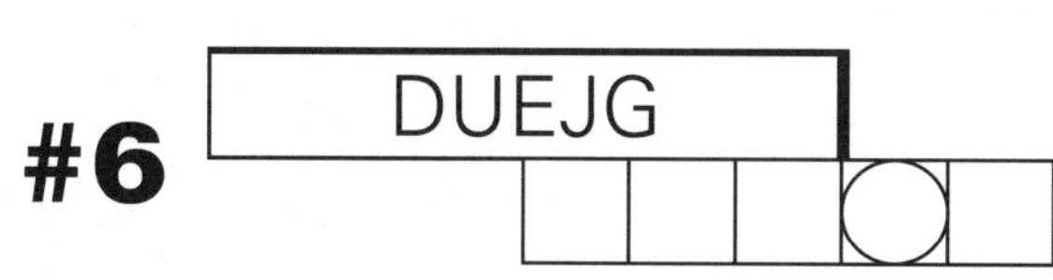

Arrange the circled letters to solve the mystery answer.

MYSTERY ANSWER

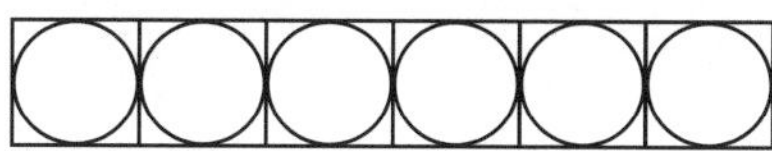

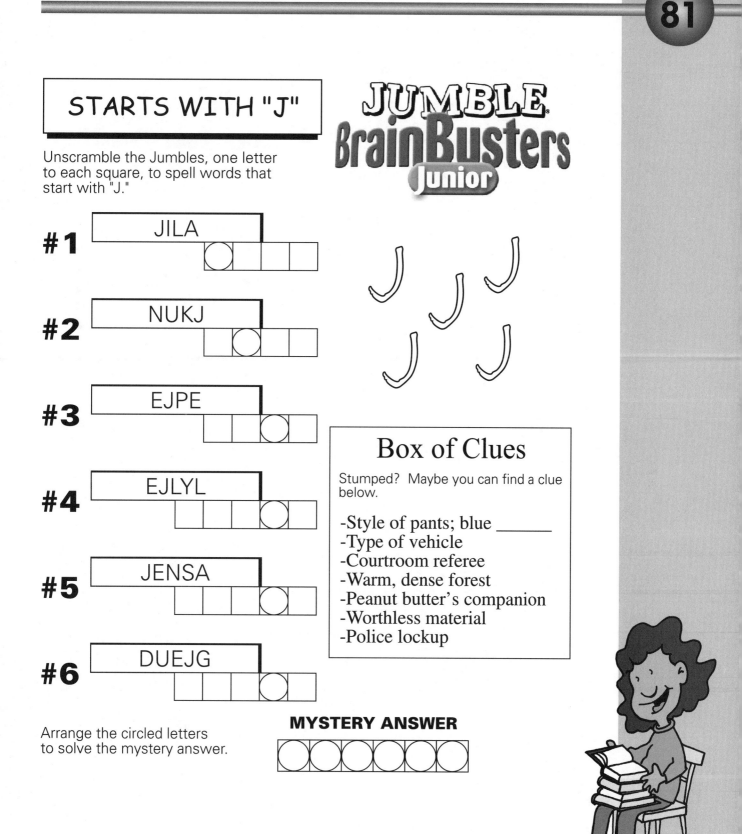

PUZZLE

82

THE HUMAN BODY

Unscramble the Jumbles, one letter to each square, to spell words related to the human body.

#1

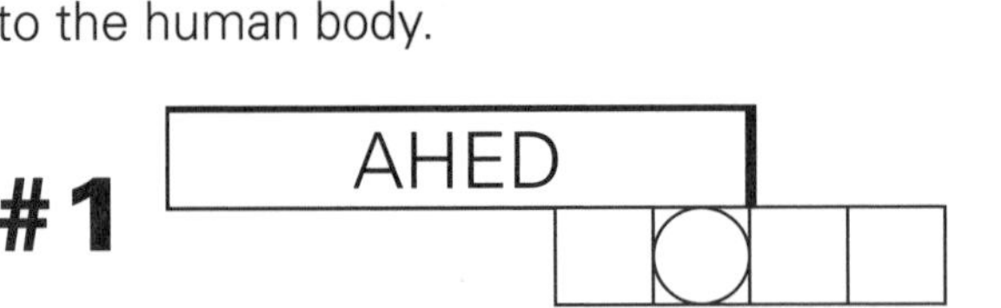

#2

#3

#4

#5

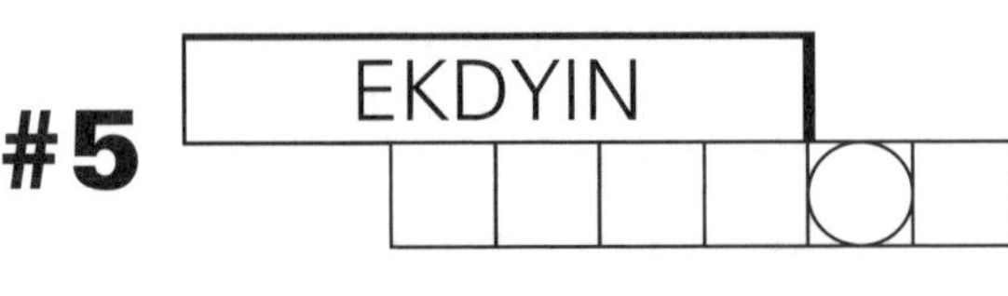

#6

UMLSEC

Interesting Human Body Facts

It takes the human eye up to an hour to adapt completely to seeing in the dark.

Blue eyes are the most sensitive to light. Dark brown eyes are the least sensitive.

Arrange the circled letters to solve the mystery answer.

MYSTERY ANSWER

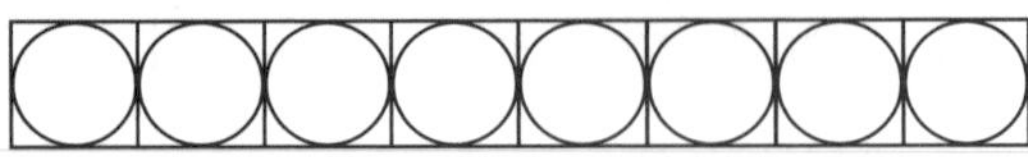

PUZZLE

83

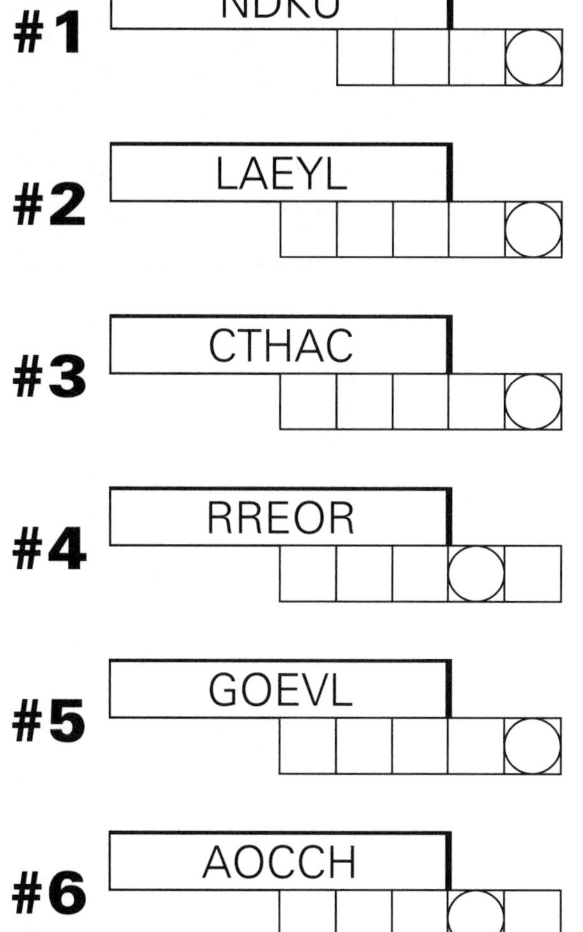

SPORTS

Unscramble the Jumbles, one letter to each square, to spell words related to sports.

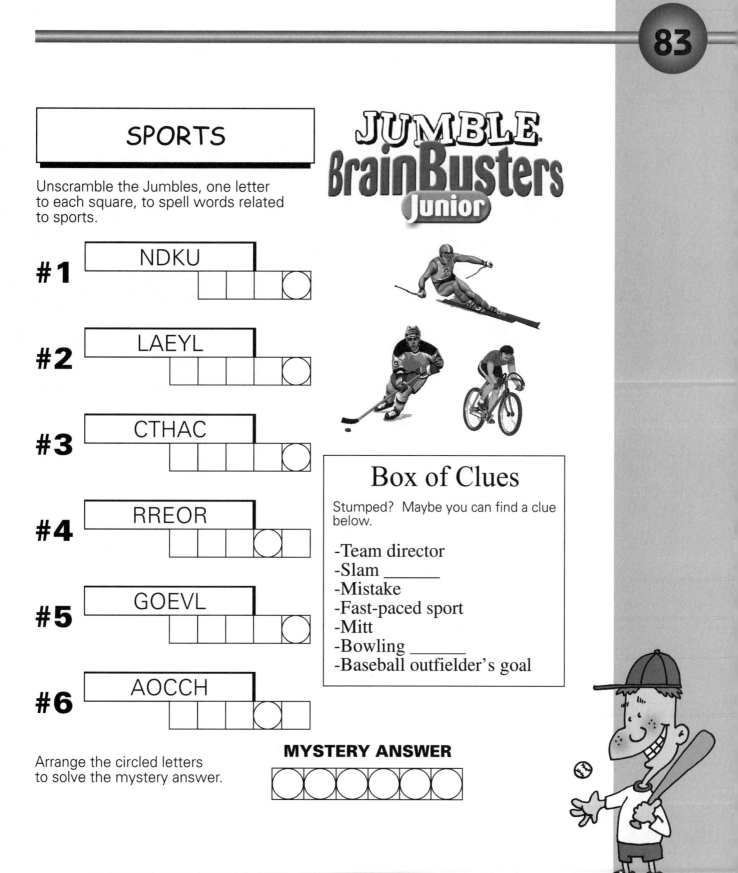

#1 NDKU

#2 LAEYL

#3 CTHAC

#4 RREOR

#5 GOEVL

#6 AOCCH

Box of Clues

Stumped? Maybe you can find a clue below.

-Team director
-Slam ______
-Mistake
-Fast-paced sport
-Mitt
-Bowling ______
-Baseball outfielder's goal

Arrange the circled letters to solve the mystery answer.

MYSTERY ANSWER

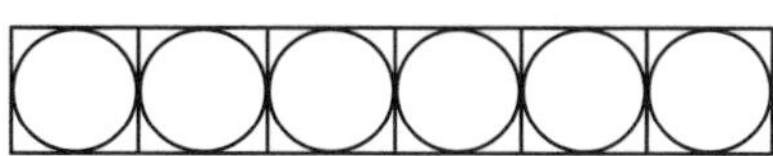

PUZZLE 84

ANIMALS

Unscramble the Jumbles, one letter to each square, to spell names of animals.

#1 PHIOP

#2 ZLIADR

#3 BRAITB

#4 LGZIZYR

#5 FIGRFEA

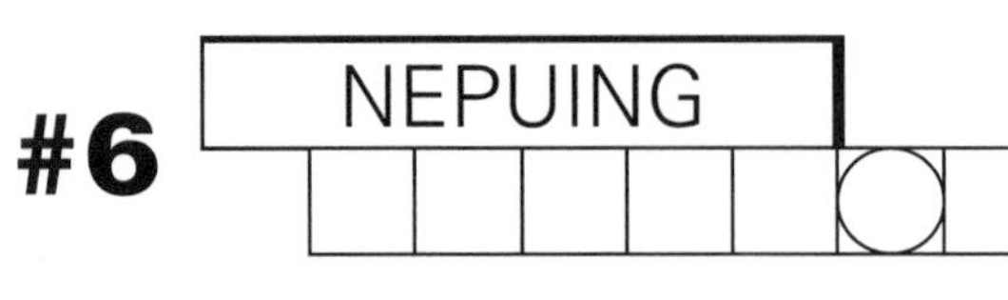

#6 NEPUING

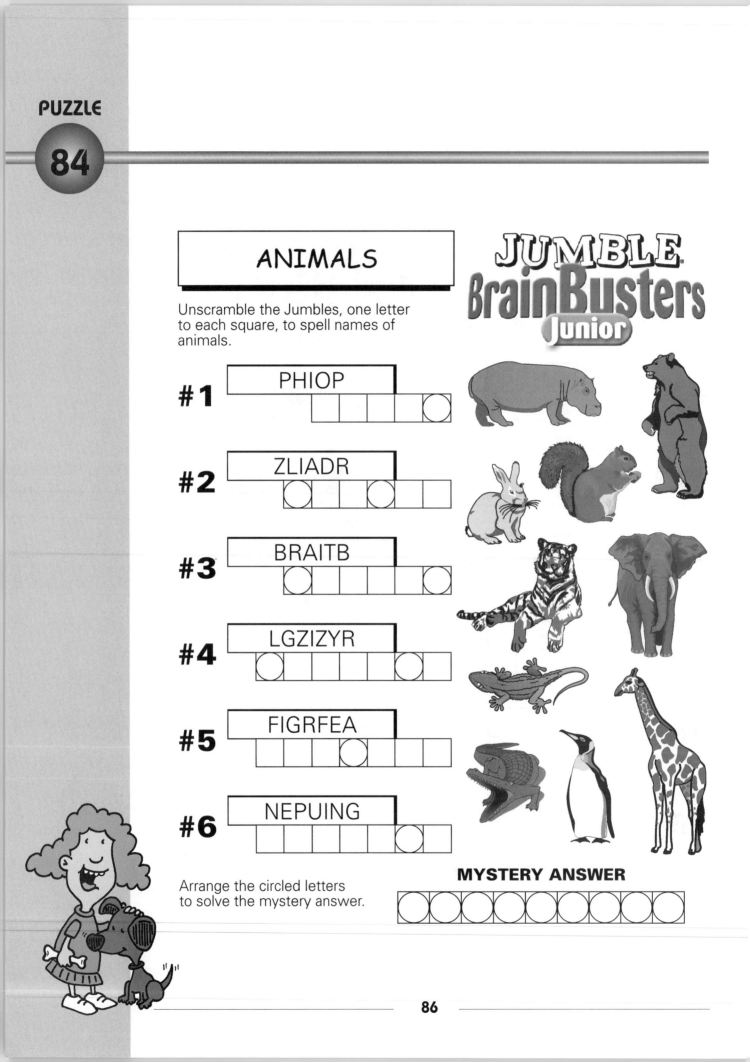

Arrange the circled letters to solve the mystery answer.

MYSTERY ANSWER

MATH

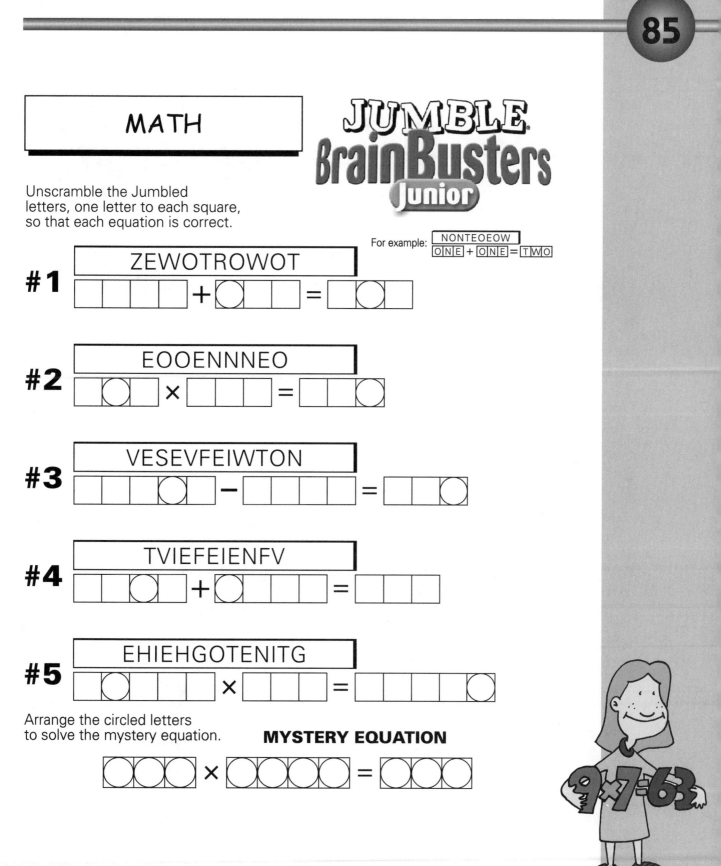

JUMBLE BrainBusters Junior

Unscramble the Jumbled letters, one letter to each square, so that each equation is correct.

For example: NONTEOEOW
ONE + ONE = TWO

#1 ZEWOTROWOT

☐☐☐☐ + ◯☐☐ = ☐◯☐

#2 EOOENNNEO

☐◯☐ × ☐☐☐ = ☐☐◯

#3 VESEVFEIWTON

☐☐☐◯☐ − ☐☐☐☐ = ☐☐◯

#4 TVIEFEIENFV

☐☐◯☐ + ◯☐☐☐ = ☐☐☐

#5 EHIEHGOTENITG

☐◯☐☐☐ × ☐☐☐ = ☐☐☐☐◯

Arrange the circled letters to solve the mystery equation.

MYSTERY EQUATION

◯◯◯ × ◯◯◯◯ = ◯◯◯

PUZZLE

86

COMPUTERS

JUMBLE BrainBusters Junior

Unscramble the Jumbles, one letter to each square, to spell words related to computers.

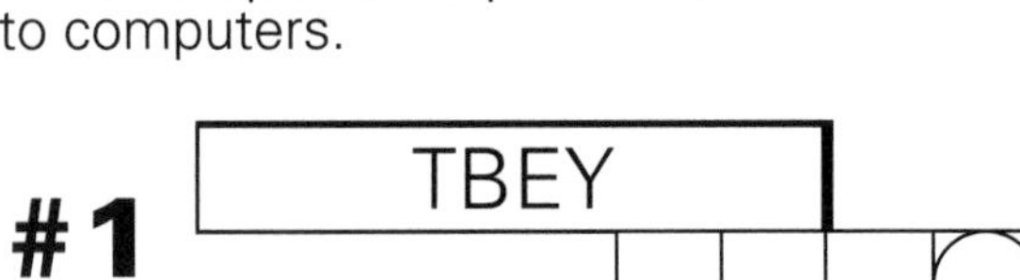

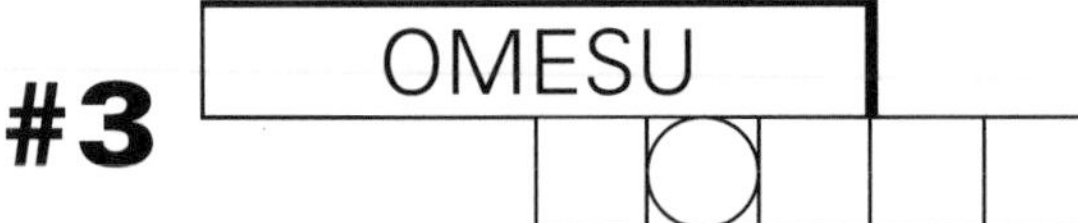

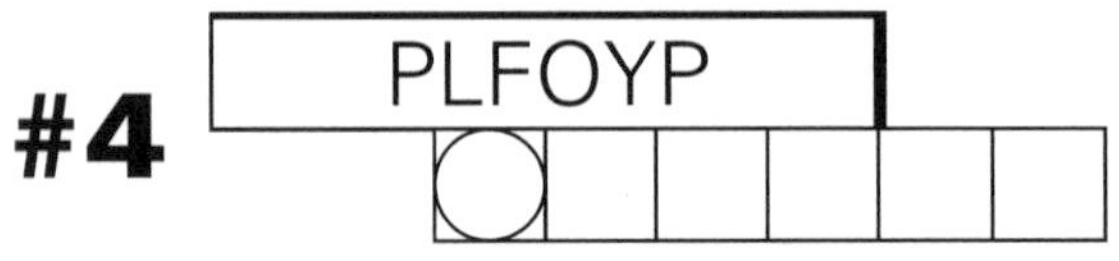

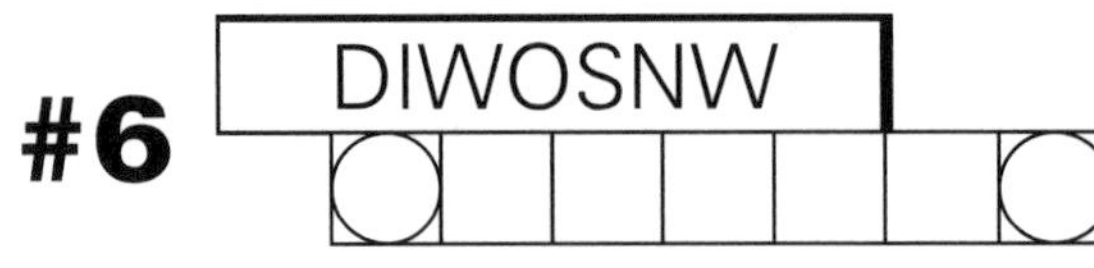

Box of Clues

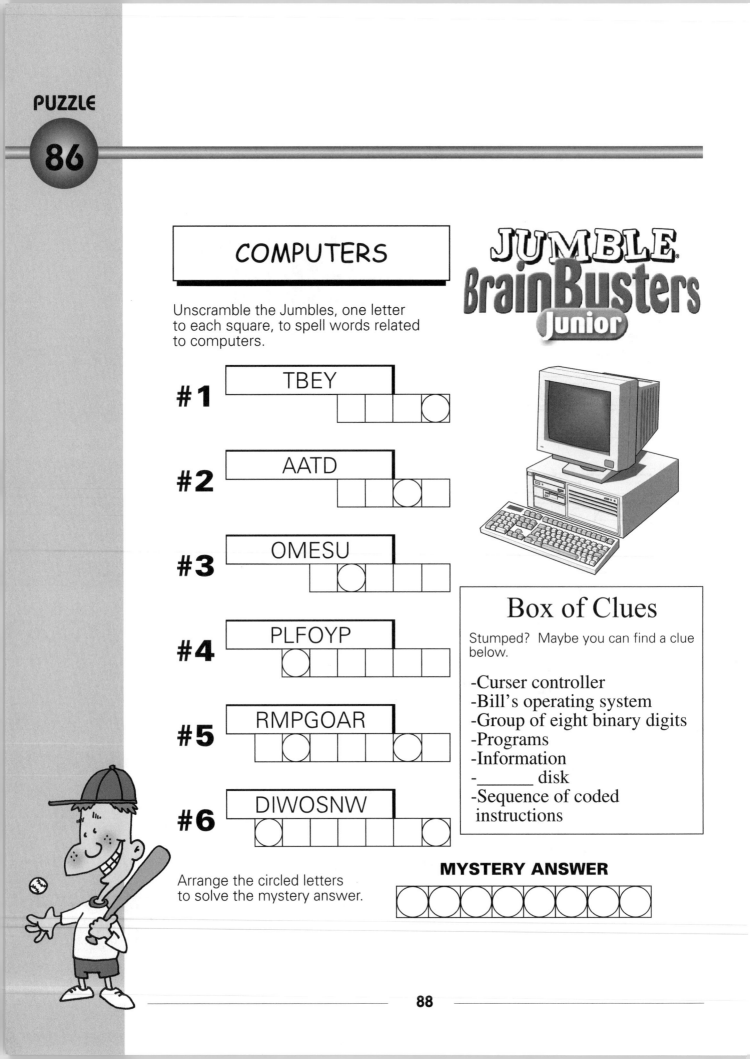

Stumped? Maybe you can find a clue below.

-Curser controller
-Bill's operating system
-Group of eight binary digits
-Programs
-Information
-_______ disk
-Sequence of coded instructions

Arrange the circled letters to solve the mystery answer.

MYSTERY ANSWER

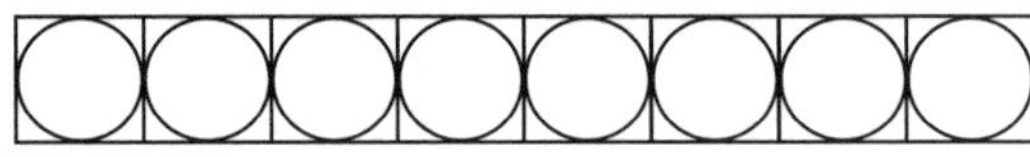

PUZZLE

87

EUROPEAN COUNTRIES

Unscramble the Jumbles, one letter to each square, to spell names of European countries.

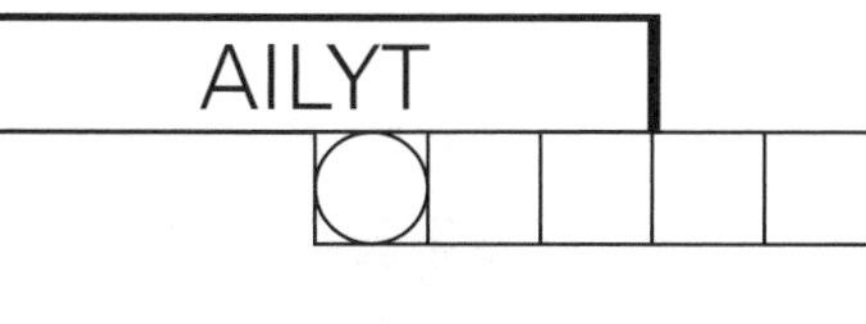

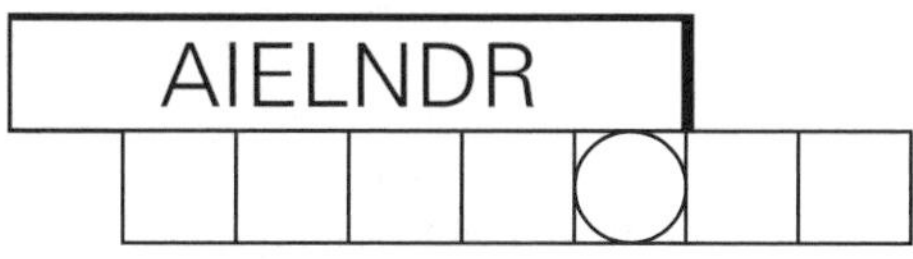

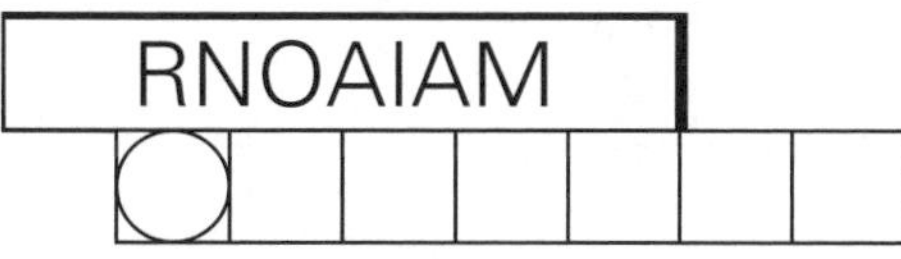

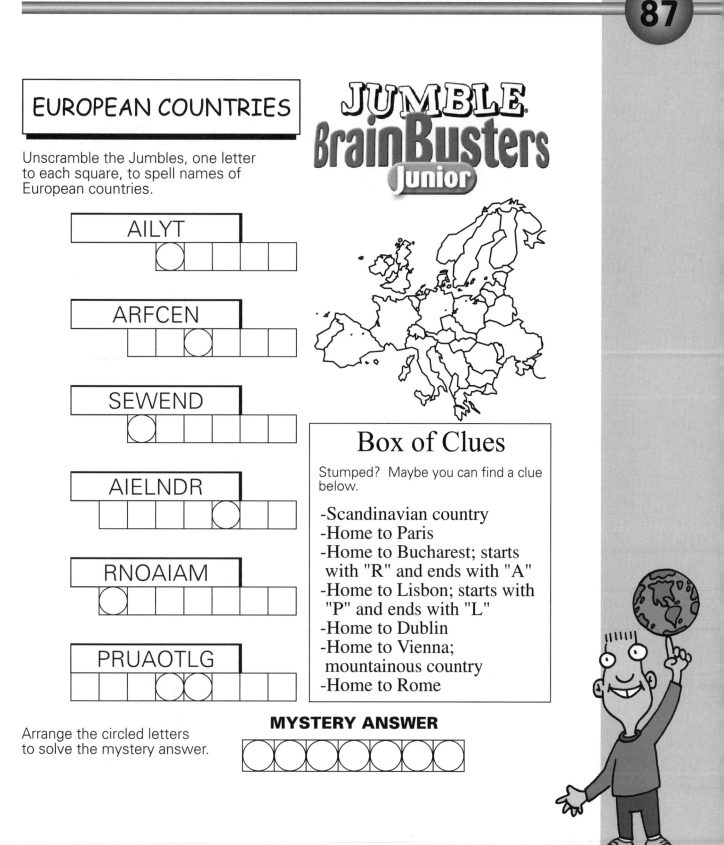

Box of Clues

Stumped? Maybe you can find a clue below.

-Scandinavian country
-Home to Paris
-Home to Bucharest; starts with "R" and ends with "A"
-Home to Lisbon; starts with "P" and ends with "L"
-Home to Dublin
-Home to Vienna; mountainous country
-Home to Rome

MYSTERY ANSWER

Arrange the circled letters to solve the mystery answer.

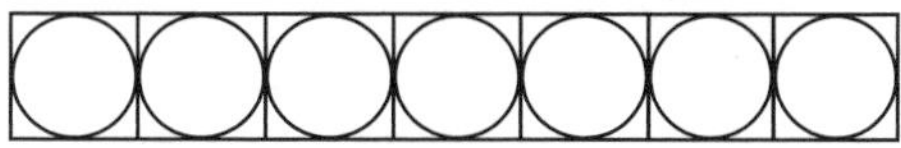

PUZZLE

88

PLANTS

Unscramble the Jumbles, one letter to each square, to spell words related to plants.

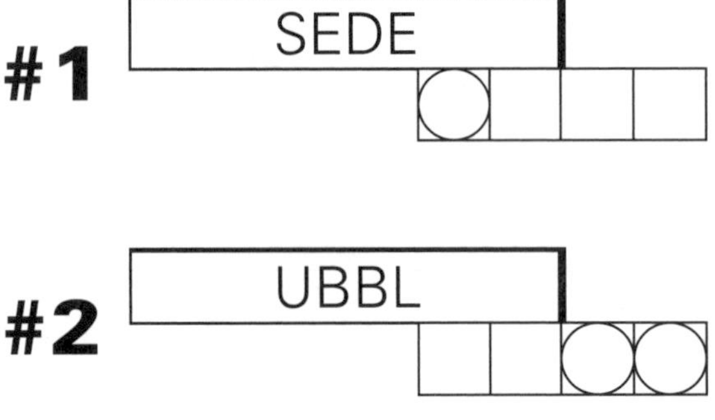

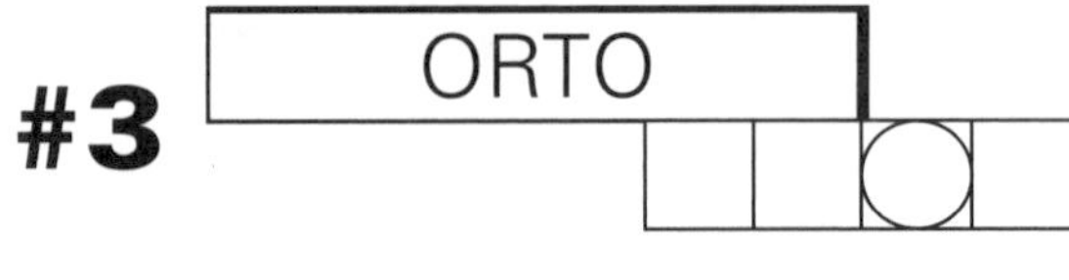

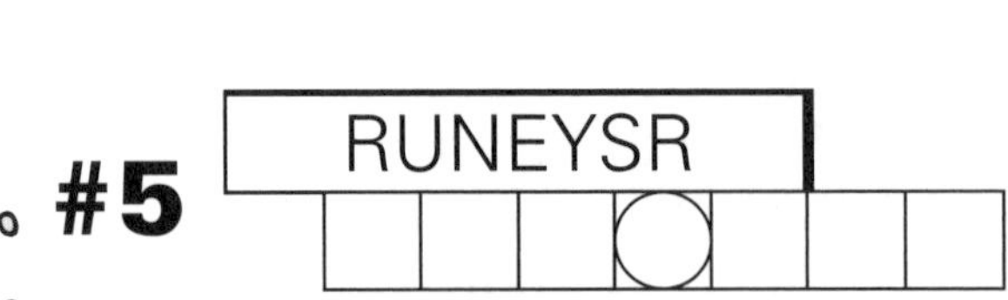

Box of Clues

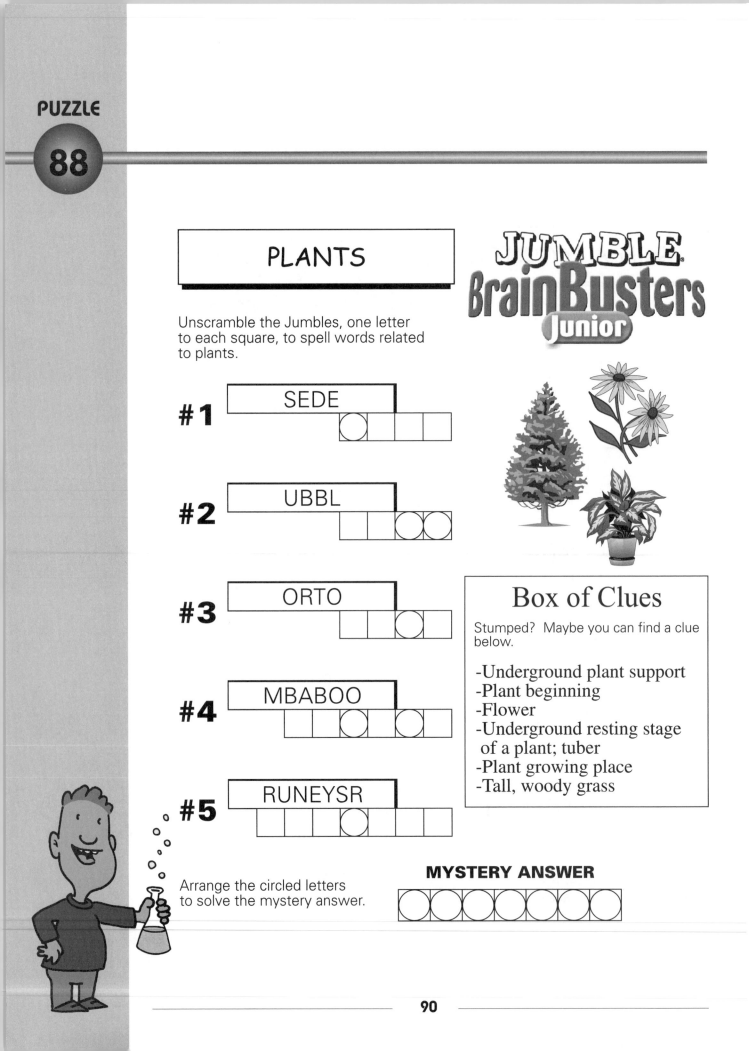

Stumped? Maybe you can find a clue below.

- Underground plant support
- Plant beginning
- Flower
- Underground resting stage of a plant; tuber
- Plant growing place
- Tall, woody grass

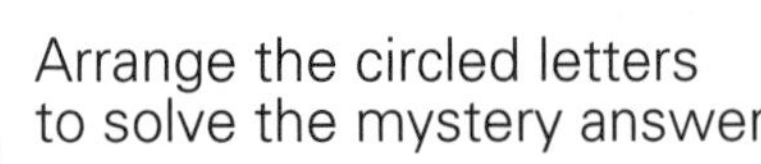

Arrange the circled letters to solve the mystery answer.

MYSTERY ANSWER

AUTOMOBILES

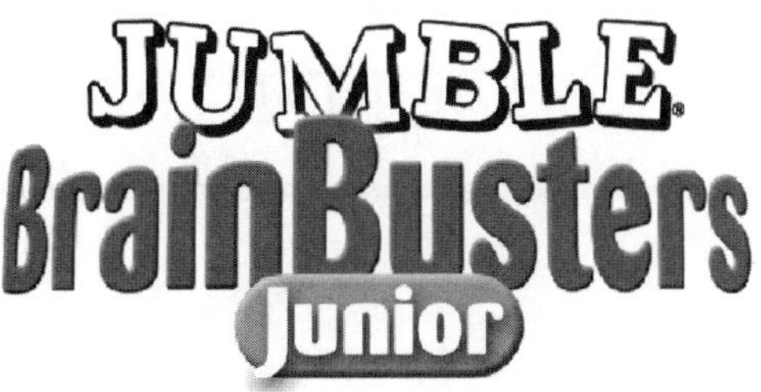

Unscramble the Jumbles, one letter to each square, to spell words related to automobiles.

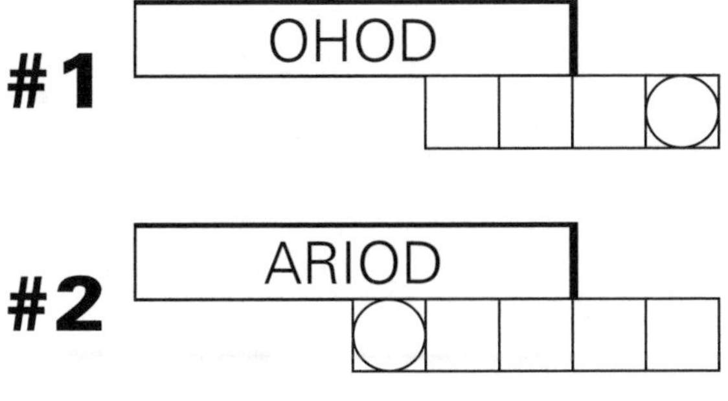

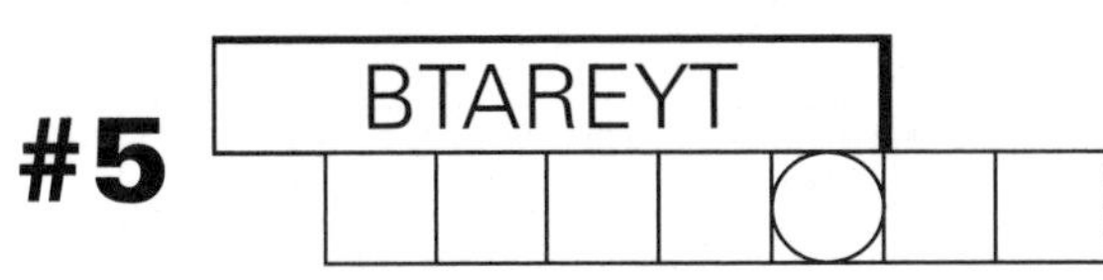

#6 FFELRUM

Box of Clues

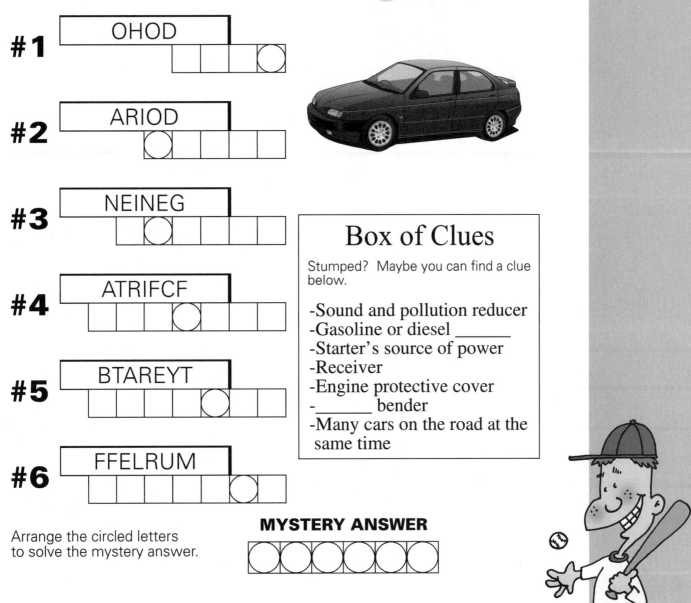

Stumped? Maybe you can find a clue below.

- Sound and pollution reducer
- Gasoline or diesel ______
- Starter's source of power
- Receiver
- Engine protective cover
- ______ bender
- Many cars on the road at the same time

Arrange the circled letters to solve the mystery answer.

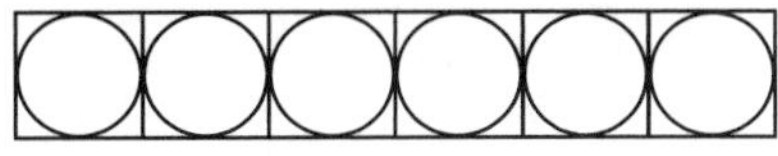

PUZZLE

90

COUNTRIES

JUMBLE BrainBusters Junior

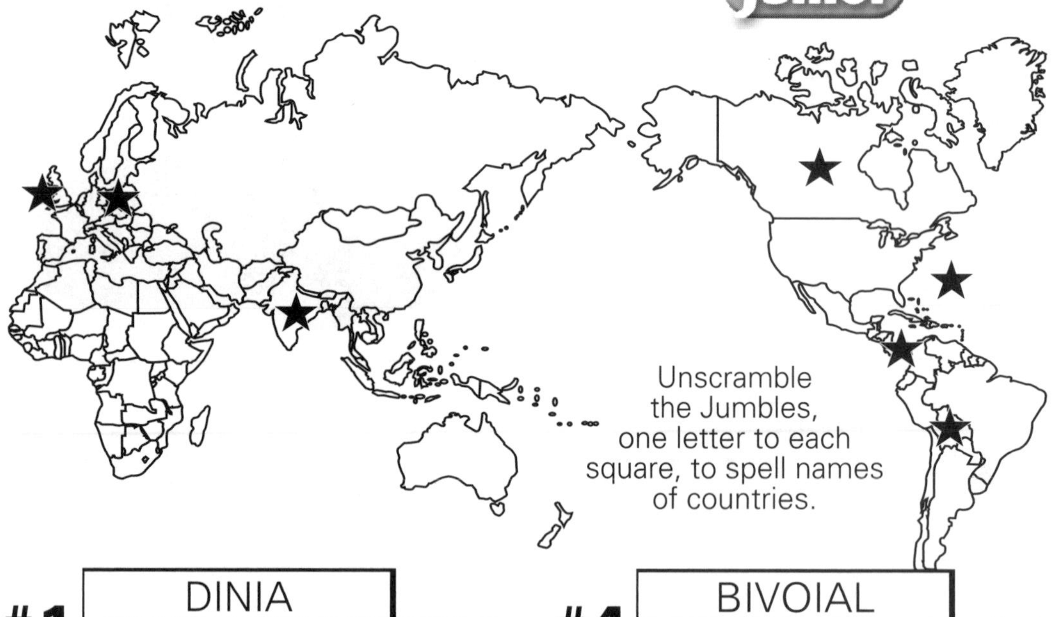

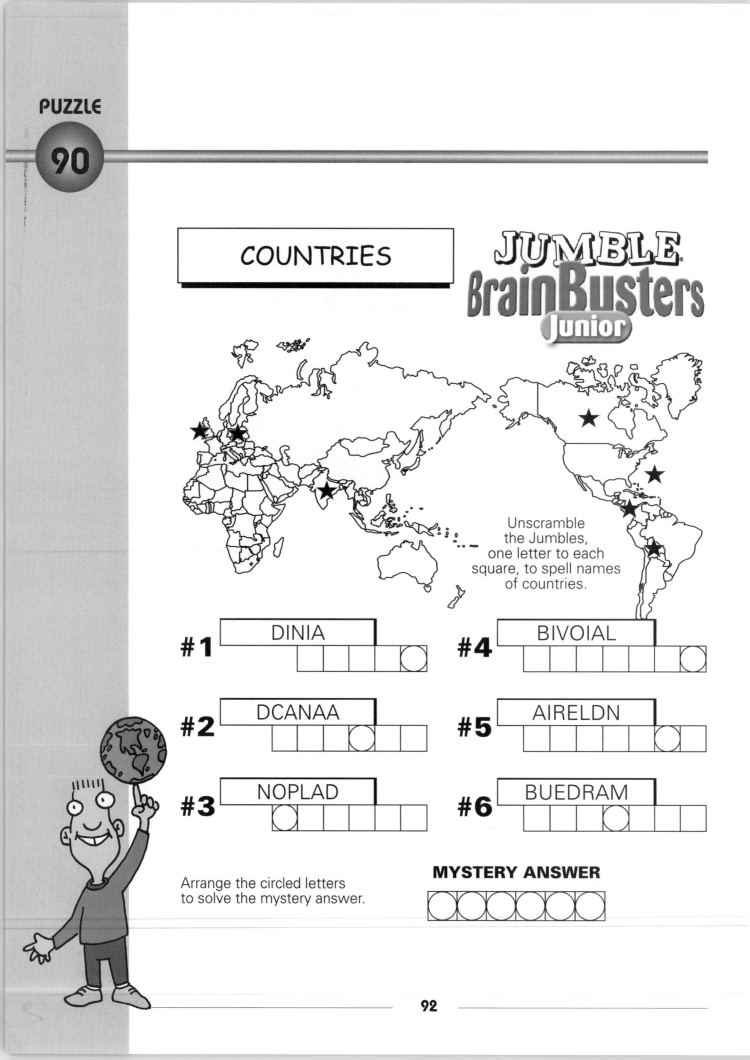

Unscramble the Jumbles, one letter to each square, to spell names of countries.

#1 DINIA

#2 DCANAA

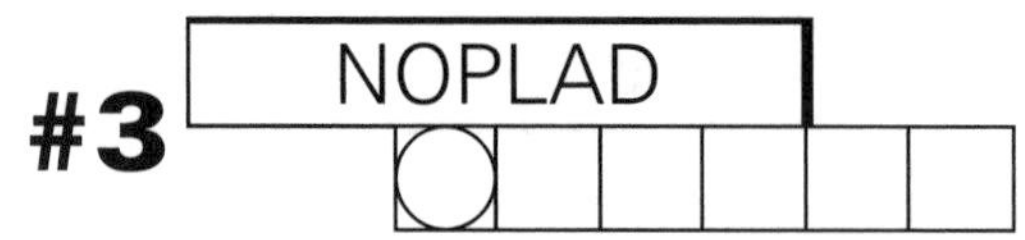

#3 NOPLAD

#4 BIVOIAL

#5 AIRELDN

#6 BUEDRAM

Arrange the circled letters to solve the mystery answer.

MYSTERY ANSWER

PUZZLE 91

TIME LINE

JUMBLE BrainBusters Junior

Unscramble the Jumbles, one letter to each square, to spell words as suggested by the time line.

#1 1732 ______ of George Washington

#2 1846 Elias Howe invents the ______ machine

#3 1888 Eastman produces first Kodak ______

#4 1912 Titanic sinks in the ______

#5 1922 ______ Union established

#6 1986 Hole discovered in ______ layer

#1 TBIHR

#2 EIWSNG

#3 ECRAAM

#4 LTAAICNT

#5 OSIETV

#6 ZEONO

Arrange the circled letters to solve the mystery answer.

1954 ______ divided into North and South

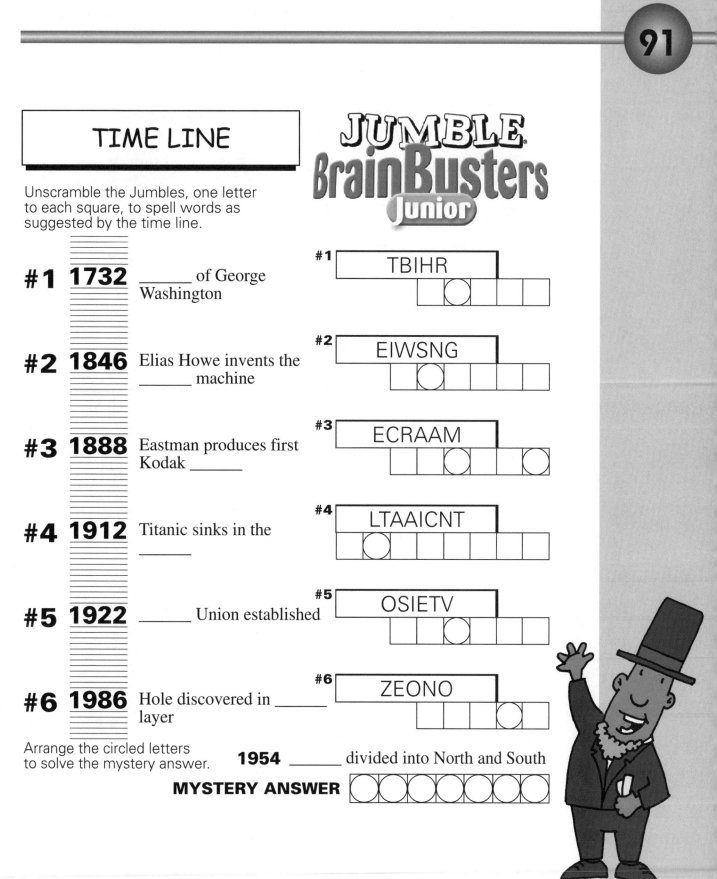

MYSTERY ANSWER

PUZZLE 92

STARTS WITH "K"

Unscramble the Jumbles, one letter to each square, to spell words that start with "K."

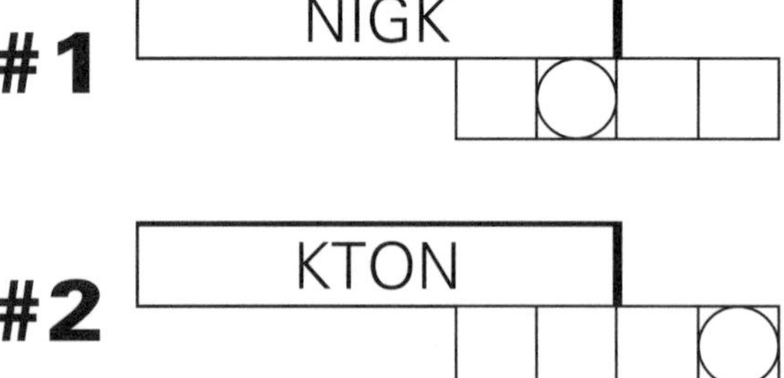

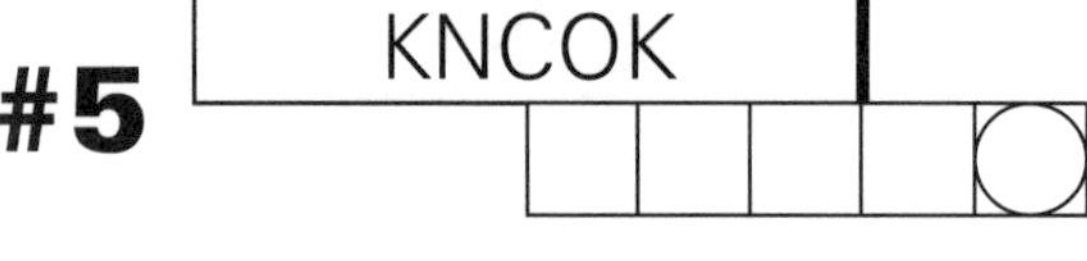

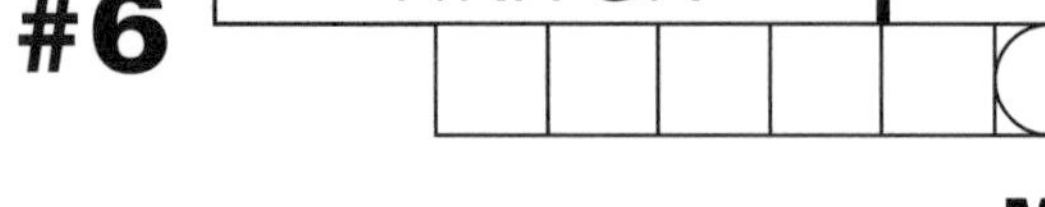

Box of Clues

Stumped? Maybe you can find a clue below.

-Chess piece
-Strike with a sharp blow
-Cutting tool
-Young cat
-Male monarch
-Grasp, understand
-Tangle, snarl

Arrange the circled letters to solve the mystery answer.

MYSTERY ANSWER

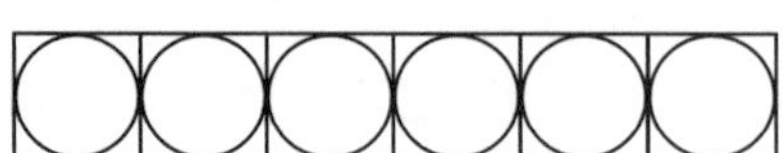

ELEMENTS

JUMBLE® BrainBusters Junior

Unscramble the Jumbles, one letter to each square, to spell names of elements.

#1 OCEPRP

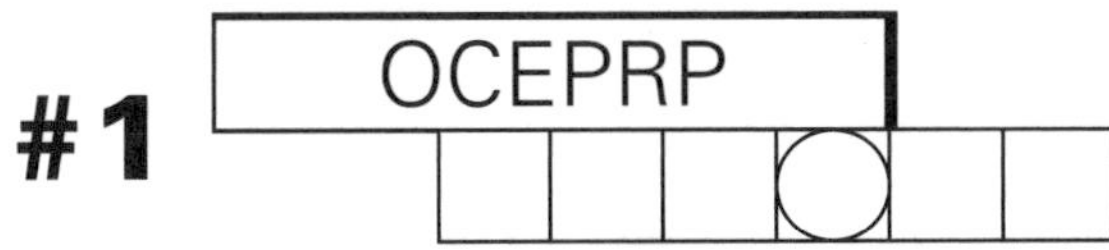

#2 BOCATL

#3 UOSIMD

#4 CILINSO

#5 LCAIMUC

Arrange the circled letters to solve the mystery answer.

MYSTERY ANSWER

THE PERIODIC TABLE

Name
Actinium
Aluminum
Americium
Antimony
Argon
Arsenic
Astatine
Barium
Berkelium
Beryllium
Bismuth
Bohrium
Boron
Bromine
Cadmium
Calcium
Californium
Carbon
Cerium
Cesium
Chlorine
Chromium
Cobalt
Copper
Curium
Dubnium
Dysprosium
Einsteinium
Erbium
Europium
Fermium
Fluorine
Francium
Gadolinium
Gallium
Germanium
Gold
Hafnium
Hassium
Helium
Holmium
Hydrogen
Indium
Iodine
Iridium
Iron
Krypton
Lanthanum
Lawrencium
Lead
Lithium
Lutetium
Magnesium
Manganese
Meitnerium
Mendelevium
Mercury
Molybdenum
Neodymium
Neon
Neptunium
Nickel
Niobium
Nitrogen
Nobelium
Osmium
Oxygen
Palladium
Phosphorus
Platinum
Plutonium
Polonium
Potassium
Potassium
Praseodymium
Promethium
Protactinium
Radium
Radon
Rhenium
Rhodium
Rubidium
Ruthenium
Rutherfordium
Samarium
Scandium
Seaborgium
Selenium
Silicon
Silver
Sodium
Strontium
Sulfur
Tantalum
Technetium
Tellurium
Terbium
Thallium
Thorium
Thulium
Tin
Titanium
Tungsten
Uranium
Vanadium
Xenon
Ytterbium
Yttrium
Zinc
Zirconium

PUZZLE

94

BASEBALL

Unscramble the Jumbles, one letter to each square, to spell words related to baseball.

#1

#2

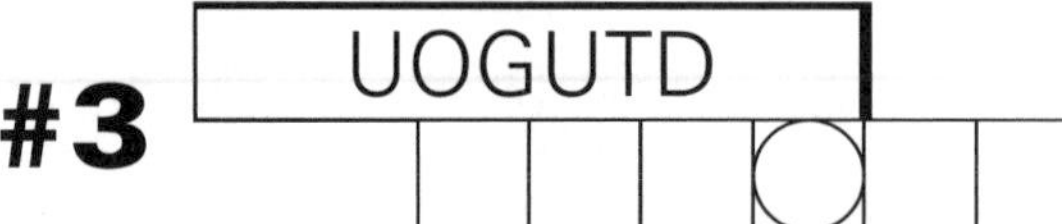

#3

#4

#5

#6

ADIOMDN

Box of Clues

Stumped? Maybe you can find a clue below.

-Pitcher's partner
-Type of hit
-Pitcher's goal
-Waiting and watching area
-Left field, first base, pitcher or catcher
-Bases four-sided shape
-Catcher's partner

Arrange the circled letters to solve the mystery answer.

MYSTERY ANSWER

NOUNS

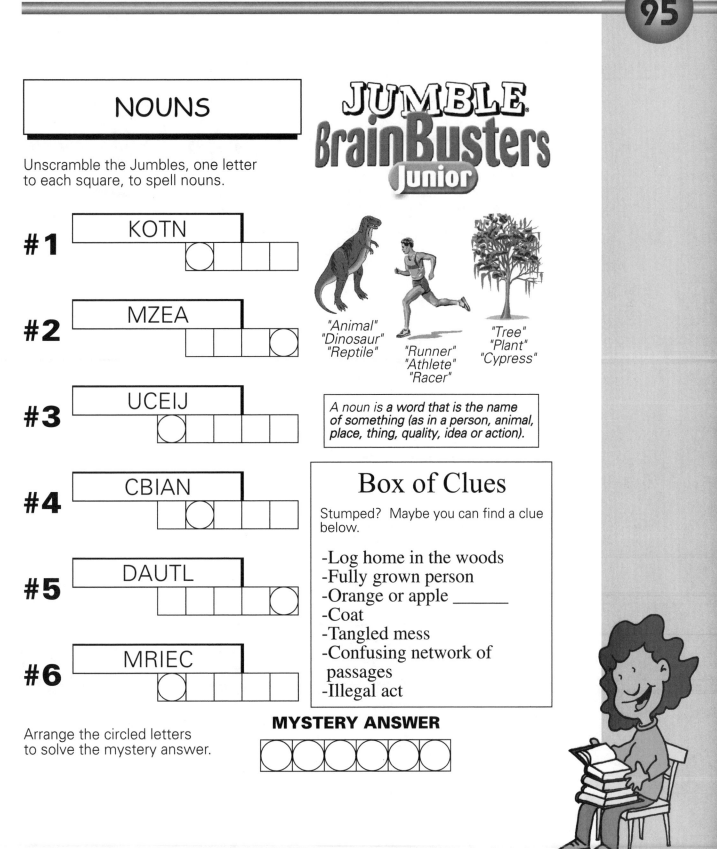

JUMBLE BrainBusters Junior

Unscramble the Jumbles, one letter to each square, to spell nouns.

#1 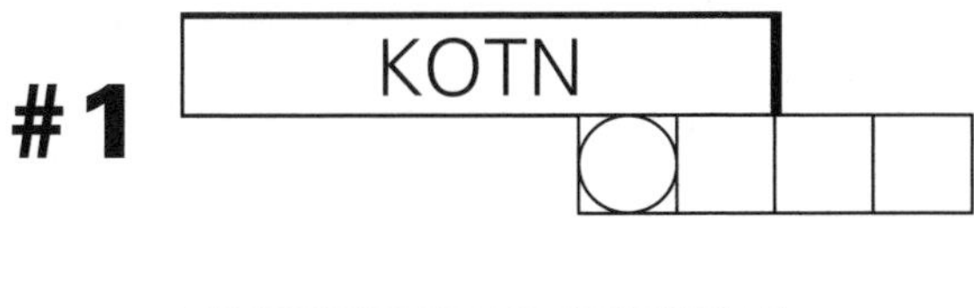

#2 

#3 

#4 

#5 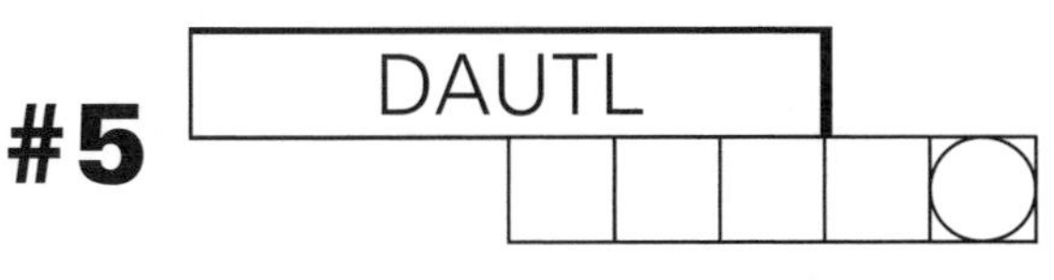

#6 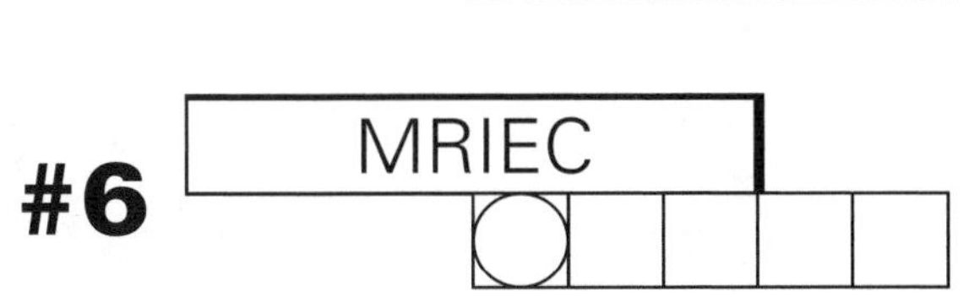

A noun is a word that is the name of something (as in a person, animal, place, thing, quality, idea or action).

Box of Clues

Stumped? Maybe you can find a clue below.

- Log home in the woods
- Fully grown person
- Orange or apple ______
- Coat
- Tangled mess
- Confusing network of passages
- Illegal act

Arrange the circled letters to solve the mystery answer.

MYSTERY ANSWER

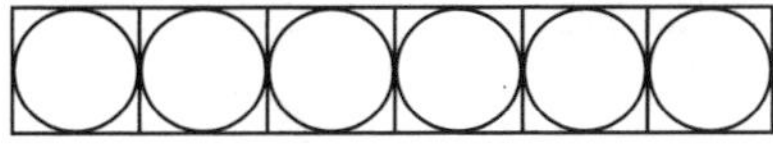

PUZZLE

96

MATH

JUMBLE BrainBusters Junior

Unscramble the Jumbled letters, one letter to each square, so that each equation is correct.

For example: NONTEOEOW
ONE + ONE = TWO

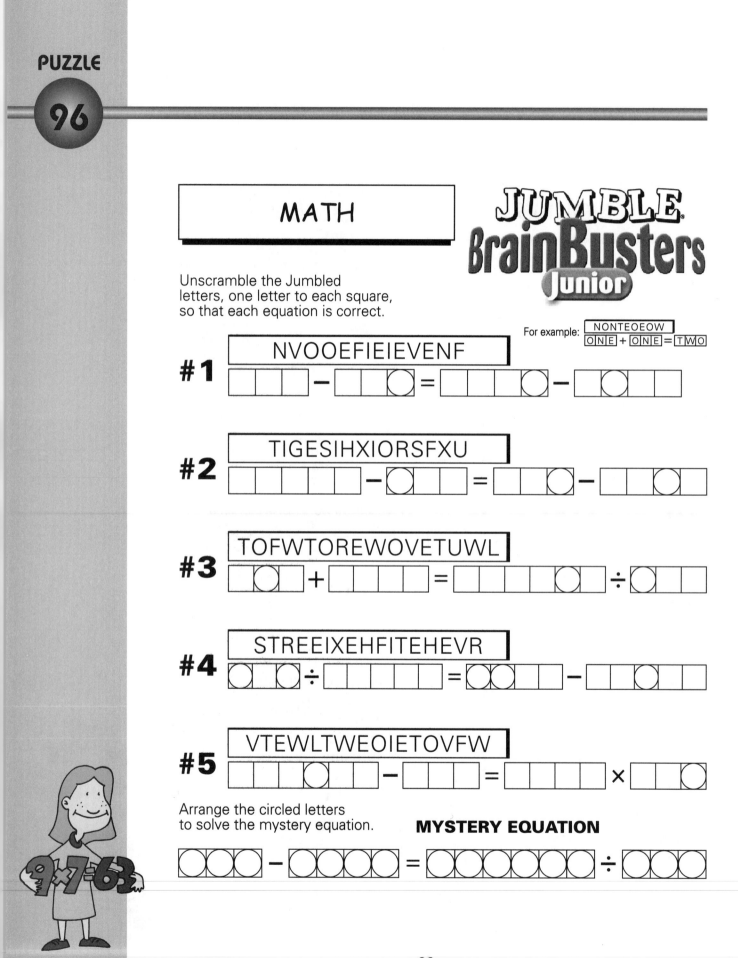

#1 NVOOEFIEIEVENF

☐☐☐ – ☐☐◯ = ☐☐☐◯ – ☐◯☐☐

#2 TIGESIHXIORSFXU

☐☐☐☐☐ – ◯☐☐ = ☐☐◯ – ☐☐◯☐

#3 TOFWTOREWOVETUWL

☐◯☐ + ☐☐☐☐ = ☐☐☐☐◯☐ ÷ ◯☐☐

#4 STREEIXEHFITEHEVR

◯☐◯ ÷ ☐☐☐☐☐ = ◯◯☐☐ – ☐☐◯☐☐

#5 VTEWLTWEOIETOVFW

☐☐☐◯☐☐ – ☐☐☐ = ☐☐☐☐ × ☐☐◯

Arrange the circled letters to solve the mystery equation.

MYSTERY EQUATION

◯◯◯ – ◯◯◯◯◯ = ◯◯◯◯◯◯◯ ÷ ◯◯◯

PUZZLE 97

MEANS THE OPPOSITE

Unscramble the Jumbles, one letter to each square, to spell pairs of words that have opposite or nearly opposite meanings.

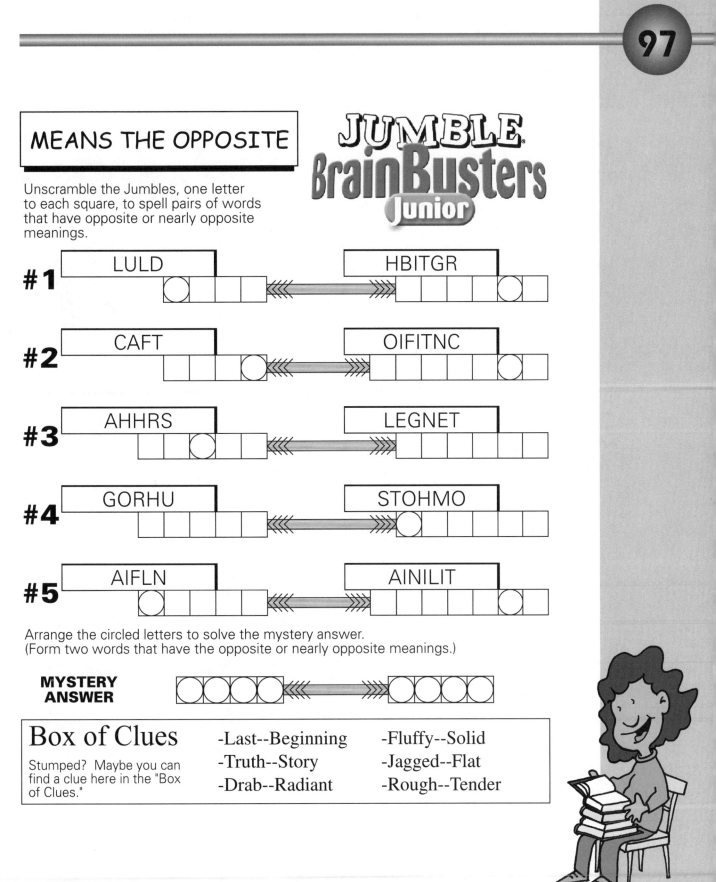

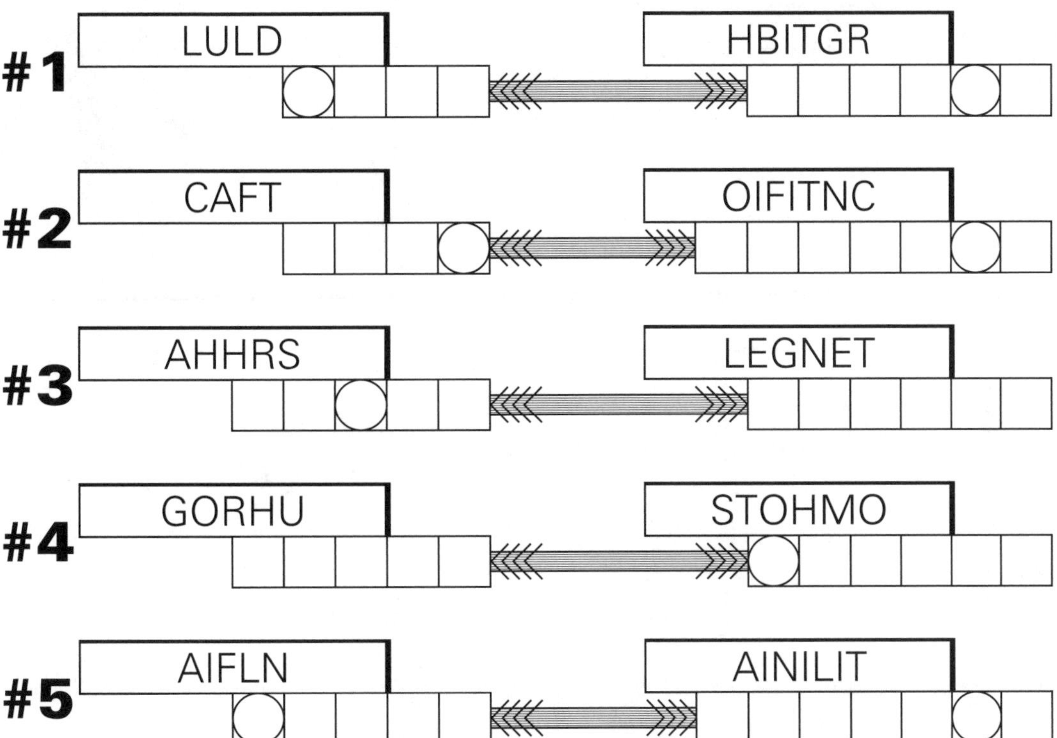

Arrange the circled letters to solve the mystery answer.
(Form two words that have the opposite or nearly opposite meanings.)

MYSTERY ANSWER

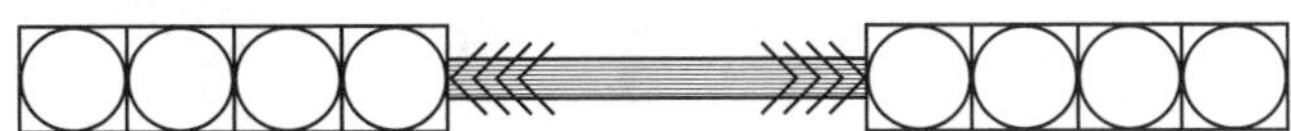

Box of Clues

Stumped? Maybe you can find a clue here in the "Box of Clues."

- -Last--Beginning
- -Truth--Story
- -Drab--Radiant
- -Fluffy--Solid
- -Jagged--Flat
- -Rough--Tender

PUZZLE

98

CLOTHING

Jumble BrainBusters Junior

Unscramble the Jumbles, one letter to each square, to spell words related to clothing.

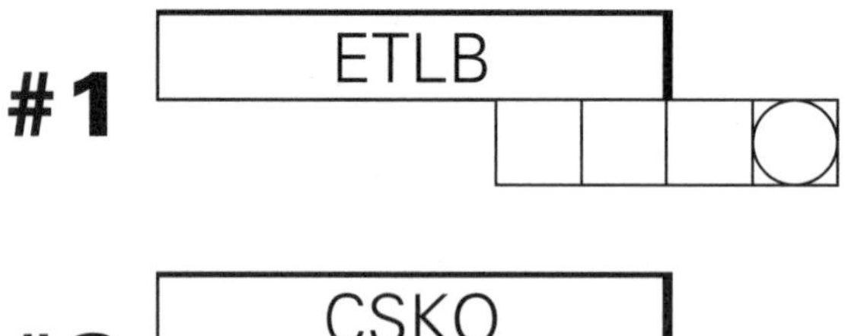

#1 ETLB

#2 CSKO

#3 AJESN

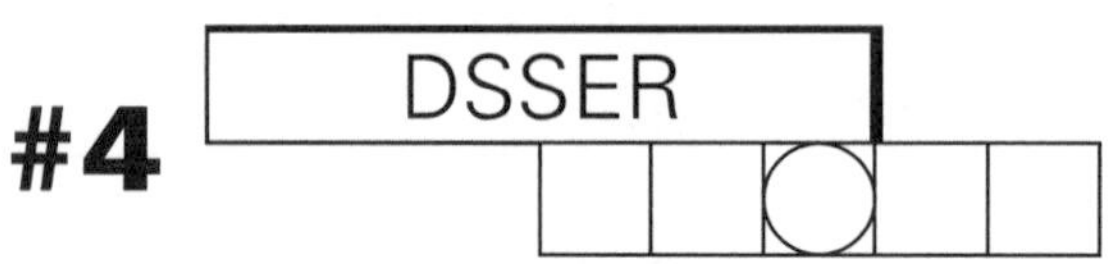

#4 DSSER

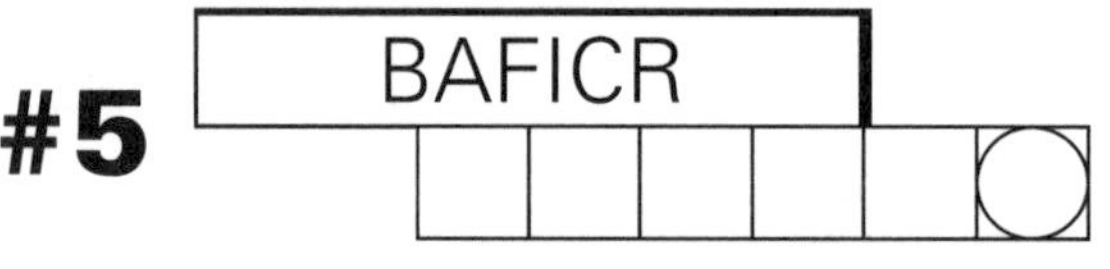

#5 BAFICR

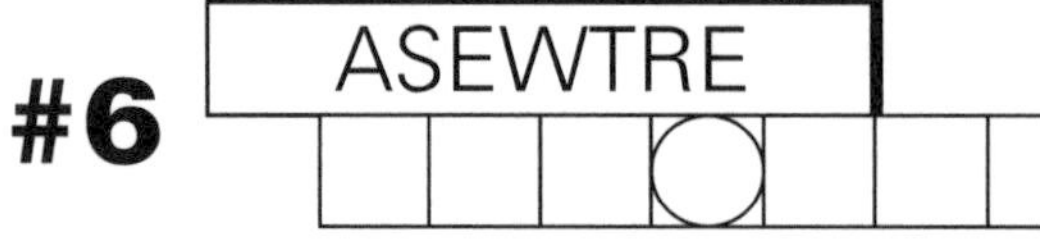

#6 ASEWTRE

Box of Clues

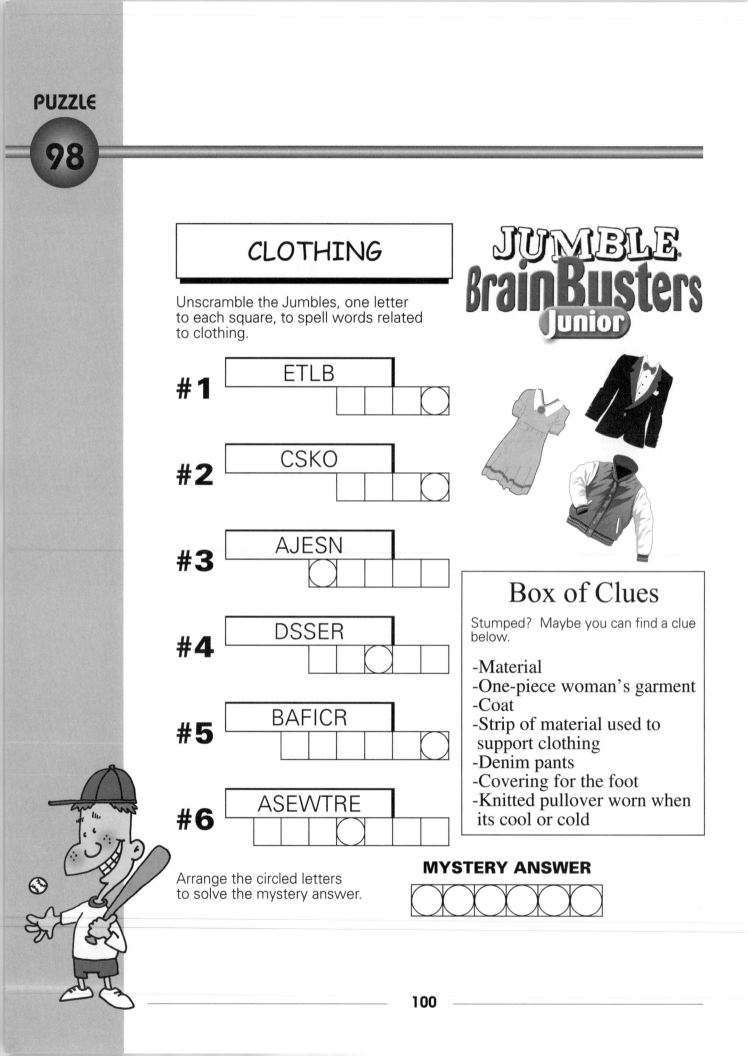

Stumped? Maybe you can find a clue below.

-Material
-One-piece woman's garment
-Coat
-Strip of material used to support clothing
-Denim pants
-Covering for the foot
-Knitted pullover worn when its cool or cold

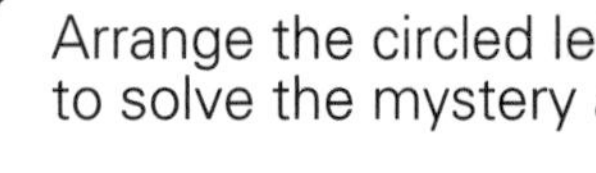

Arrange the circled letters to solve the mystery answer.

MYSTERY ANSWER

ADVERBS

JUMBLE BrainBusters Junior

Unscramble the Jumbles, one letter to each square, to spell adverbs.

#1 MDIYL

#2 DRULYE

#3 OSLLYW

#4 GLIHLYT

#5 TOMNLYH

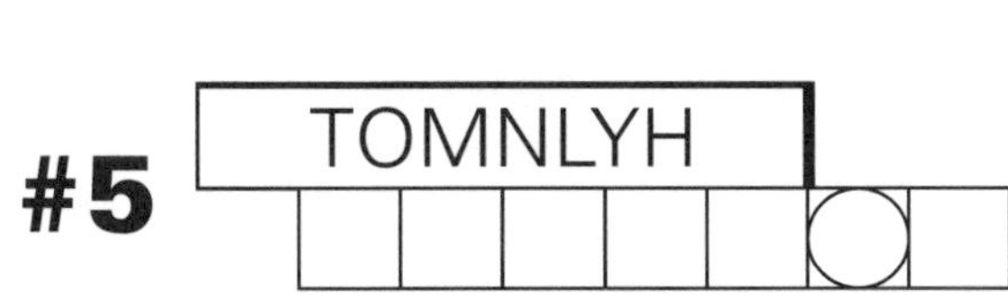

Arrange the circled letters to solve the mystery answer.

MYSTERY ANSWER

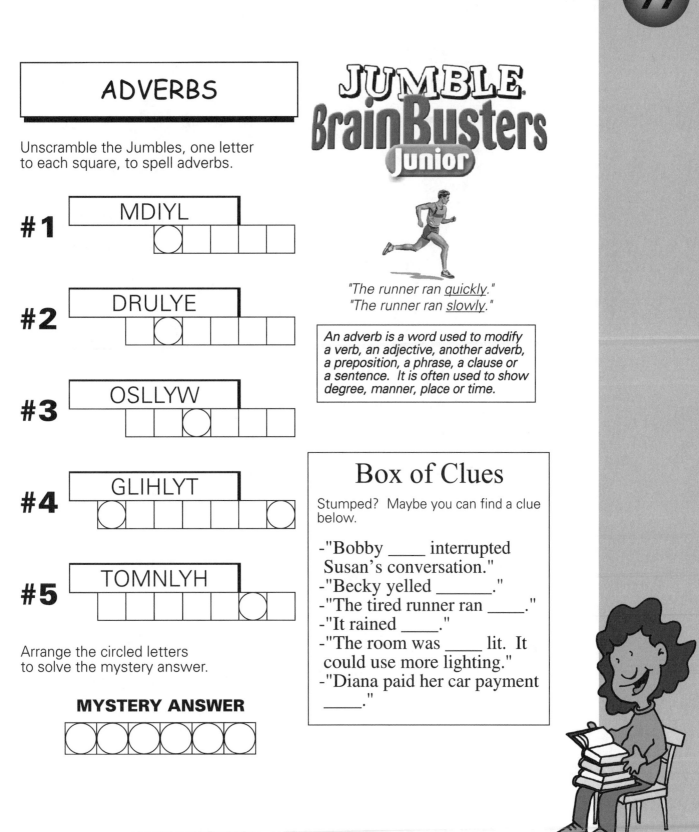

"The runner ran quickly."
"The runner ran slowly."

An adverb is a word used to modify a verb, an adjective, another adverb, a preposition, a phrase, a clause or a sentence. It is often used to show degree, manner, place or time.

Box of Clues

Stumped? Maybe you can find a clue below.

-"Bobby ____ interrupted Susan's conversation."
-"Becky yelled ______."
-"The tired runner ran ____."
-"It rained ____."
-"The room was ____ lit. It could use more lighting."
-"Diana paid her car payment ____."

PUZZLE

100

ELEMENTS

JUMBLE BrainBusters Junior

An element is a fundamental substance consisting of atoms of only one kind that cannot be broken down into simpler substances.

THE PERIODIC TABLE

Atomic # / Atomic Symbol

1 H																	2 He
3 Li	4 Be											5 B	6 C	7 N ★	8 O ★	9 F	10 Ne
11 Na	12 Mg											13 Al	14 Si	15 P	16 S	17 Cl	18 Ar
19 K	20 Ca	21 Sc	22 Ti	23 V	24 Cr	25 Mn	26 Fe ★	27 Co ★	28 Ni	29 Cu	30 Zn ★	31 Ga	32 Ge	33 As	34 Se	35 Br	36 Kr
37 Rb	38 Sr	39 Y	40 Zr	41 Nb	42 Mo	43 Tc	44 Ru	45 Rh	46 Pd	47 Ag	48 Cd	49 In	50 Sn	51 Sb	52 Te	53 I	54 Xe
55 Cs	56 Ba	57-71 Lathanide series (rare earth elements)	72 Hf	73 Ta	74 W	75 Re	76 Os	77 Ir	78 Pt	79 Au ★	80 Hg	81 Tl	82 Pb	83 Bi	84 Po	85 At	86 Rn
87 Fr	88 Ra ★	89-103 Actinide series (radioactive rare earth elements)	104 Unq	105 Unp	106 Unh	107 Uns		108 Une									

Unscramble the Jumbles, one letter to each square, to spell names of elements.

#1 ZICN

#2 RNIO

#3 ODLG

#4 OYNXEG

#5 BCLTAO

#6 ARDIMU

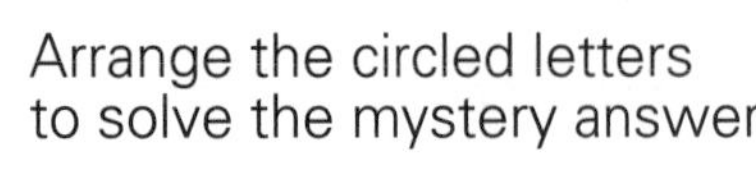

Arrange the circled letters to solve the mystery answer.

MYSTERY ANSWER

POETRY

JUMBLE BrainBusters Junior

Unscramble the Jumbles, one letter to each square, to spell words found in the poem.

#1 ONSG

#2 RBDNA

#3 WNYAAY

#4 DRISB

#5 ROWM

MORNING SERENADE

by Kim E. Nolan

There's a _____#1 outside my window
Little birds they chirp away
It's this tune I hear each morning
That cues a _____#2-new day

Sometimes the song is lonely
Sometimes the song is gay
Sometimes it even wakes me
But I love it _____#3

I could stay in bed and listen
Instead I rise and stretch
Just like my little friends the _____#4
I have a _____#5 to catch

Arrange the circled letters to solve the mystery answer. (The mystery answer is not in the poem.)

MYSTERY ANSWER

PUZZLE

102

WEATHER

Unscramble the Jumbles, one letter to each square, to spell words related to weather.

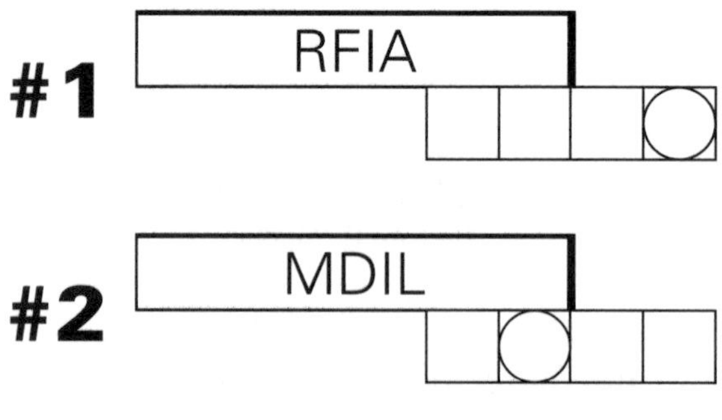

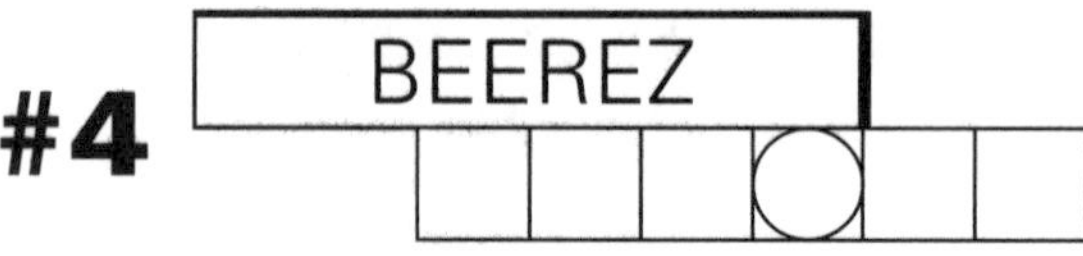

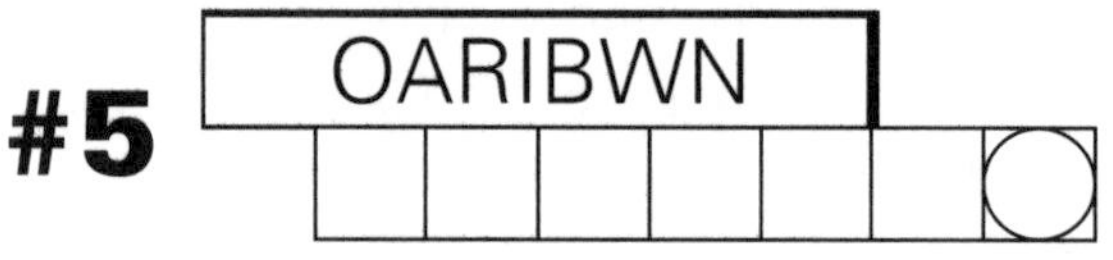

Box of Clues

Stumped? Maybe you can find a clue below.

- -Light wind
- -Colorful weather display
- -Cold or warm ______
- -Prediction
- -Tornado nickname
- -Warm
- -Not stormy, fine

Arrange the circled letters to solve the mystery answer.

MYSTERY ANSWER

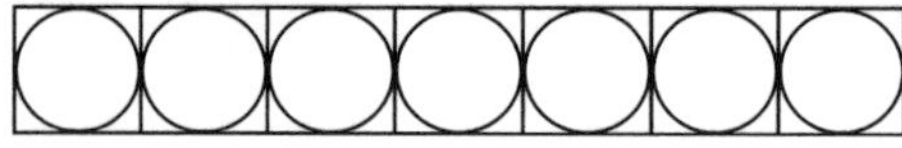

NOUNS

JUMBLE BrainBusters Junior

Unscramble the Jumbles, one letter to each square, to spell nouns.

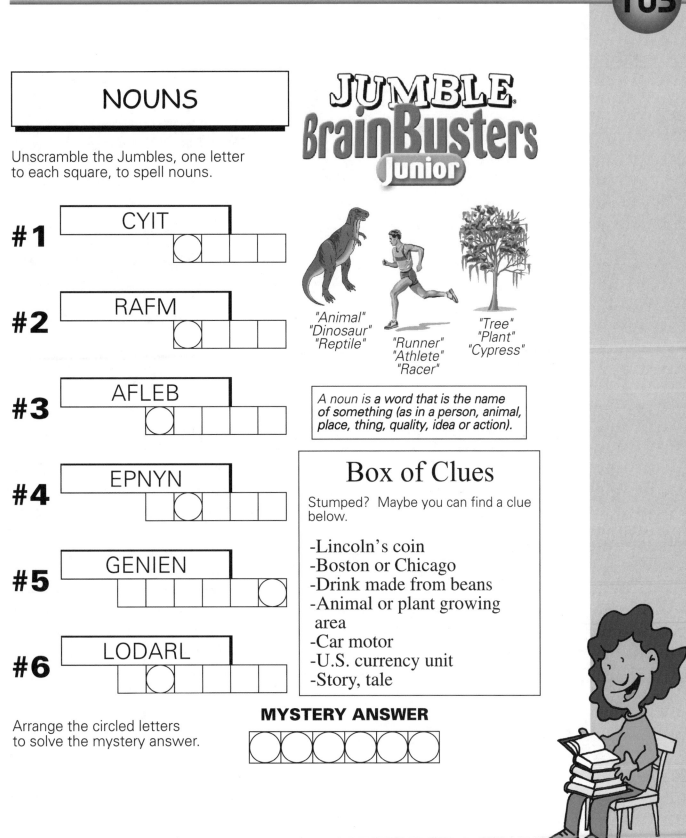

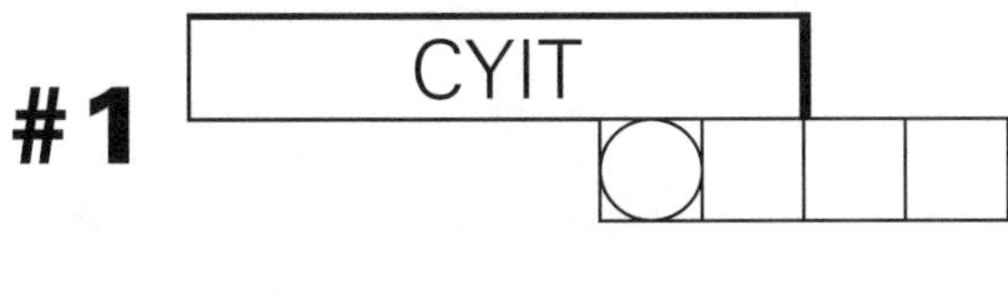

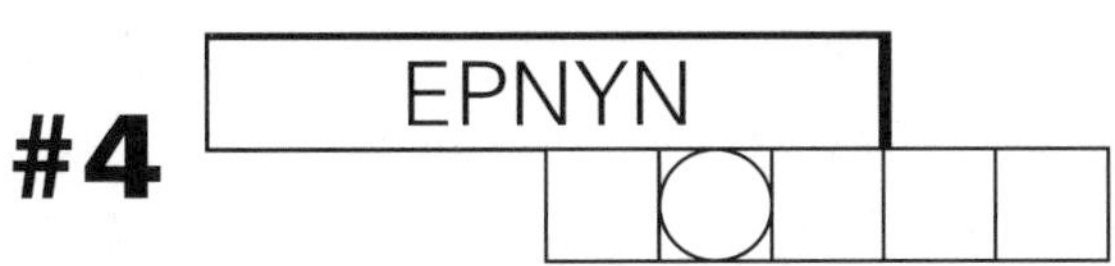

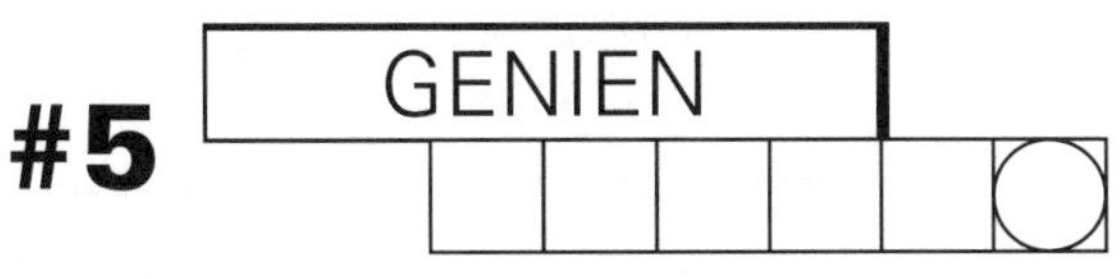

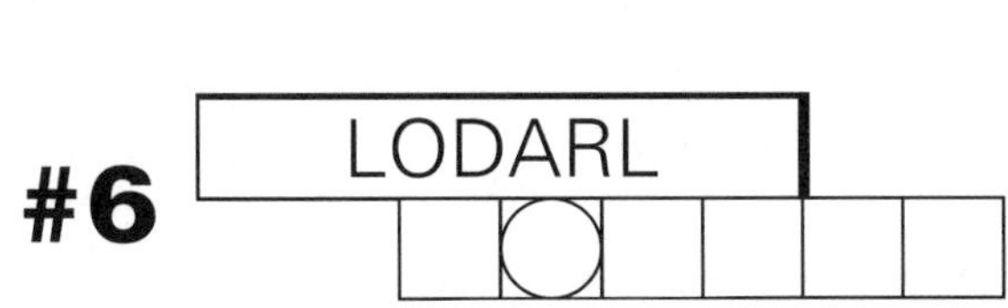

A noun is a word that is the name of something (as in a person, animal, place, thing, quality, idea or action).

Box of Clues

Stumped? Maybe you can find a clue below.

- -Lincoln's coin
- -Boston or Chicago
- -Drink made from beans
- -Animal or plant growing area
- -Car motor
- -U.S. currency unit
- -Story, tale

MYSTERY ANSWER

Arrange the circled letters to solve the mystery answer.

PUZZLE

104

ALL ABOUT MUSIC

Unscramble the Jumbles, one letter to each square, to spell words related to music.

#1 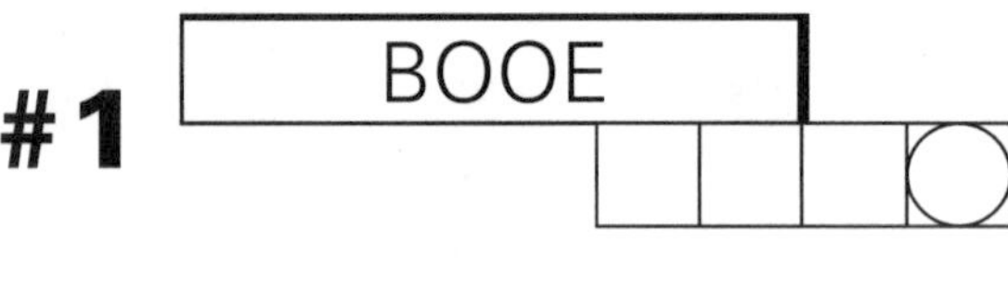

#2 

#3 VNIOIL

#4 

#5 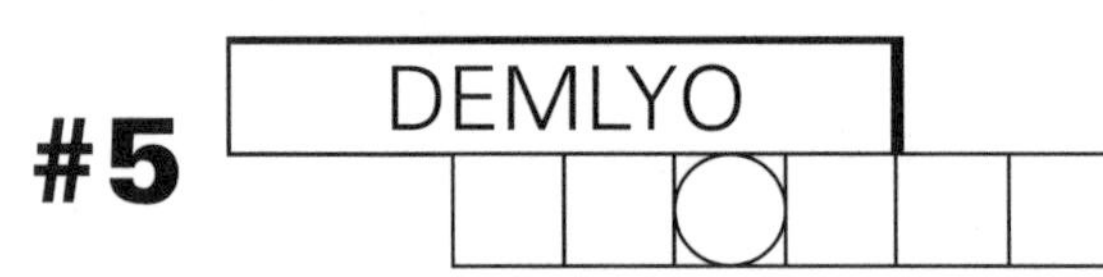

Box of Clues

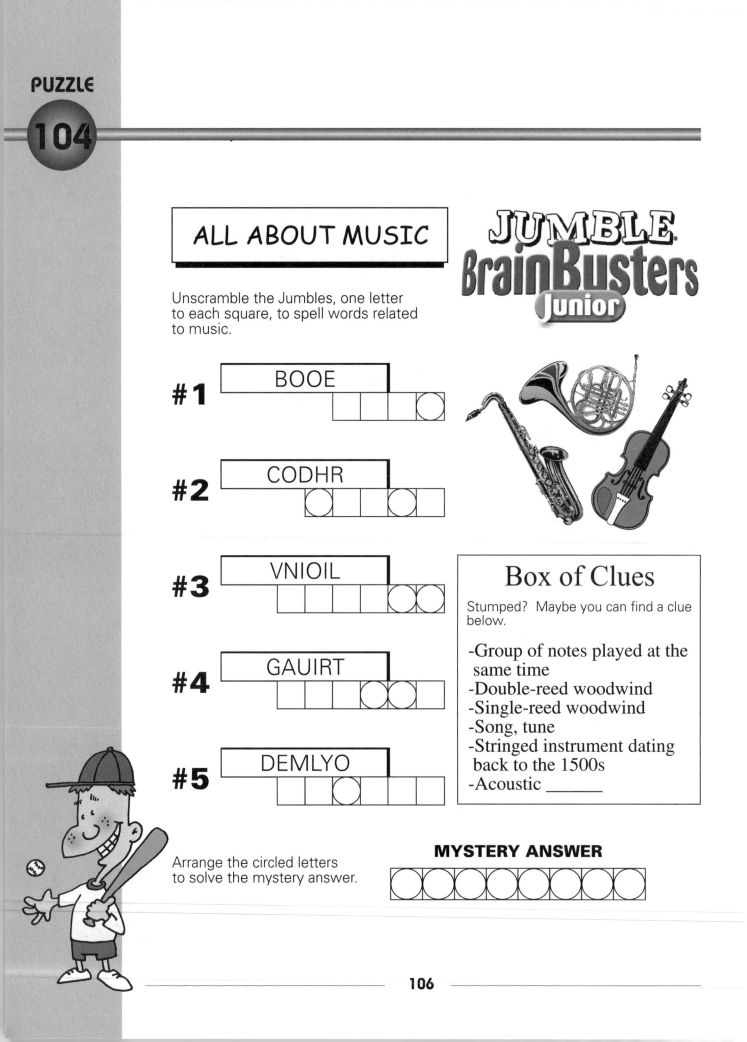

Stumped? Maybe you can find a clue below.

- Group of notes played at the same time
- Double-reed woodwind
- Single-reed woodwind
- Song, tune
- Stringed instrument dating back to the 1500s
- Acoustic ______

Arrange the circled letters to solve the mystery answer.

ABBREVIATED WORDS

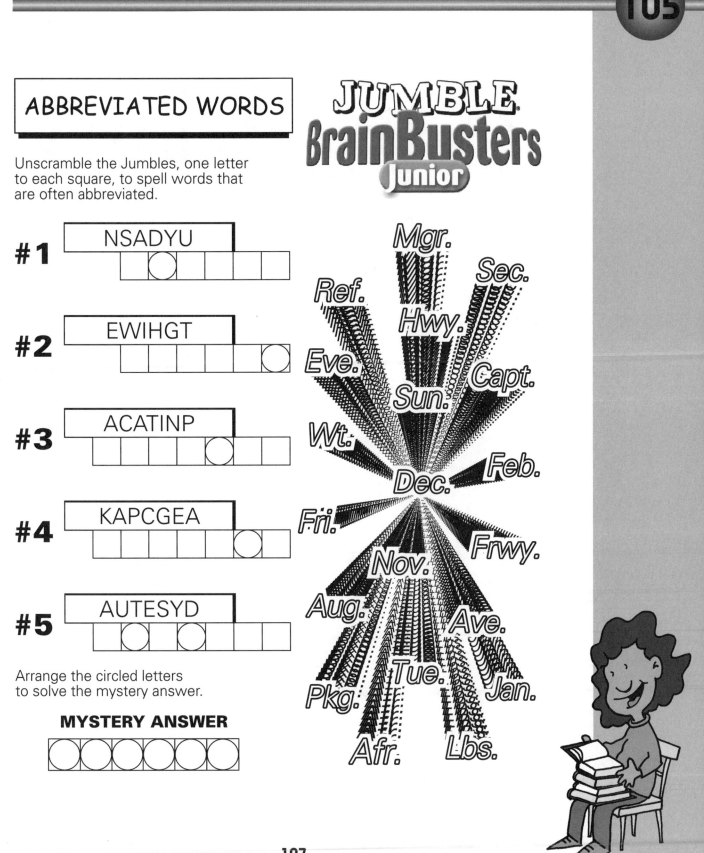

Unscramble the Jumbles, one letter to each square, to spell words that are often abbreviated.

#1 NSADYU

#2 EWIHGT

#3 ACATINP

#4 KAPCGEA

#5 AUTESYD

Mgr. Sec. Ref. Hwy. Eve. Capt. Sun. Wt. Feb. Dec. Fri. Frwy. Nov. Aug. Ave. Tue. Pkg. Jan. Afr. Lbs.

Arrange the circled letters to solve the mystery answer.

MYSTERY ANSWER

PUZZLE

106

U.S. STATE CAPITALS

Unscramble the Jumbles, one letter to each square, to spell names of U.S. state capitals.

#1

#2

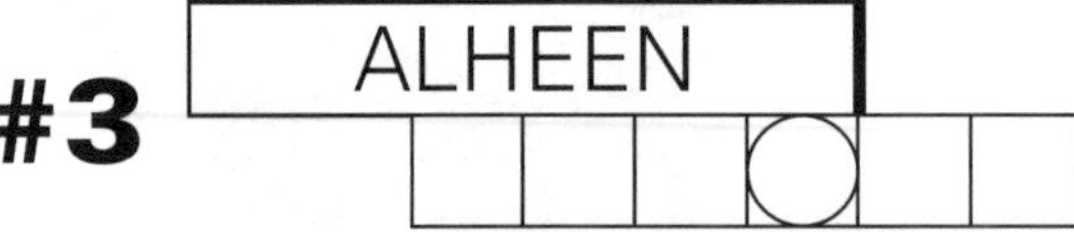

#3

#4

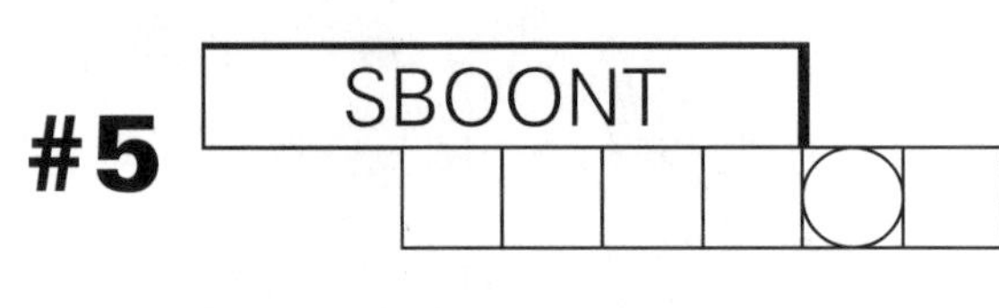

#5

#6

JSCONAK

Box of Clues

Stumped? Maybe you can find a clue below.

- -The capital of Kansas
- -The capital of Mississippi
- -The capital of New York
- -The capital of Texas
- -The capital of Montana
- -The capital of Massachusetts
- -The capital of South Dakota

Arrange the circled letters to solve the mystery answer.

MYSTERY ANSWER

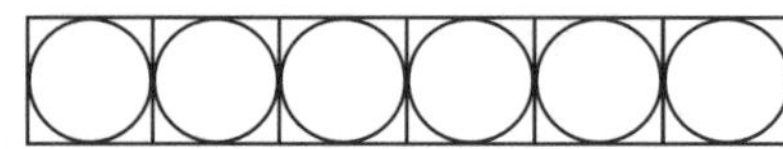

STARTS WITH "N"

JUMBLE BrainBusters Junior

Unscramble the Jumbles, one letter to each square, to spell words that start with "N."

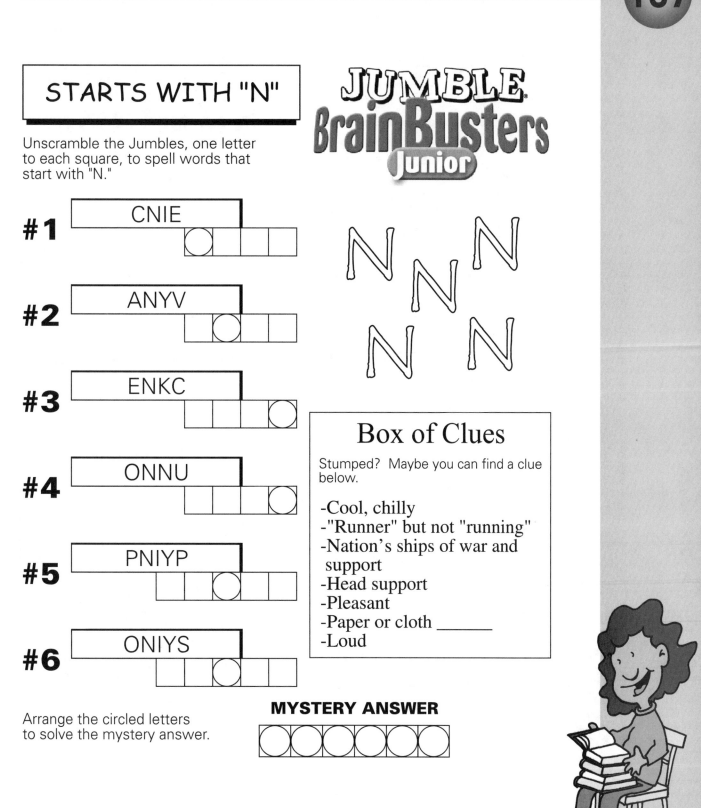

#1 CNIE

#2 ANYV

#3 ENKC

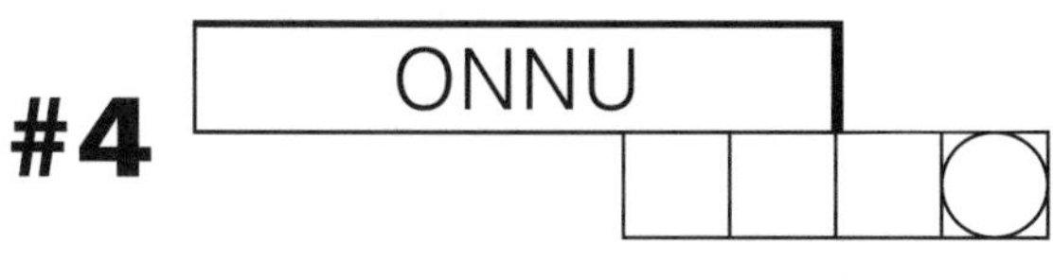
#4 ONNU

#5 PNIYP

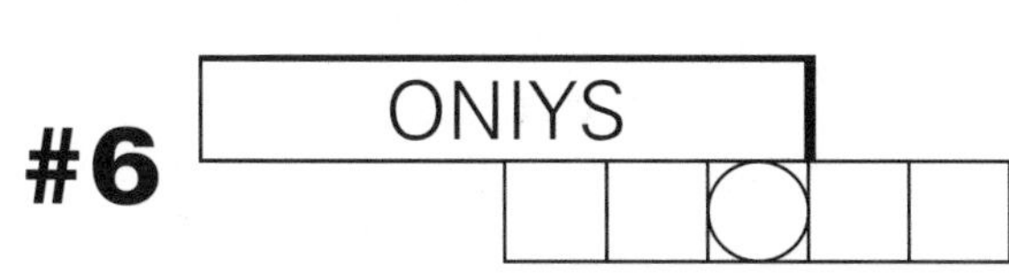
#6 ONIYS

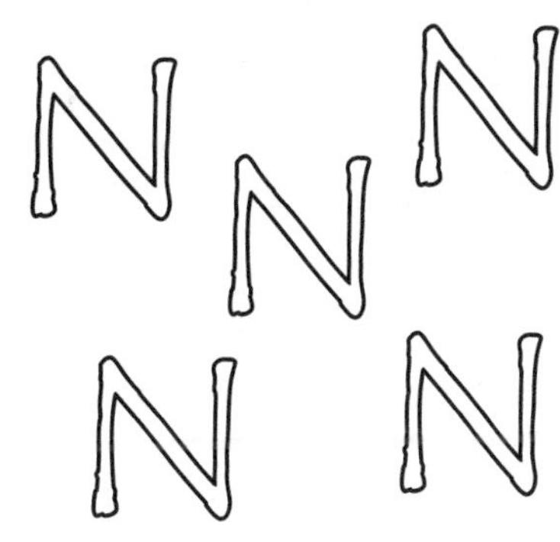

Box of Clues

Stumped? Maybe you can find a clue below.

-Cool, chilly
-"Runner" but not "running"
-Nation's ships of war and support
-Head support
-Pleasant
-Paper or cloth ______
-Loud

Arrange the circled letters to solve the mystery answer.

MYSTERY ANSWER

PUZZLE 108

FAMOUS ATHLETES

Unscramble the Jumbles, one letter to each square, to spell last names of famous athletes.

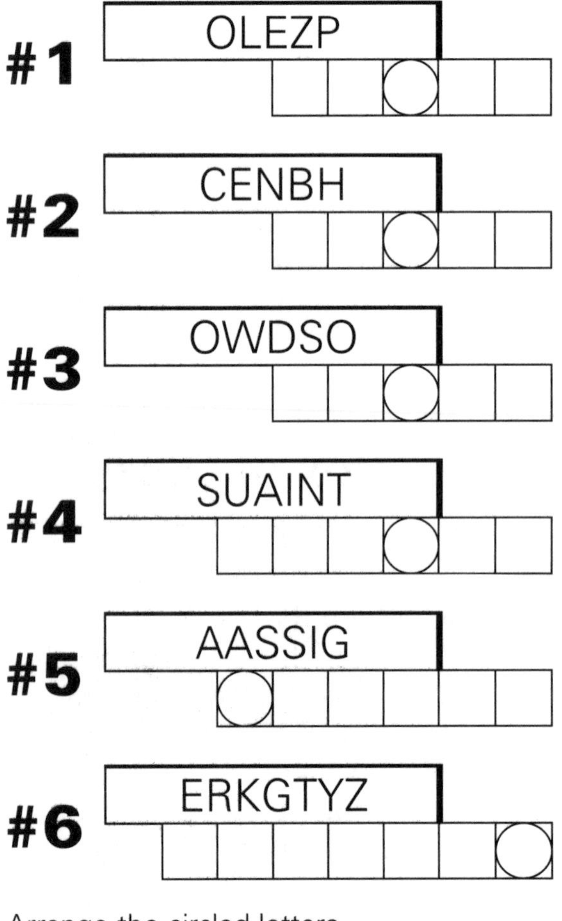

Arrange the circled letters to solve the mystery answer.

MYSTERY ANSWER

Box of Clues

Stumped? Maybe you can find a clue below.

- -Golfer Nancy ______ (or actress Jennifer)
- -Golfing "feline" (feline=cat)
- -Hockey player Wayne ______
- -Tennis player Andre ______
- -Tracy ______; tennis player who shares her last name with the capital of Texas
- -Walter ______
- -Johnny ______; baseball player who shares his last name with something you can sit on

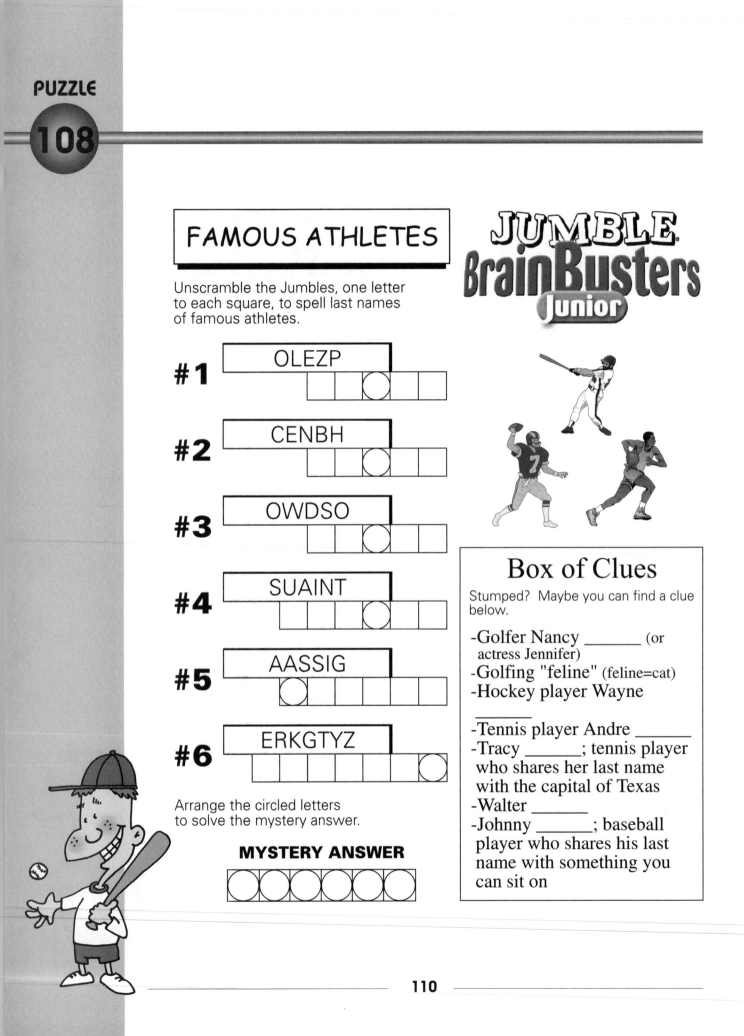

THE HUMAN BODY

JUMBLE® BrainBusters Junior

Unscramble the Jumbles, one letter to each square, to spell words related to the human body.

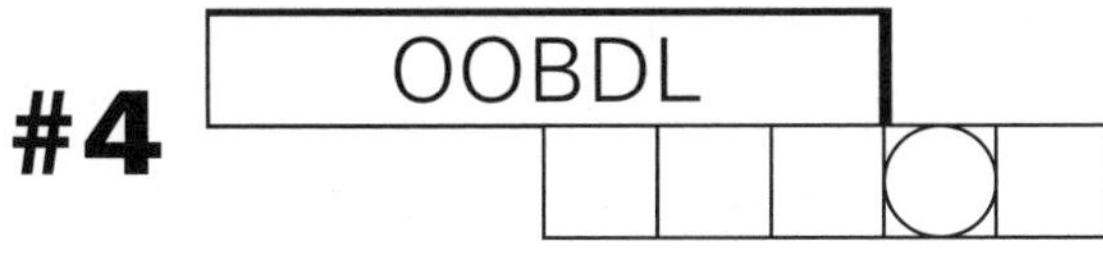

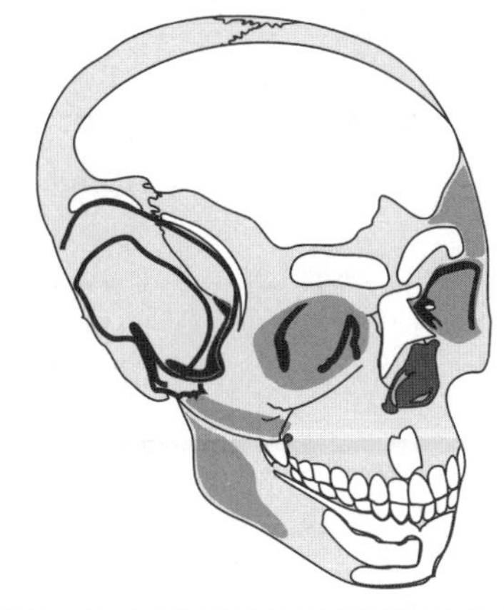

Box of Clues

Stumped? Maybe you can find a clue below.

-Starts with "M"; ends with "H"
-Starts with "H"; ends with "R"
-Starts with "C"; ends with "T"
-Starts with "B"; ends with "D"
-Starts with "T"; ends with "H"
-Starts with "S"; ends with "H"
-Starts with "A"; ends with "Y"

Arrange the circled letters to solve the mystery answer.

MYSTERY ANSWER

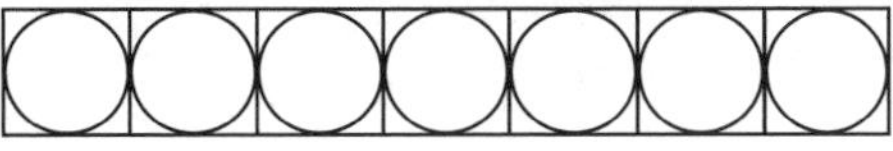

PUZZLE 110

DOUBLE CONSONANTS

JUMBLE BrainBusters Junior

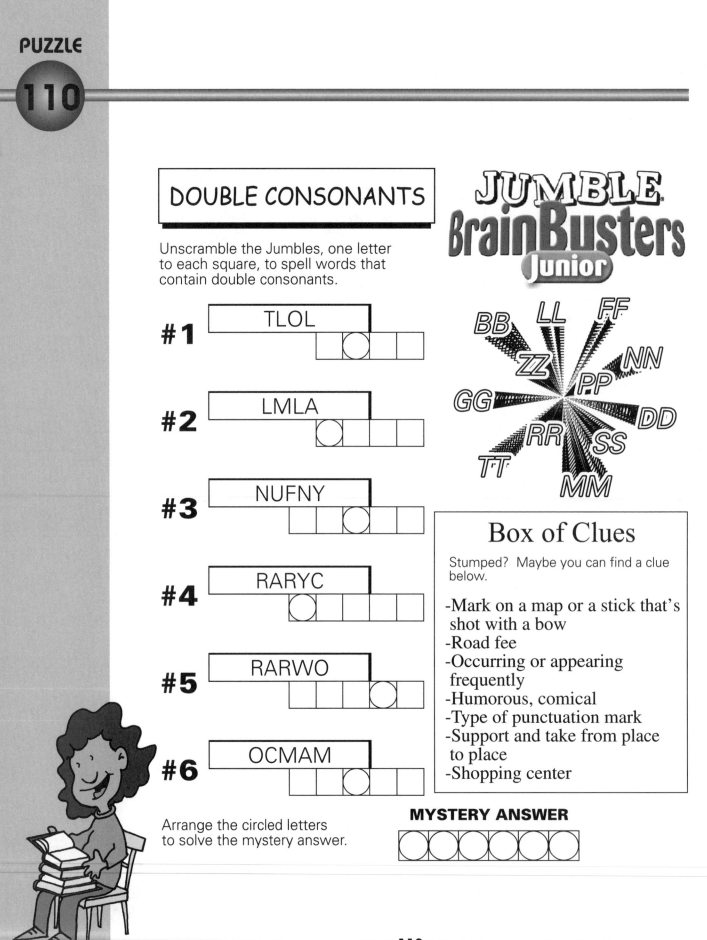

Unscramble the Jumbles, one letter to each square, to spell words that contain double consonants.

#1 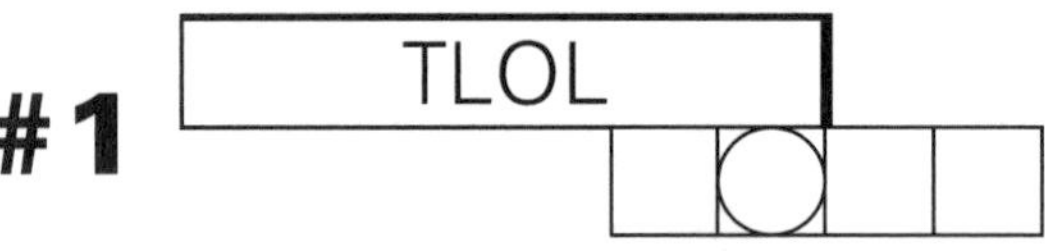

#2 

#3 

#4 

#5 

#6 

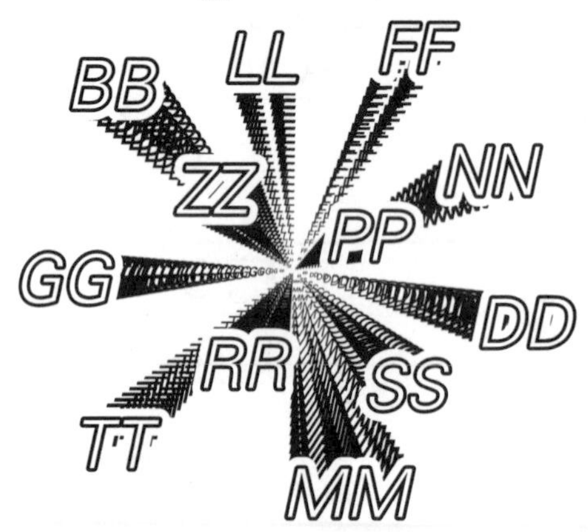

Box of Clues

Stumped? Maybe you can find a clue below.

- Mark on a map or a stick that's shot with a bow
- Road fee
- Occurring or appearing frequently
- Humorous, comical
- Type of punctuation mark
- Support and take from place to place
- Shopping center

Arrange the circled letters to solve the mystery answer.

MYSTERY ANSWER

U.S. CITIES

JUMBLE BrainBusters Junior

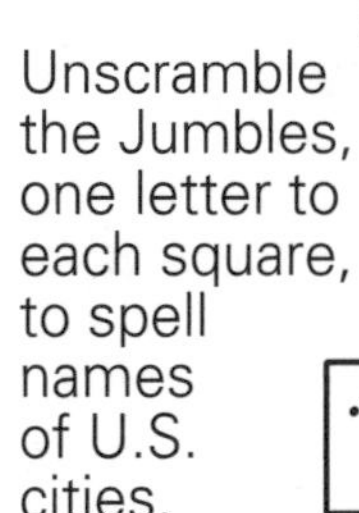

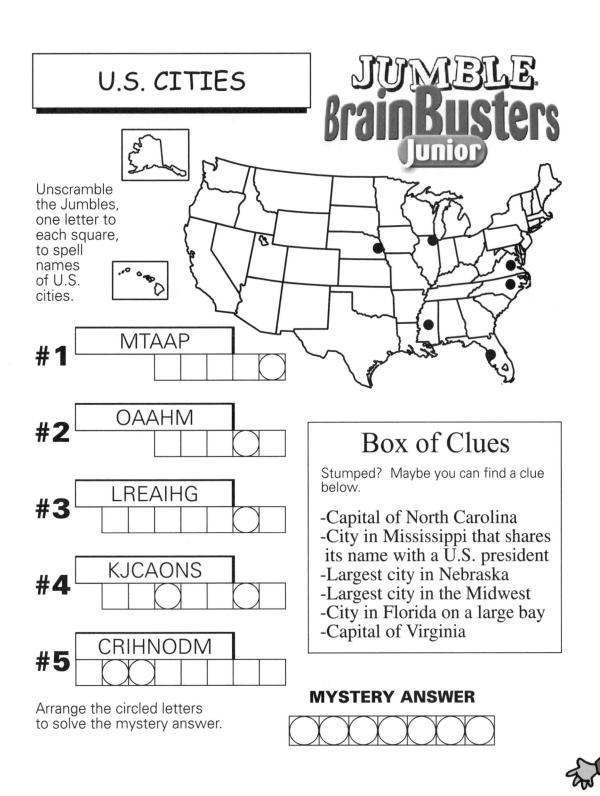

Unscramble the Jumbles, one letter to each square, to spell names of U.S. cities.

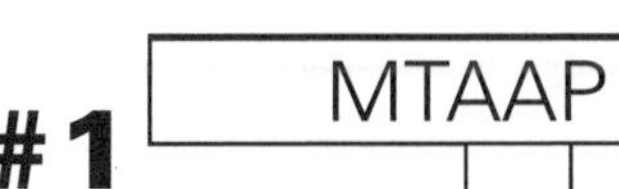

#1 MTAAP

#2 OAAHM

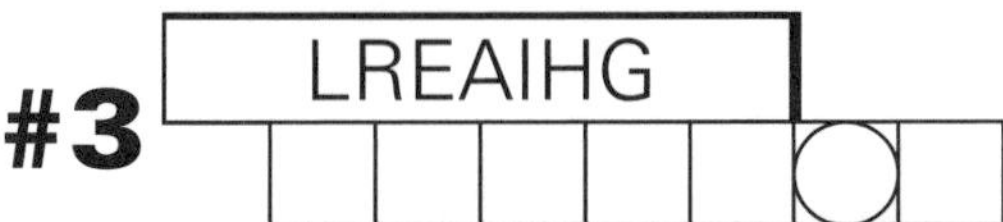

#3 LREAIHG

#4 KJCAONS

#5 CRIHNODM

Arrange the circled letters to solve the mystery answer.

Box of Clues

Stumped? Maybe you can find a clue below.

- -Capital of North Carolina
- -City in Mississippi that shares its name with a U.S. president
- -Largest city in Nebraska
- -Largest city in the Midwest
- -City in Florida on a large bay
- -Capital of Virginia

MYSTERY ANSWER

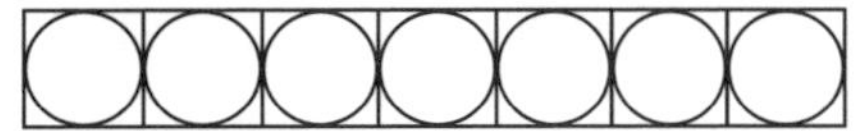

PUZZLE

112

MEANS THE SAME

JUMBLE BrainBusters Junior

Unscramble the Jumbles, one letter to each square, to spell pairs of words that have the same or similar meanings.

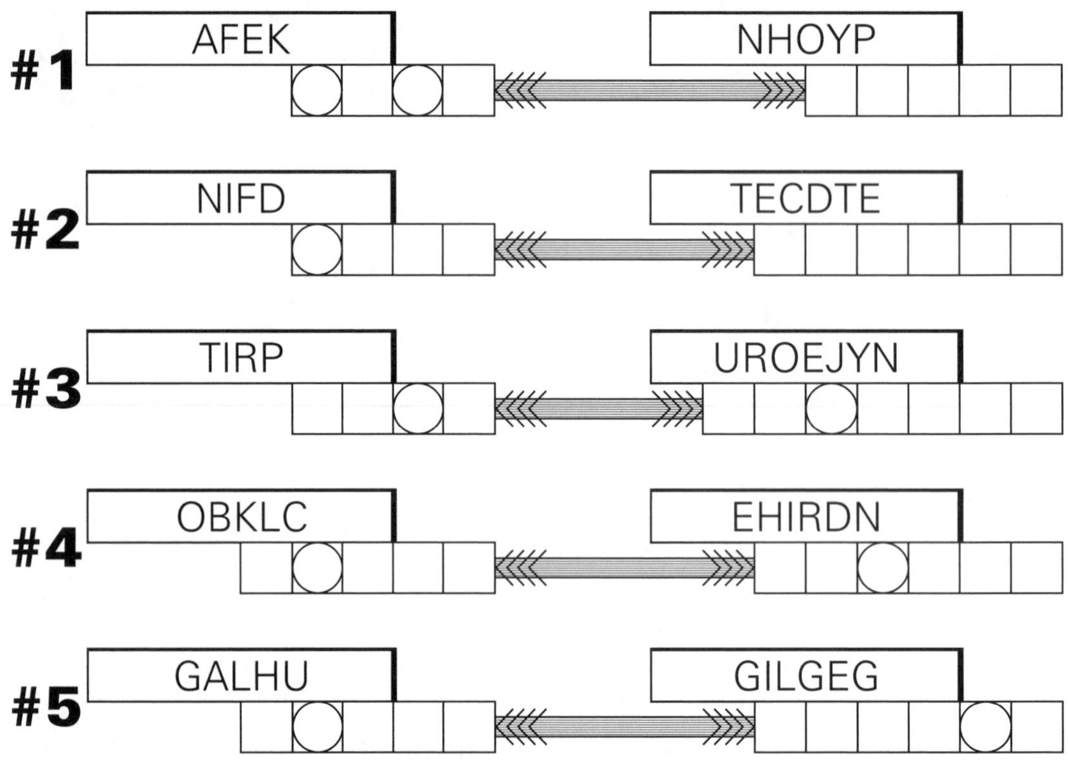

Arrange the circled letters to solve the mystery answer.
(Form two words that have the same or similar meanings.)

Box of Clues

Stumped? Maybe you can find a clue here in the "Box of Clues."

- -Bomb, flop
- -Chuckle
- -Voyage, expedition
- -Hamper, obstruct
- -Spot, catch
- -Not real

PUZZLE 113

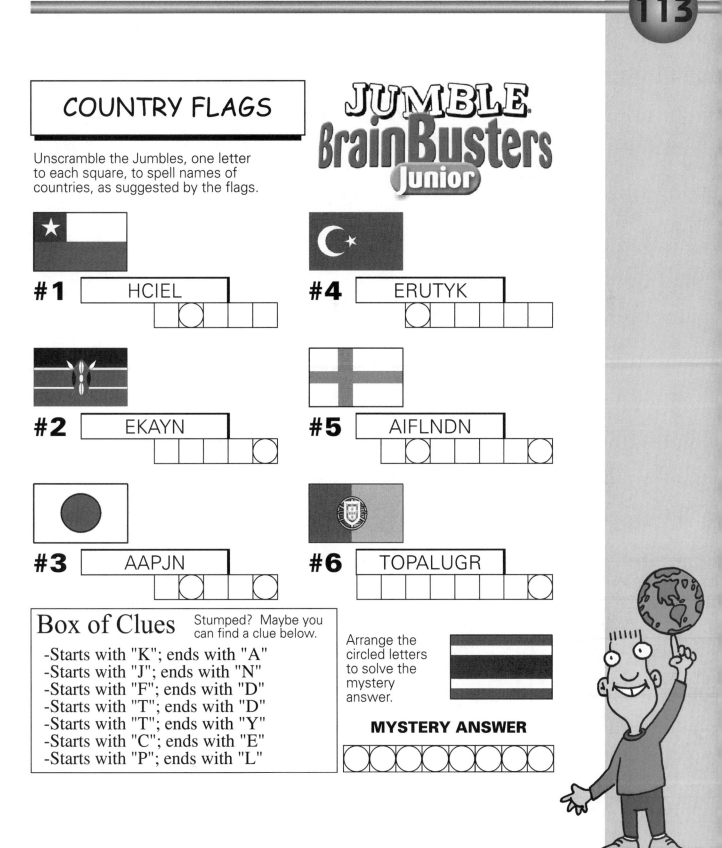

COUNTRY FLAGS

Unscramble the Jumbles, one letter to each square, to spell names of countries, as suggested by the flags.

#1 HCIEL

#4 ERUTYK

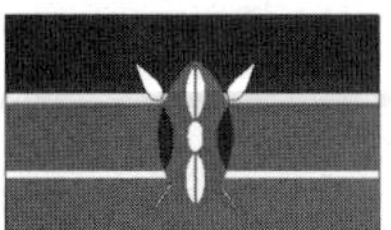

#2 EKAYN

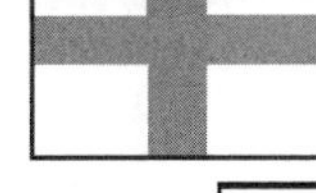

#5 AIFLNDN

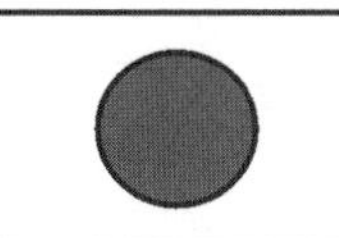

#3 AAPJN

#6 TOPALUGR

Box of Clues Stumped? Maybe you can find a clue below.

- -Starts with "K"; ends with "A"
- -Starts with "J"; ends with "N"
- -Starts with "F"; ends with "D"
- -Starts with "T"; ends with "D"
- -Starts with "T"; ends with "Y"
- -Starts with "C"; ends with "E"
- -Starts with "P"; ends with "L"

Arrange the circled letters to solve the mystery answer.

MYSTERY ANSWER

PUZZLE 114

STARTS WITH "R"

Unscramble the Jumbles, one letter to each square, to spell words that start with "R."

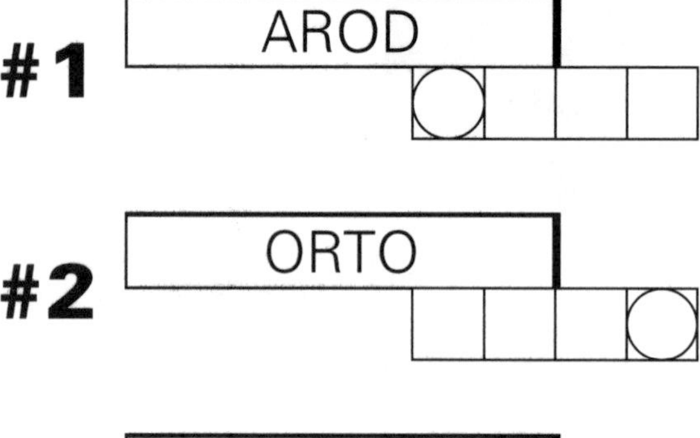

#1 AROD

#2 ORTO

#3 VRIRE

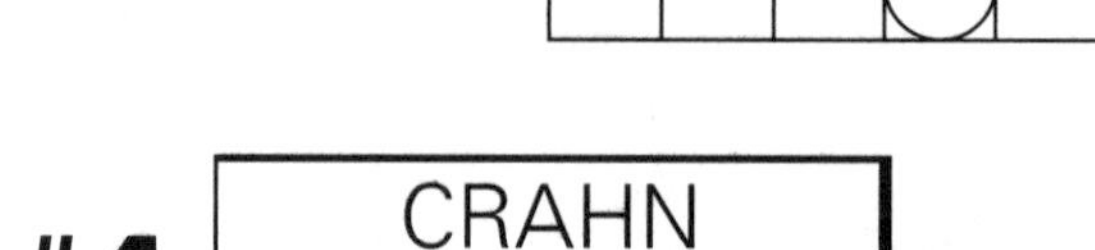

#4 CRAHN

Box of Clues

Stumped? Maybe you can find a clue below.

- -Plant support
- -Horse farm
- -Street
- -Rat or mouse
- -Basketball's shape
- -Human-looking machine
- -The Ohio ______

#5 OOTBR

#6 RUDNO

Arrange the circled letters to solve the mystery answer.

MYSTERY ANSWER

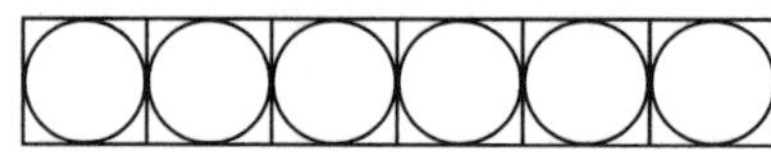

JUMBLE BrainBusters Junior

FOOD

Unscramble the Jumbles, one letter to each square, to spell words related to food.

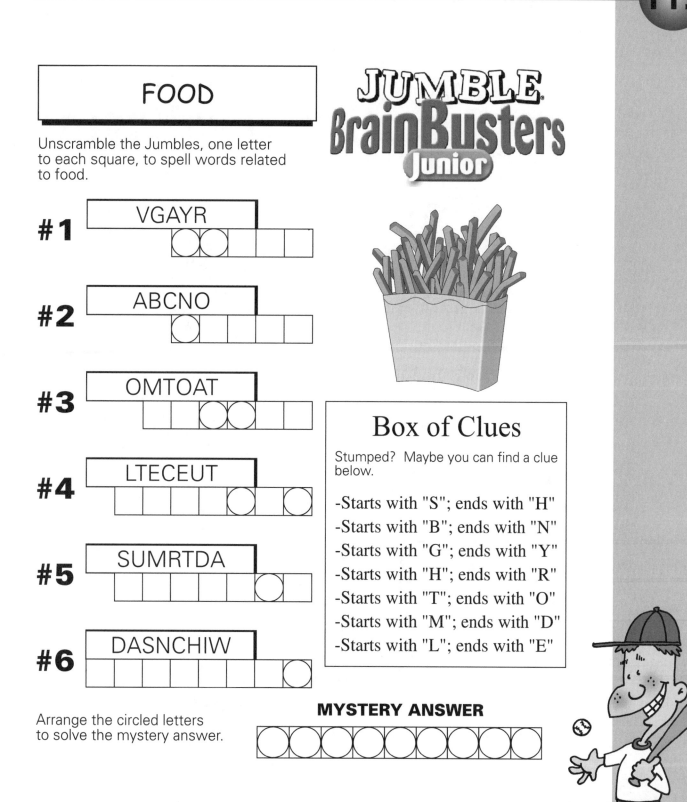

#1 VGAYR

#2 ABCNO

#3 OMTOAT

#4 LTECEUT

#5 SUMRTDA

#6 DASNCHIW

Box of Clues

Stumped? Maybe you can find a clue below.

- -Starts with "S"; ends with "H"
- -Starts with "B"; ends with "N"
- -Starts with "G"; ends with "Y"
- -Starts with "H"; ends with "R"
- -Starts with "T"; ends with "O"
- -Starts with "M"; ends with "D"
- -Starts with "L"; ends with "E"

Arrange the circled letters to solve the mystery answer.

MYSTERY ANSWER

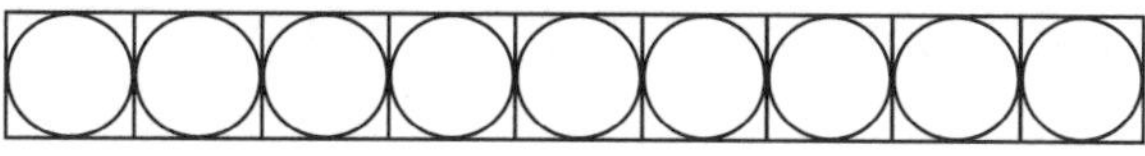

MAMMALS

JUMBLE BrainBusters Junior

Unscramble the Jumbles, one letter to each square, to spell names of mammals.

#1 PADAN

#2 MAELC

#3 SOOEM

#4 VEEBRA

#5 POEGRH

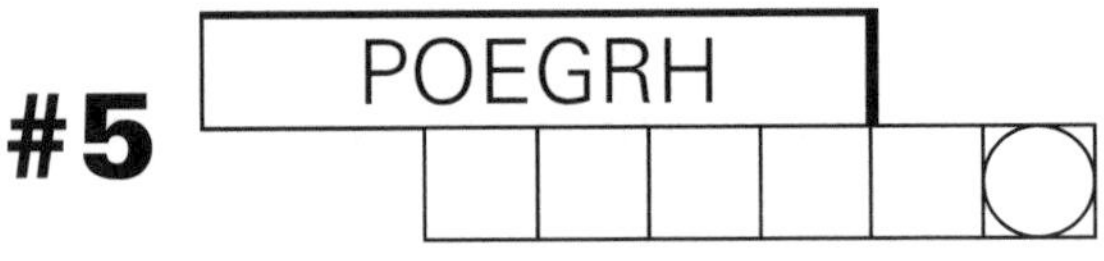

#6 CARCONO

Box of Clues

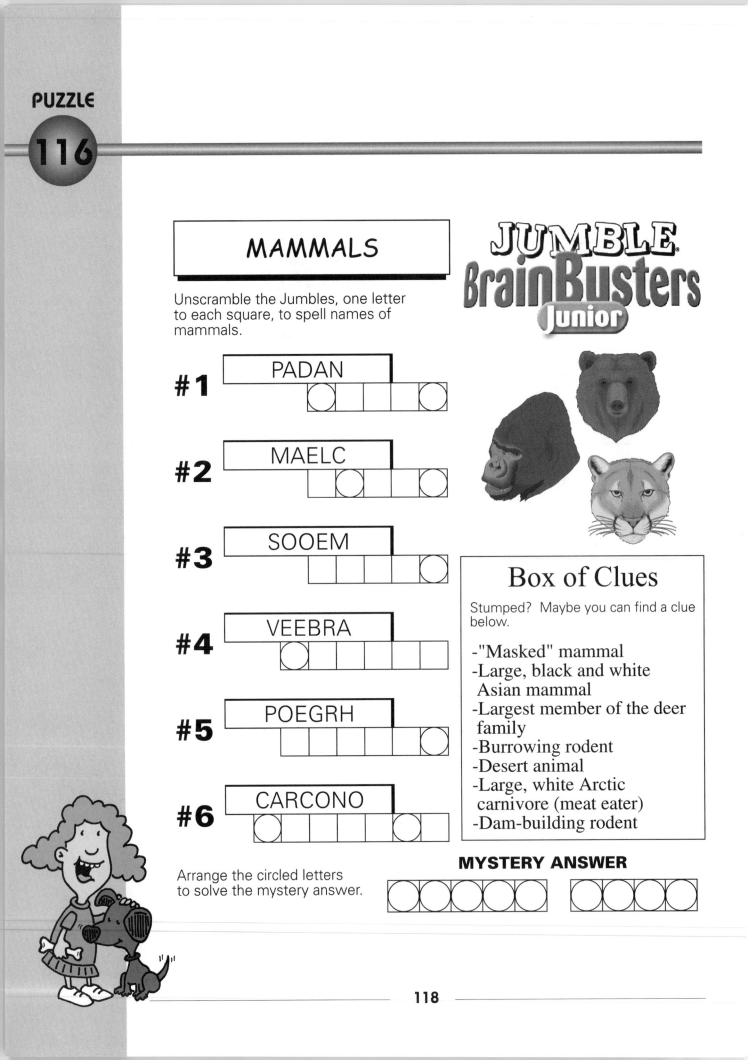

Stumped? Maybe you can find a clue below.

- "Masked" mammal
- Large, black and white Asian mammal
- Largest member of the deer family
- Burrowing rodent
- Desert animal
- Large, white Arctic carnivore (meat eater)
- Dam-building rodent

Arrange the circled letters to solve the mystery answer.

MYSTERY ANSWER

U.S. CITIES

JUMBLE BrainBusters Junior

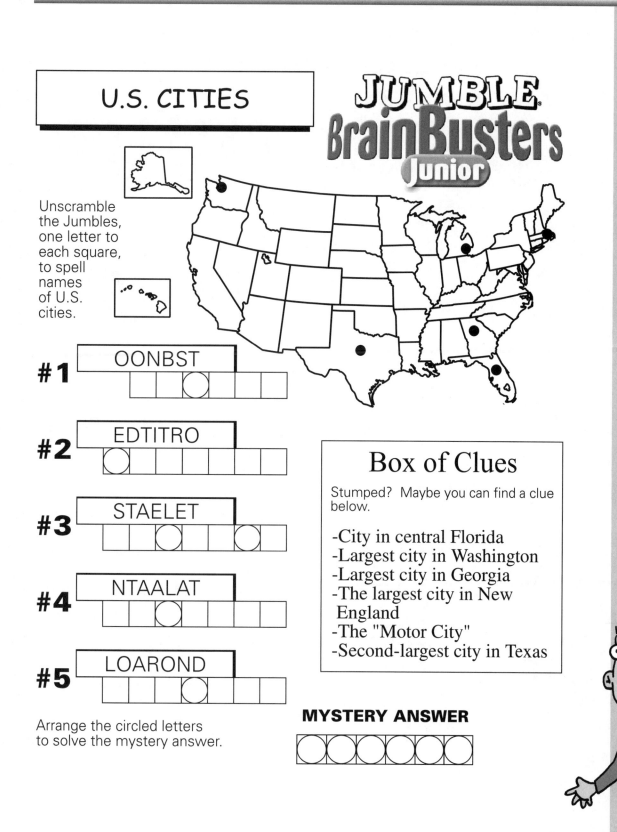

Unscramble the Jumbles, one letter to each square, to spell names of U.S. cities.

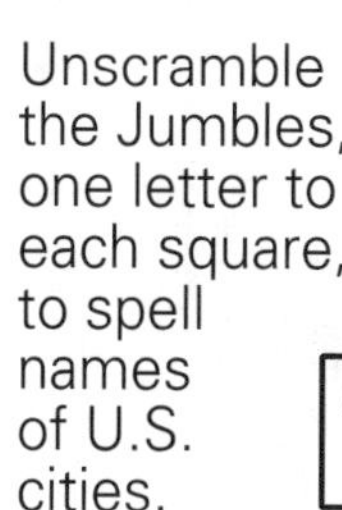

#1 OONBST

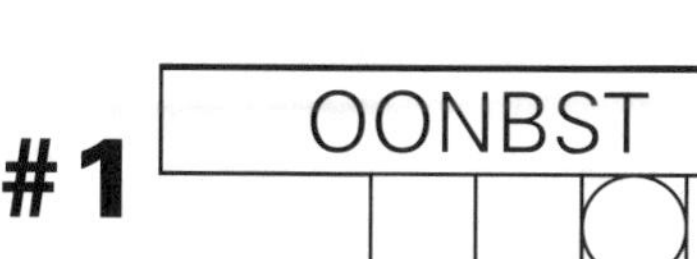

#2 EDTITRO

#3 STAELET

#4 NTAALAT

#5 LOAROND

Arrange the circled letters to solve the mystery answer.

Box of Clues

Stumped? Maybe you can find a clue below.

- City in central Florida
- Largest city in Washington
- Largest city in Georgia
- The largest city in New England
- The "Motor City"
- Second-largest city in Texas

MYSTERY ANSWER

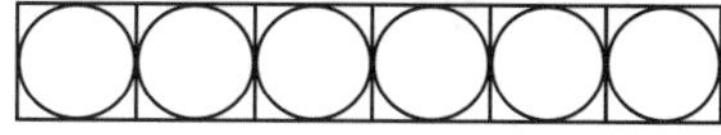

STARTS WITH A VOWEL

Unscramble the Jumbles, one letter to each square, to spell words that start with vowels (a,e,i,o,u).

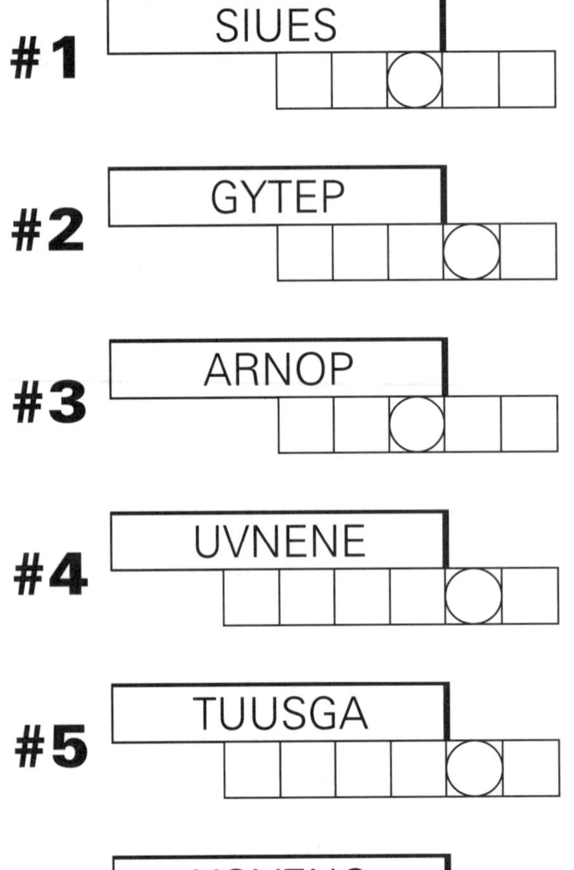

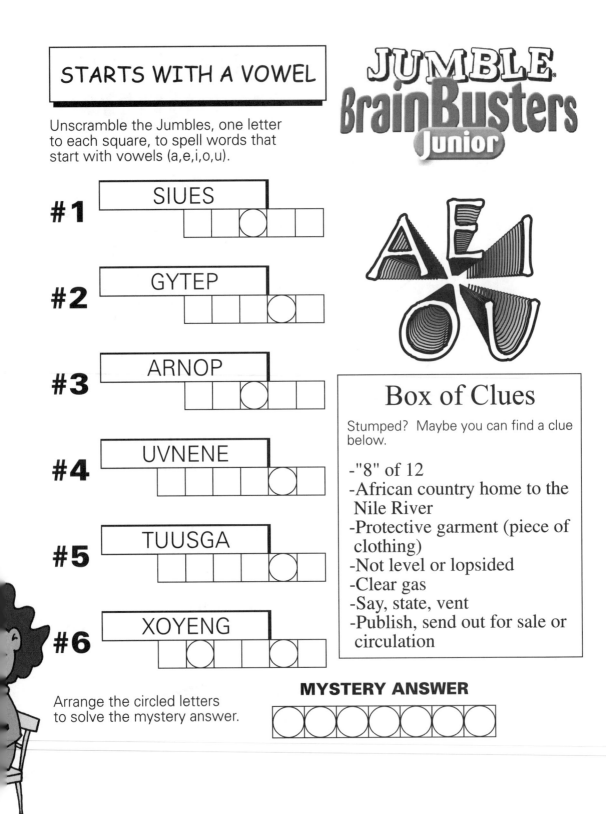

Box of Clues

Stumped? Maybe you can find a clue below.

-"8" of 12
-African country home to the Nile River
-Protective garment (piece of clothing)
-Not level or lopsided
-Clear gas
-Say, state, vent
-Publish, send out for sale or circulation

MYSTERY ANSWER

Arrange the circled letters to solve the mystery answer.

BIRDS

JUMBLE® BrainBusters Junior

Unscramble the Jumbles, one letter to each square, to spell names of birds.

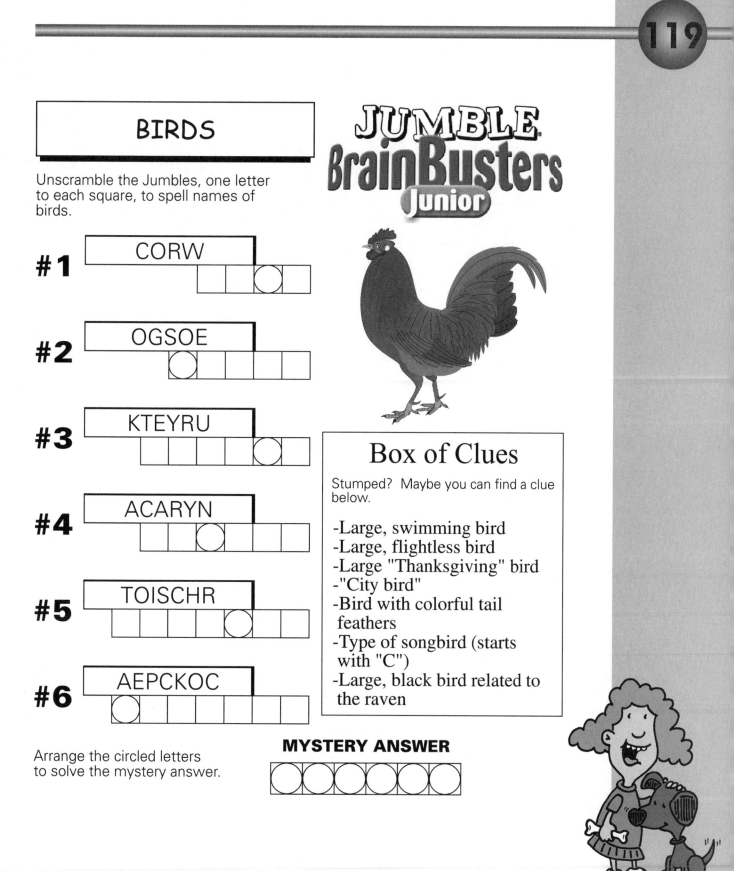

#1 CORW

#2 OGSOE

#3 KTEYRU

#4 ACARYN

#5 TOISCHR

#6 AEPCKOC

Box of Clues

Stumped? Maybe you can find a clue below.

- -Large, swimming bird
- -Large, flightless bird
- -Large "Thanksgiving" bird
- -"City bird"
- -Bird with colorful tail feathers
- -Type of songbird (starts with "C")
- -Large, black bird related to the raven

Arrange the circled letters to solve the mystery answer.

MYSTERY ANSWER

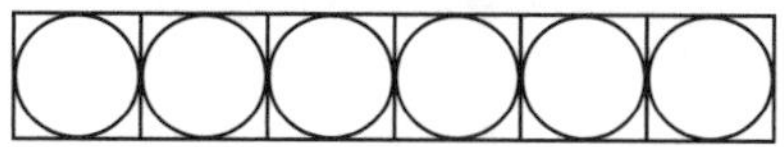

RHYMING WORDS

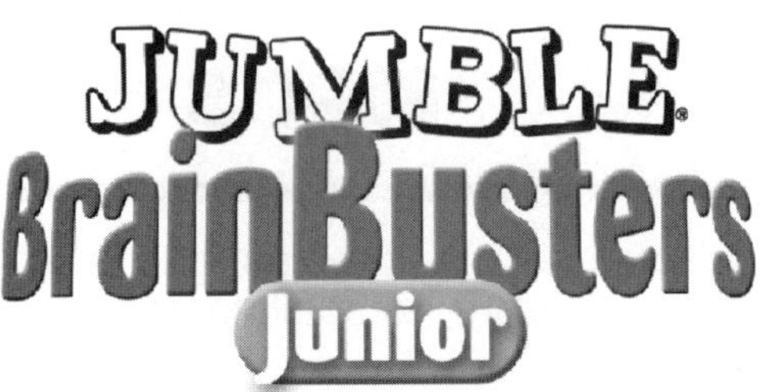

Unscramble the Jumbles, one letter to each square, to spell pairs of words that rhyme.

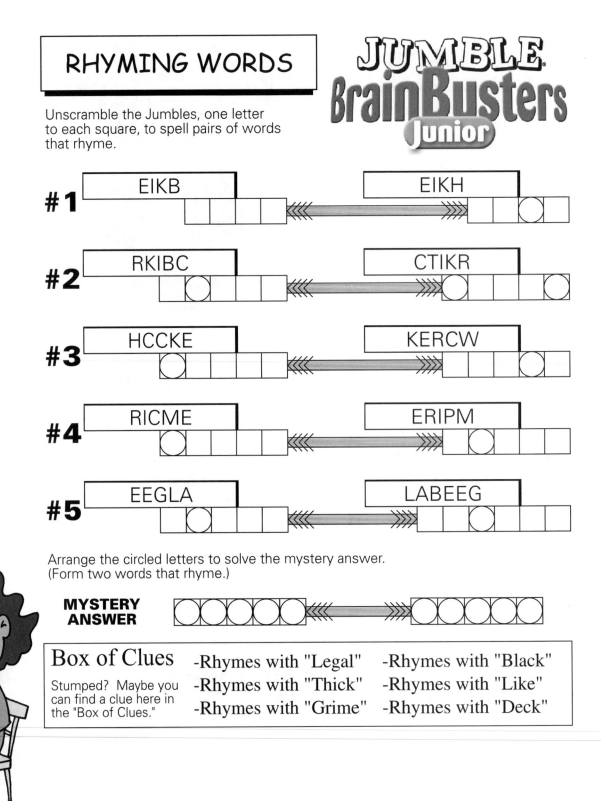

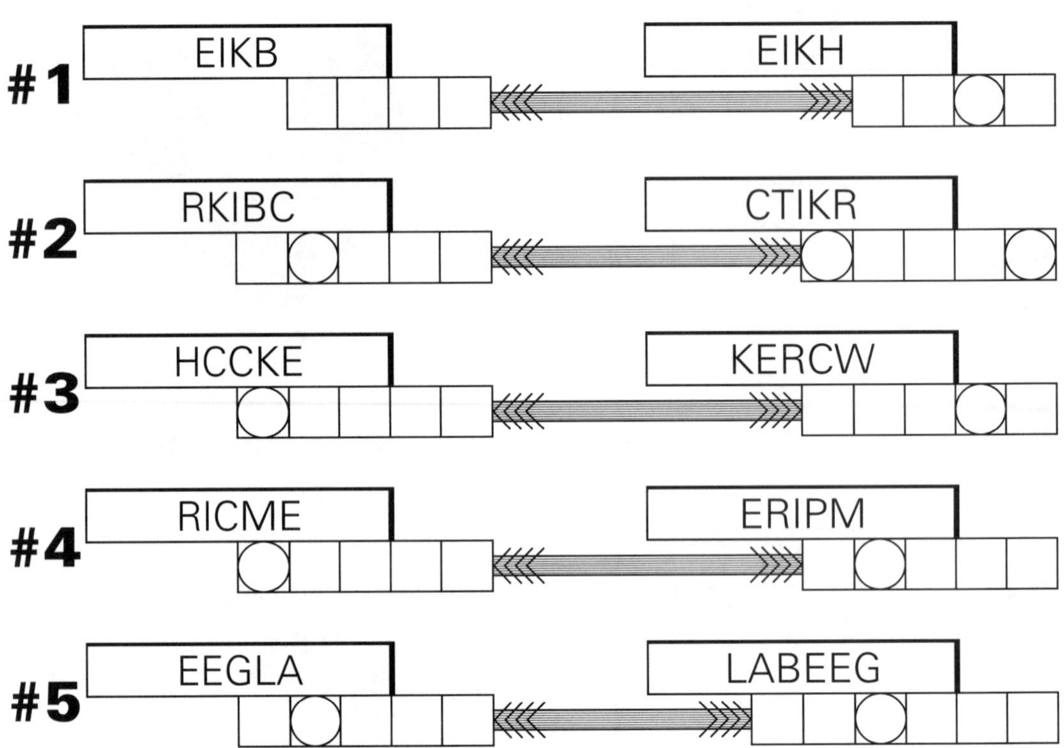

Arrange the circled letters to solve the mystery answer. (Form two words that rhyme.)

MYSTERY ANSWER

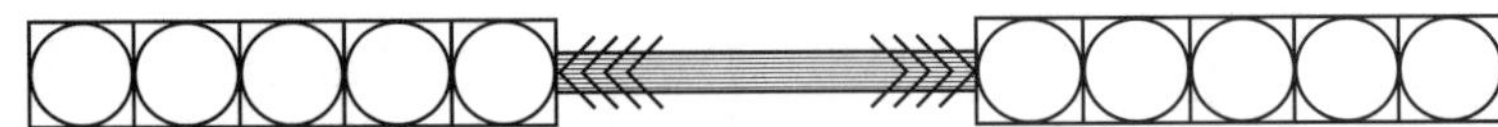

Box of Clues

Stumped? Maybe you can find a clue here in the "Box of Clues."

-Rhymes with "Legal"
-Rhymes with "Thick"
-Rhymes with "Grime"
-Rhymes with "Black"
-Rhymes with "Like"
-Rhymes with "Deck"

state capitals

animals

JUMBLE®

BrainBusters Junior II

ADVANCED PUZZLES

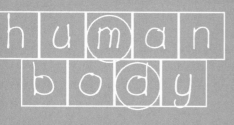

human body

outer space

money

sports

PUZZLE

121

MONEY

Unscramble the Jumbles, one letter to each square, to spell words related to money.

JUMBLE BrainBusters Junior

#1 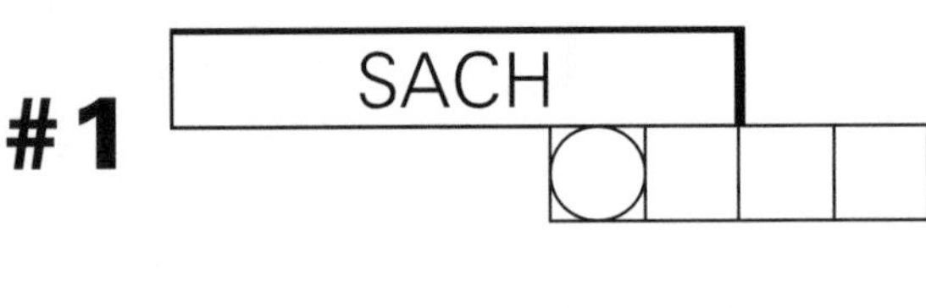
SACH

#2 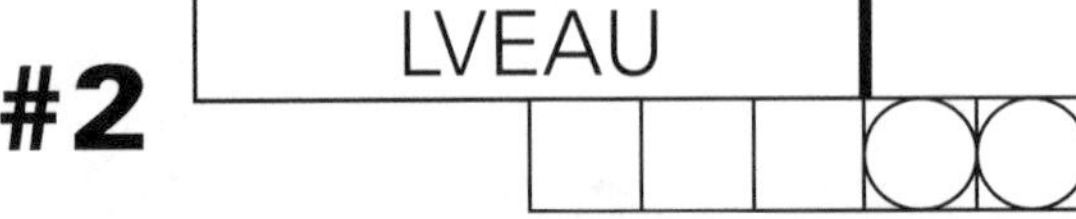
LVEAU

#3 
NEYNP

#4 
FRNCA

#5 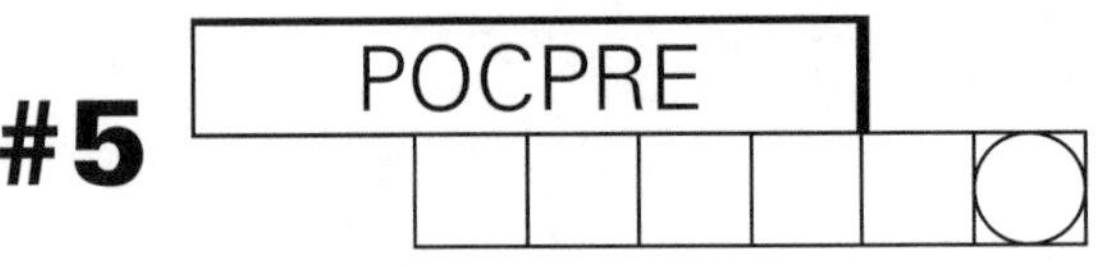
POCPRE

#6 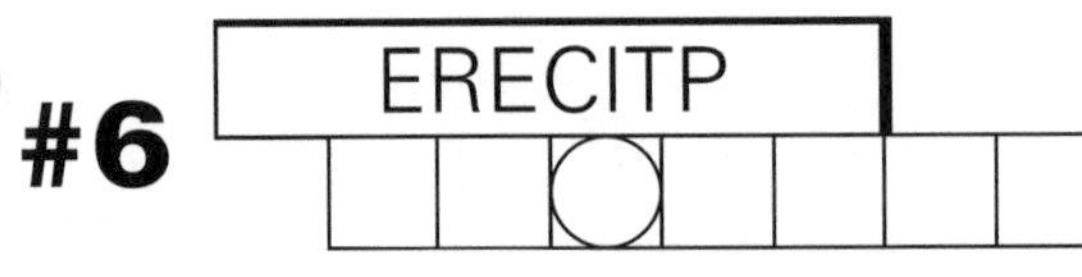
ERECITP

Box of Clues

Stumped? Maybe you can find a clue below.

- -Money in circulation
- -French money unit that rhymes with "tank"
- -Worth
- -Cold, hard ______
- -Written record of a purchase
- -U.S. coin
- -Coin metal

Arrange the circled letters to solve the mystery answer.

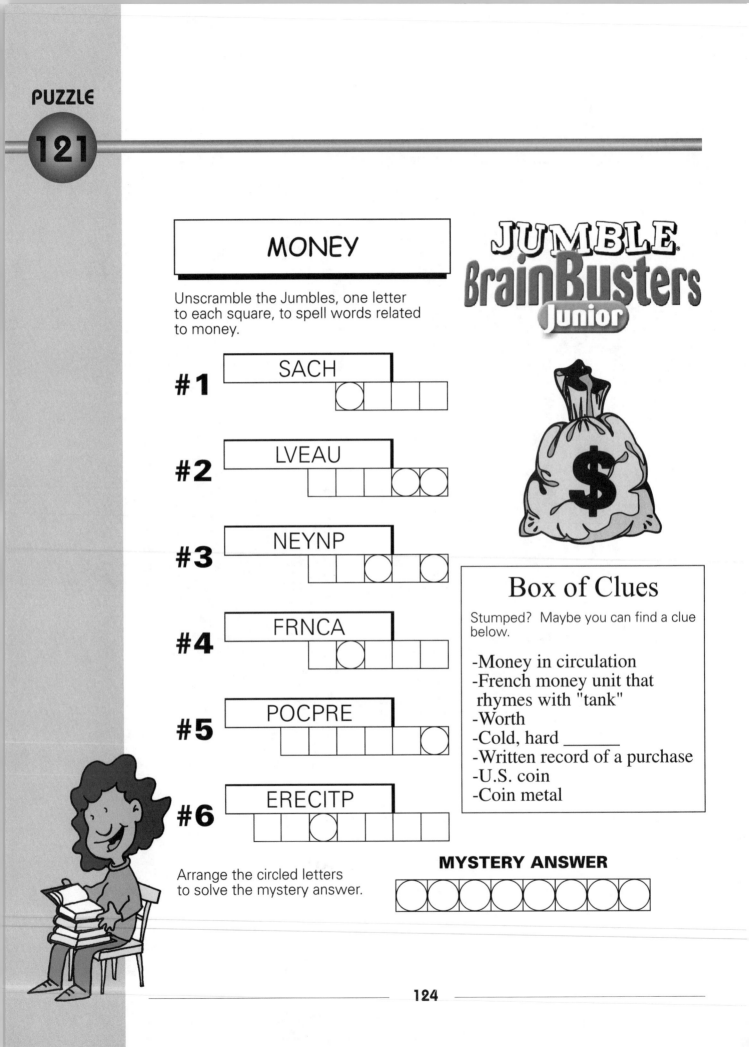

MYSTERY ANSWER

PUZZLE 122

MATH

Unscramble the Jumbled letters, one letter to each square, so that each equation is correct.

For example: NONTEOEOW
ONE + ONE = TWO

#1 XSISIEOZXR

□□□ − □□□ = □□□□

#2 GTOFOWUERITH

□□□ × □□□□ = □□□□□

#3 OFEIHGWTUROT

□□□□□ ÷ □□□ = □□□□

#4 ETNETRHETTIYHR

□□□ × □□□□□ = □□□□□□

#5 TFEIYEITFNFV

□□□□□ ÷ □□□ = □□□□

Arrange the circled letters to solve the mystery equation.

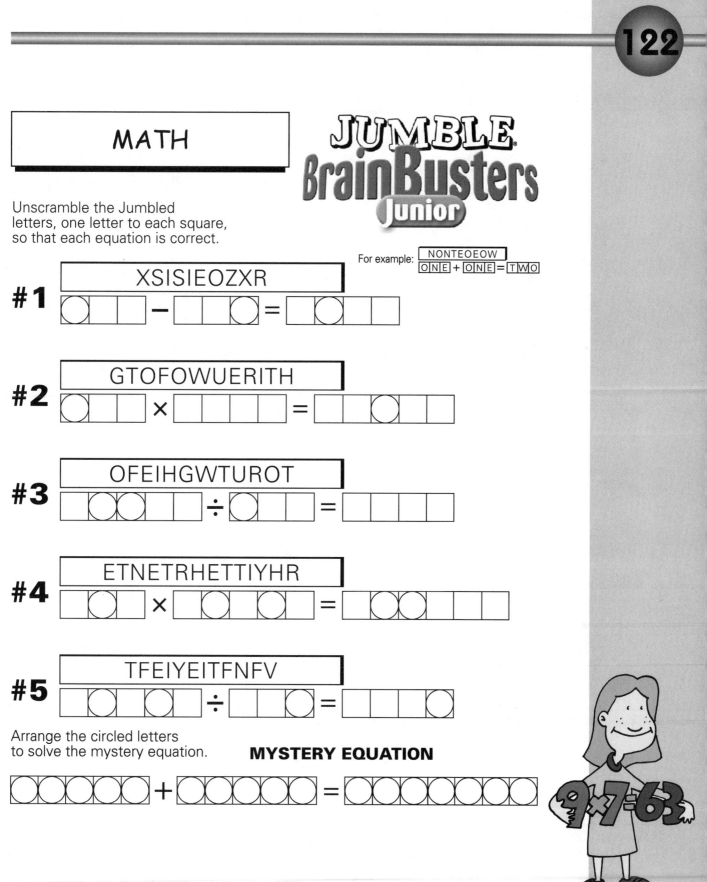

MYSTERY EQUATION

□□□□□ + □□□□□ = □□□□□□□

PUZZLE 123

OUTER SPACE

Unscramble the Jumbles, one letter to each square, to spell words related to outer space.

#1

#2

#3
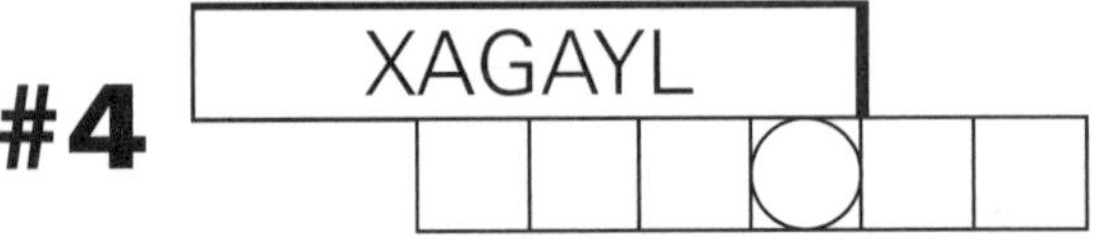

#4
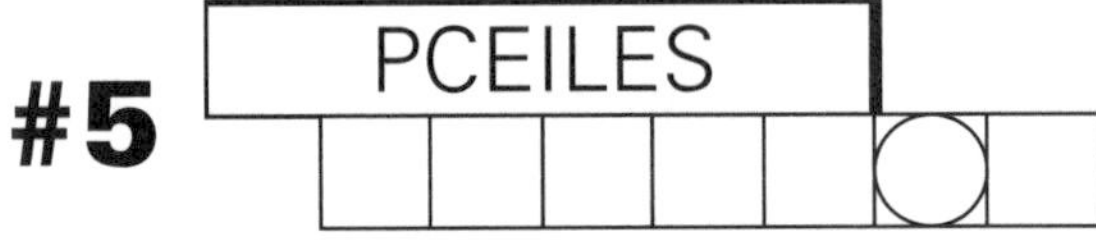

#5
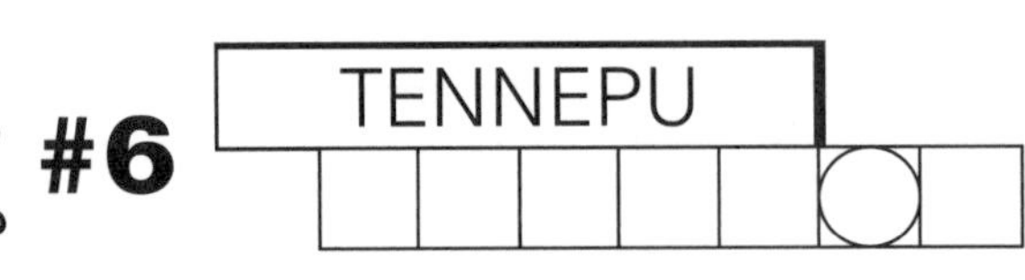

#6
TENNEPU

Box of Clues

Stumped? Maybe you can find a clue below.

-Large collection of stars and their planets
-Home to the moon Titan
-Total or partial ______
-Smallest planet
-______ Space Telescope
-Pluto's inner neighbor
-Relating to the Moon

Arrange the circled letters to solve the mystery answer.

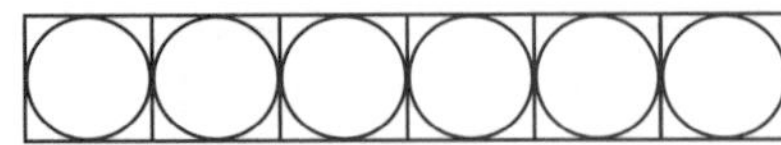

PUZZLE 124

U.S. CITIES

JUMBLE BrainBusters Junior

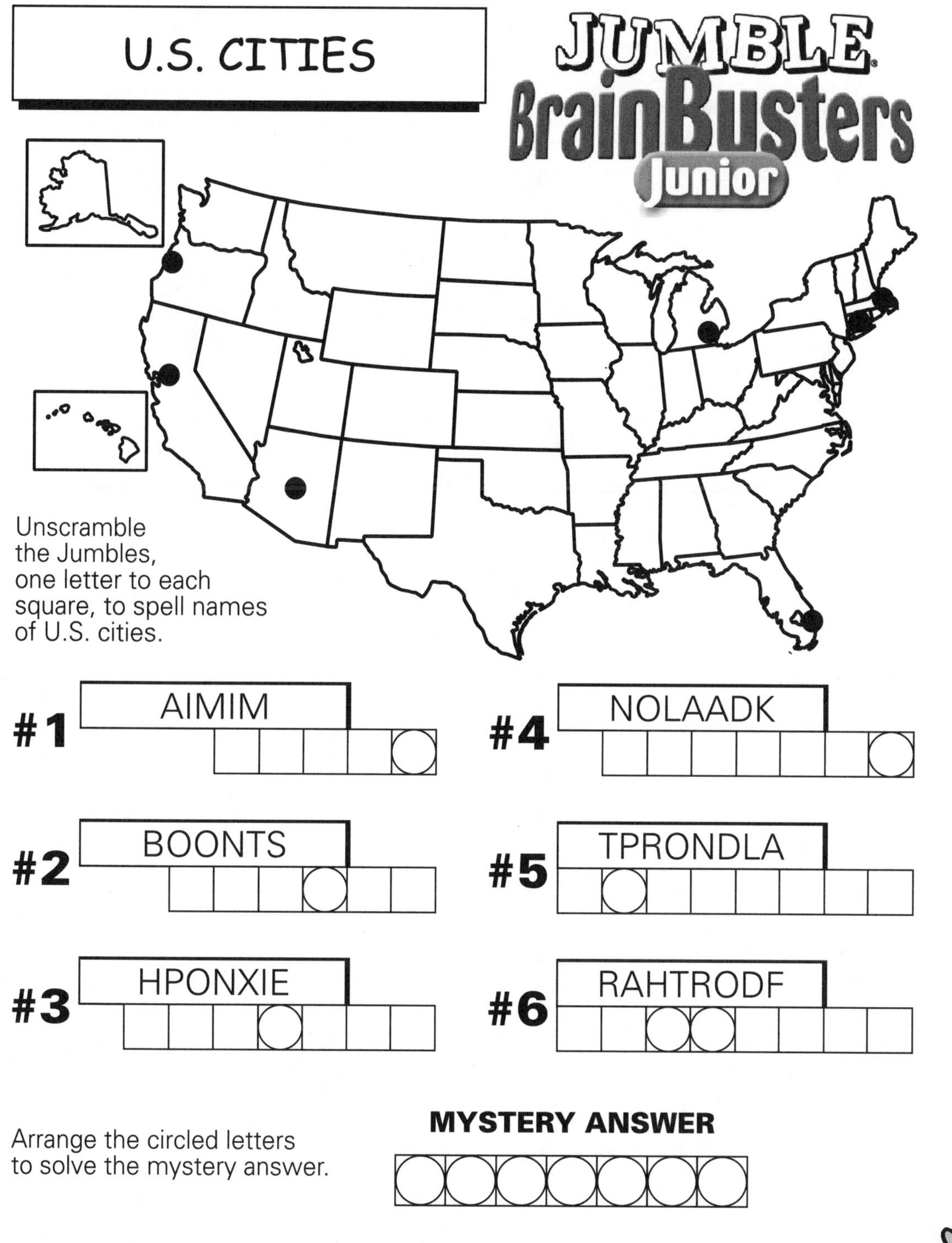

Unscramble the Jumbles, one letter to each square, to spell names of U.S. cities.

#1 AIMIM

#2 BOONTS

#3 HPONXIE

#4 NOLAADK

#5 TPRONDLA

#6 RAHTRODF

Arrange the circled letters to solve the mystery answer.

MYSTERY ANSWER

PUZZLE

125

ADJECTIVES

JUMBLE BrainBusters Junior

Unscramble the Jumbles, one letter to each square, to spell adjectives.

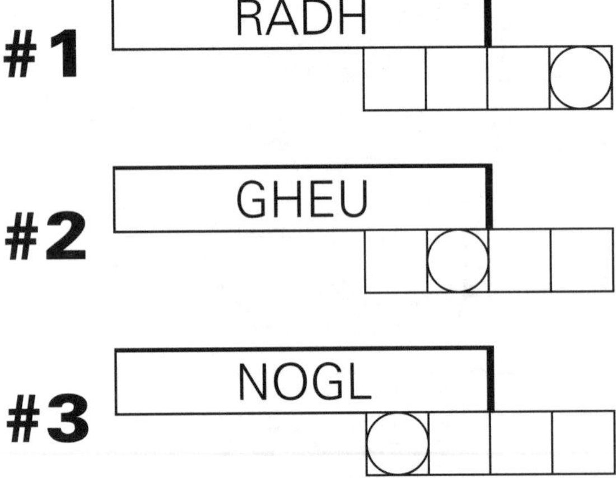

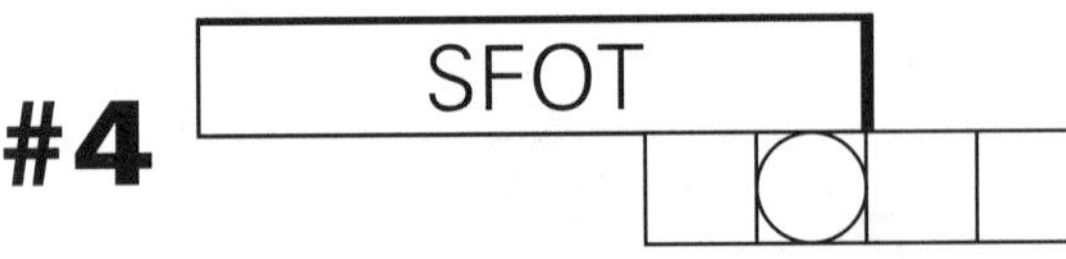

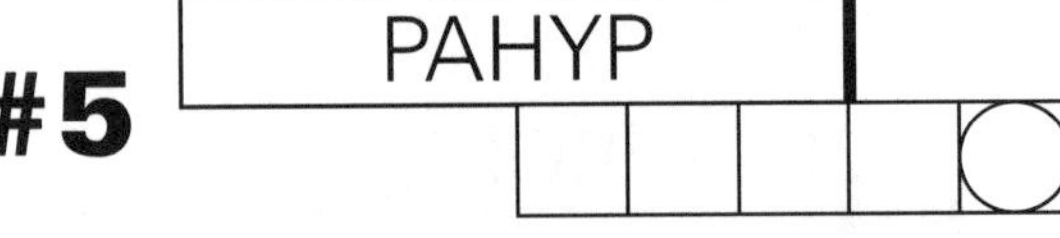

Arrange the circled letters to solve the mystery answer.

MYSTERY ANSWER

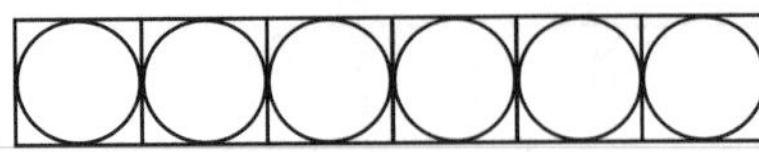

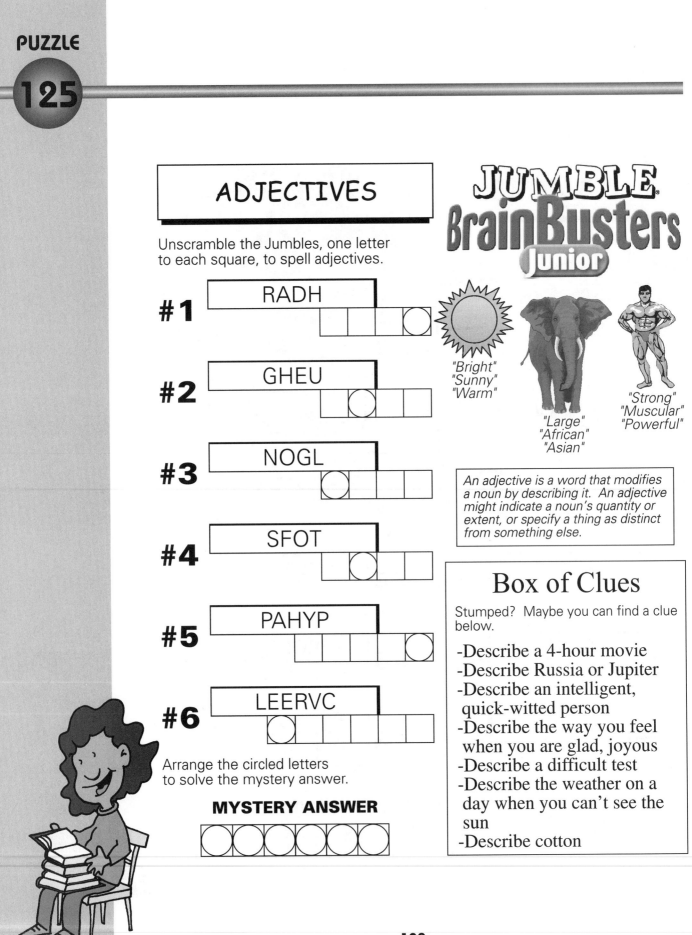

"Bright"
"Sunny"
"Warm"

"Large"
"African"
"Asian"

"Strong"
"Muscular"
"Powerful"

An adjective is a word that modifies a noun by describing it. An adjective might indicate a noun's quantity or extent, or specify a thing as distinct from something else.

Box of Clues

Stumped? Maybe you can find a clue below.

-Describe a 4-hour movie
-Describe Russia or Jupiter
-Describe an intelligent, quick-witted person
-Describe the way you feel when you are glad, joyous
-Describe a difficult test
-Describe the weather on a day when you can't see the sun
-Describe cotton

ELEMENTS

Unscramble the Jumbles, one letter to each square, to spell names of elements.

#1 DIONIE

#2 ACOLTB

#3 POCERP

#4 DRAIMU

#5 LSIONIC

Arrange the circled letters to solve the mystery answer.

MYSTERY ANSWER

JUMBLE BrainBusters Junior

THE PERIODIC TABLE

H — Atomic # — Atomic Symbol

H																	He
Li	Be											B	C	N	O	F	Ne
Na	Mg											Al	Si	P	S	Cl	Ar
K	Ca	Sc	Ti	V	Cr	Mn	Fe	Co	Ni	Cu	Zn	Ga	Ge	As	Se	Br	Kr
Rb	Sr	Y	Zr	Nb	Mo	Tc	Ru	Rh	Pd	Ag	Cd	In	Sn	Sb	Te	I	Xe
Cs	Ba		Hf	Ta	W	Re	Os	Ir	Pt	Au	Hg	Tl	Pb	Bi	Po	At	Rn
Fr	Ra		Unq	Unp	Unh	Uns		Une									

Name
Actinium
Aluminum
Americium
Antimony
Argon
Arsenic
Astatine
Barium
Berkelium
Beryllium
Bismuth
Bohrium
Boron
Bromine
Cadmium
Calcium
Californium
Carbon
Cerium
Cesium
Chlorine
Chromium
Cobalt
Copper
Curium
Dubnium
Dysprosium
Einsteinium
Erbium
Europium
Fermium
Fluorine
Francium
Gadolinium
Gallium
Germanium
Gold
Hafnium
Hassium
Helium
Holmium
Hydrogen
Indium
Iodine
Iridium
Iron
Krypton
Lanthanum
Lawrencium
Lead
Lithium
Lutetium
Magnesium
Manganese
Meitnerium
Mendelevium
Mercury
Molybdenum
Neodymium
Neon
Neptunium
Nickel
Niobium
Nitrogen
Nobelium
Osmium
Oxygen
Palladium
Phosphorus
Platinum
Plutonium
Polonium
Potassium
Potassium
Praseodymium
Promethium
Protactinium
Radium
Radon
Rhenium
Rhodium
Rubidium
Ruthenium
Rutherfordium
Samarium
Scandium
Seaborgium
Selenium
Silicon
Silver
Sodium
Strontium
Sulfur
Tantalum
Technetium
Tellurium
Terbium
Thallium
Thorium
Thulium
Tin
Titanium
Tungsten
Uranium
Vanadium
Xenon
Ytterbium
Yttrium
Zinc
Zirconium

PUZZLE 127

COUNTRIES

JUMBLE BrainBusters Junior

Unscramble the Jumbles, one letter to each square, to spell names of countries.

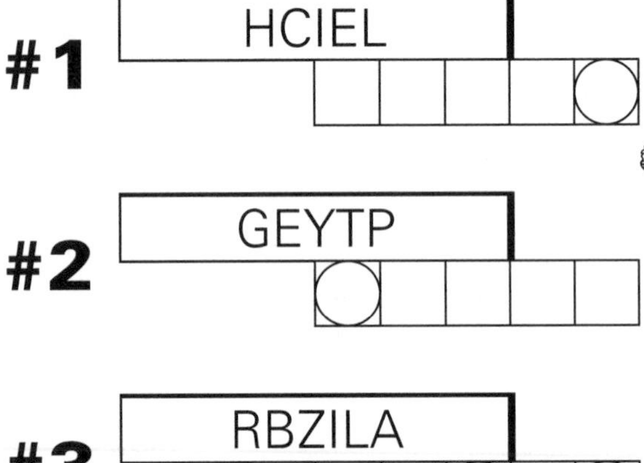

#1 HCIEL

#2 GEYTP

#3 RBZILA

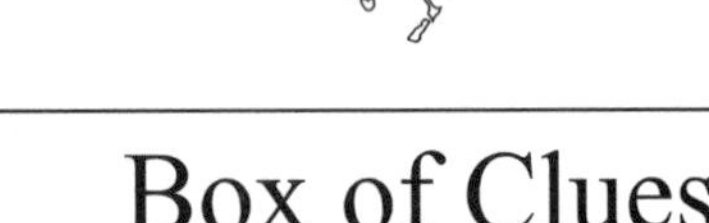

Box of Clues

Stumped? Maybe you can find a clue below.

-African country that is home to Cairo
-Most populous South American country
-Central American country
-Country in the South Pacific
-South American country that starts with "C" and ends with "E"
-Scandinavian country; home to Oslo
-Home to London and Birmingham

#4 AANPMA

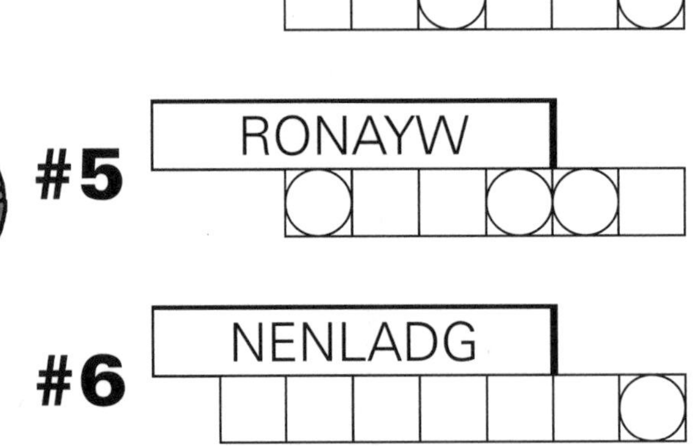

#5 RONAYW

#6 NENLADG

MYSTERY ANSWER

Arrange the circled letters to solve the mystery answer.

PUZZLE 128

STARTS WITH "S"

Unscramble the Jumbles, one letter to each square, to spell words that start with "S."

#1 
SFEA

#2 
USLLK

#3 
ASLDA

#4 
RCAYS

#5 
LSELM

#6 
MSKEO

Box of Clues

Stumped? Maybe you can find a clue below.

-Frightening
-One of four time periods
-Secure
-Nose function
-Caesar ______
-Brain protection
-Fire fumes

Arrange the circled letters to solve the mystery answer.

MYSTERY ANSWER

PUZZLE

129

ANIMALS

Unscramble the Jumbles, one letter to each square, to spell names of animals.

JUMBLE BrainBusters Junior

#1
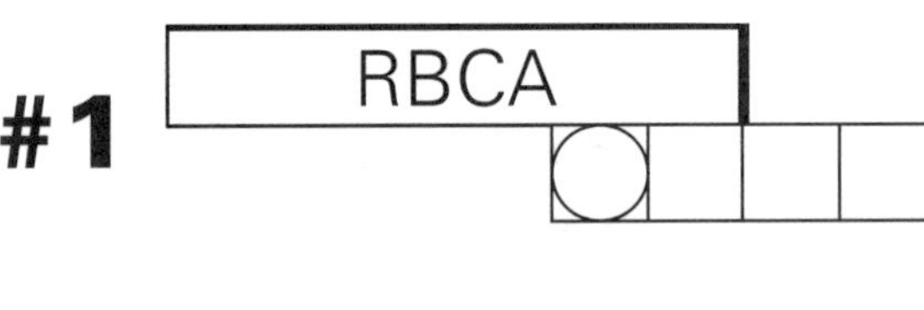

#2

#3

#4

#5

#6
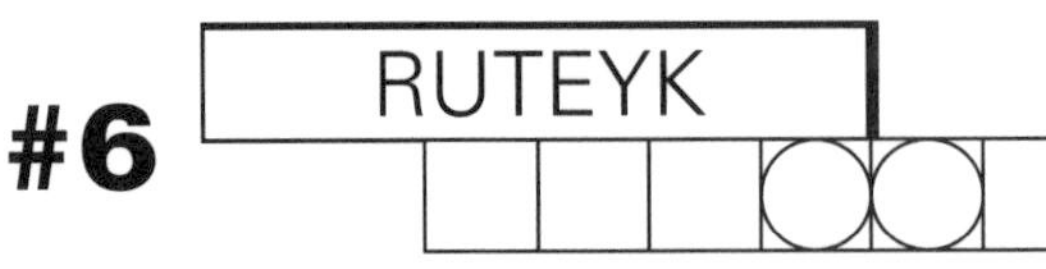

Box of Clues

Stumped? Maybe you can find a clue below.

- -Black and white Asian mammal
- -Large, black bird related to the raven
- -Type of crustacean
- -Farm bird
- -"Thanksgiving" bird
- -Large, water-loving mammal
- -Chameleon or iguana

Arrange the circled letters to solve the mystery answer.

MYSTERY ANSWER

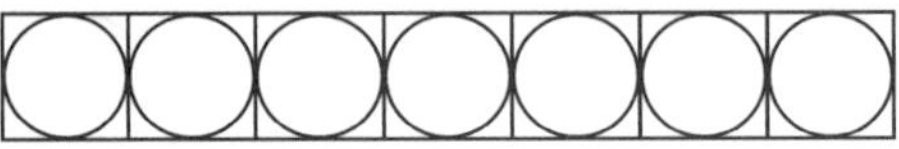

PUZZLE 130

TIME LINE

JUMBLE BrainBusters Junior

Unscramble the Jumbles, one letter to each square, to spell words as suggested by the time line.

#1 1687 Isaac ______ published his *Principia*

#1 WNEONT

#2 1791 Death of ______ (composer)

#2 AOZMRT

#3 1949 Creation of East and West ______

#3 AEGRNYM

#4 1953 Hillary and Tenzing reach top of ______

#4 EVESTRE

#5 1961 South ______ becomes a republic

#5 FIRACA

#6 1990 Iraq invades ______

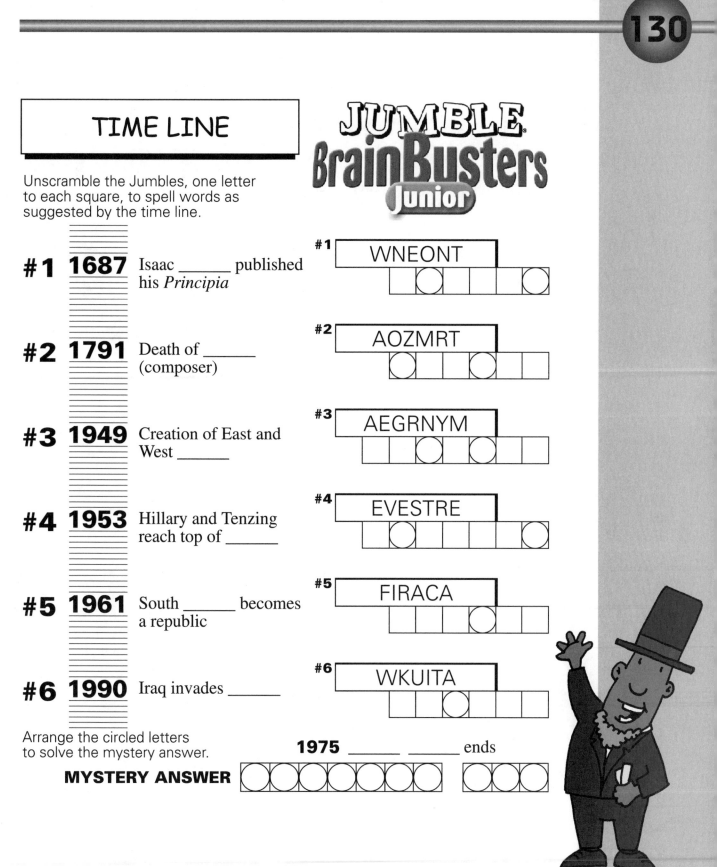

#6 WKUITA

Arrange the circled letters to solve the mystery answer.

1975 ______ ______ ends

MYSTERY ANSWER

PUZZLE

131

ALL ABOUT MUSIC

JUMBLE BrainBusters Junior

Unscramble the Jumbles, one letter to each square, to spell words related to music.

#1 OOBE

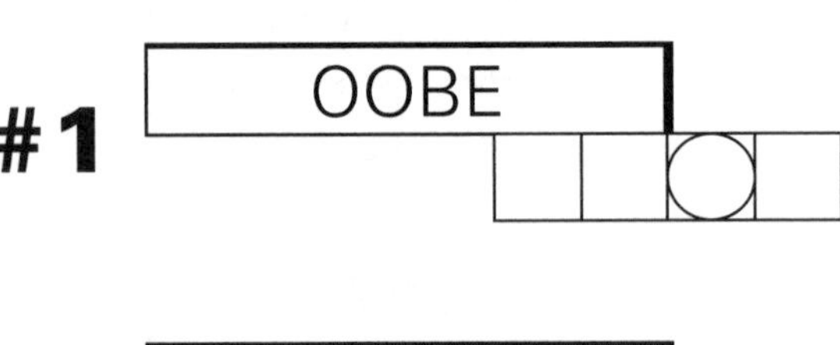

#2 PIONA

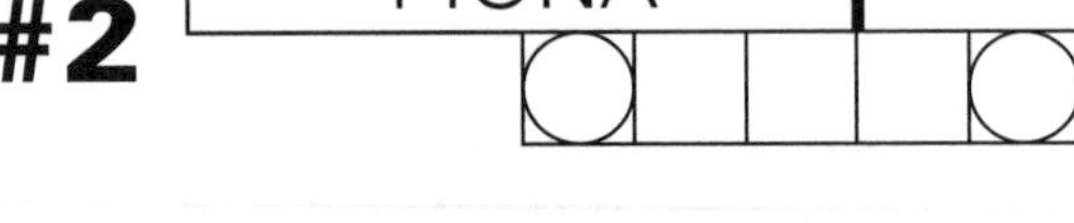

#3 HCODR

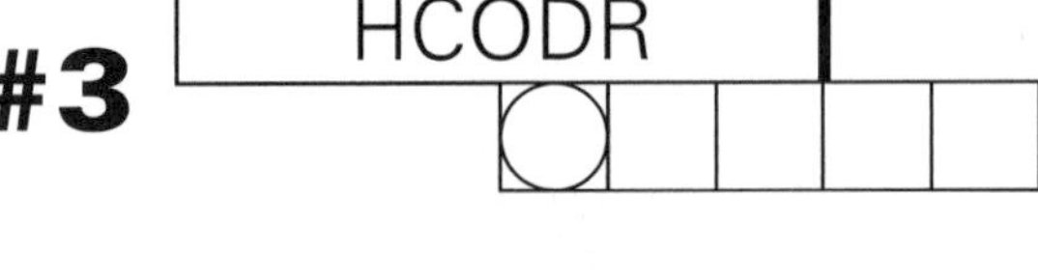

#4 UICSM

#5 LVIOIN

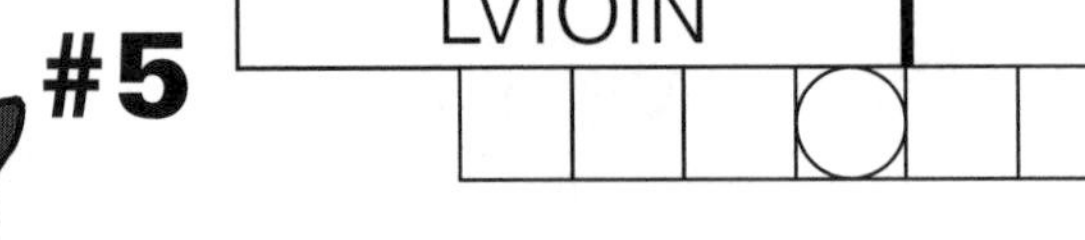

Interesting Music Facts

Rap star Vanilla Ice's real name is Robert Van Winkle.

"Happy Birthday to You" is the most frequently sung song in the western world.

Arrange the circled letters to solve the mystery answer.

MYSTERY ANSWER

PUZZLE 132

SPORTS

JUMBLE BrainBusters Junior

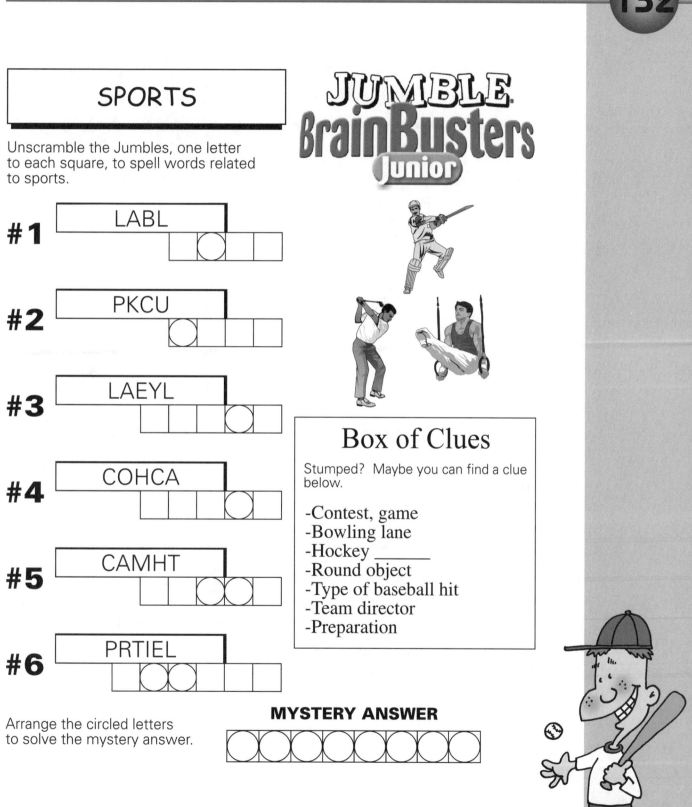

Unscramble the Jumbles, one letter to each square, to spell words related to sports.

#1 LABL

#2 PKCU

#3 LAEYL

#4 COHCA

#5 CAMHT

#6 PRTIEL

Box of Clues

Stumped? Maybe you can find a clue below.

-Contest, game
-Bowling lane
-Hockey ______
-Round object
-Type of baseball hit
-Team director
-Preparation

MYSTERY ANSWER

Arrange the circled letters to solve the mystery answer.

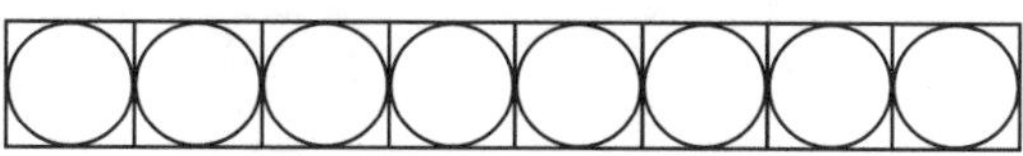

PUZZLE
133

PLANET EARTH

Unscramble the Jumbles, one letter to each square, to spell words related to Planet Earth.

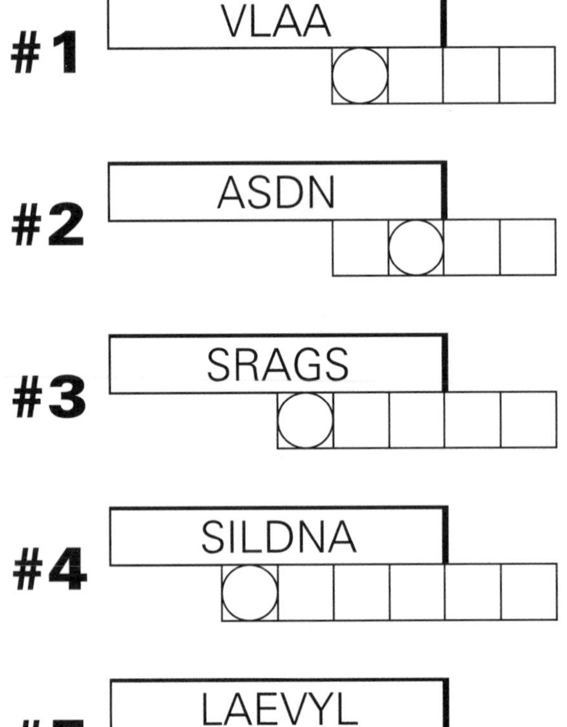

Box of Clues

Stumped? Maybe you can find a clue below.

-Beach material
-Crust, outermost layer
-Frozen river
-Isolated, surround land area
-Plant with slender leaves
-Depression, low area
-Volcano output

Arrange the circled letters to solve the mystery answer.

MYSTERY ANSWER

U.S. PRESIDENTS

JUMBLE BrainBusters Junior

Unscramble the Jumbles, one letter to each square, to spell last names of U.S. presidents.

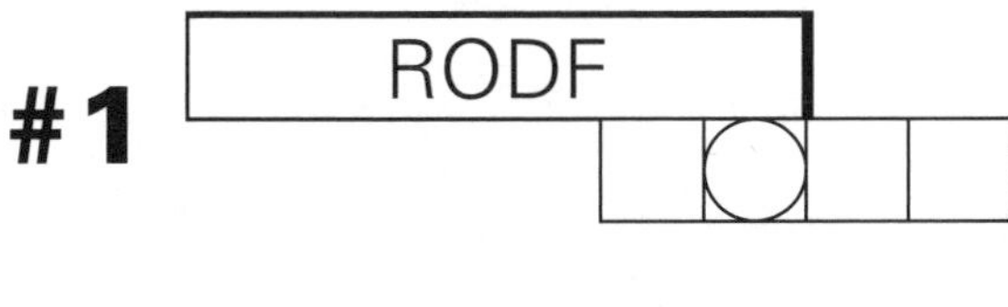

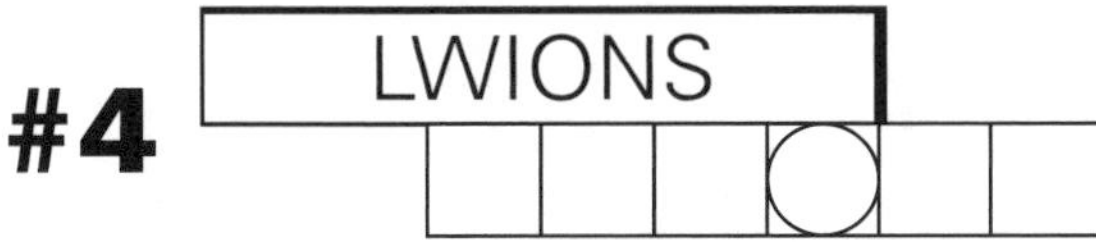

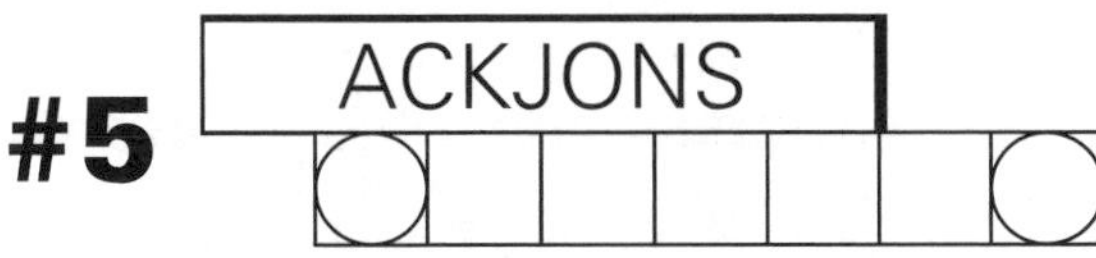

PRESIDENTS OF THE UNITED STATES OF AMERICA

1789-1797 George Washington
1797-1801 John Adams
1801-1809 Thomas Jefferson
1809-1817 James Madison
1817-1825 James Monroe
1825-1829 John Quincy Adams
1829-1837 Andrew Jackson
1837-1841 Martin Van Buren
1841 William Henry Harrison
1841-1845 John Tyler
1845-1849 James Polk
1849-1850 Zachary Taylor
1850-1853 Millard Fillmore
1853-1857 Franklin Pierce
1857-1861 James Buchanan
1861-1865 Abraham Lincoln
1865-1869 Andrew Johnson
1869-1877 Ulysses S. Grant
1877-1881 Rutherford B. Hayes
1881 James A. Garfield
1881-1885 Chester A. Arthur
1885-1889 Stephen Grover Cleveland
1889-1893 Benjamin Harrison
1893-1897 Grover Cleveland
1897-1901 William McKinley
1901-1909 Theodore (Teddy) Roosevelt
1909-1913 William Howard Taft
1913-1921 Thomas Woodrow Wilson
1921-1923 Warren G. Harding
1923-1929 John Calvin Coolidge
1929-1933 Herbert Hoover
1933-1945 Franklin D. Roosevelt
1945-1953 Harry S. Truman
1953-1961 Dwight David Eisenhower
1961-1963 John Fitzgerald Kennedy
1963-1969 Lyndon B. Johnson
1969-1974 Richard M. Nixon
1974-1977 Gerald R. Ford
1977-1981 James (Jimmy) Carter
1981-1989 Ronald Reagan
1989-1993 George W. Bush
1993-2001 William Jefferson Clinton
2001- George Walker Bush

Arrange the circled letters to solve the mystery answer.

MYSTERY ANSWER

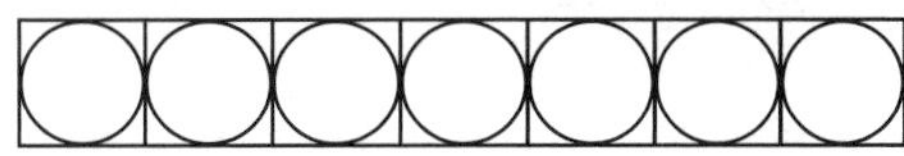

PUZZLE

135

THE HUMAN BODY

JUMBLE BrainBusters Junior

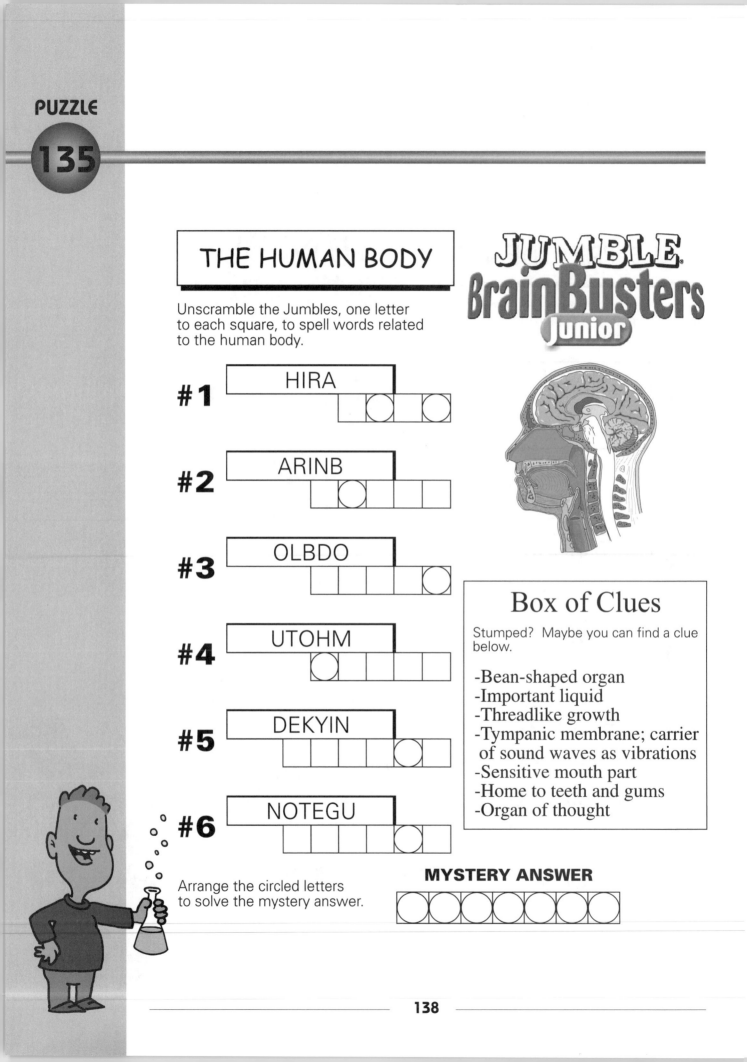

Unscramble the Jumbles, one letter to each square, to spell words related to the human body.

#1

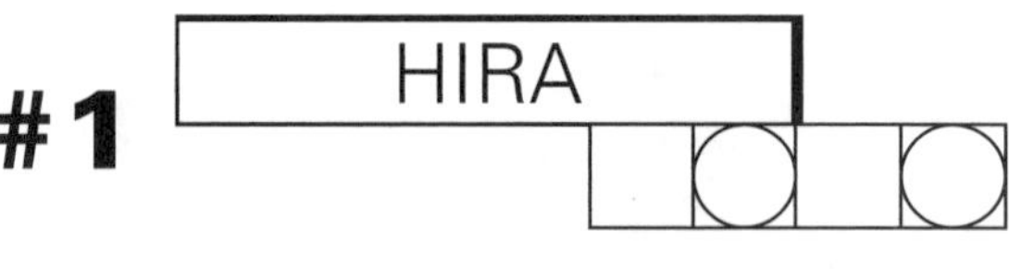

#2

#3

#4

#5

#6

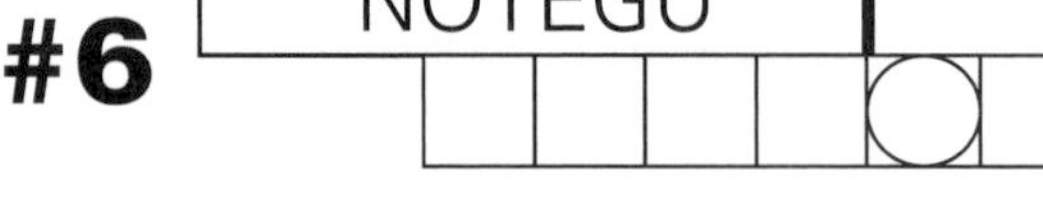

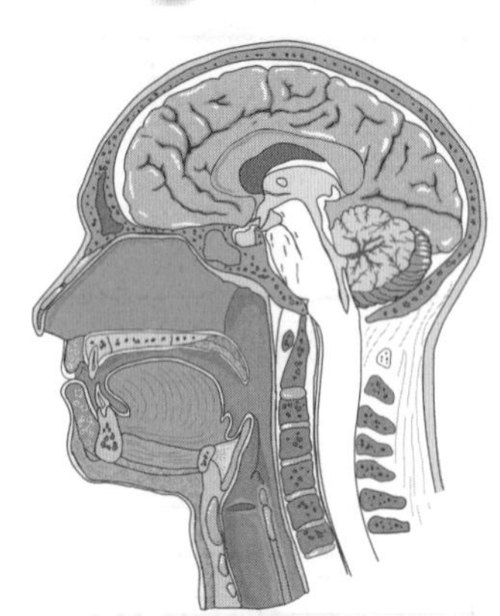

Box of Clues

Stumped? Maybe you can find a clue below.

- -Bean-shaped organ
- -Important liquid
- -Threadlike growth
- -Tympanic membrane; carrier of sound waves as vibrations
- -Sensitive mouth part
- -Home to teeth and gums
- -Organ of thought

Arrange the circled letters to solve the mystery answer.

MYSTERY ANSWER

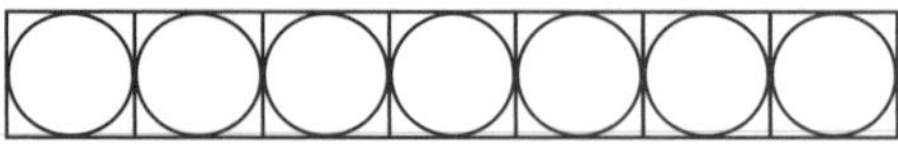

STARTS WITH "W"

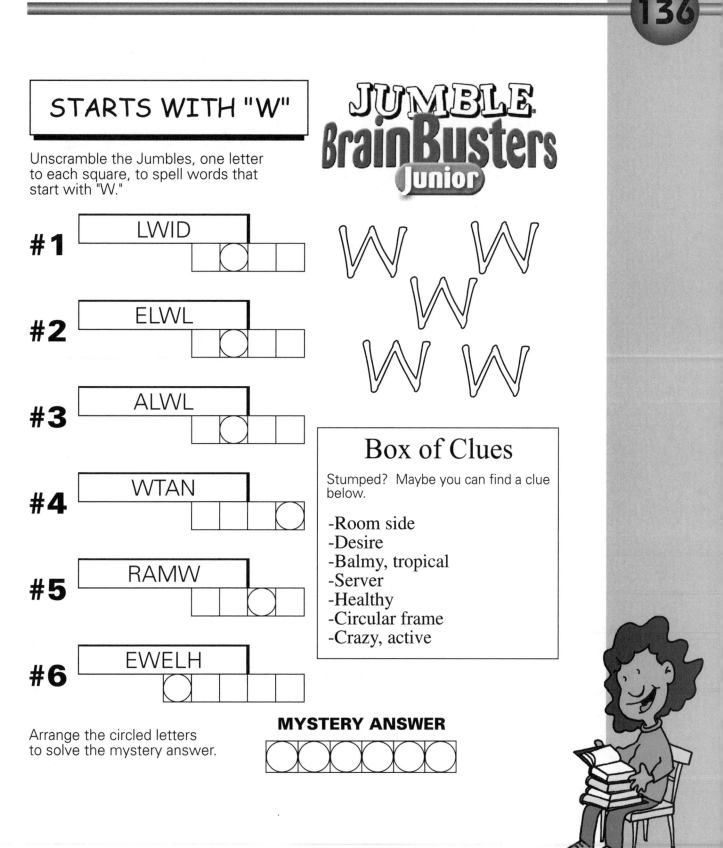

Unscramble the Jumbles, one letter to each square, to spell words that start with "W."

#1 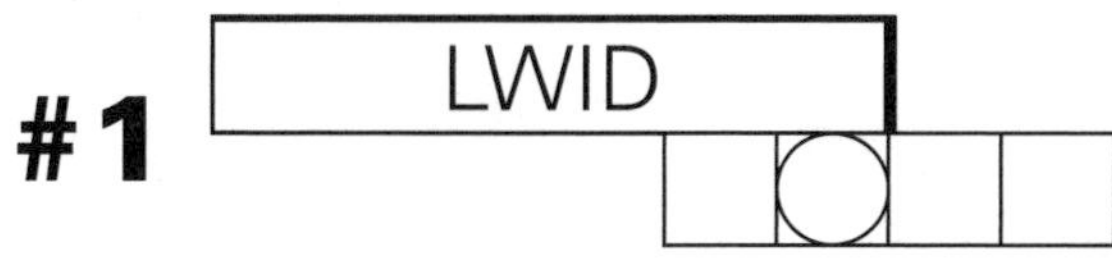

#2 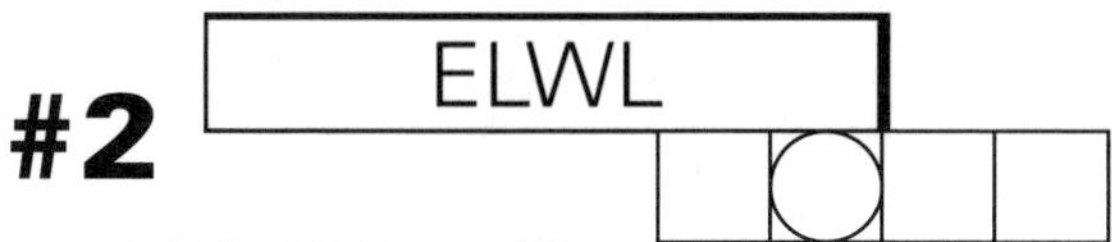

#3 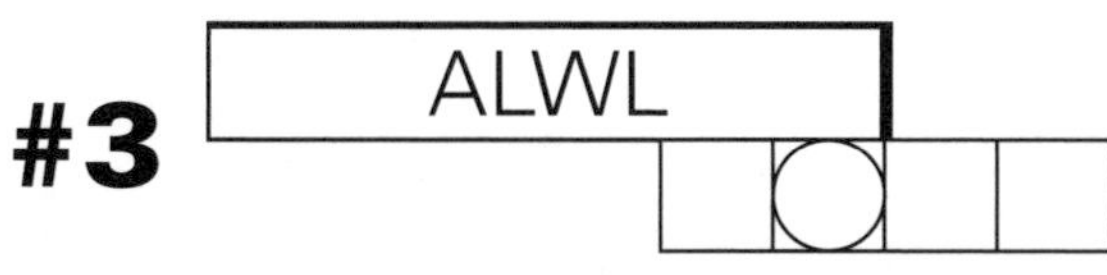

#4 

#5 

#6 

Box of Clues

Stumped? Maybe you can find a clue below.

-Room side
-Desire
-Balmy, tropical
-Server
-Healthy
-Circular frame
-Crazy, active

Arrange the circled letters to solve the mystery answer.

MYSTERY ANSWER

PUZZLE

137

JUMBLE BrainBusters Junior

BASKETBALL

Unscramble the Jumbles, one letter to each square, to spell words related to basketball.

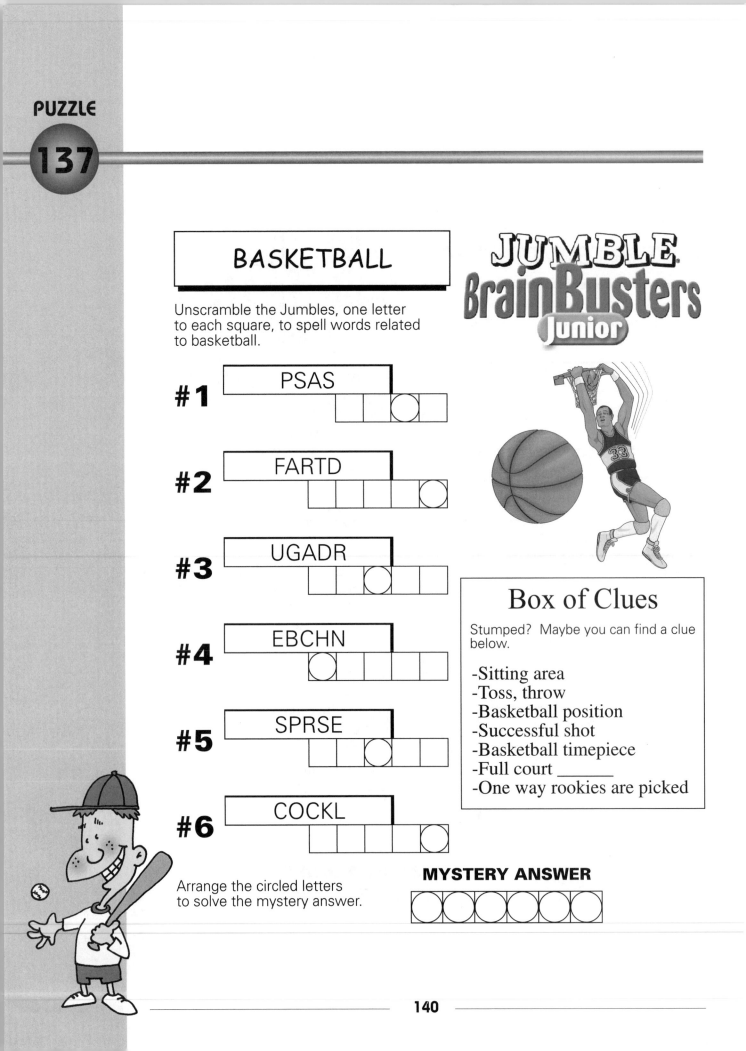

#1
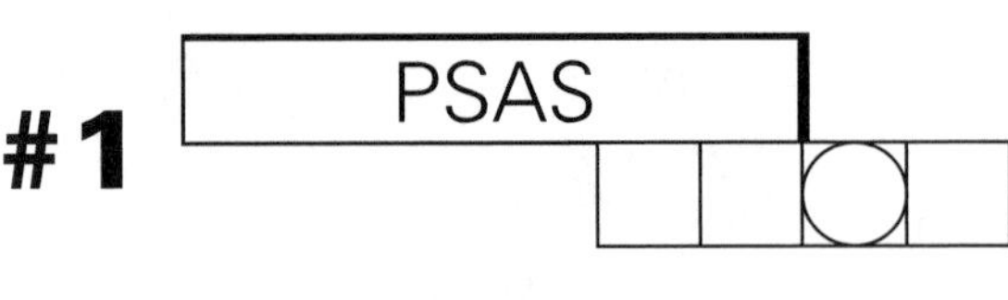

#2

#3

#4

#5
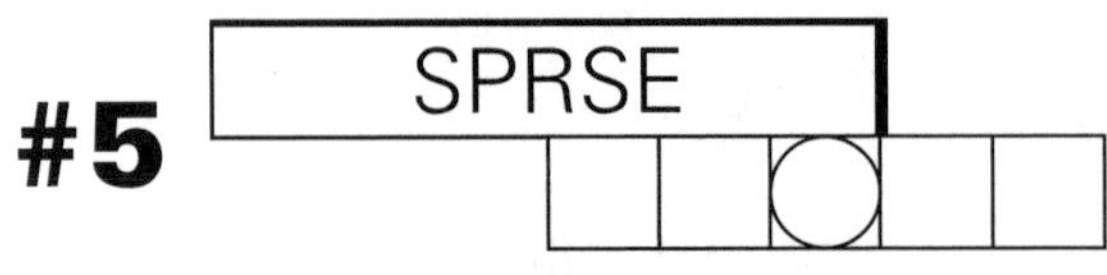

#6

Box of Clues

Stumped? Maybe you can find a clue below.

- -Sitting area
- -Toss, throw
- -Basketball position
- -Successful shot
- -Basketball timepiece
- -Full court ______
- -One way rookies are picked

Arrange the circled letters to solve the mystery answer.

MYSTERY ANSWER

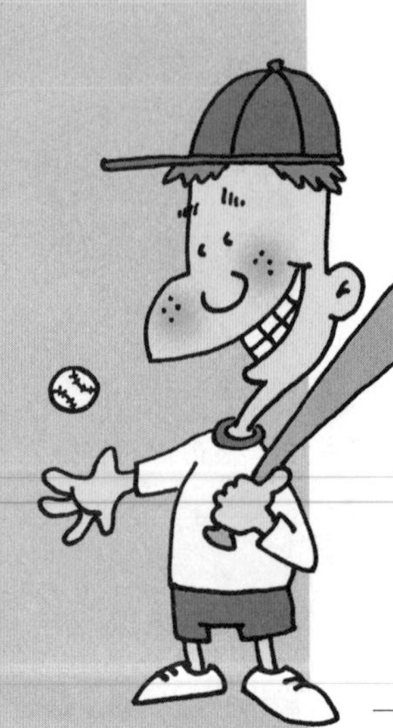

U.S. STATES

Unscramble the Jumbles, one letter to each square, to spell names of U.S. states.

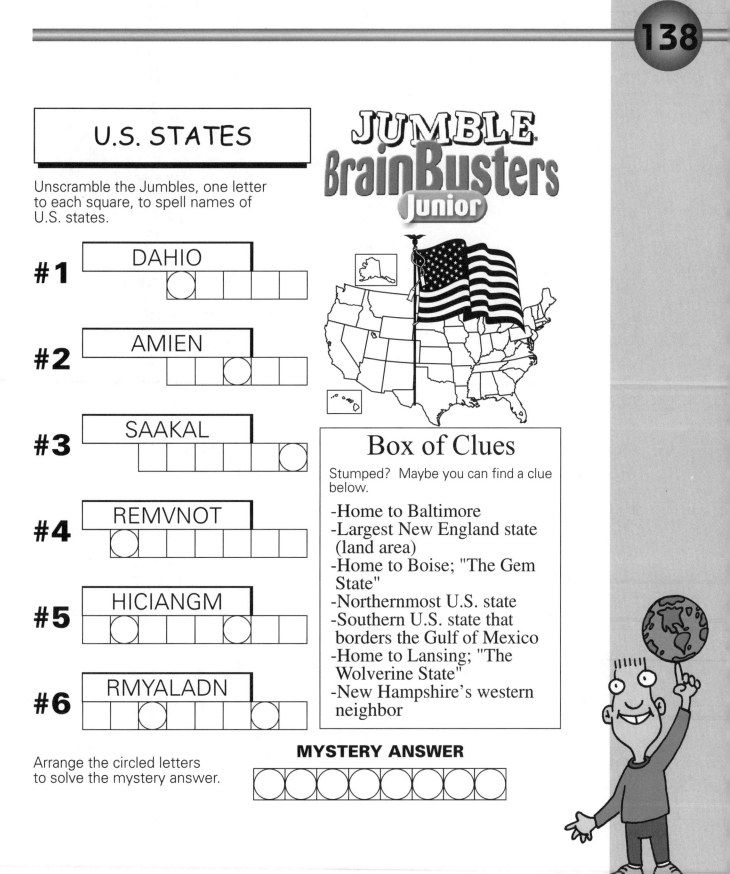

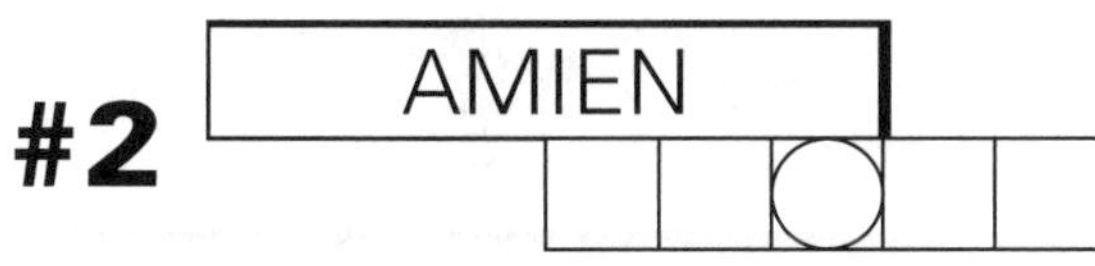

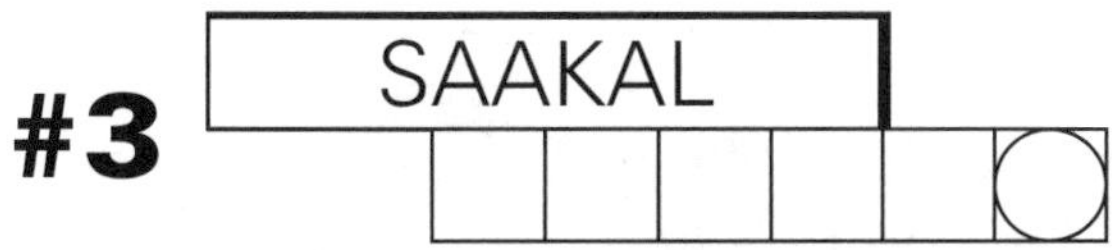

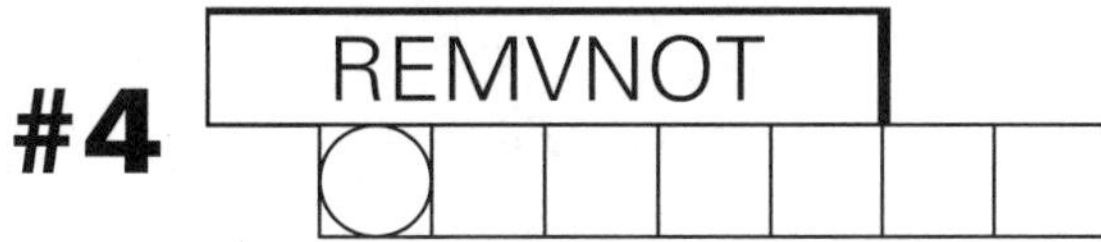

JUMBLE BrainBusters Junior

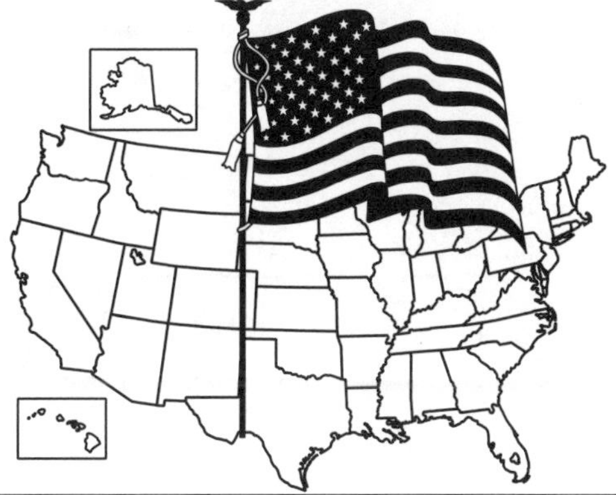

Box of Clues

Stumped? Maybe you can find a clue below.

- -Home to Baltimore
- -Largest New England state (land area)
- -Home to Boise; "The Gem State"
- -Northernmost U.S. state
- -Southern U.S. state that borders the Gulf of Mexico
- -Home to Lansing; "The Wolverine State"
- -New Hampshire's western neighbor

MYSTERY ANSWER

Arrange the circled letters to solve the mystery answer.

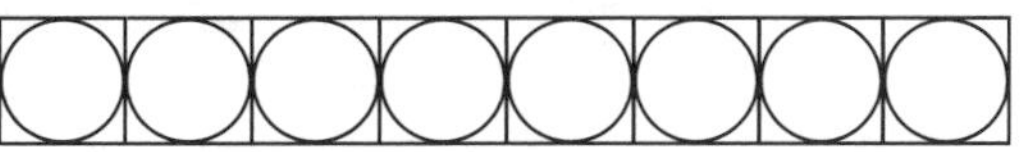

PUZZLE 139

JUMBLE BrainBusters Junior

POETRY

Unscramble the Jumbles, one letter to each square, to spell words found in the poem.

#1 SIKC

#2 UYOR

#3 SDIETG

#4 AHIR

#5 CSTEH

#6 CMOONM

MYTHS by Kim E. Nolan

Don't make that face
It just might stick
If you sleep with wet hair
You're sure to get ____ #1

If you swallow ____ #2 gum
It'll take years to ____ #3
Eating your vegetables
Will put ____ #4 on your ____ #5

There's one ____ #6 theme
That you can probably hear
That not all things said
Are as true as they appear

Arrange the circled letters to solve the mystery answer. (The mystery answer is not in the poem.)

MYSTERY ANSWER

PUZZLE 140

OCCUPATIONS

JUMBLE BrainBusters Junior

Unscramble the Jumbles, one letter to each square, to spell occupations.

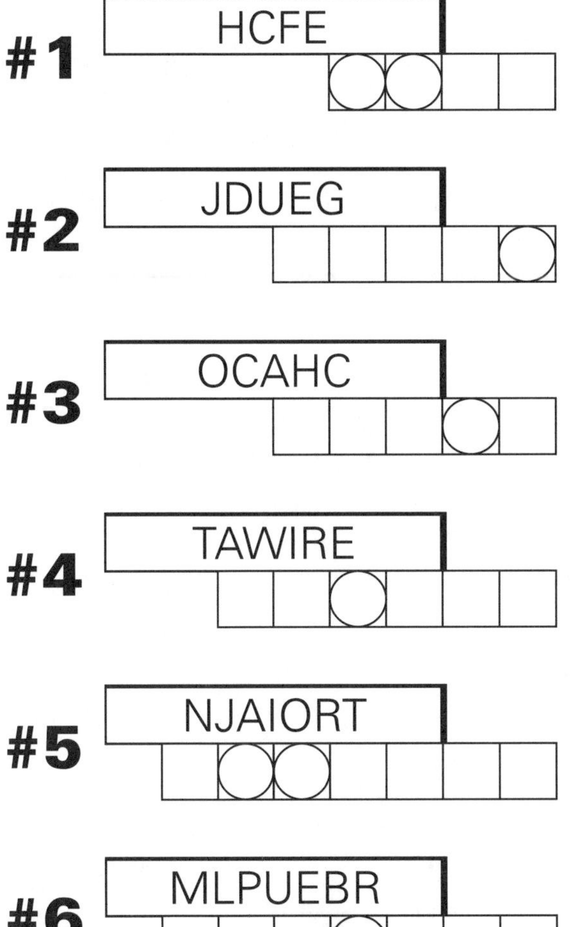

Box of Clues

Stumped? Maybe you can find a clue below.

-Starts with "C"; ends with "H"
-Starts with "J"; ends with "R"
-Starts with "M"; ends with "C"
-Starts with "C"; ends with "F"
-Starts with "W"; ends with "R"
-Starts with "J"; ends with "E"
-Starts with "P"; ends with "R"

MYSTERY ANSWER

Arrange the circled letters to solve the mystery answer.

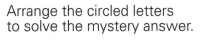

PUZZLE

141

LARGE CITIES

JUMBLE BrainBusters Junior

Unscramble the Jumbles, one letter to each square, to spell names of large cities.

#1
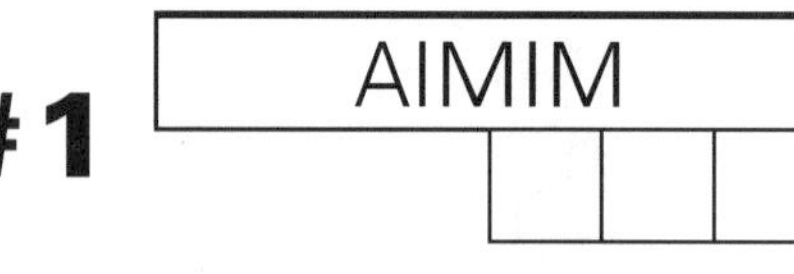

#2

#3

#4
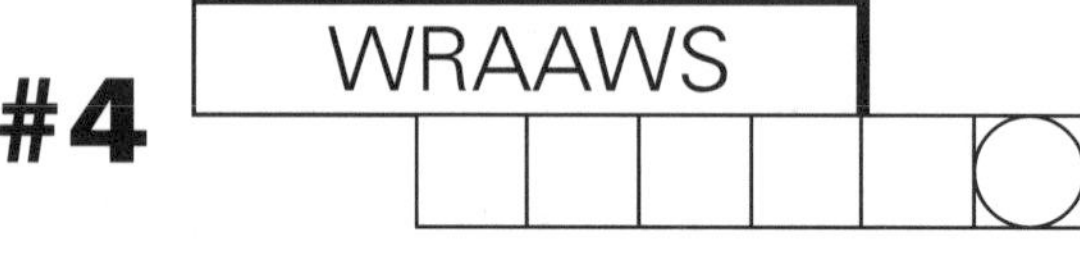

#5

#6
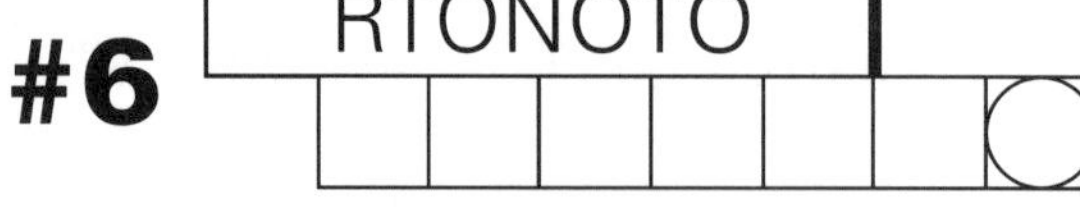

Box of Clues

Stumped? Maybe you can find a clue below.

- -Largest city in Australia
- -Largest U.S. city bordering the Great Lakes
- -Largest city in the largest country
- -Large Canadian city
- -Large city in Florida
- -Home to Big Ben; Largest city in England

Arrange the circled letters to solve the mystery answer.

MYSTERY ANSWER

CLOTHING

JUMBLE BrainBusters Junior

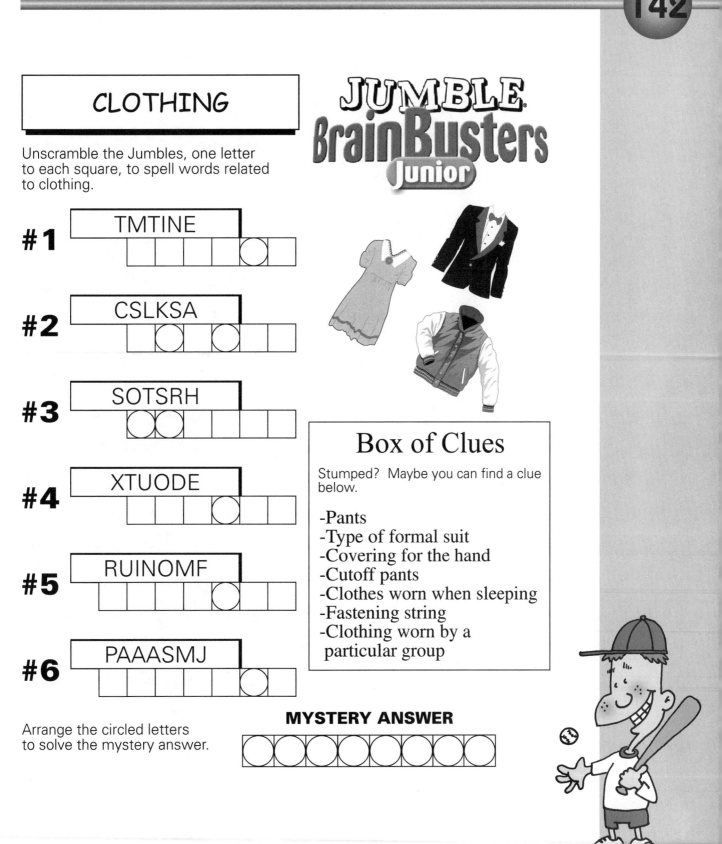

Unscramble the Jumbles, one letter to each square, to spell words related to clothing.

#1 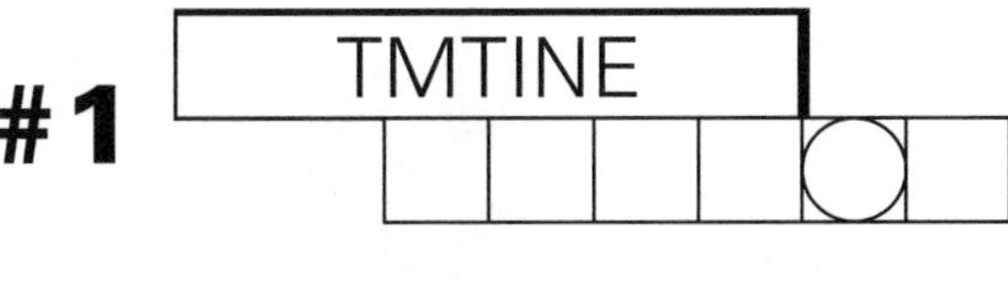

#2 

#3 

#4 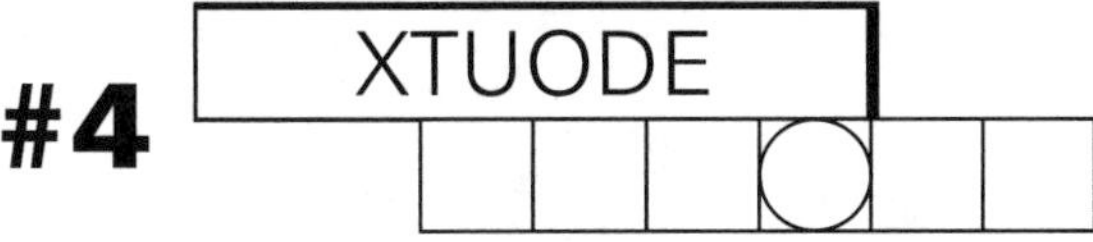

#5 

#6 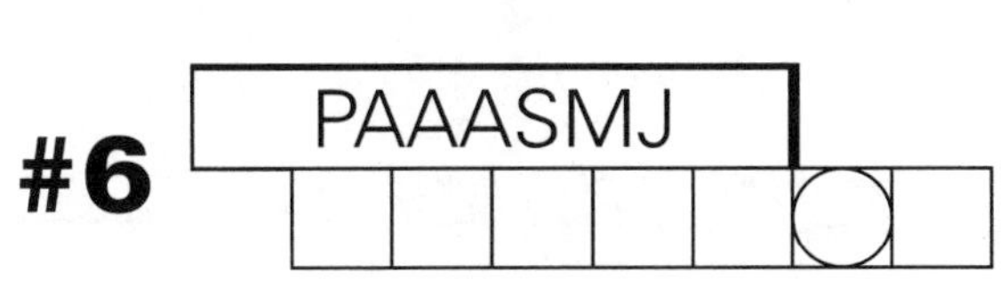

Box of Clues

Stumped? Maybe you can find a clue below.

-Pants
-Type of formal suit
-Covering for the hand
-Cutoff pants
-Clothes worn when sleeping
-Fastening string
-Clothing worn by a particular group

MYSTERY ANSWER

Arrange the circled letters to solve the mystery answer.

PUZZLE

143

ABBREVIATED WORDS

Unscramble the Jumbles, one letter to each square, to spell words that are often abbreviated.

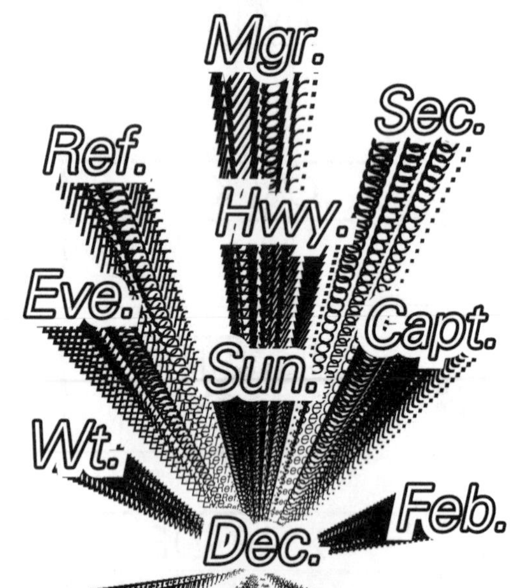

#1 GWIHTE

#2 DTESAUY

#3 MAAERGN

#4 UEBRAFYR

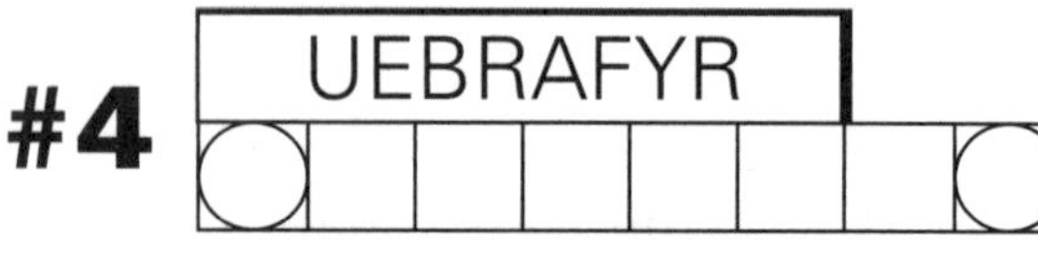

#5 NOMEEVRB

Arrange the circled letters to solve the mystery answer.

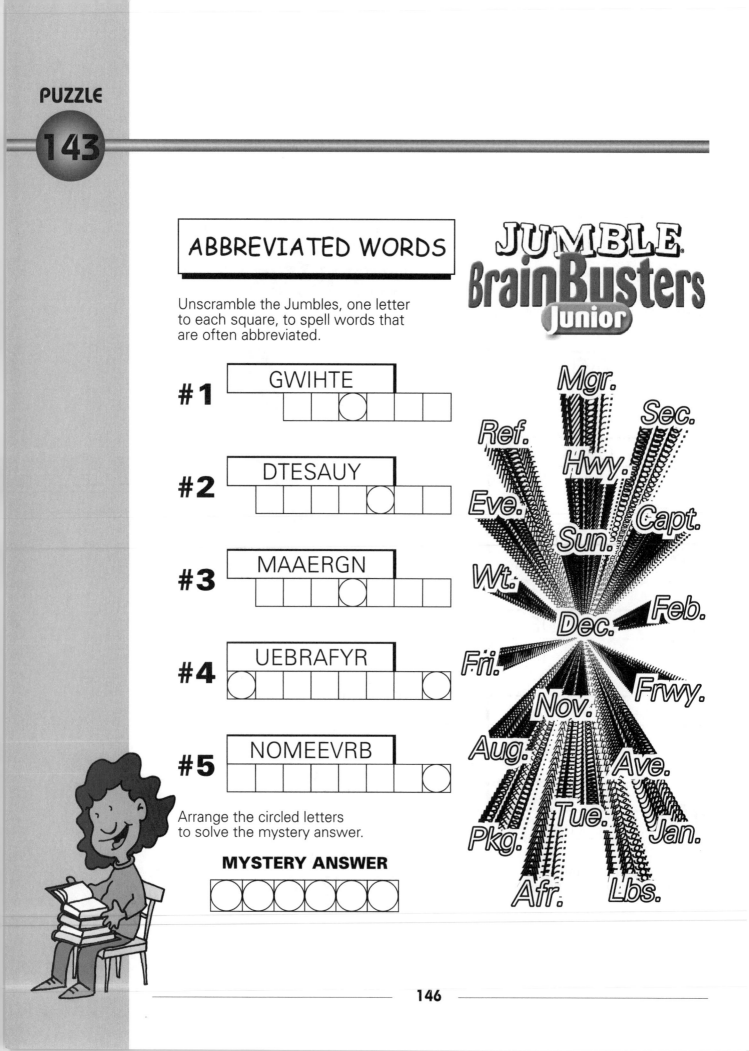

MYSTERY ANSWER

U.S. PRESIDENTS

Unscramble the Jumbles, one letter to each square, to spell last names of U.S. presidents.

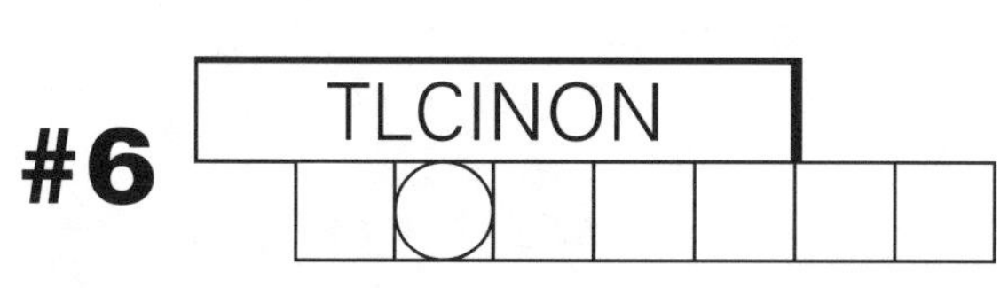

Box of Clues

Stumped? Maybe you can find a clue below.

-Starts with "C"; ends with "N"
-Starts with "T"; ends with "R"
-Starts with "H"; ends with "R"
-Starts with "T"; ends with "R"
-Starts with "G"; ends with "T"
-Starts with "L"; ends with "N"
-Starts with "H"; ends with "S"

Arrange the circled letters to solve the mystery answer.

MYSTERY ANSWER

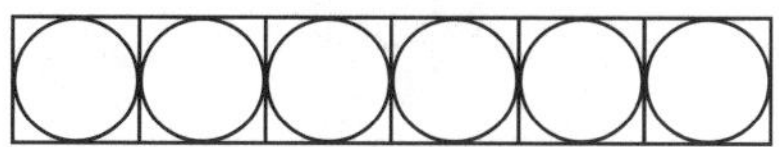

PUZZLE 145

JUMBLE® BrainBusters Junior

ADJECTIVES

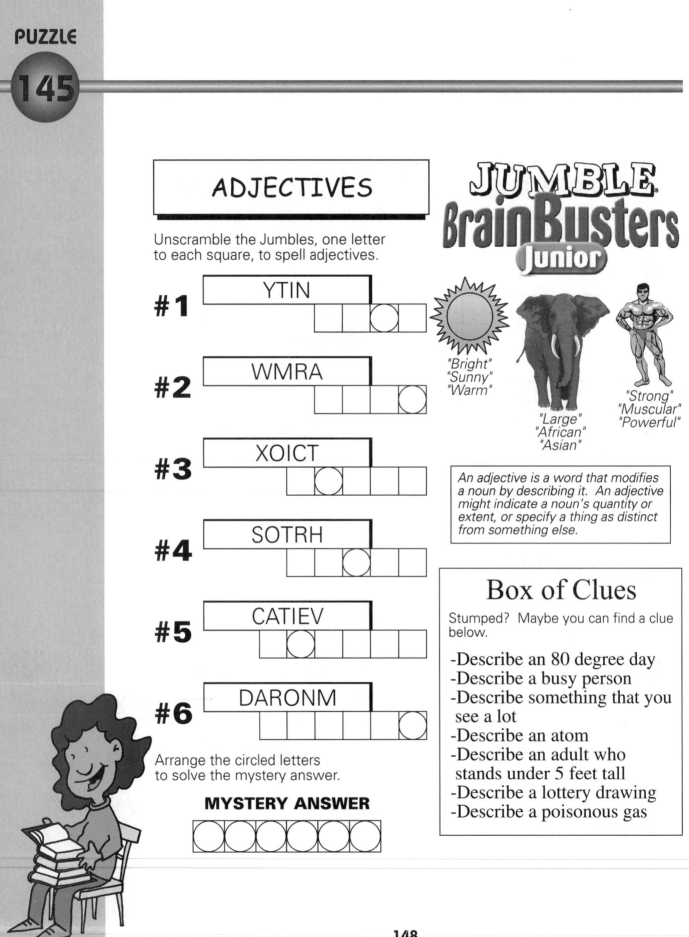

Unscramble the Jumbles, one letter to each square, to spell adjectives.

#1 YTIN

#2 WMRA

#3 XOICT

#4 SOTRH

#5 CATIEV

#6 DARONM

Arrange the circled letters to solve the mystery answer.

MYSTERY ANSWER

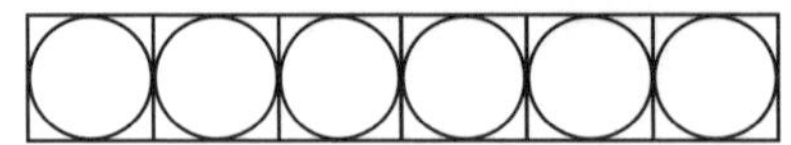

"Bright" "Sunny" "Warm"

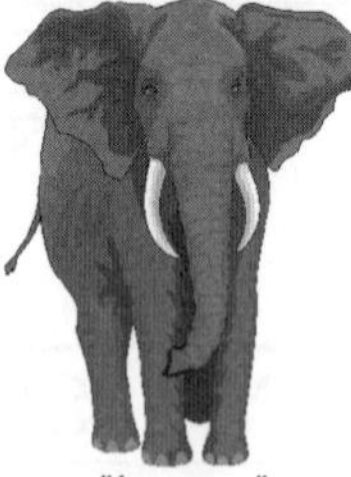

"Large" "African" "Asian"

"Strong" "Muscular" "Powerful"

An adjective is a word that modifies a noun by describing it. An adjective might indicate a noun's quantity or extent, or specify a thing as distinct from something else.

Box of Clues

Stumped? Maybe you can find a clue below.

- -Describe an 80 degree day
- -Describe a busy person
- -Describe something that you see a lot
- -Describe an atom
- -Describe an adult who stands under 5 feet tall
- -Describe a lottery drawing
- -Describe a poisonous gas

JUMBLE BrainBusters Junior

ANIMALS

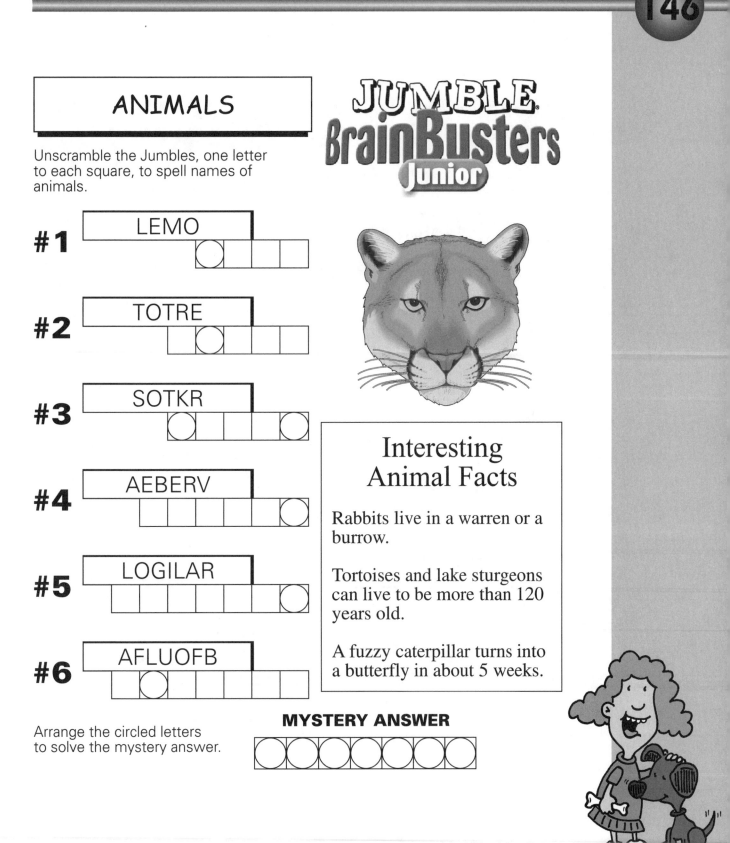

Unscramble the Jumbles, one letter to each square, to spell names of animals.

#1 LEMO

#2

#3

#4
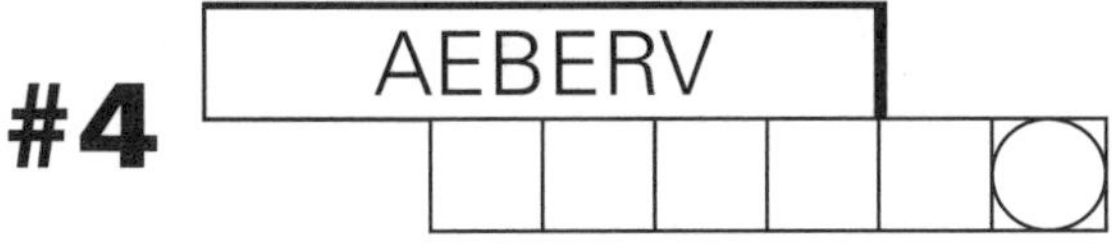

#5
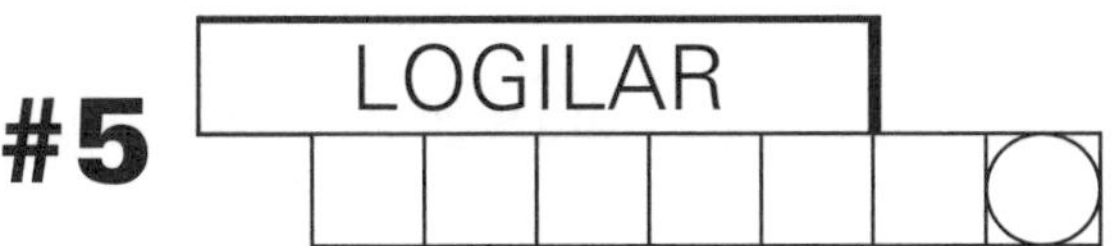

#6
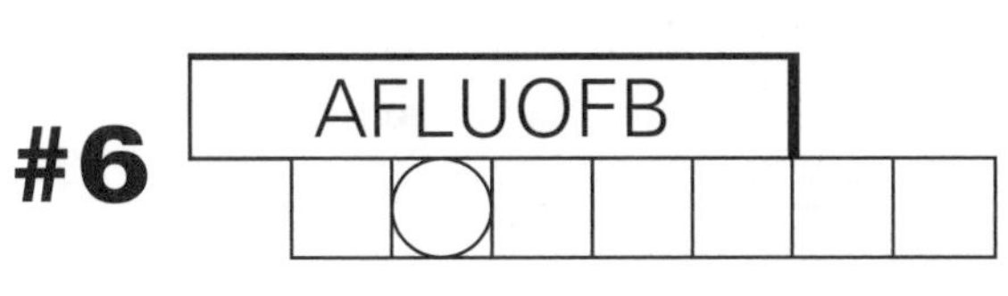

Interesting Animal Facts

Rabbits live in a warren or a burrow.

Tortoises and lake sturgeons can live to be more than 120 years old.

A fuzzy caterpillar turns into a butterfly in about 5 weeks.

Arrange the circled letters to solve the mystery answer.

MYSTERY ANSWER

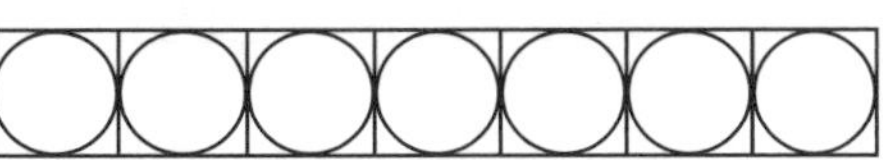

PUZZLE

147

U.S. STATE CAPITALS

Unscramble the Jumbles, one letter to each square, to spell names of U.S. state capitals.

#1 OBIES

#2 PTOKAE

#3 LIASNGN

#4 GUUATAS

#5 NRTEOTN

#6 CNOODRC

Box of Clues

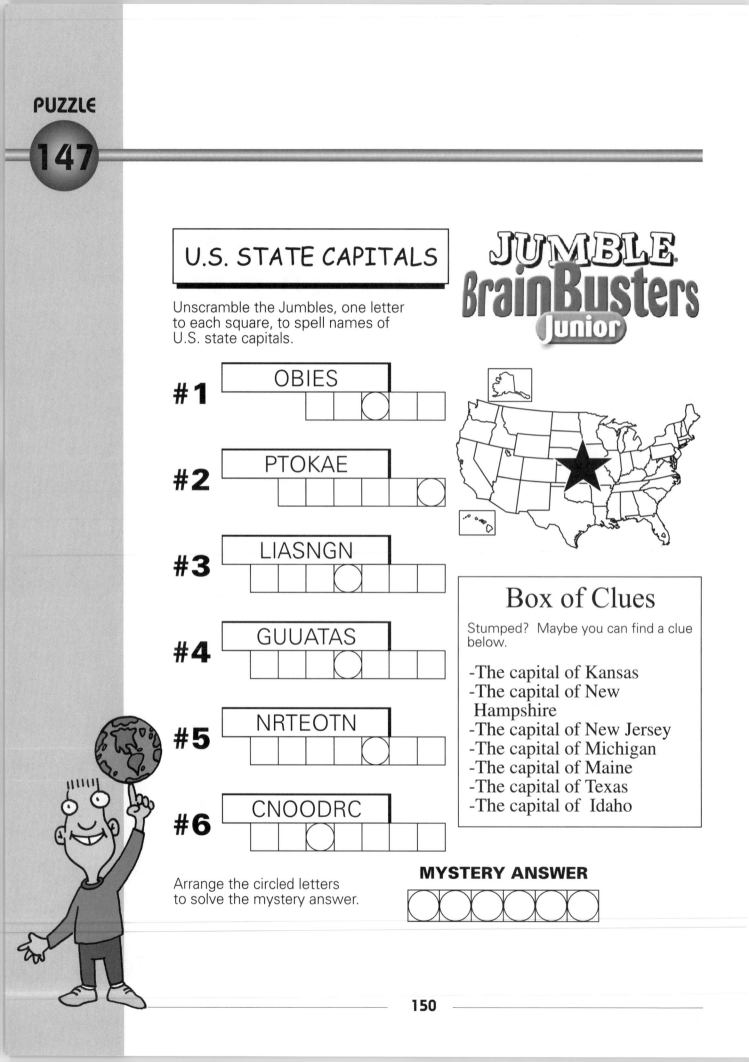

Stumped? Maybe you can find a clue below.

- -The capital of Kansas
- -The capital of New Hampshire
- -The capital of New Jersey
- -The capital of Michigan
- -The capital of Maine
- -The capital of Texas
- -The capital of Idaho

Arrange the circled letters to solve the mystery answer.

MYSTERY ANSWER

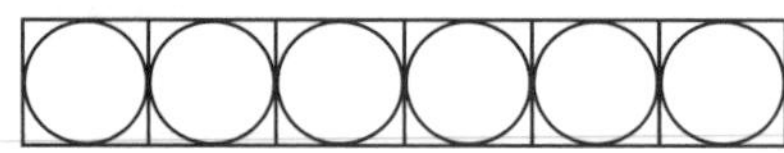

BASEBALL

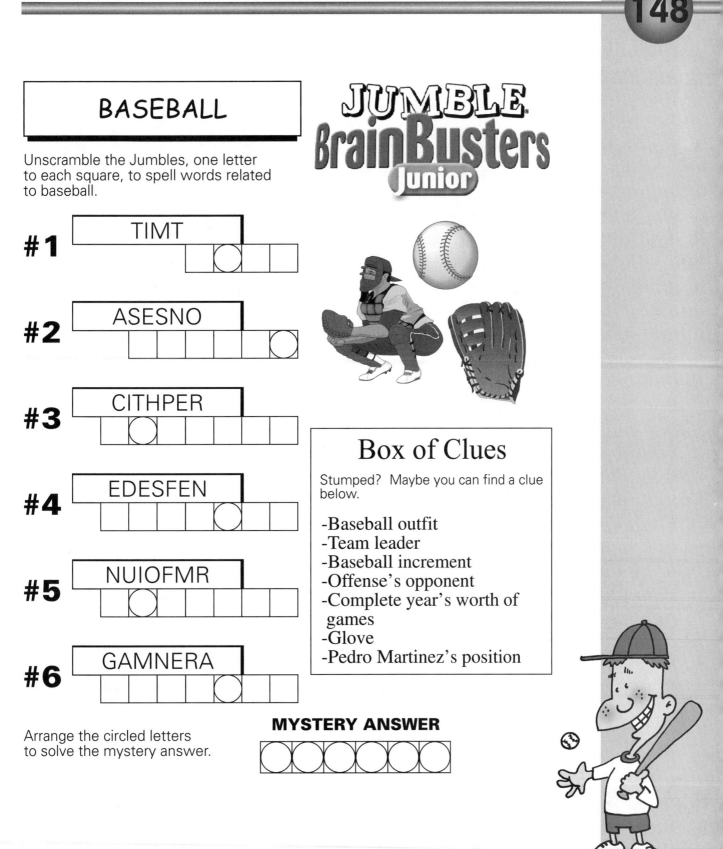

Unscramble the Jumbles, one letter to each square, to spell words related to baseball.

#1 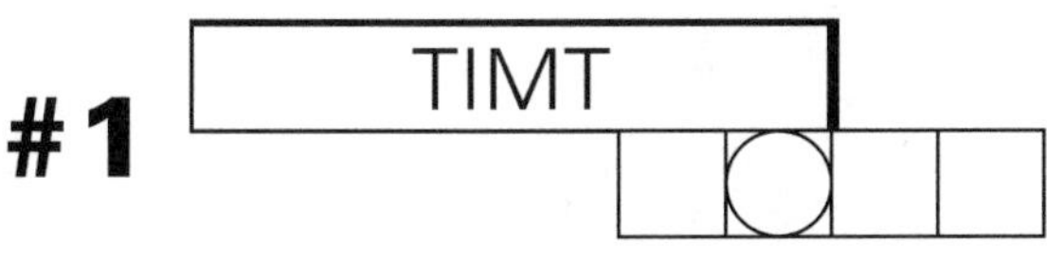

#2 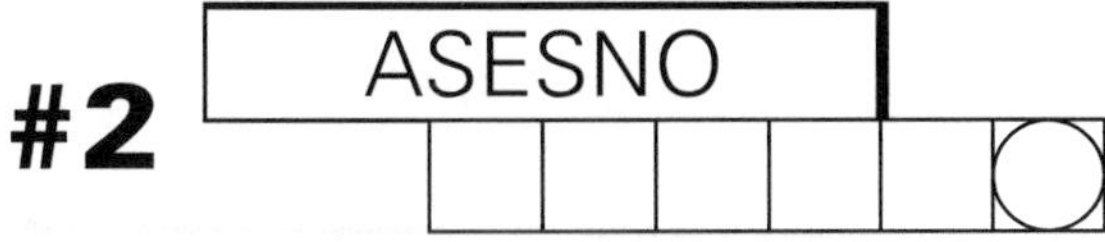

#3 

#4 

#5 

#6 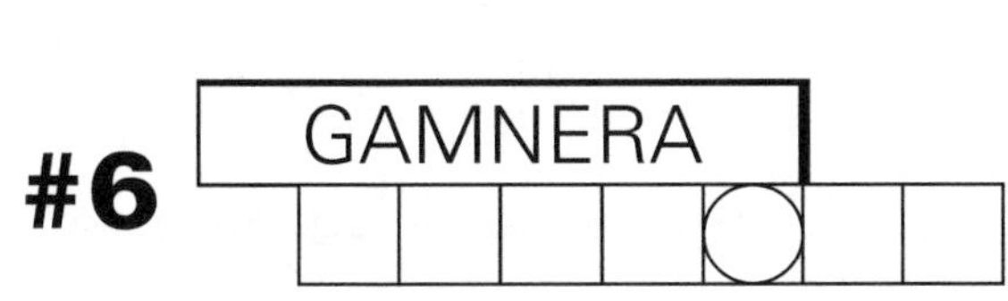

Box of Clues

Stumped? Maybe you can find a clue below.

-Baseball outfit
-Team leader
-Baseball increment
-Offense's opponent
-Complete year's worth of games
-Glove
-Pedro Martinez's position

Arrange the circled letters to solve the mystery answer.

MYSTERY ANSWER

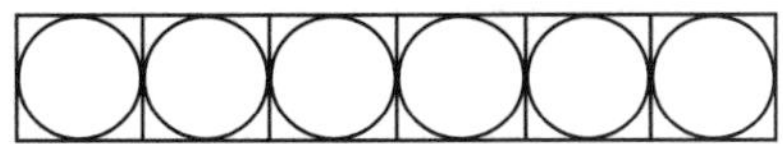

PUZZLE

149

COUNTRY FLAGS

Unscramble the Jumbles, one letter to each square, to spell names of countries, as suggested by the flags.

#1 UCAB

#4 AAIAJMC

#2 RSIAY

#5 RDCEUOA

#3 OJDNAR

#6 LOCOIBAM

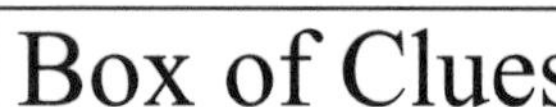

Box of Clues

Stumped? Maybe you can find a clue below.

-Starts with "C"; ends with "A"
-Starts with "J"; ends with "N"
-Starts with "C"; ends with "A"
-Starts with "J"; ends with "A"
-Starts with "C"; ends with "A"
-Starts with "E"; ends with "R"
-Starts with "S"; ends with "A"

Arrange the circled letters to solve the mystery answer.

MYSTERY ANSWER

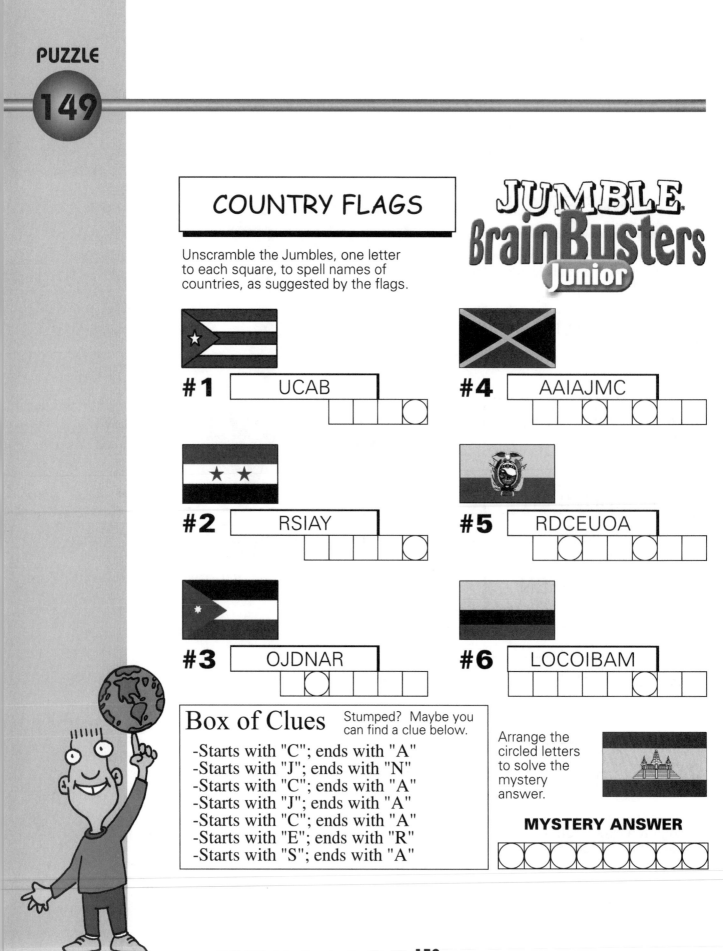

WEATHER

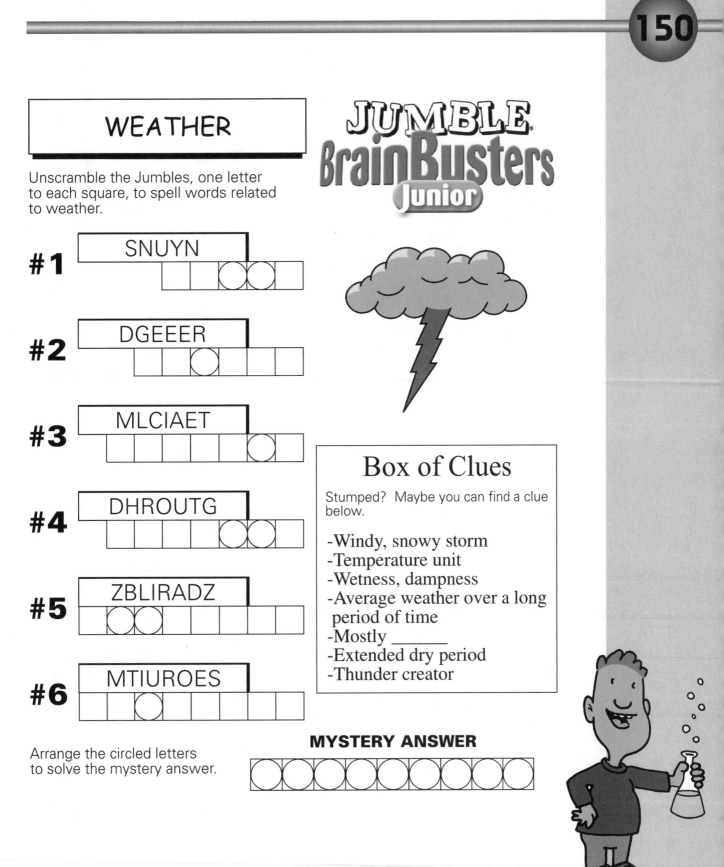

JUMBLE BrainBusters Junior

Unscramble the Jumbles, one letter to each square, to spell words related to weather.

#1 SNUYN
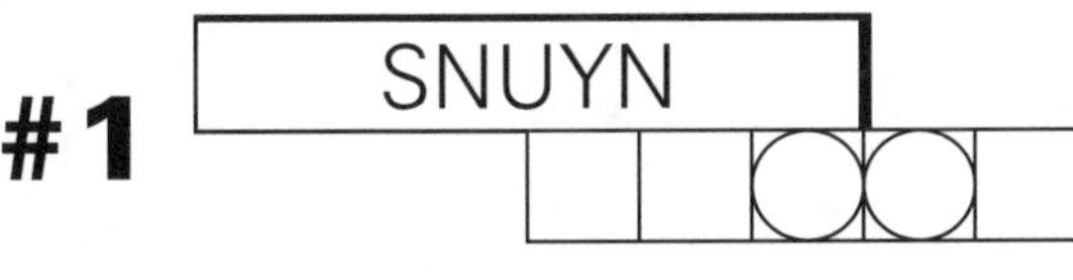

#2 DGEEER
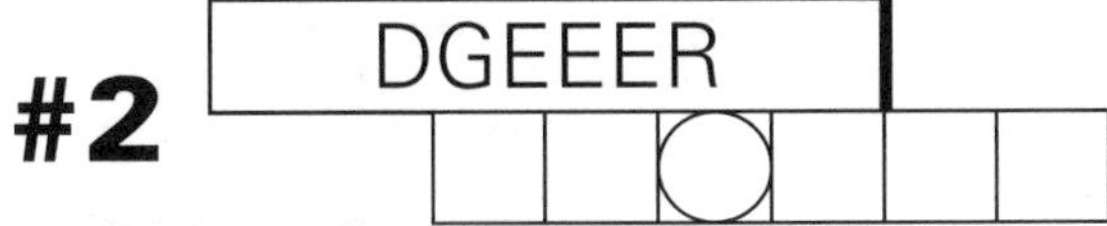

#3 MLCIAET

#4 DHROUTG
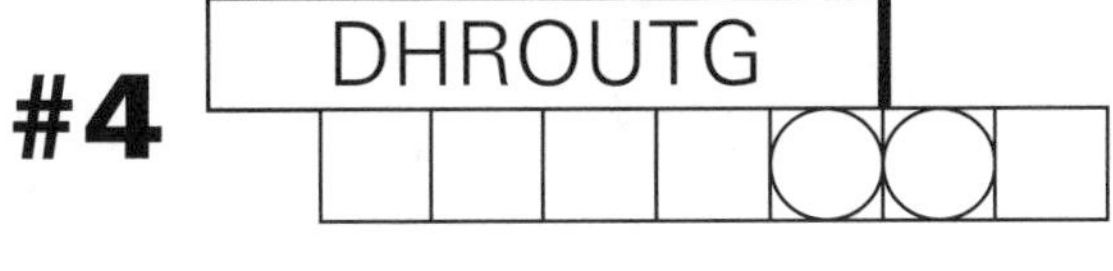

#5 ZBLIRADZ

#6 MTIUROES

Box of Clues

Stumped? Maybe you can find a clue below.

-Windy, snowy storm
-Temperature unit
-Wetness, dampness
-Average weather over a long period of time
-Mostly ______
-Extended dry period
-Thunder creator

Arrange the circled letters to solve the mystery answer.

MYSTERY ANSWER

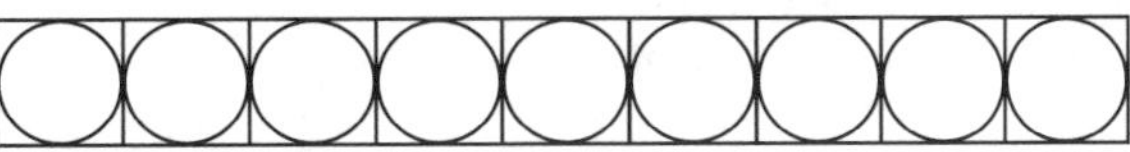

PUZZLE 151

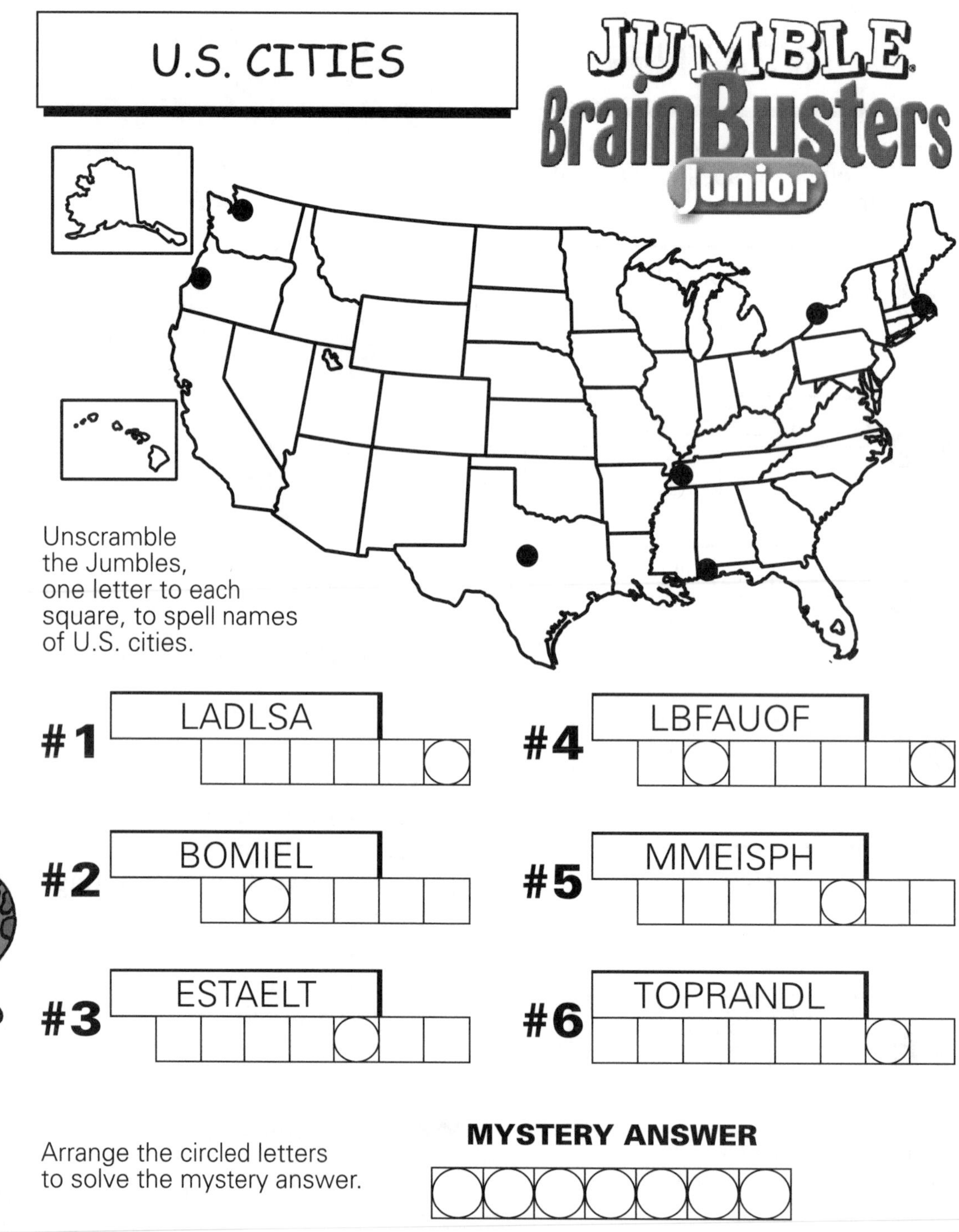

U.S. CITIES

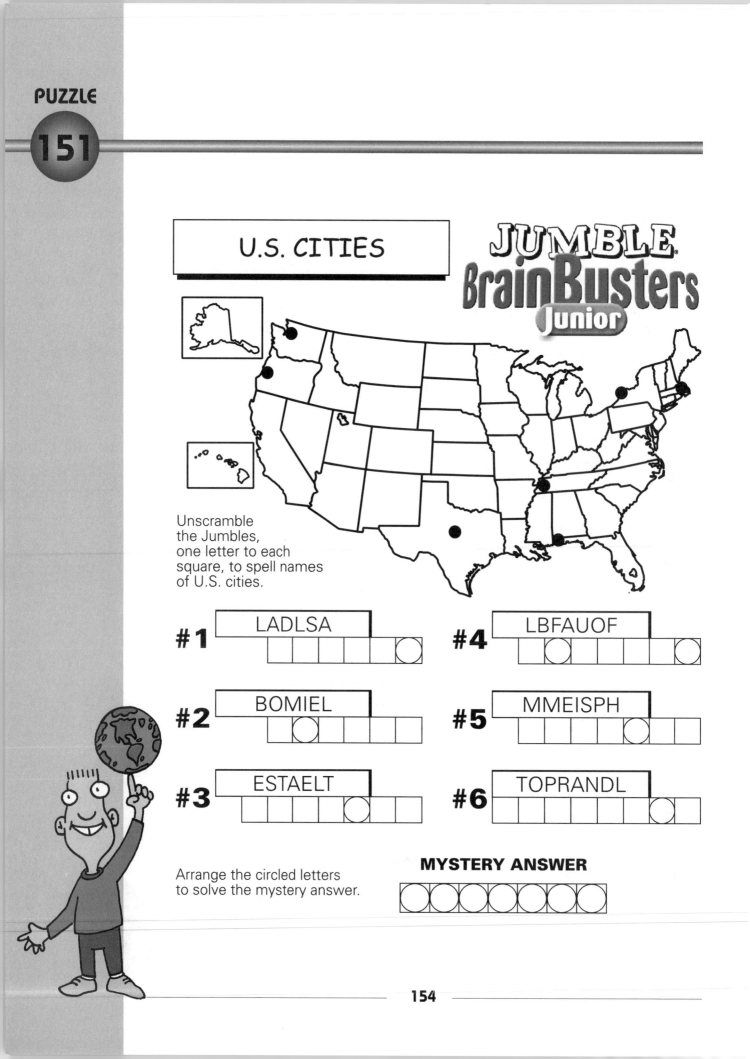

Unscramble the Jumbles, one letter to each square, to spell names of U.S. cities.

#1 LADLSA

#2 BOMIEL

#3 ESTAELT

#4 LBFAUOF

#5 MMEISPH

#6 TOPRANDL

MYSTERY ANSWER

Arrange the circled letters to solve the mystery answer.

PLANET EARTH

JUMBLE BrainBusters Junior

Unscramble the Jumbles, one letter to each square, to spell words related to Planet Earth.

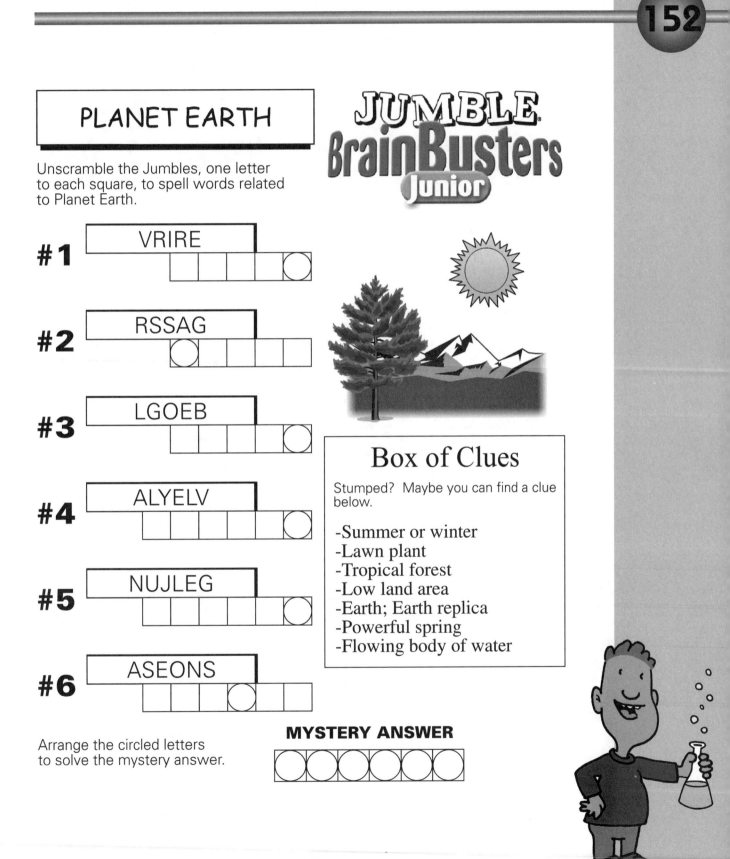

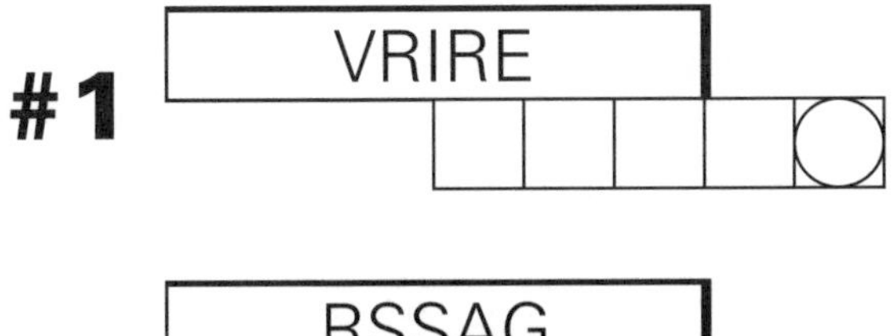

#2

#3

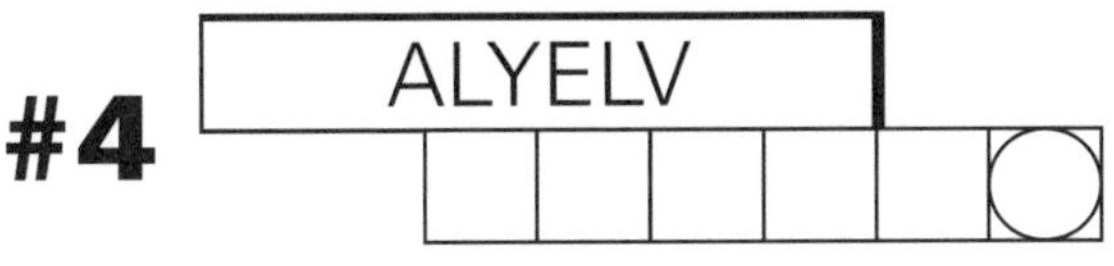

#4

#5

#6

Box of Clues

Stumped? Maybe you can find a clue below.

- -Summer or winter
- -Lawn plant
- -Tropical forest
- -Low land area
- -Earth; Earth replica
- -Powerful spring
- -Flowing body of water

Arrange the circled letters to solve the mystery answer.

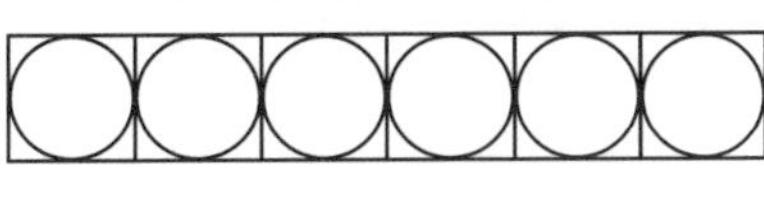

PUZZLE

153

STARTS WITH "Y"

Unscramble the Jumbles, one letter to each square, to spell words that start with "Y."

#1
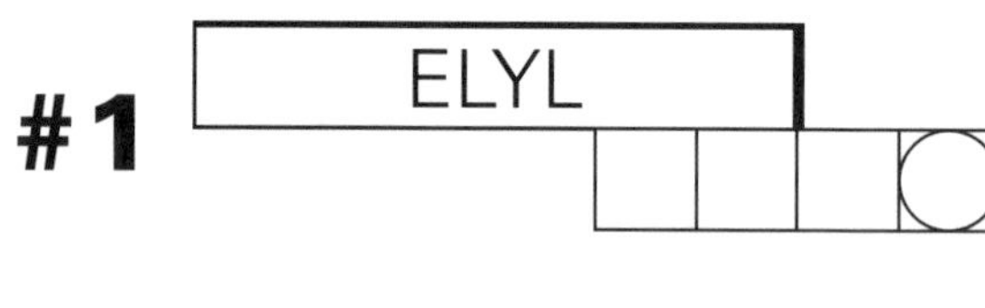

#2

#3

#4

#5
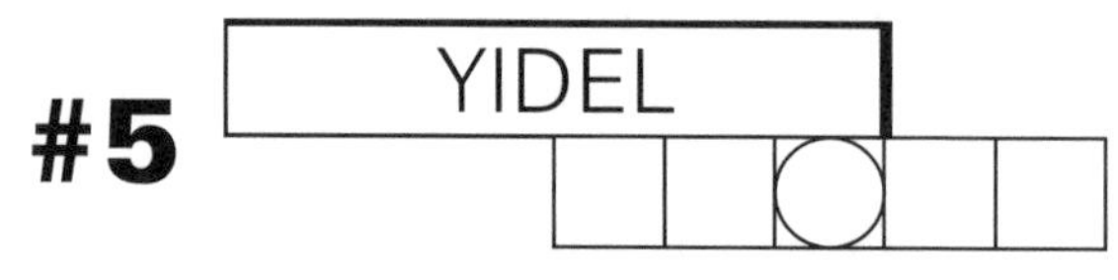

#6

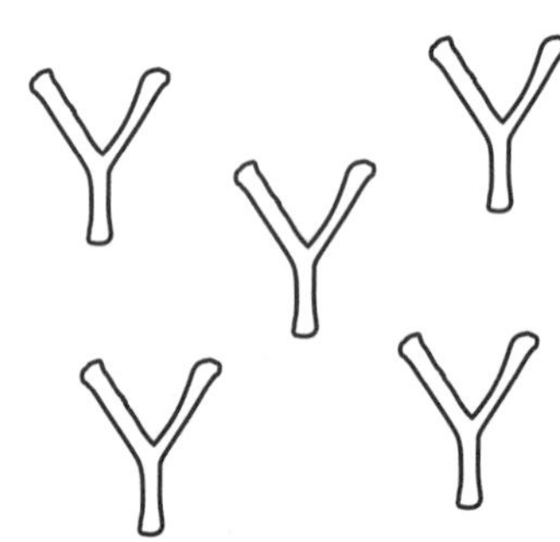

Box of Clues

Stumped? Maybe you can find a clue below.

-Tired mouth action
-Egg center
-Youngster
-Give way, concede
-Type of mental and physical exercise
-Light color
-Scream

Arrange the circled letters to solve the mystery answer.

MYSTERY ANSWER

SOUTH AMERICA

JUMBLE BrainBusters Junior

Unscramble the Jumbles, one letter to each square, to spell words related to South America.

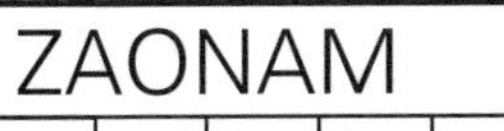

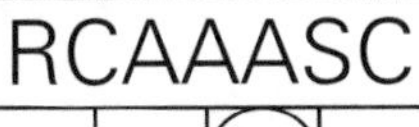

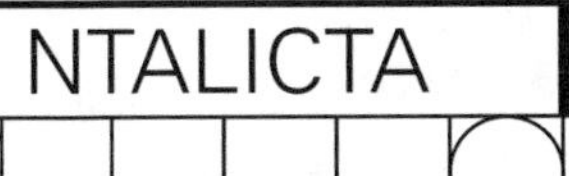

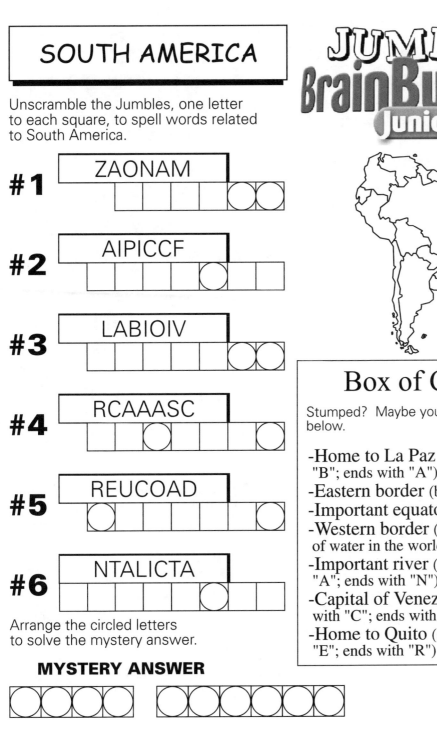

Arrange the circled letters to solve the mystery answer.

MYSTERY ANSWER

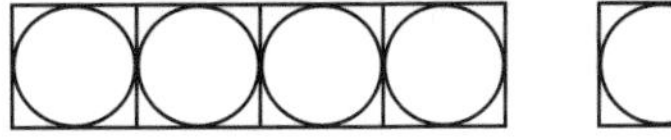
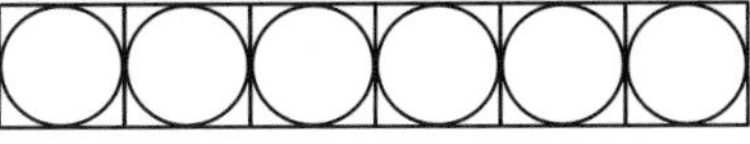

Box of Clues

Stumped? Maybe you can find a clue below.

-Home to La Paz (starts with "B"; ends with "A")
-Eastern border (body of water)
-Important equatorial region
-Western border (largest body of water in the world)
-Important river (starts with "A"; ends with "N")
-Capital of Venezuela (starts with "C"; ends with "S")
-Home to Quito (starts with "E"; ends with "R")

PUZZLE

155

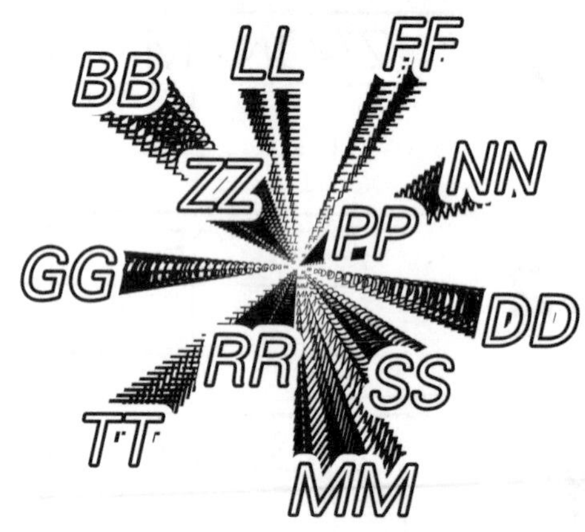

DOUBLE CONSONANTS

JUMBLE BrainBusters Junior

Unscramble the Jumbles, one letter to each square, to spell words that contain double consonants.

#1 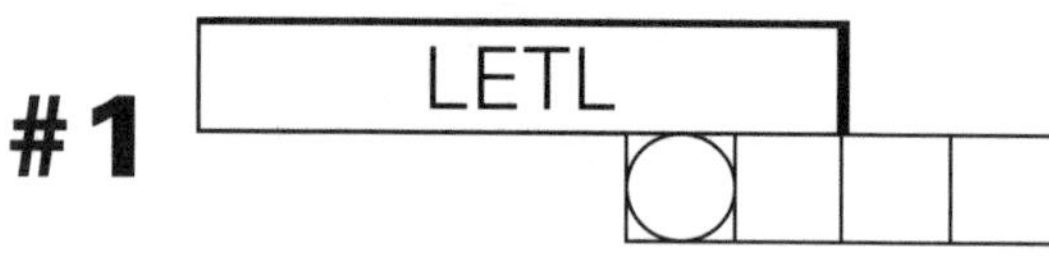

#2 

#3 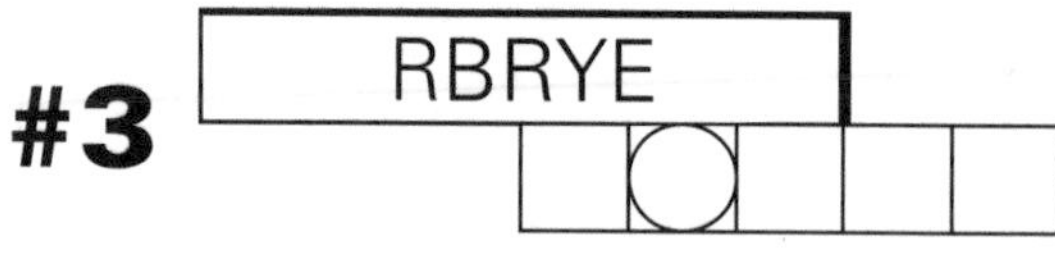

#4 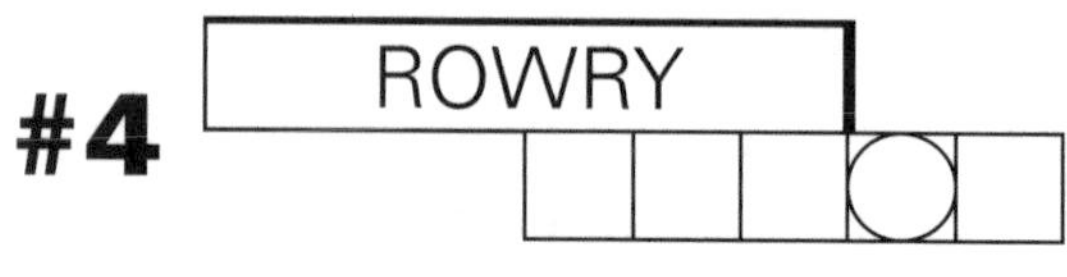

#5 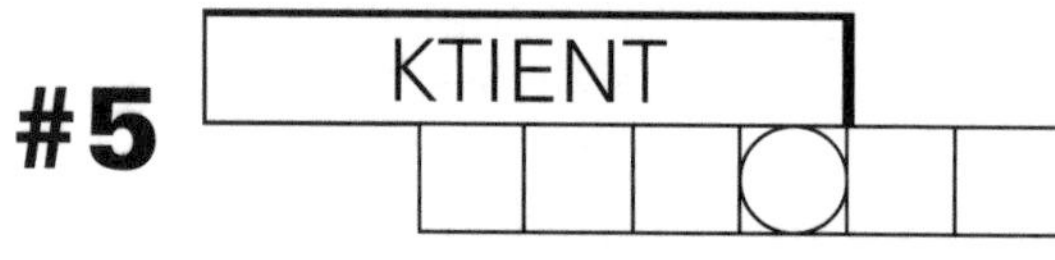

#6 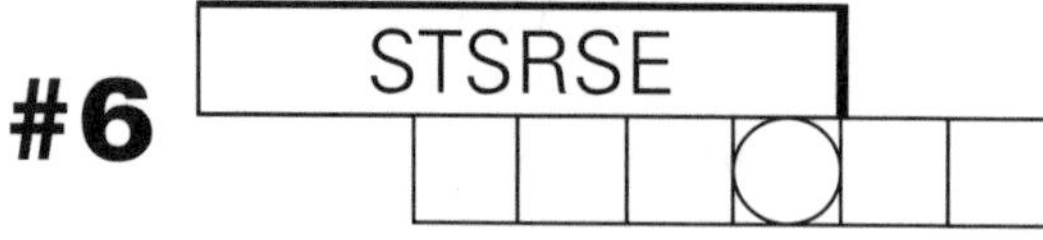

Box of Clues

Stumped? Maybe you can find a clue below.

-Young feline (cat)
-Bowling ______
-Small pulpy fruit
-Tension
-Improved
-Reveal, make known
-Fret, feel concern

Arrange the circled letters to solve the mystery answer.

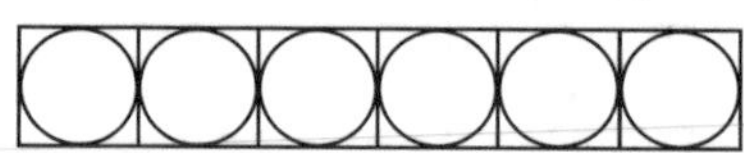

PUZZLE

156

FOOD

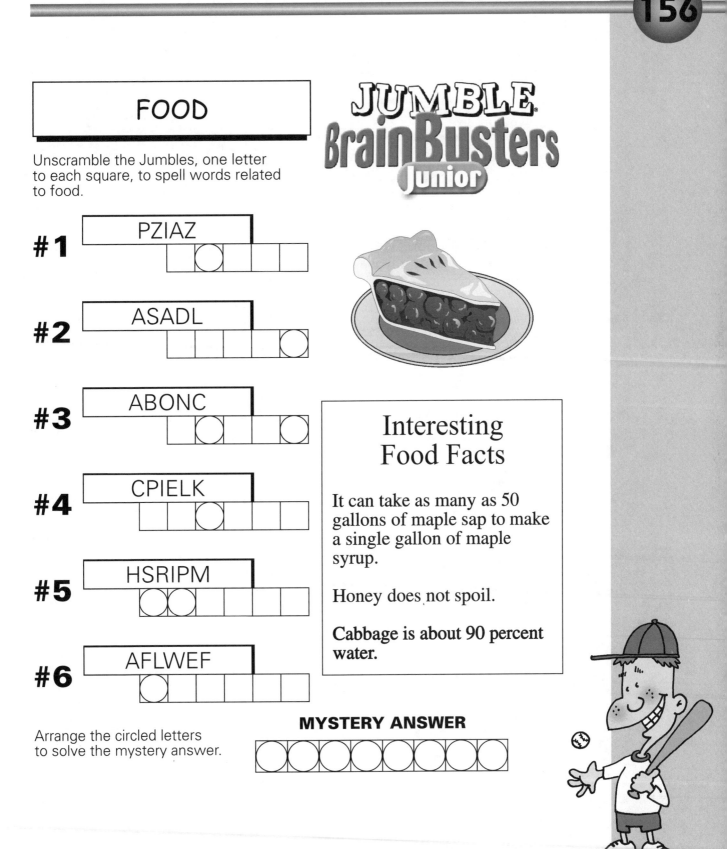

Unscramble the Jumbles, one letter to each square, to spell words related to food.

#1

#2
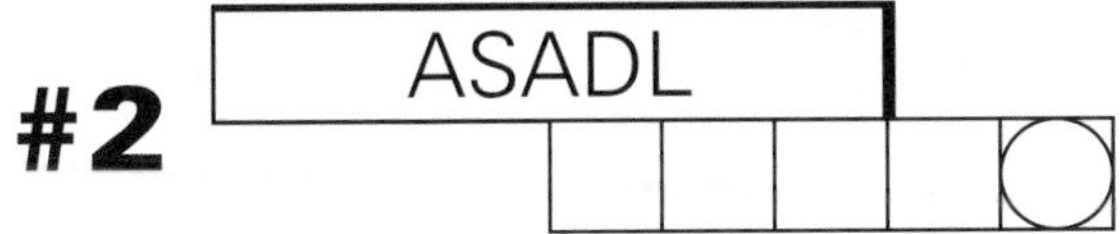

#3
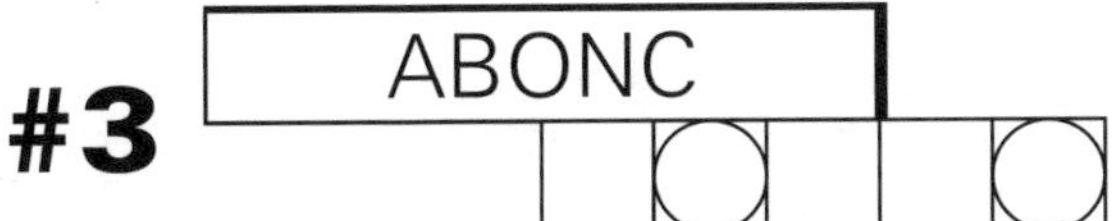

#4
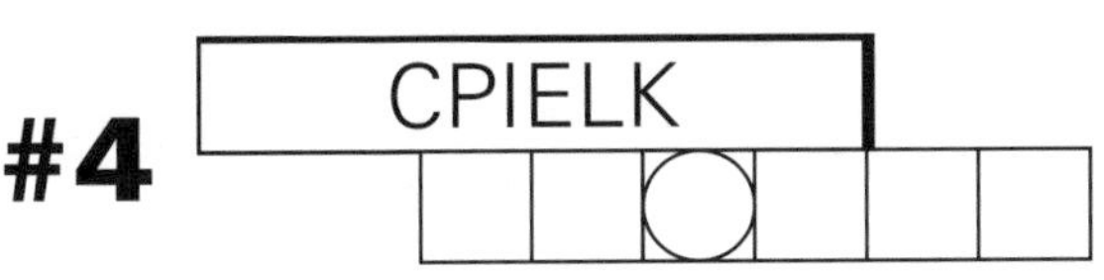

#5

#6

Interesting Food Facts

It can take as many as 50 gallons of maple sap to make a single gallon of maple syrup.

Honey does not spoil.

Cabbage is about 90 percent water.

MYSTERY ANSWER

Arrange the circled letters to solve the mystery answer.

PUZZLE

157

TIME LINE

Unscramble the Jumbles, one letter to each square, to spell words as suggested by the time line.

#1 **1768** James Cook makes his first voyage to the ______

#1 APIFCIC

#2 **1781** William Herschel discovers ______ (planet)

#2 RUNUSA

#3 **1812** Napoleon Bonaparte invades ______

#3 USIASR

#4 **1841** British annex New ______

#4 LEZAADN

#5 **1927** Lindbergh crosses the ______ in an airplane

#5 LATATICN

#6 **1982** ______ disc introduced

#6 MCOACTP

Arrange the circled letters to solve the mystery answer.

1914 ______ ______ opens

MYSTERY ANSWER

U.S. STATES

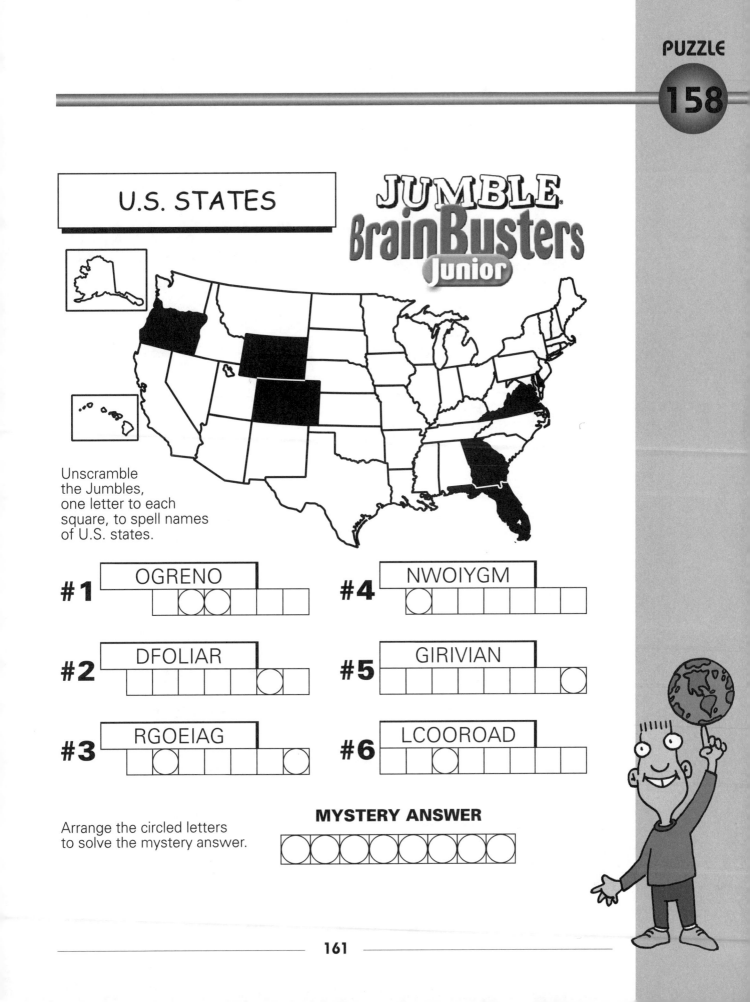

JUMBLE BrainBusters Junior

Unscramble the Jumbles, one letter to each square, to spell names of U.S. states.

#1 OGRENO

#2 DFOLIAR

#3 RGOEIAG

#4 NWOIYGM

#5 GIRIVIAN

#6 LCOOROAD

Arrange the circled letters to solve the mystery answer.

MYSTERY ANSWER

PUZZLE

159

THE HUMAN BODY

Jumble BrainBusters Junior

Unscramble the Jumbles, one letter to each square, to spell words related to the human body.

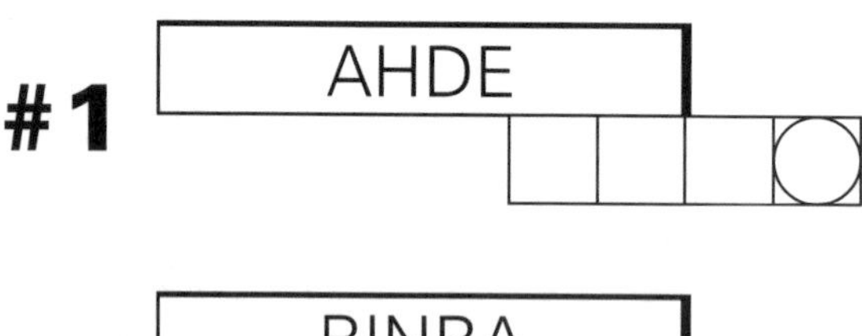

#1

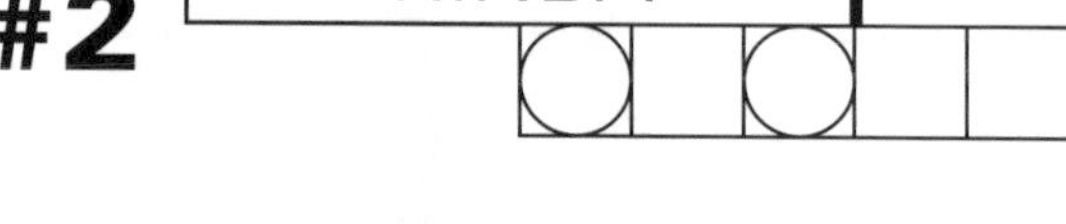

#2

#3

#4

#5

#6

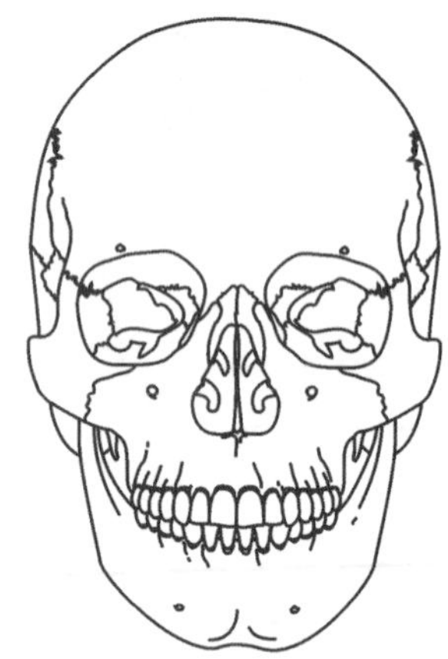

Box of Clues

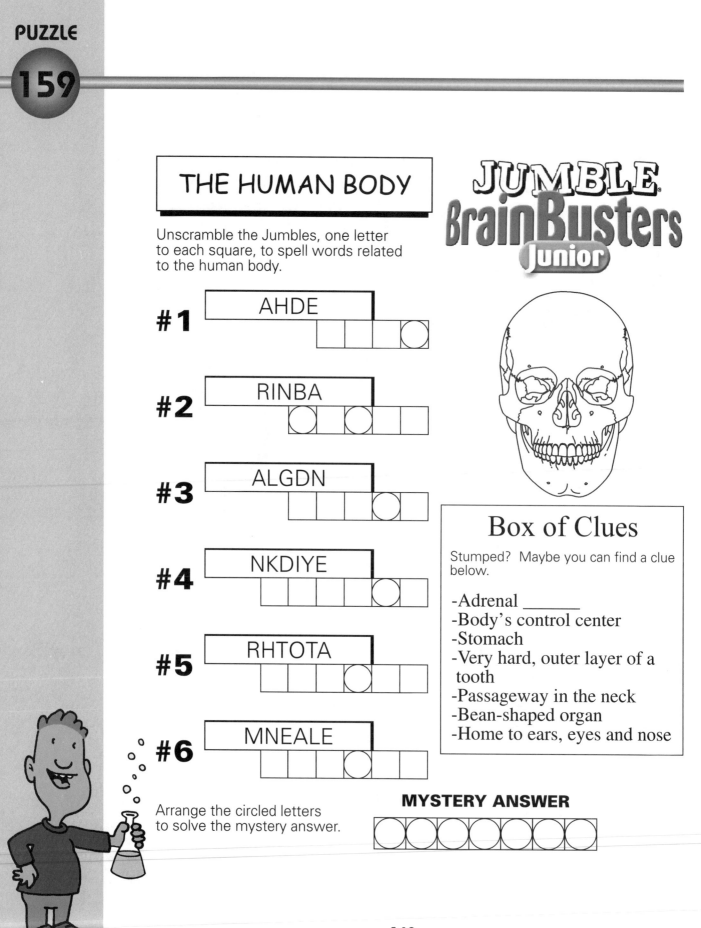

Stumped? Maybe you can find a clue below.

- -Adrenal ______
- -Body's control center
- -Stomach
- -Very hard, outer layer of a tooth
- -Passageway in the neck
- -Bean-shaped organ
- -Home to ears, eyes and nose

Arrange the circled letters to solve the mystery answer.

MYSTERY ANSWER

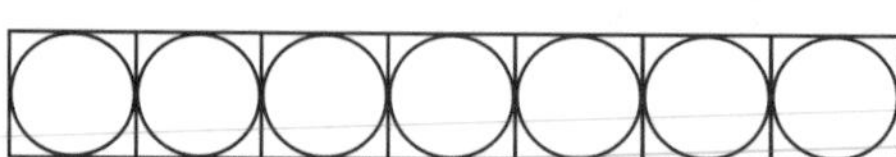

COUNTRIES

JUMBLE BrainBusters Junior

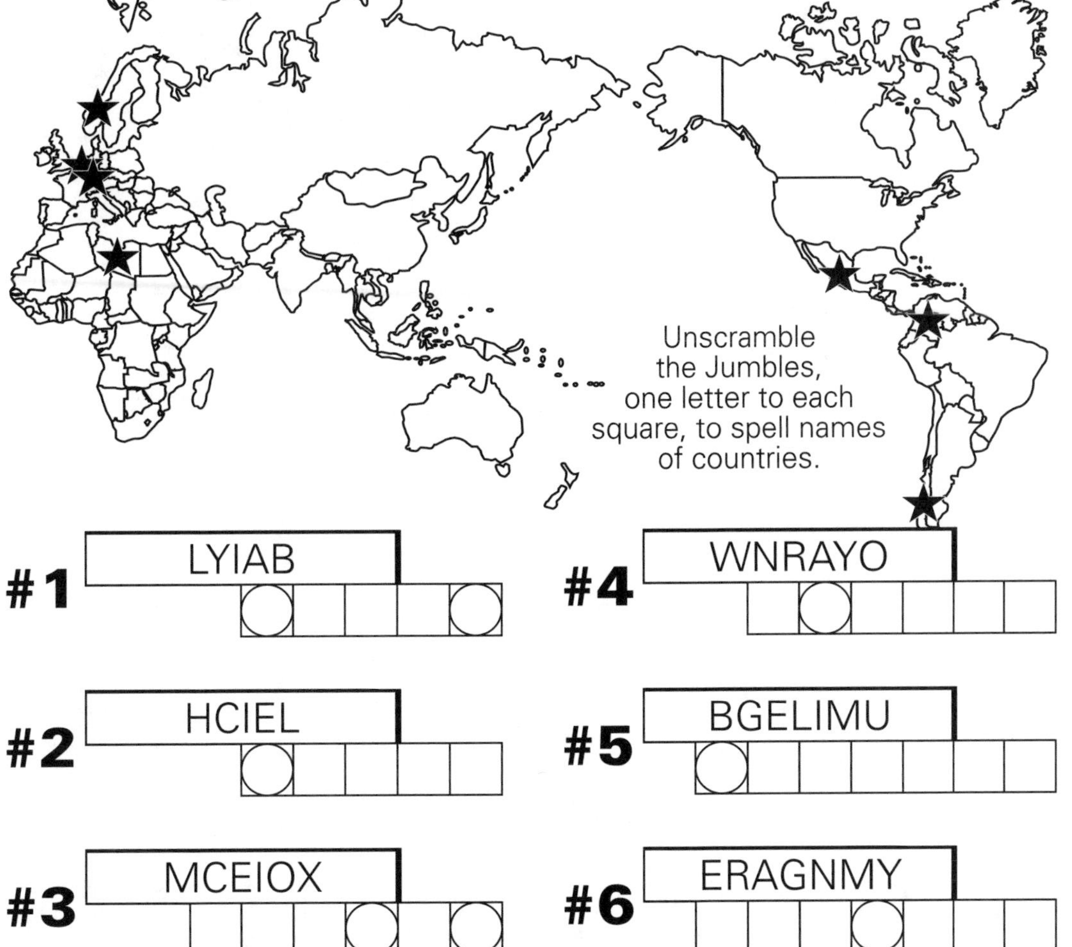

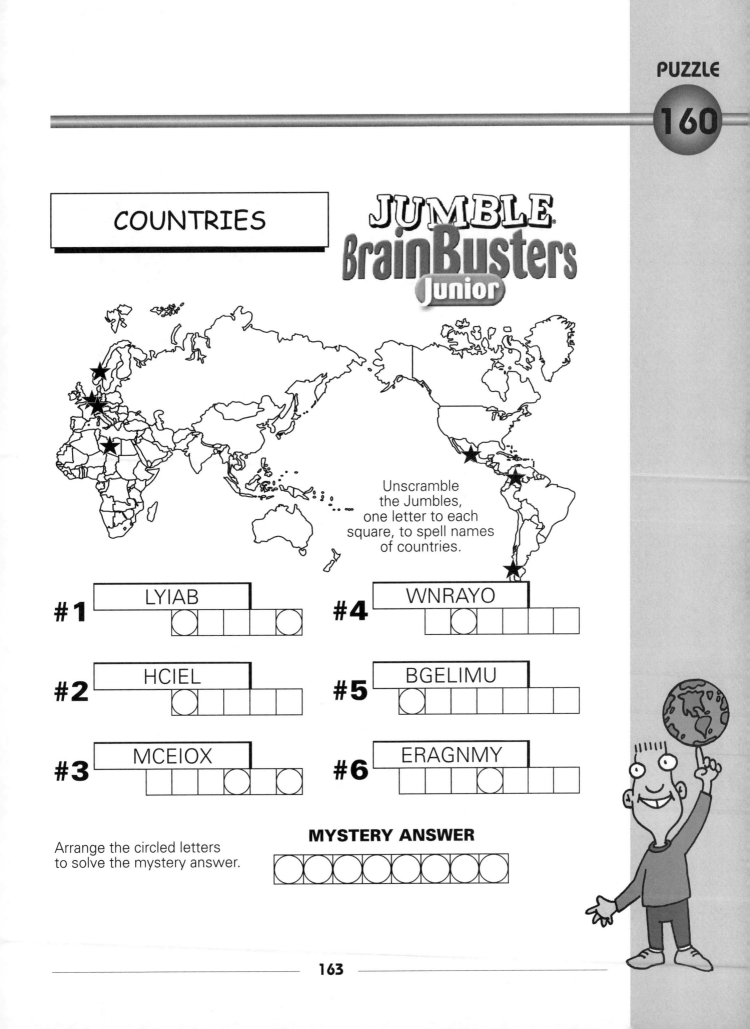

Unscramble the Jumbles, one letter to each square, to spell names of countries.

#1 LYIAB

#2 HCIEL

#3 MCEIOX

#4 WNRAYO

#5 BGELIMU

#6 ERAGNMY

MYSTERY ANSWER

Arrange the circled letters to solve the mystery answer.

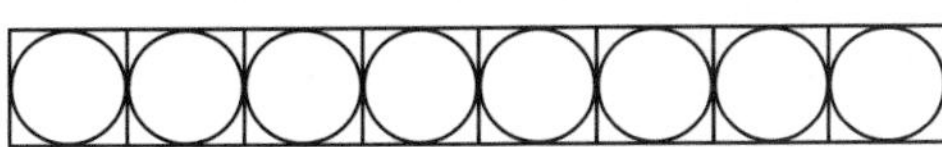

PUZZLE 161

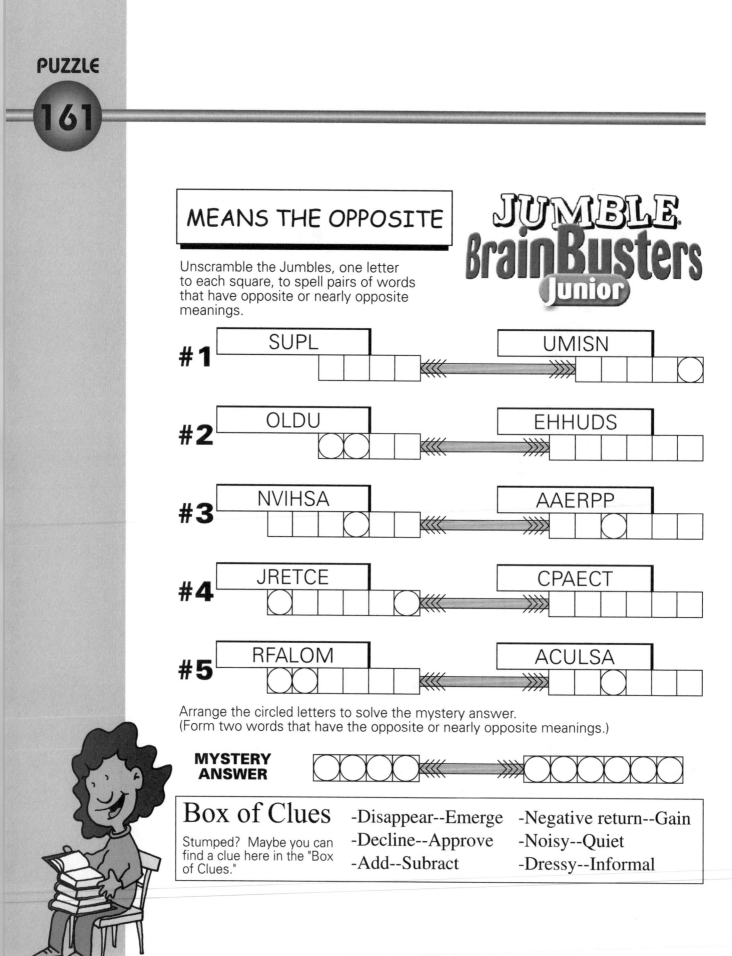

MEANS THE OPPOSITE

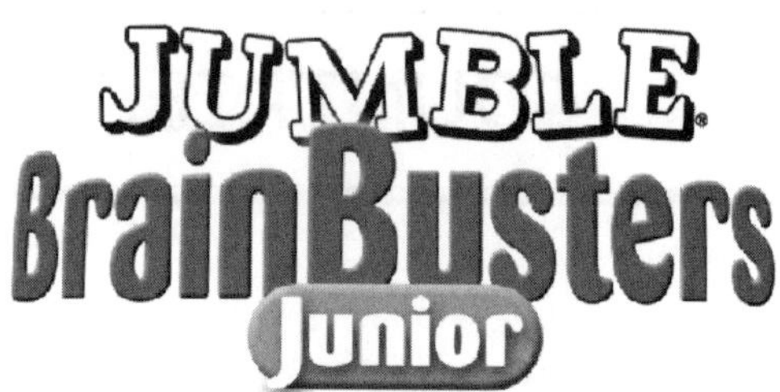

Unscramble the Jumbles, one letter to each square, to spell pairs of words that have opposite or nearly opposite meanings.

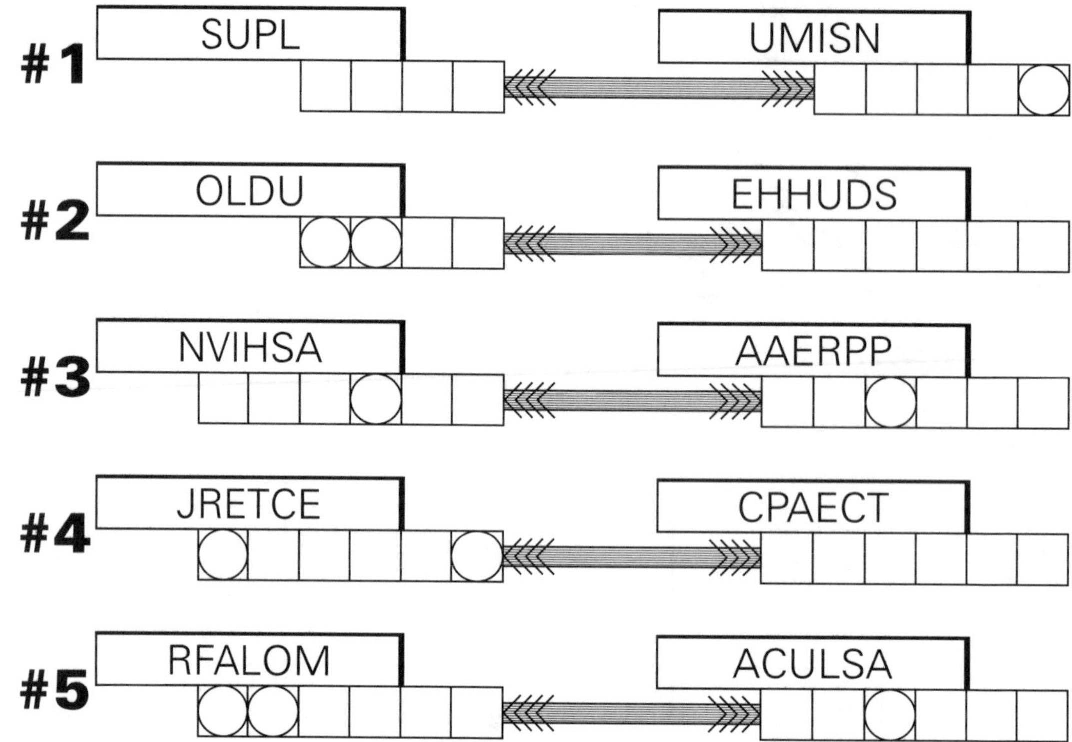

Arrange the circled letters to solve the mystery answer.
(Form two words that have the opposite or nearly opposite meanings.)

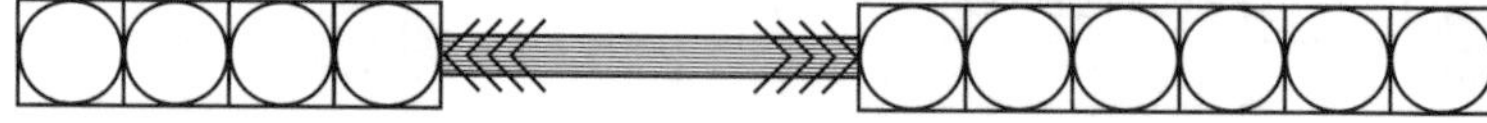

Box of Clues

Stumped? Maybe you can find a clue here in the "Box of Clues."

-Disappear--Emerge
-Decline--Approve
-Add--Subract
-Negative return--Gain
-Noisy--Quiet
-Dressy--Informal

EUROPEAN COUNTRIES

JUMBLE BrainBusters Junior

Unscramble the Jumbles, one letter to each square, to spell names of European countries.

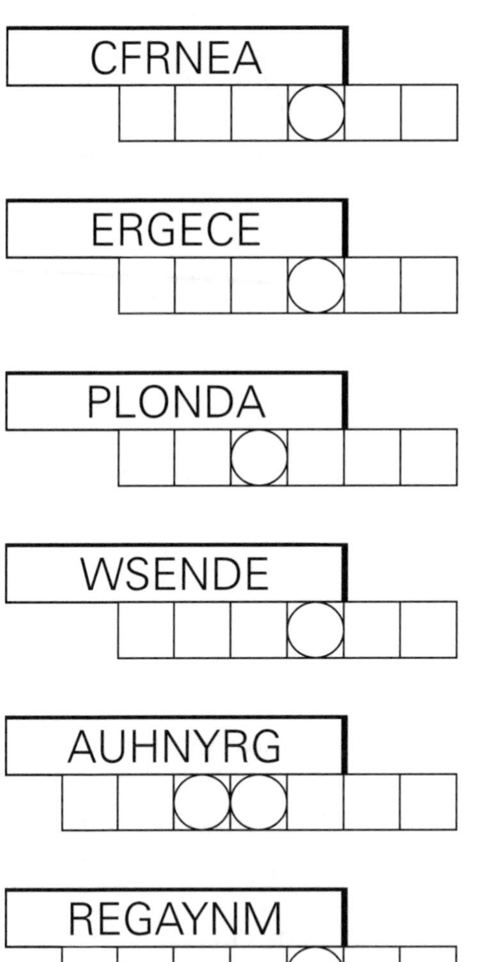

Box of Clues

Stumped? Maybe you can find a clue below.

-Starts with "P"; ends with "D"
-Starts with "G"; ends with "Y"
-Starts with "F"; ends with "E"
-Starts with "E"; ends with "D"
-Starts with "G"; ends with "E"
-Starts with "H"; ends with "Y"
-Starts with "S"; ends with "N"

MYSTERY ANSWER

Arrange the circled letters to solve the mystery answer.

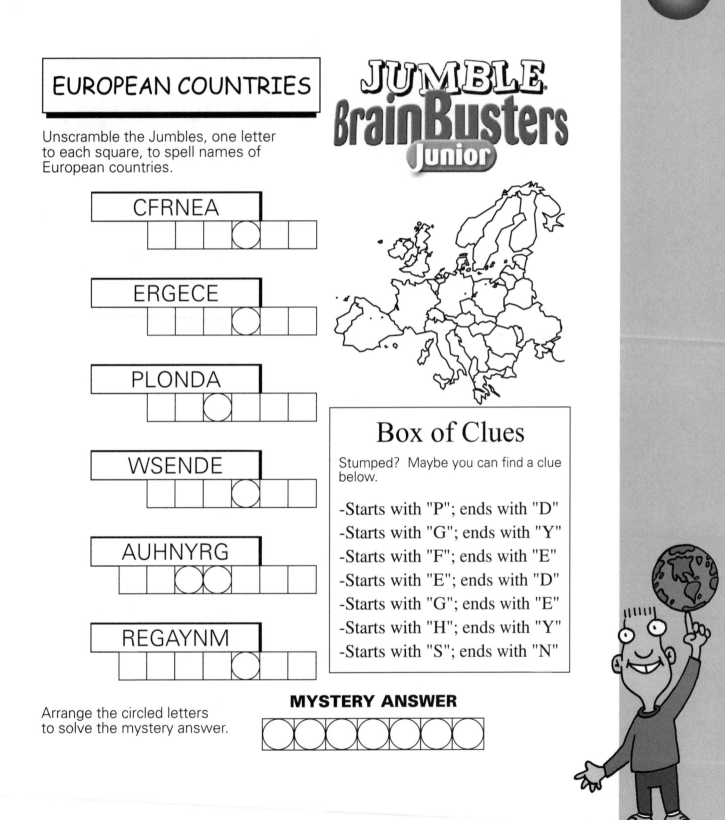

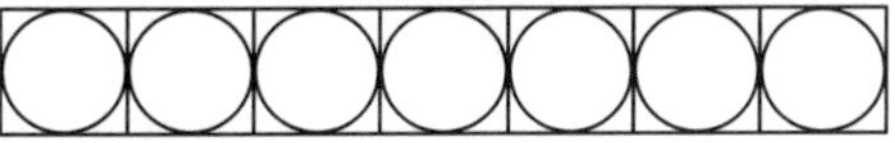

PUZZLE

163

DOGS

Unscramble the Jumbles, one letter to each square, to spell names of dogs.

#1 SUKHY

#2 BERXO

#3 PSAIELN

#4 LUBLOGD

#5 SPHEERDH

Box of Clues

Stumped? Maybe you can find a clue below.

-Cocker or springer ______
-Stocky, short-haired dog with square head
-Hunting dog with drooping ears
-Heavy-coated Arctic work dog
-Medium-sized dog of German origin (sounds like a fighter)
-German ______

Arrange the circled letters to solve the mystery answer.

MYSTERY ANSWER

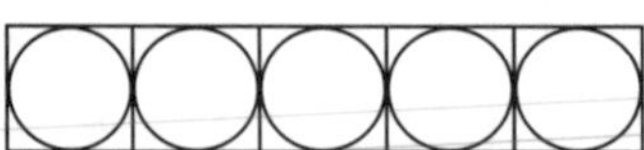

LARGE CITIES

Unscramble the Jumbles, one letter to each square, to spell names of large cities.

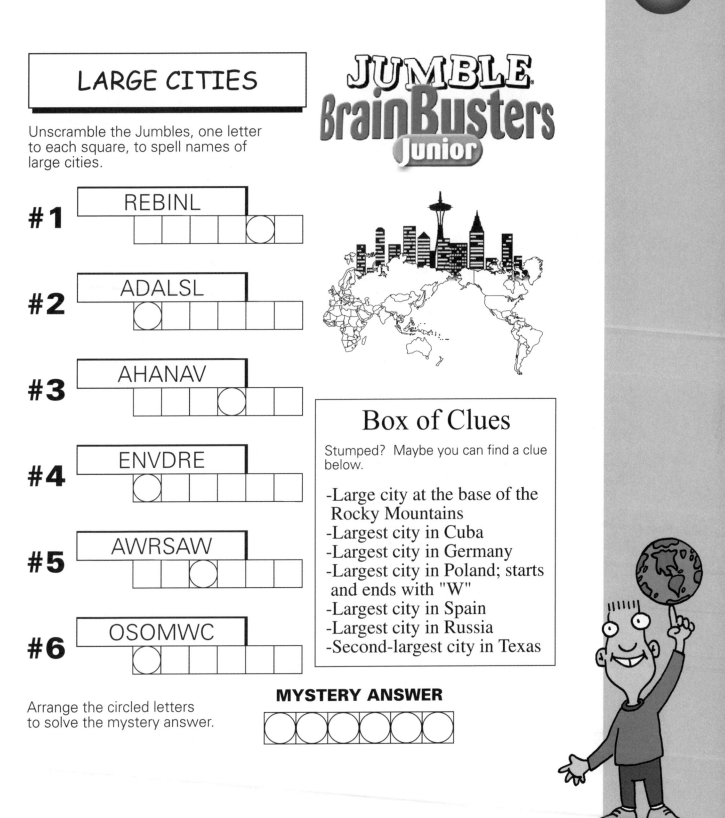

#1

#2

#3

#4

#5

#6
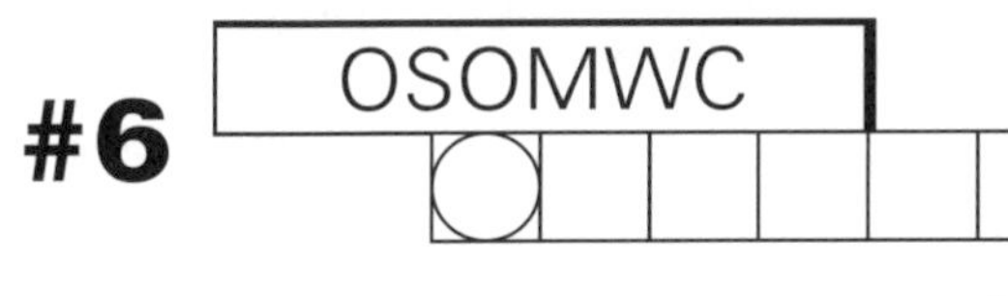

Box of Clues

Stumped? Maybe you can find a clue below.

- -Large city at the base of the Rocky Mountains
- -Largest city in Cuba
- -Largest city in Germany
- -Largest city in Poland; starts and ends with "W"
- -Largest city in Spain
- -Largest city in Russia
- -Second-largest city in Texas

Arrange the circled letters to solve the mystery answer.

MYSTERY ANSWER

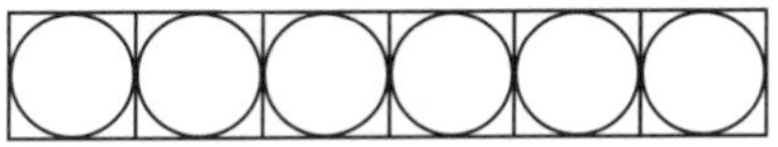

PUZZLE 165

OUTER SPACE

Unscramble the Jumbles, one letter to each square, to spell words related to outer space.

#1 GLITH

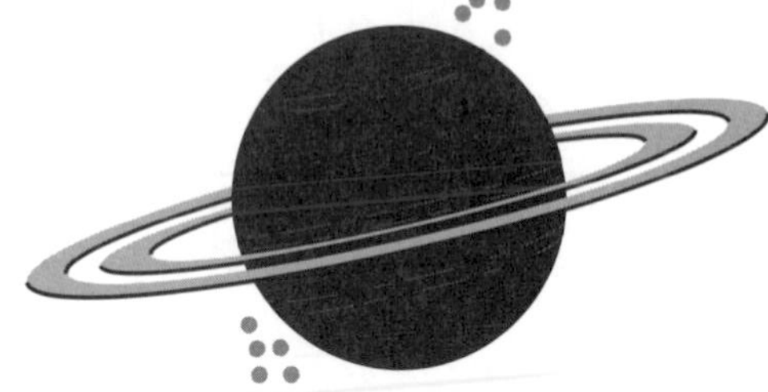

#2

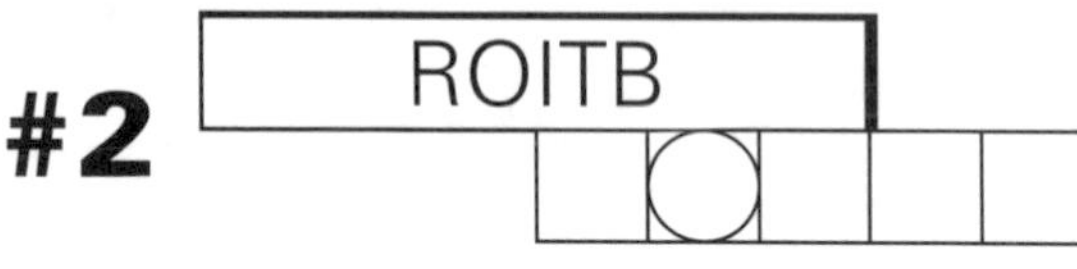

#3

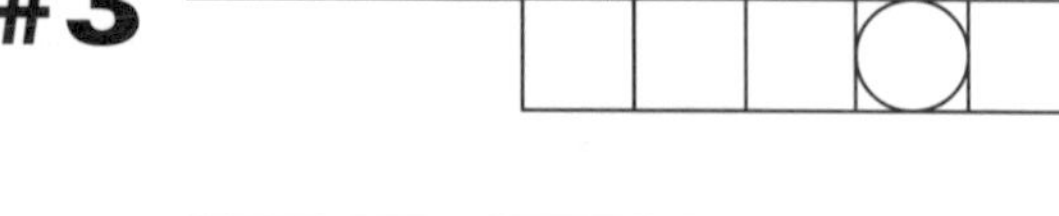

#4

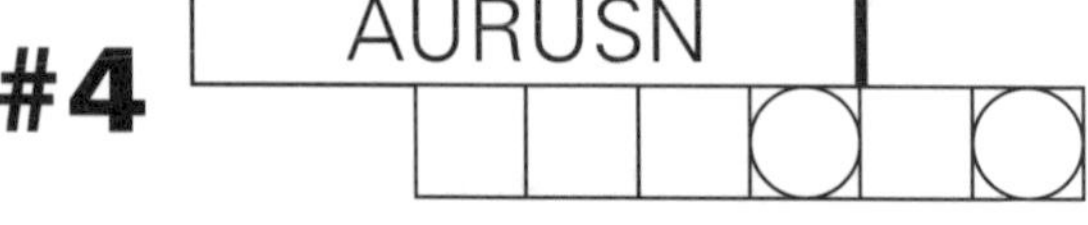

#5

#6

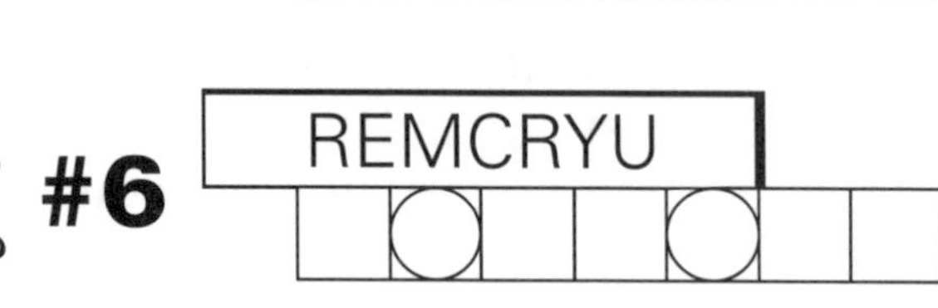

Stumped? Maybe you can find a clue below.

-Halley's ______
-Universal attractive force
-Star's bright output
-Moon motion
-Cosmos
-Home to the moon Miranda
-Closest planet to the sun

Arrange the circled letters to solve the mystery answer.

MYSTERY ANSWER

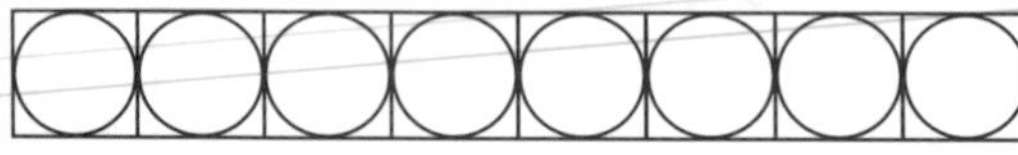

PUZZLE 166

COUNTRIES

Unscramble the Jumbles, one letter to each square, to spell names of countries.

#1 NEKYA

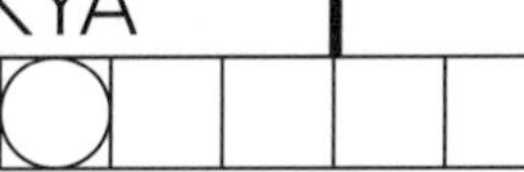

#2 PGEYT

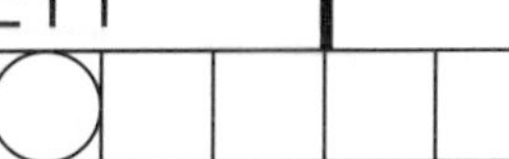

#3 RNACFE

#4 EAUDCOR

#5 TIEVNMA

#6 OMCROOC

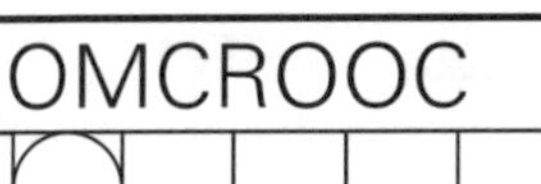

Box of Clues

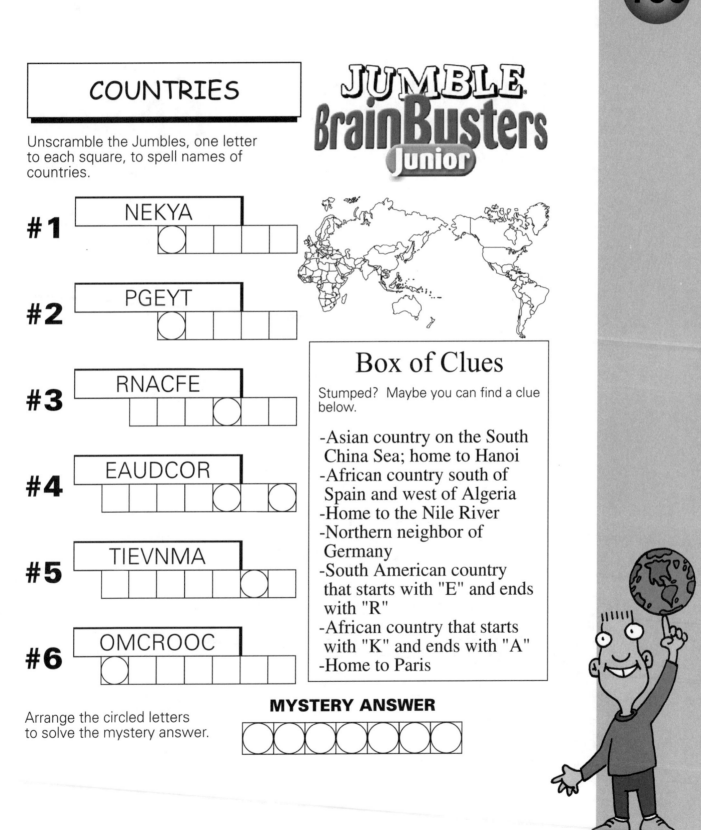

Stumped? Maybe you can find a clue below.

- Asian country on the South China Sea; home to Hanoi
- African country south of Spain and west of Algeria
- Home to the Nile River
- Northern neighbor of Germany
- South American country that starts with "E" and ends with "R"
- African country that starts with "K" and ends with "A"
- Home to Paris

MYSTERY ANSWER

Arrange the circled letters to solve the mystery answer.

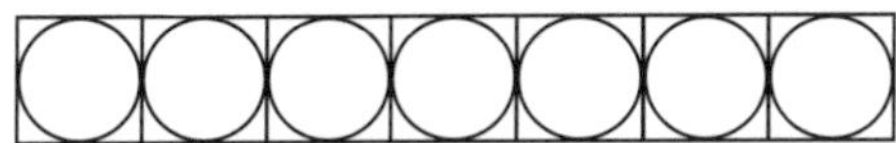

PUZZLE 167

MEANS THE SAME

JUMBLE BrainBusters Junior

Unscramble the Jumbles, one letter to each square, to spell pairs of words that have the same or similar meanings.

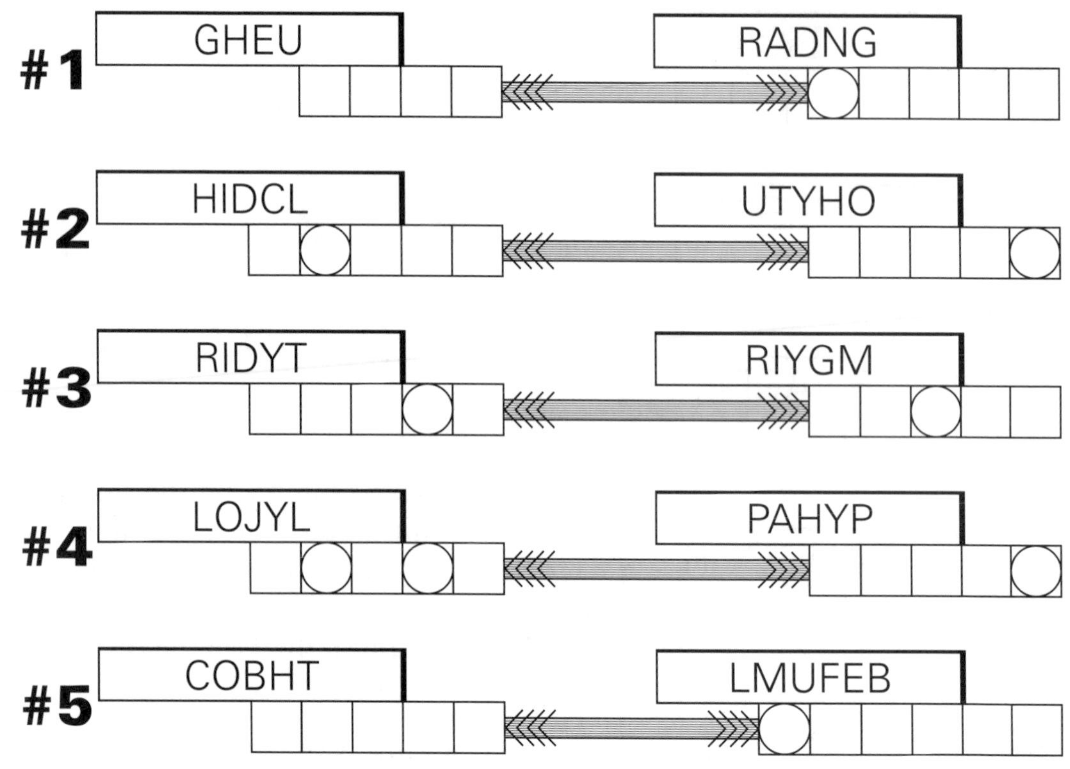

Arrange the circled letters to solve the mystery answer.
(Form two words that have the same or similar meanings.)

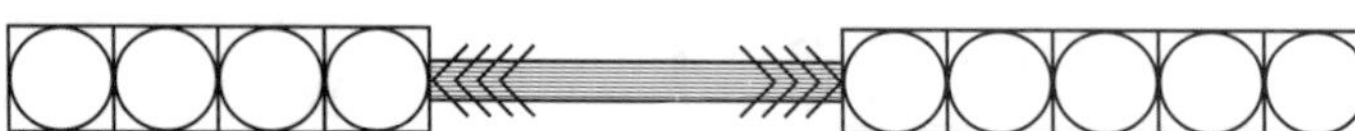

Box of Clues

Stumped? Maybe you can find a clue here in the "Box of Clues."

- -Filthy
- -Young person
- -Joyous
- -Blunder
- -Way up in the air
- -Big, majestic

SPORTS

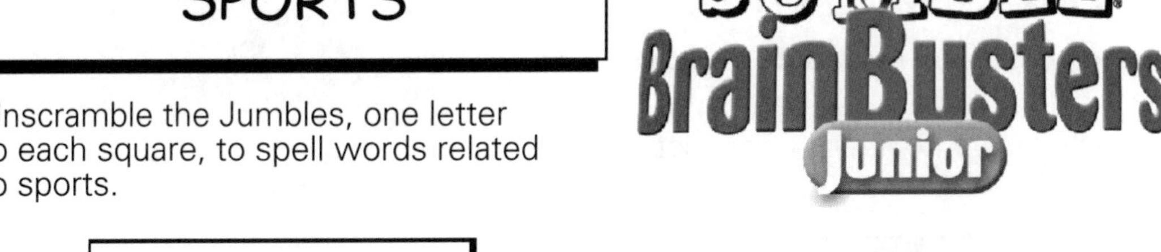

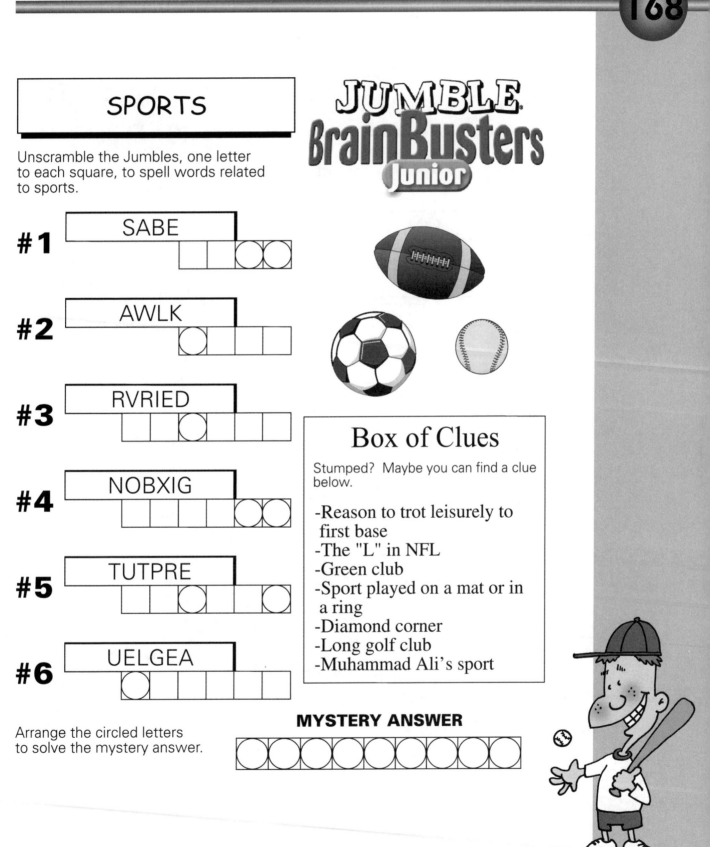

Unscramble the Jumbles, one letter to each square, to spell words related to sports.

#1
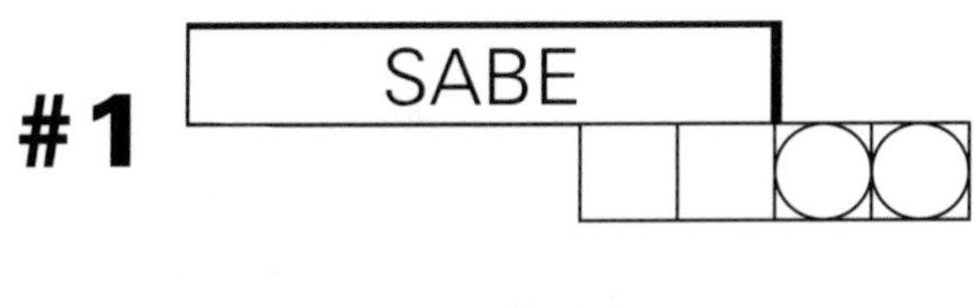

#2

#3

#4
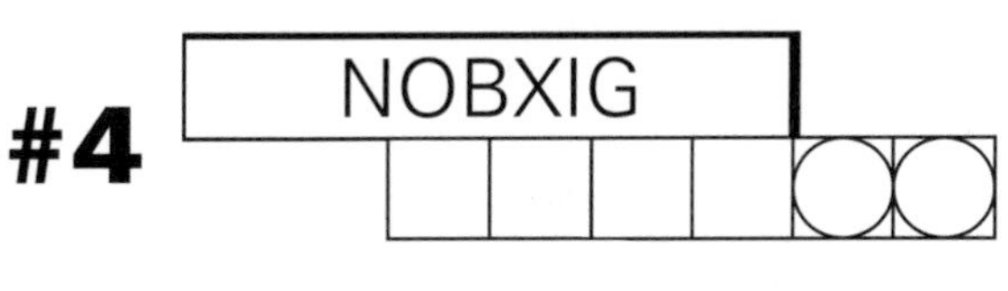

#5

#6

Box of Clues

Stumped? Maybe you can find a clue below.

- -Reason to trot leisurely to first base
- -The "L" in NFL
- -Green club
- -Sport played on a mat or in a ring
- -Diamond corner
- -Long golf club
- -Muhammad Ali's sport

MYSTERY ANSWER

Arrange the circled letters to solve the mystery answer.

PUZZLE 169

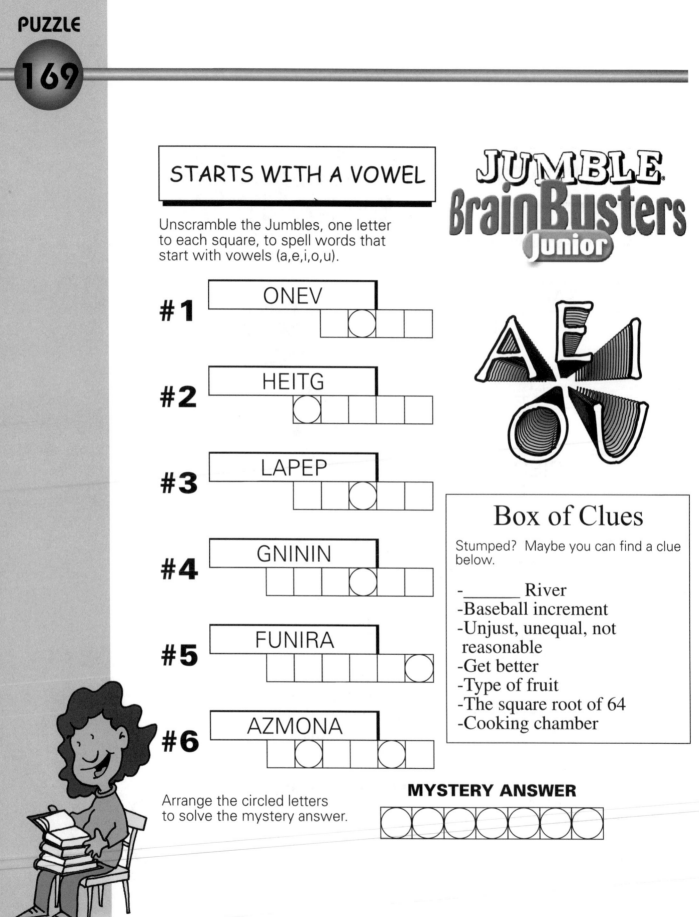

STARTS WITH A VOWEL

Unscramble the Jumbles, one letter to each square, to spell words that start with vowels (a,e,i,o,u).

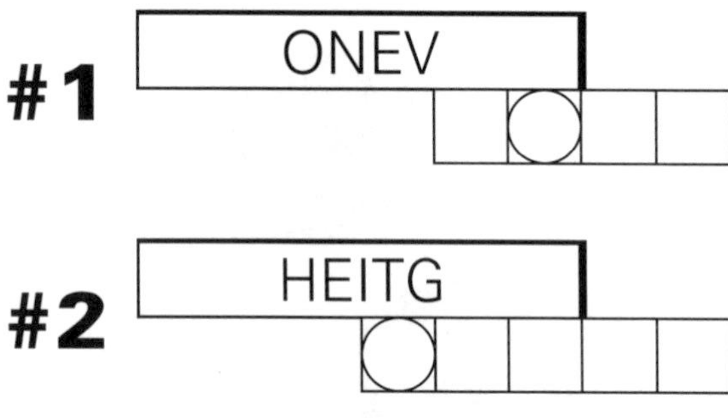

#1 ONEV

#2 HEITG

#3 LAPEP

#4 GNININ

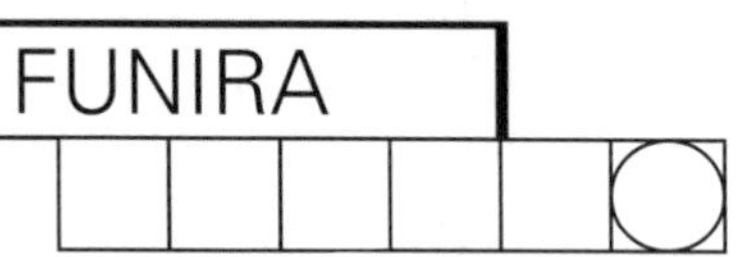

#5 FUNIRA

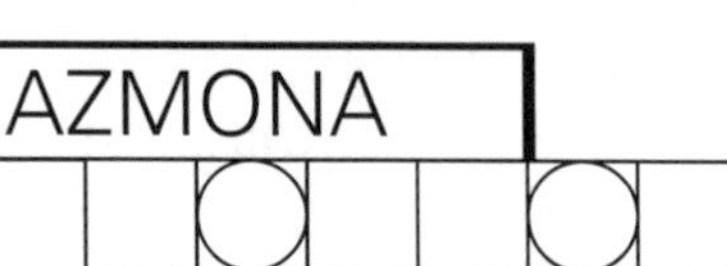

#6 AZMONA

Box of Clues

Stumped? Maybe you can find a clue below.

-______ River
-Baseball increment
-Unjust, unequal, not reasonable
-Get better
-Type of fruit
-The square root of 64
-Cooking chamber

Arrange the circled letters to solve the mystery answer.

MYSTERY ANSWER

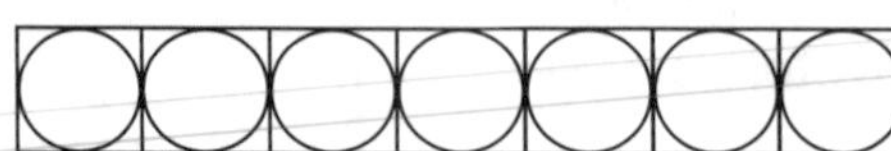

JUMBLE BrainBusters Junior

BIRDS

Unscramble the Jumbles, one letter to each square, to spell names of birds.

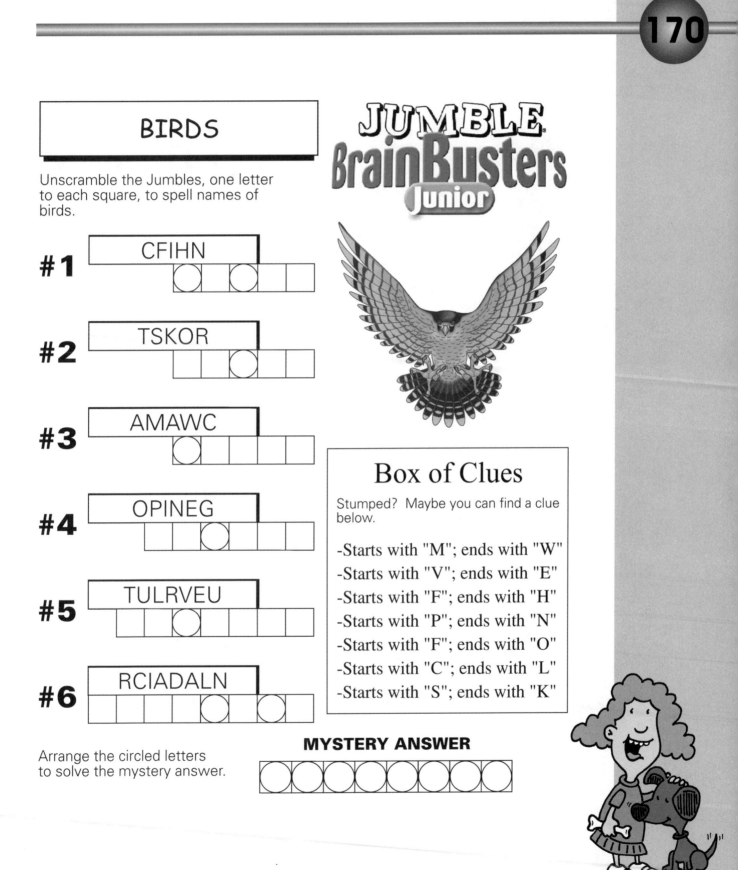

#1

#2

#3

#4

#5

#6

RCIADALN

Box of Clues

Stumped? Maybe you can find a clue below.

-Starts with "M"; ends with "W"
-Starts with "V"; ends with "E"
-Starts with "F"; ends with "H"
-Starts with "P"; ends with "N"
-Starts with "F"; ends with "O"
-Starts with "C"; ends with "L"
-Starts with "S"; ends with "K"

Arrange the circled letters to solve the mystery answer.

MYSTERY ANSWER

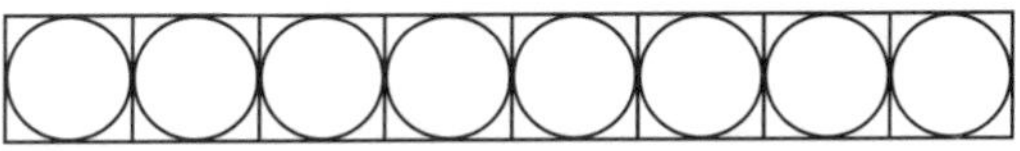

PUZZLE

171

ADVERBS

Unscramble the Jumbles, one letter to each square, to spell adverbs.

JUMBLE BrainBusters Junior

#1 LGALYD

#2 SOLYTF

#3 KEWELY

#4 RPDULYO

#5 TBIRLYHG

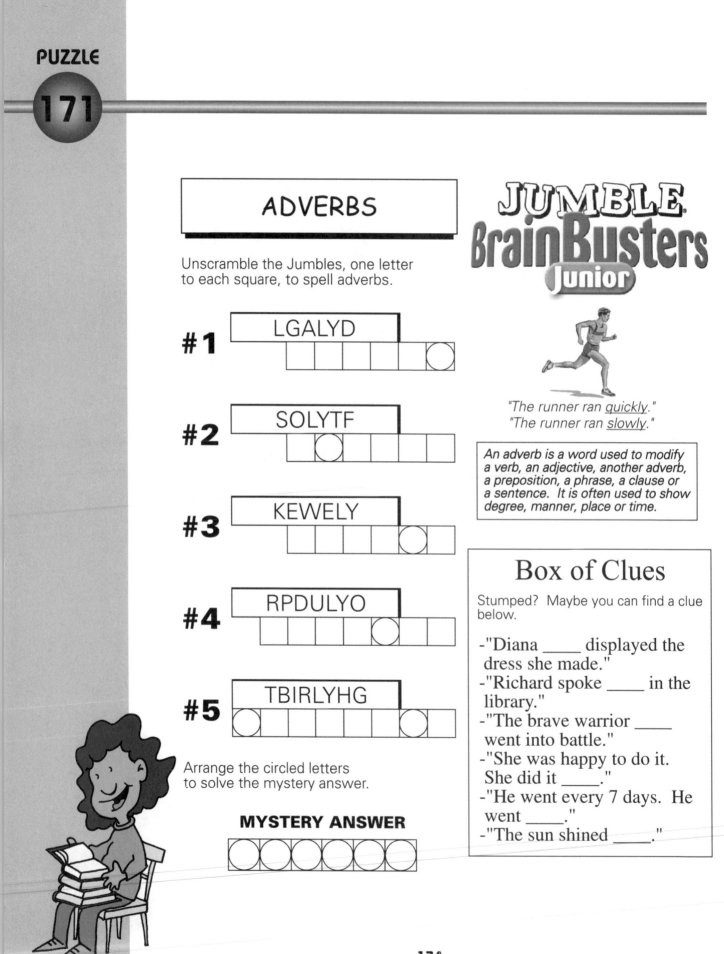

"The runner ran quickly."
"The runner ran slowly."

An adverb is a word used to modify a verb, an adjective, another adverb, a preposition, a phrase, a clause or a sentence. It is often used to show degree, manner, place or time.

Box of Clues

Stumped? Maybe you can find a clue below.

-"Diana ____ displayed the dress she made."
-"Richard spoke ____ in the library."
-"The brave warrior ____ went into battle."
-"She was happy to do it. She did it ____."
-"He went every 7 days. He went ____."
-"The sun shined ____."

Arrange the circled letters to solve the mystery answer.

MYSTERY ANSWER

ELEMENTS

JUMBLE BrainBusters Junior

An element is a fundamental substance consisting of atoms of only one kind that cannot be broken down into simpler substances.

Atomic #
Atomic Symbol

THE PERIODIC TABLE

1 H																	2 ★ He
3 Li	4 Be											5 B	6 C	7 ★ N	8 ★ O	9 F	10 Ne
11 ★ Na	12 Mg											13 Al	14 Si	15 P	16 ★ S	17 Cl	18 Ar
19 K	20 Ca	21 Sc	22 Ti	23 V	24 Cr	25 Mn	26 Fe	27 Co	28 Ni	29 Cu	30 Zn	31 Ga	32 Ge	33 As	34 Se	35 Br	36 Kr
37 Rb	38 Sr	39 Y	40 Zr	41 Nb	42 Mo	43 Tc	44 Ru	45 Rh	46 Pd	47 Ag	48 Cd	49 In	50 Sn	51 Sb	52 Te	53 ★ I	54 Xe
55 Cs	56 Ba	57-71 Lathanide series (rare earth elements)	72 Hf	73 Ta	74 W	75 Re	76 Os	77 Ir	78 Pt	79 Au	80 ★ Hg	81 Tl	82 Pb	83 Bi	84 Po	85 At	86 Rn
87 Fr	88 Ra	89-103 Actinide series (radioactive rare earth elements)	104 Unq	105 Unp	106 Unh	107 Uns		108 Une									

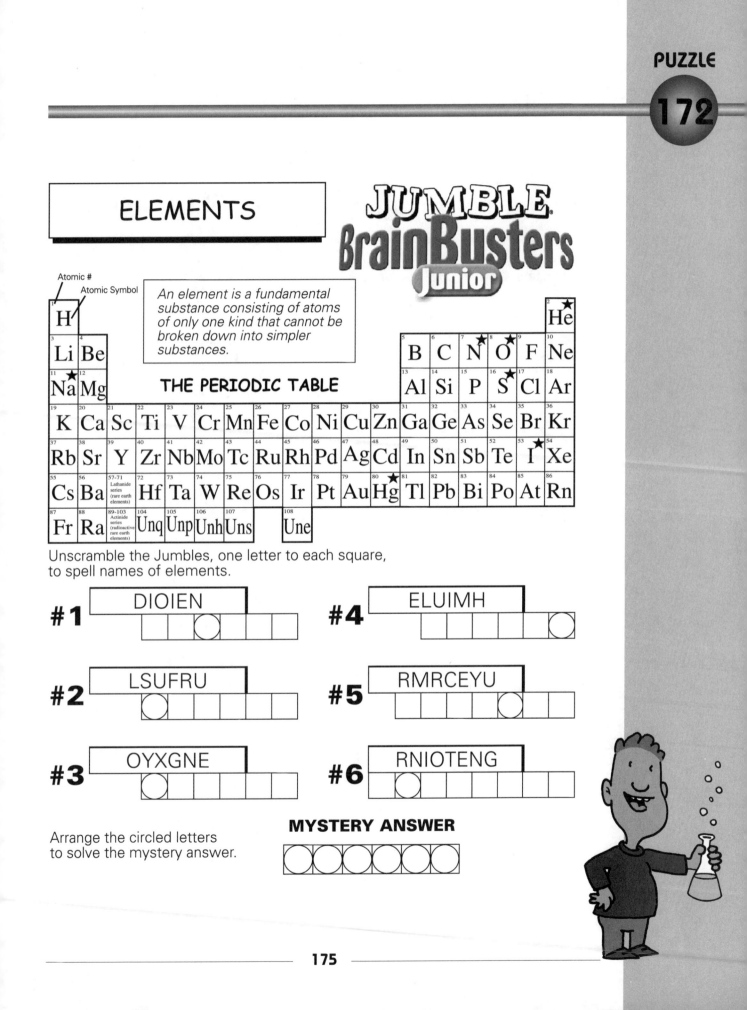

Unscramble the Jumbles, one letter to each square, to spell names of elements.

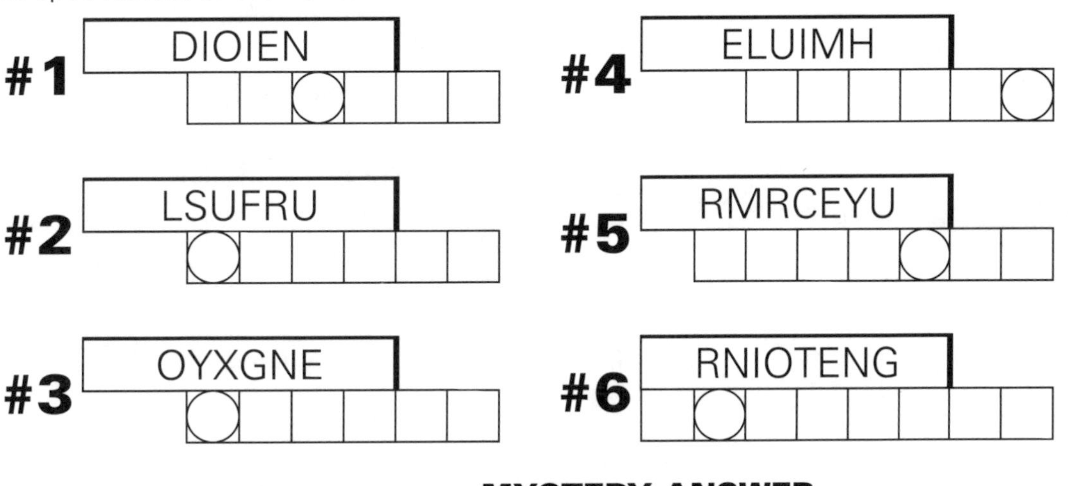

MYSTERY ANSWER

Arrange the circled letters to solve the mystery answer.

PUZZLE

173

U.S. PRESIDENTS

Unscramble the Jumbles, one letter to each square, to spell last names of U.S. presidents.

#1 FTAT

#2 DFRO

#3 ARNGT

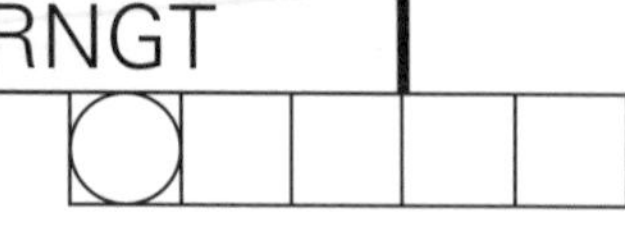

#4 OOHERV

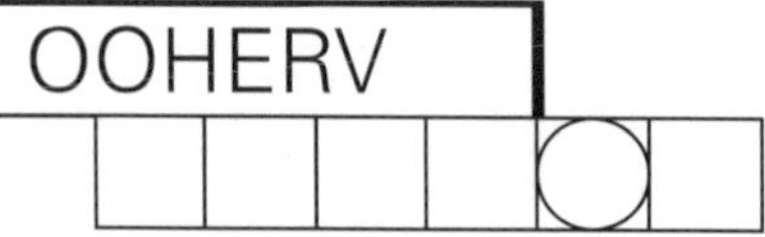

#5 NENDEKY

#6 KAOJSNC

Box of Clues

Stumped? Maybe you can find a clue below.

-President on the $50 bill
-William Howard ______
-40th U.S. president
-John F. ______
-38th U.S. president
-Andrew ______
-Herbert ______

Arrange the circled letters to solve the mystery answer.

MYSTERY ANSWER

ABBREVIATED WORDS

Unscramble the Jumbles, one letter to each square, to spell words that are often abbreviated.

#1 NSCEDO

#2 TAPCINA

#3 NJUARYA

#4 RFEEYWA

#5 MEDECREB

Arrange the circled letters to solve the mystery answer.

MYSTERY ANSWER

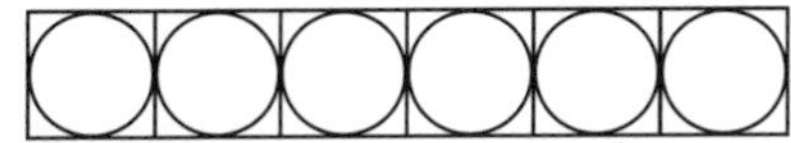

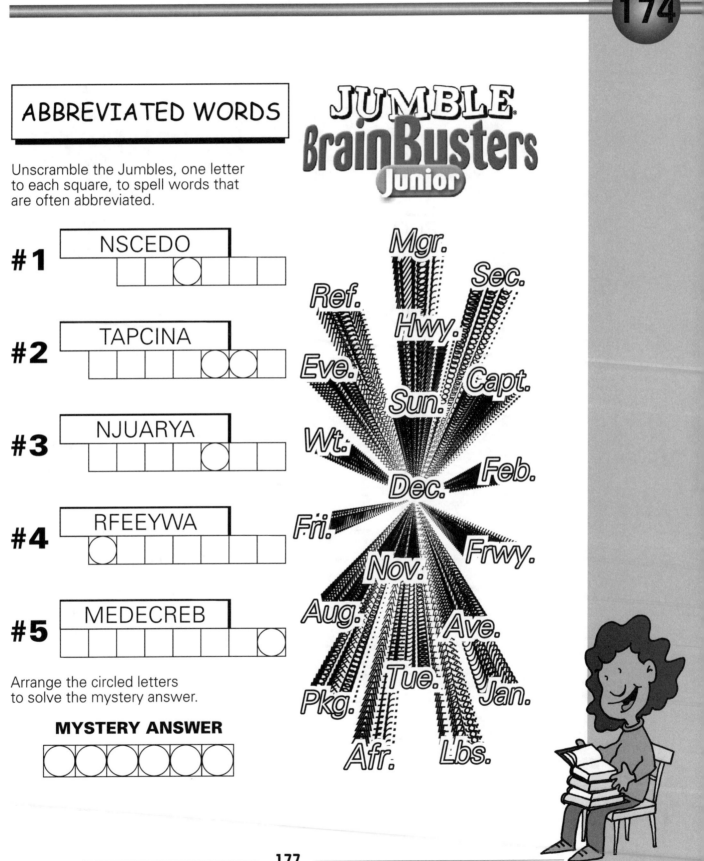

PUZZLE

175

OUTER SPACE

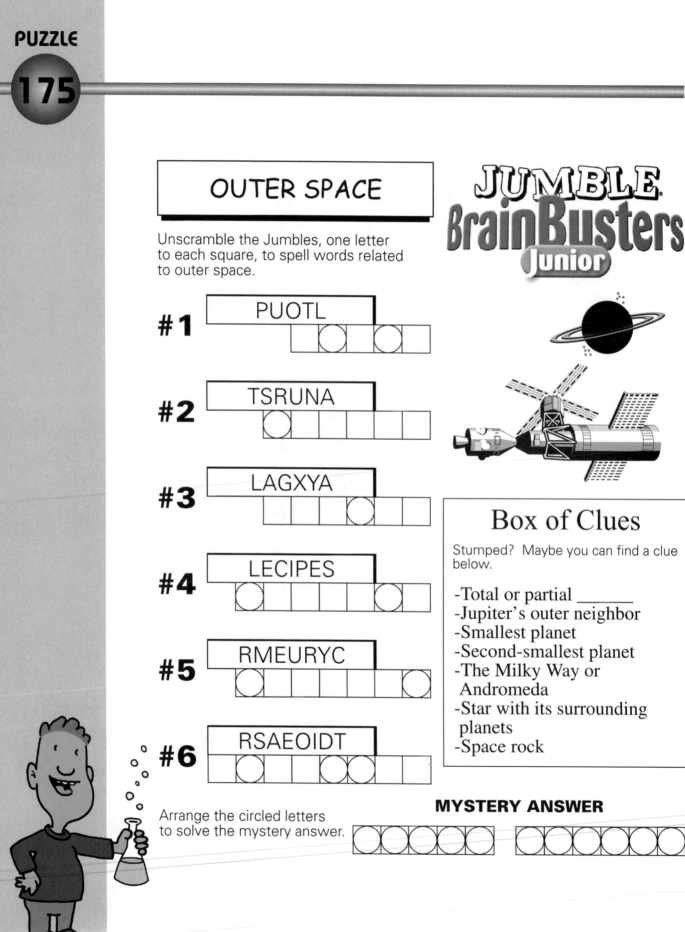

Unscramble the Jumbles, one letter to each square, to spell words related to outer space.

#1
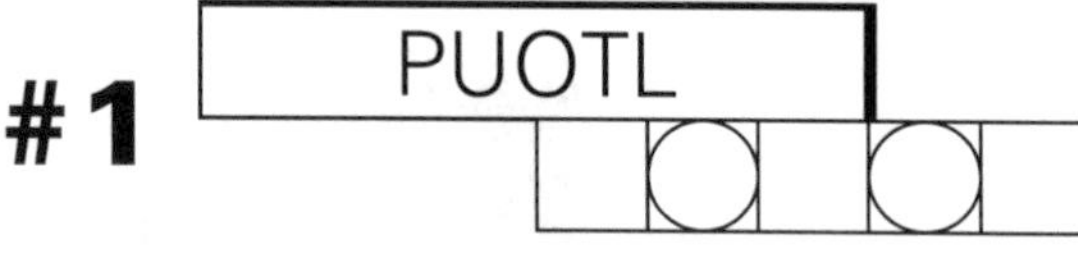

#2

#3
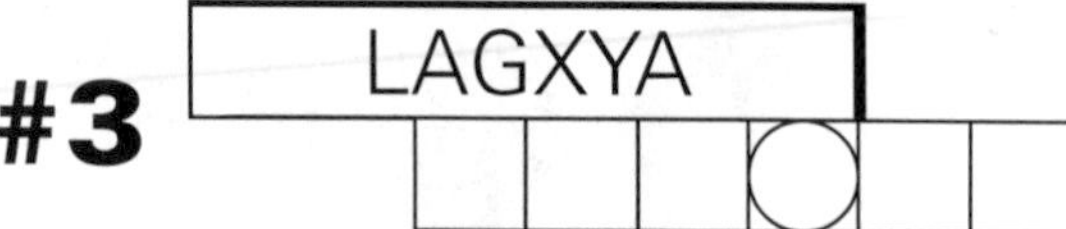

#4
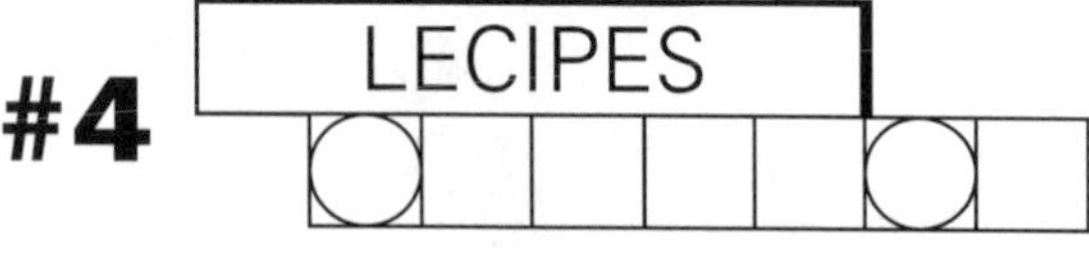

#5
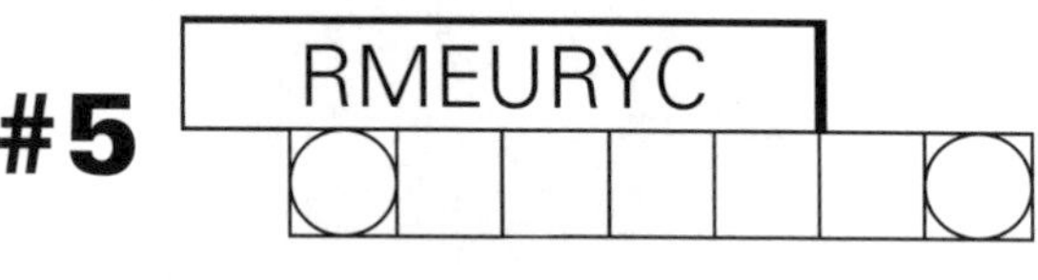

#6
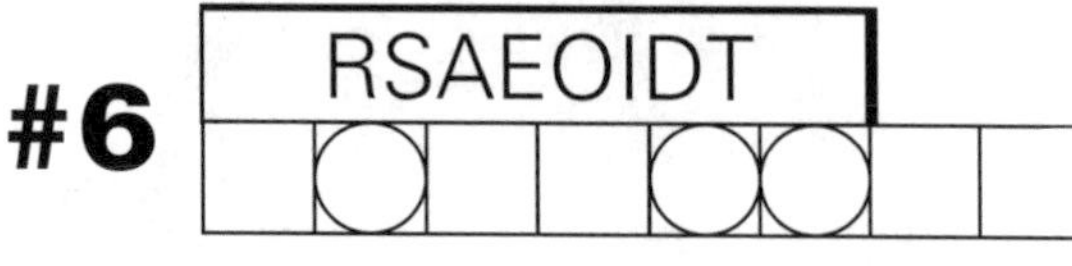

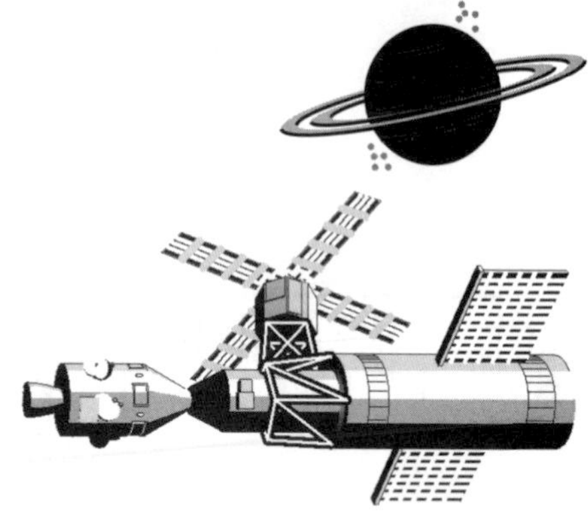

Box of Clues

Stumped? Maybe you can find a clue below.

-Total or partial ______
-Jupiter's outer neighbor
-Smallest planet
-Second-smallest planet
-The Milky Way or Andromeda
-Star with its surrounding planets
-Space rock

Arrange the circled letters to solve the mystery answer.

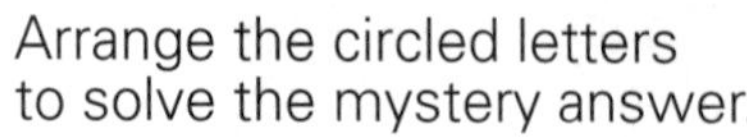

MYSTERY ANSWER

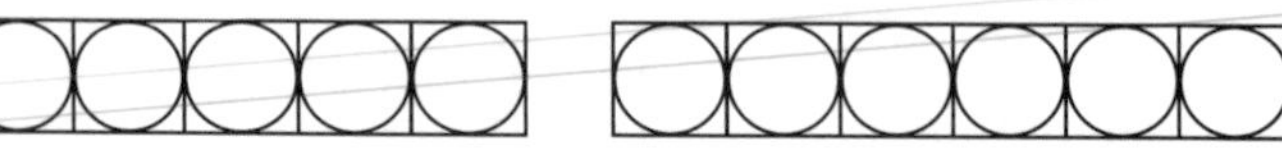

LARGE CITIES

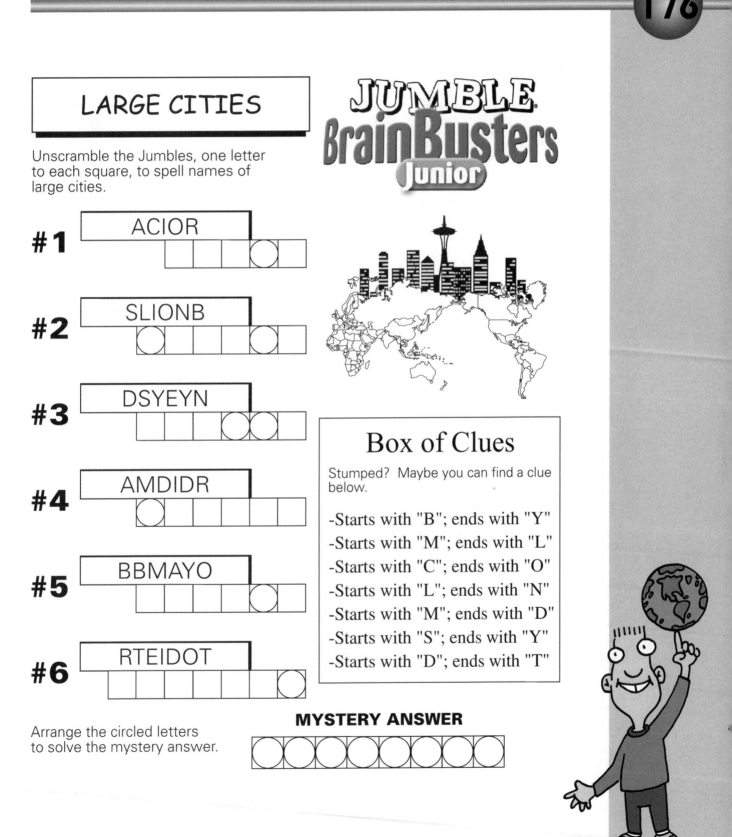

Unscramble the Jumbles, one letter to each square, to spell names of large cities.

#1 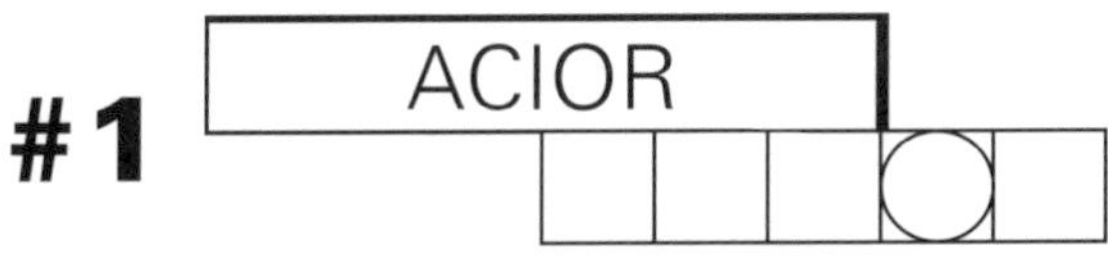

#2 

#3 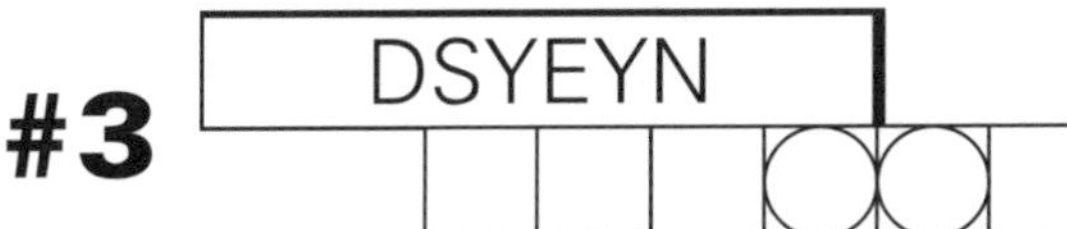

#4 

#5 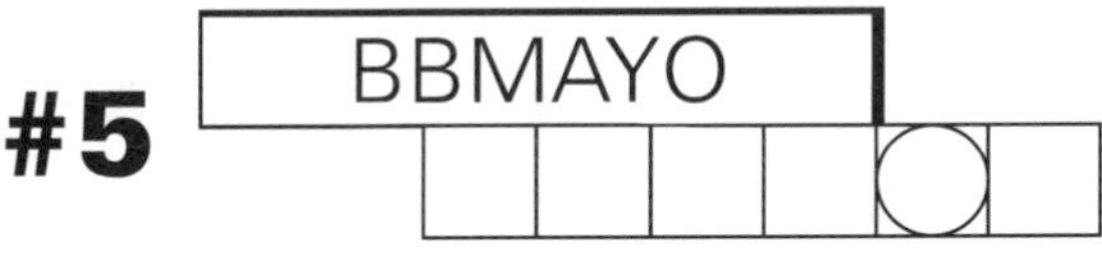

#6 

Box of Clues

Stumped? Maybe you can find a clue below.

-Starts with "B"; ends with "Y"
-Starts with "M"; ends with "L"
-Starts with "C"; ends with "O"
-Starts with "L"; ends with "N"
-Starts with "M"; ends with "D"
-Starts with "S"; ends with "Y"
-Starts with "D"; ends with "T"

Arrange the circled letters to solve the mystery answer.

MYSTERY ANSWER

PUZZLE

177

MATH

JUMBLE BrainBusters Junior

Unscramble the Jumbled letters, one letter to each square, so that each equation is correct.

For example: NONTEOEOW
ONE + ONE = TWO

#1 XSIZSIREOX

□□□ – □□□ = □□□□

#2 ESVZEENVROEENS

□□□□□ – □□□□ = □□□□□

#3 HTETGIGNOEIHE

□□□□□ ÷ □□□□□ = □□□

#4 TGEITEOWSIEHNXT

□□□□□ × □□□ = □□□□□□□

#5 TFYIFFITOYNHNDERDEFU

□□□□□ + □□□□□ = □□□ □□□□□□□

Arrange the circled letters to solve the mystery equation.

MYSTERY EQUATION

□□□ + □□□ = □□□ □□□□□

9×7=63

COUNTRY FLAGS

Unscramble the Jumbles, one letter to each square, to spell names of countries, as suggested by the flags.

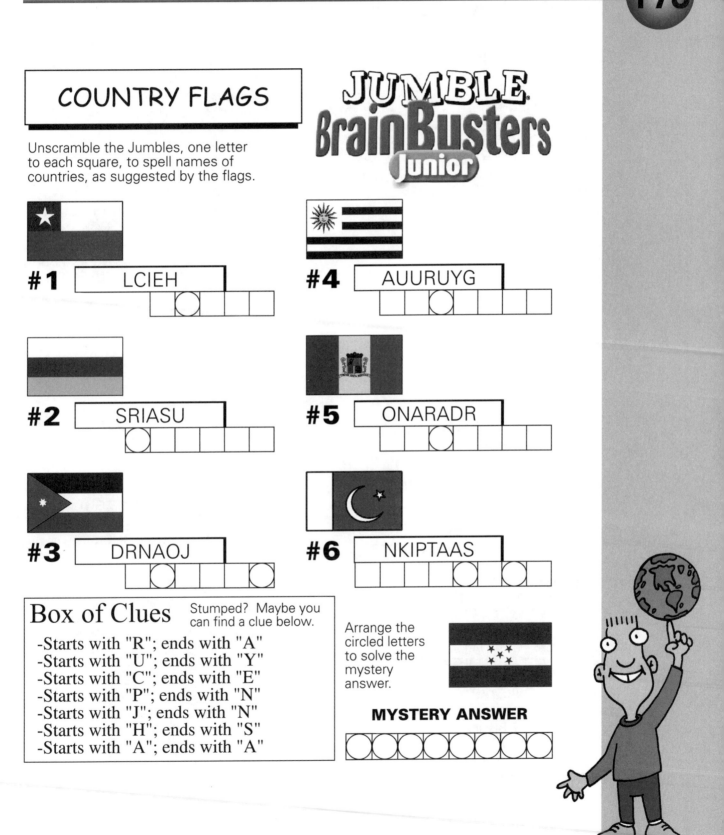

#1 LCIEH

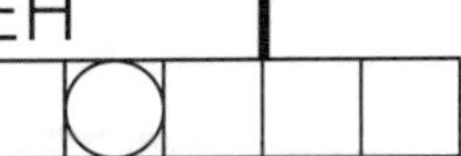

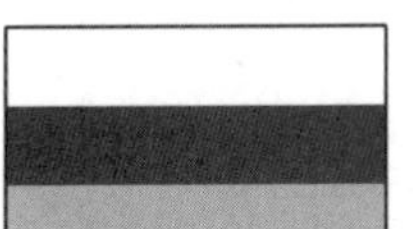

#2 SRIASU

#3 DRNAOJ

#4 AUURUYG

#5 ONARADR

#6 NKIPTAAS

Box of Clues

Stumped? Maybe you can find a clue below.

- -Starts with "R"; ends with "A"
- -Starts with "U"; ends with "Y"
- -Starts with "C"; ends with "E"
- -Starts with "P"; ends with "N"
- -Starts with "J"; ends with "N"
- -Starts with "H"; ends with "S"
- -Starts with "A"; ends with "A"

Arrange the circled letters to solve the mystery answer.

MYSTERY ANSWER

ANSWERS

1. **Jumbles:** #1. FROG #2. SKUNK #3. SHEEP #4. MOOSE #5. TURKEY #6. CHICKEN
Answer: MONKEY

2. **Jumbles:** #1. AUSTIN #2. ALBANY #3. BOSTON #4. RALEIGH #5. LANSING #6. JACKSON
Answer: ATLANTA

3. **Jumbles:** #1. IVORY #2. ADULT #3. UPPER #4. ERROR #5. OUNCE #6. AUTHOR
Answer: ORCHARD

4. **Jumbles:** #1. NIXON #2. REAGAN #3. TAYLOR #4. HOOVER #5. CLINTON
Answer: LINCOLN

5. **Jumbles:** #1. MULE #2. TIGER #3. HIPPO #4. SKUNK #5. MOUSE #6. RABBIT
Answer: ELEPHANT

6. **Jumbles:** #1. RICH #2. DARK #3. GOOD #4. NOISY #5. FRESH #6. AWFUL
Answer: NARROW

7. **Jumbles:** #1. FIVE + FIVE = TEN
#2. TEN – TEN = ZERO
#3. FOUR – TWO = TWO
#4. ONE + SIX = SEVEN
#5. THREE + THREE = SIX
Answer: ONE + THREE = FOUR

8. **Jumbles:** #1. CUBA #2. ITALY #3. JAPAN #4. CANADA #5. FRANCE #6. MEXICO
Answer: POLAND

9. **Jumbles:** #1. BILL #2. CASH #3. LOAN #4. VAULT #5. INVEST #6. CHARGE
Answer: INTEREST

10. **Jumbles:** #1. PLUTO #2. SATURN #3. SYSTEM #4. JUPITER #5. MERCURY
Answer: COMET

11. **Jumbles:** #1. CHOP CROP #2. HAIR FLARE #3. HOUND SOUND #4. MIGHT TIGHT #5. DRESS STRESS
Answer: MATH PATH

12. **Jumbles:** #1. BOISE #2. JUNEAU #3. LINCOLN #4. TRENTON #5. CONCORD #6. RICHMOND
Answer: COLUMBIA

13. **Jumbles:** #1. HAWAII #2. RADIO #3. SOVIET #4. FLIGHT #5. CUBA #6. AFRICA
Answer: CIVIL WAR

14. **Jumbles:** #1. CHEF #2. CHOP #3. KNIFE #4. GRILL #5. BROIL
Answer: RECIPE

15. **Jumbles:** #1. IRON #2. BORON #3. SULFUR #4. CALCIUM #5. HYDROGEN
Answer: MERCURY

16. **Jumbles:** #1. REDS #2. MAGIC #3. KNICKS #4. GIANTS #5. TIGERS #6. EAGLES
Answer: INDIANS

17. **Jumbles:** #1. FERN #2. ROOT #3. TRUNK #4. WATER #5. NEEDLE
Answer: FLOWER

18. **Jumbles:** #1. CUBA #2. INDIA #3. JAPAN #4. RUSSIA #5. FRANCE #6. POLAND
Answer: CANADA

19. **Jumbles:** #1. HARP #2. HORN #3. POLKA #4. BANJO #5. GUITAR
Answer: PIANO

20. **Jumbles:** #1. OHIO #2. IOWA #3. ARIZONA #4. GEORGIA #5. MONTANA #6. KENTUCKY
Answer: MICHIGAN

21. **Jumbles:** #1. BELL #2. BAND #3. BODY #4. BOOM #5. BRICK #6. BLOCK
Answer: BAKERY

22. **Jumbles:** #1. DUCK #2. RHINO #3. ZEBRA #4. GOOSE #5. CAMEL #6. BUFFALO
Answer: RACCOON

23. **Jumbles:** #1. IDAHO #2. MAINE #3. NEVADA #4. KANSAS #5. FLORIDA
Answer: ALASKA

24. **Jumbles:** #1. LONDON #2. HALLEY #3. ITALY #4. JAPAN #5. KOREAN #6. NIXON
Answer: JOHN KENNEDY

25. **Jumbles:** #1. WIND #2. SNOW #3. FOGGY #4. STORM #5. CLOUDY
Answer: SUNNY

26. **Jumbles:** #1. HOUR POWER #2. STAND BLAND #3. JOKER BROKER #4. WEDGE PLEDGE #5. FRIGHT BRIGHT
Answer: FROWN BROWN

27. **Jumbles:** #1. MENU #2. CLICK #3. MODEM #4. DELETE #5. CURSOR #6. MEMORY
Answer: MONITOR

28. **Jumbles:** #1. FOOT #2. TEETH #3. THUMB #4. THROAT #5. MUSCLE
Answer: MOUTH

29. **Jumbles:** #1. EIGHT + TWO = TEN
#2. FOUR + FOUR = EIGHT
#3. NINE + THREE = TWELVE
#4. ONE + TWO + ONE = FOUR
#5. TEN – ZERO + TEN = TWENTY
Answer: ONE + ONE + EIGHT = TEN

30. **Jumbles:** #1. DIRT #2. HOLE #3. FOOT #4. EAGLE #5. TOOTH #6. WORLD
Answer: LETTER

31. **Jumbles:** #1. TRUNK #2. GAUGE #3. WHEEL #4. PICKUP #5. FENDER #6. BUMPER
Answer: ENGINE

32. **Jumbles:** #1. FORD #2. ADAMS #3. CLINTON #4. HARDING #5. JACKSON
Answer: GRANT

33. **Jumbles:** #1. HILL #2. GRASS #3. BEACH #4. WATER #5. VALLEY
Answer: RIVER

34. **Jumbles:** #1. HAIL #2. DAMP #3. FLOOD #4. HUMID #5. CHILLY
Answer: CLOUDY

35. **Jumbles:** #1. SUCH #2. BREEZE #3. DINNER #4. CAKE #5. MONEY
Answer: SOMEDAY

36. **Jumbles:** #1. COOK #2. PILOT #3. GUARD #4. COACH #5. BARBER #6. AUTHOR
Answer: DOCTOR

37. **Jumbles:** #1. DARK #2. DOWN #3. DIGIT #4. DIRTY #5. DRESS #6. DINNER
Answer: DISNEY

38. **Jumbles:** #1. FISH #2. HAWK #3. PANDA #4. LIZARD #5. TURTLE #6. TURKEY
Answer: WALRUS

39. **Jumbles:** #1. FISH #2. BEEF #3. CAKE #4. JELLY #5. APPLE
Answer: CHEESE

40. **Jumbles:** #1. LUNG #2. HAND #3. BONE #4. BRAIN #5. TOOTH
Answer: BLOOD

41. **Jumbles:** #1. BILLS #2. BULLS #3. TWINS #4. EXPOS #5. ROYALS #6. FALCONS
Answer: COWBOYS

42. **Jumbles:** #1. ONE – ONE = ZERO
#2. ONE + THREE = FOUR
#3. SIX – THREE = THREE
#4. FOUR + ZERO = FOUR
#5. FIVE + TWO = SEVEN
Answer: TWO + THREE = FIVE

43. **Jumbles:** #1. LIGHT #2. TRUNK #3. WATER #4. CACTUS #5. BAMBOO
Answer: BRANCH

44. **Jumbles:** #1. INDIA #2. BRAZIL #3. GREECE #4. SWEDEN #5. AUSTRIA #6. PORTUGAL
Answer: RUSSIA

45. **Jumbles:** #1. DRUM #2. PIANO #3. FLUTE #4. TEMPO #5. GUITAR
Answer: TRUMPET

46. **Jumbles:** #1. OHIO #2. NEVADA #3. OREGON #4. FLORIDA #5. ARIZONA #6. MICHIGAN
Answer: COLORADO

47. **Jumbles:** #1. BIRTH #2. FLORIDA #3. WORLD #4. POLAND #5. SHUTTLE #6. RUSSIA
Answer: BERLIN WALL

48. **Jumbles:** #1. FRUIT #2. FUDGE #3. DONUT #4. TURKEY #5. BANANA #6. POPCORN
Answer: PUDDING

49. **Jumbles:** #1. BIRD #2. COBB #3. DITKA #4. AARON #5. JACKSON #6. MONTANA
Answer: JORDAN

50. **Jumbles:** #1. BONE #2. ANKLE #3. PULSE #4. CHEST #5. STOMACH #6. ABDOMEN
Answer: MUSCLE

51. **Jumbles:** #1. PILL #2. PULL #3. ERROR #4. SMELL #5. PRETTY #6. BUBBLE
Answer: PEPPER

52. **Jumbles:** #1. SUIT #2. SOCK #3. SHIRT #4. PANTS #5. SCARF #6. BLOUSE
Answer: OUTFIT

53. **Jumbles:** #1. CHILE #2. BRAZIL #3. TURKEY #4. MEXICO #5. IRELAND #6. ENGLAND
Answer: GREECE

54. **Jumbles:** #1. LAND #2. CAVE #3. ORBIT #4. SWAMP #5. ISLAND #6. JUNGLE
Answer: MOUNTAIN

55. **Jumbles:** #1. INDIA #2. EGYPT #3. GREECE #4. PANAMA #5. BOLIVIA #6. BELGIUM
Answer: LIBERIA

56. **Jumbles:** #1. RICH POOR
#2. MILD CHILLY #3. BASE SUMMIT
#4. HAPPY GLOOMY
#5. DETACH COMBINE
Answer: CALM STORMY

57. **Jumbles:** #1. FIGHT #2. RUGBY #3. SERIES #4. ROOKIE #5. RUNNER #6. DEFENSE
Answer: REFEREE

58. **Jumbles:** #1. HORN #2. MENU #3. WOOD #4. CHILD #5. PAPER #6. STORY
Answer: COUNTRY

59. **Jumbles:** #1. HELENA #2. RALEIGH #3. PHOENIX #4. CONCORD #5. BISMARCK #6. HONOLULU
Answer: LANSING

60. **Jumbles:** #1. OBEY #2. EJECT #3. UNION #4. INFANT #5. ATTACK #6. INCOME
Answer: OBJECT

61. **Jumbles:** #1. HALF #2. PUNT #3. KICKER #4. JERSEY #5. HUDDLE #6. FUMBLE
Answer: HELMET

62. **Jumbles:** #1. FISH #2. FULL #3. FIFTH #4. FLUNK #5. FUSSY #6. FROWN
Answer: FOSSIL

63. **Jumbles:** #1. DUCK #2. DOVE #3. ROBIN #4. EAGLE #5. CHICKEN #6. PEACOCK
Answer: PENGUIN

64. **Jumbles:** #1. FRENCH #2. EGYPT #3. GERMANY #4. LAUNCH #5. POCKET #6. BRITISH
Answer: STEAM ENGINE

65. **Jumbles:** #1. DUCK #2. MULE #3. HIPPO #4. EAGLE #5. GRIZZLY #6. PANTHER
Answer: MONKEY

66. **Jumbles:** #1. POUNDS #2. SECOND #3. EVENING #4. REFEREE #5. HIGHWAY
Answer: AVENUE

67. **Jumbles:** #1. TWO × TWO = FOUR
#2. TWO × FOUR = EIGHT
#3. ONE × SEVEN = SEVEN
#4. THREE × THREE = NINE
#5. FOUR × THREE = TWELVE
Answer: TWO × TWO = FOUR × ONE

68. **Jumbles:** #1. POLK #2. NIXON #3. HAYES #4. TAYLOR #5. REAGAN #6. HARDING
Answer: KENNEDY

69. **Jumbles:** #1. FULL #2. BOLD #3. THICK #4. HEAVY #5. YOUNG #6. BRIGHT
Answer: CHUBBY

70. **Jumbles:** #1. OTTER #2. MOOSE #3. COUGAR #4. BABOON #5. WEASEL #6. GORILLA
Answer: WALRUS

71. **Jumbles:** #1. BANK #2. LOAN #3. VALUE #4. POUND #5. CHARGE #6. WALLET
Answer: DOLLAR

72. **Jumbles:** #1. IOWA #2. MAINE #3. ALASKA #4. VERMONT #5. MONTANA #6. NEBRASKA
Answer: ALABAMA

73. **Jumbles:** #1. ZINC #2. XENON #3. COBALT #4. COPPER #5. HELIUM
Answer: PLATINUM

74. **Jumbles:** #1. LOOK GLANCE
#2. PLAN SCHEME #3. SIGHT VISION
#4. ELECT CHOOSE
#5. ABRUPT SUDDEN
Answer: ILL SICK

75. **Jumbles:** #1. BASE #2. FOUL #3. CATCH #4. BLOCK #5. HOMER #6. TACKLE
Answer: FOOTBALL

76. **Jumbles:** #1. TWO + TWO = FOUR
#2. ZERO + ZERO = ZERO
#3. SIX + THREE = NINE
#4. TWENTY – TEN = TEN
#5. NINE + TWO = ELEVEN
Answer: FIVE + ONE = SIX

77. **Jumbles:** #1. WARM #2. FLAKE #3. SLUSH #4. WINDY #5. HUMID #6. STORM
Answer: THUNDER

78. **Jumbles:** #1. HIGH #2. WILD #3. THICK #4. BASIC #5. ALONE #6. SLEEPY
Answer: CHILLY

79. **Jumbles:** #1. ORBIT #2. COMET #3. SATURN #4. GALAXY #5. URANUS #6. JUPITER
Answer: MERCURY

80. **Jumbles:** #1. HAYES #2. ARTHUR #3. REAGAN #4. WILSON #5. LINCOLN #6. JOHNSON
Answer: HARRISON

81. **Jumbles:** #1. JAIL #2. JUNK #3. JEEP #4. JELLY #5. JEANS #6. JUDGE
Answer: JUNGLE

82. **Jumbles:** #1. HEAD #2. NECK #3. FOOT #4. JOINT #5. KIDNEY #6. MUSCLE
Answer: SKELETON

83. **Jumbles:** #1. DUNK #2. ALLEY #3. CATCH #4. ERROR #5. GLOVE #6. COACH
Answer: HOCKEY

84. **Jumbles:** #1. HIPPO #2. LIZARD #3. RABBIT #4. GRIZZLY #5. GIRAFFE #6. PENGUIN
Answer: ALLIGATOR

85. **Jumbles:** #1. ZERO + TWO = TWO
#2. ONE × ONE = ONE
#3. SEVEN – FIVE = TWO
#4. FIVE + FIVE = TEN
#5. EIGHT × ONE = EIGHT
Answer: TWO × FIVE = TEN

86. **Jumbles:** #1. BYTE #2. DATA #3. MOUSE #4. FLOPPY #5. PROGRAM #6. WINDOWS
Answer: SOFTWARE

87. **Jumbles:** #1. ITALY #2. FRANCE #3. SWEDEN #4. IRELAND #5. ROMANIA #6. PORTUGAL
Answer: AUSTRIA

88. **Jumbles:** #1. SEED #2. BULB #3. ROOT #4. BAMBOO #5. NURSERY
Answer: BLOSSOM

89. **Jumbles:** #1. HOOD #2. RADIO #3. ENGINE #4. TRAFFIC #5. BATTERY #6. MUFFLER
Answer: FENDER

90. **Jumbles:** #1. INDIA #2. CANADA #3. POLAND #4. BOLIVIA #5. IRELAND #6. BERMUDA
Answer: PANAMA

91. **Jumbles:** #1. BIRTH #2. SEWING #3. CAMERA #4. ATLANTIC #5. SOVIET #6. OZONE
Answer: VIETNAM

92. **Jumbles:** #1. KING #2. KNOT #3. KNOW #4. KNIFE #5. KNOCK #6. KNIGHT
Answer: KITTEN

93. **Jumbles:** #1. COPPER #2. COBALT #3. SODIUM #4. SILICON #5. CALCIUM
Answer: POTASSIUM

94. **Jumbles:** #1. STRIKE #2. DOUBLE #3. DUGOUT #4. PITCHER #5. CATCHER #6. DIAMOND
Answer: POSITION

95. **Jumbles:** #1. KNOT #2. MAZE #3. JUICE #4. CABIN #5. ADULT #6. CRIME
Answer: JACKET

96. **Jumbles:** #1. ONE – ONE = FIVE – FIVE
#2. EIGHT – SIX = SIX – FOUR
#3. TWO + FOUR = TWELVE ÷ TWO
#4. SIX ÷ THREE = FIVE – THREE
#5. TWELVE – TWO = FIVE × TWO
Answer: SIX – FOUR = TWELVE ÷ SIX

97. **Jumbles:** #1. DULL BRIGHT #2. FACT FICTION #3. HARSH GENTLE #4. ROUGH SMOOTH #5. FINAL INITIAL
Answer: SOFT HARD

98. **Jumbles:** #1. BELT #2. SOCK #3. JEANS #4. DRESS #5. FABRIC #6. SWEATER
Answer: JACKET

99. **Jumbles:** #1. DIMLY #2. RUDELY #3. SLOWLY #4. LIGHTLY #5. MONTHLY
Answer: LOUDLY

100. **Jumbles:** #1. ZINC #2. IRON #3. GOLD #4. OXYGEN #5. COBALT #6. RADIUM
Answer: NITROGEN

101. **Jumbles:** #1. SONG #2. BRAND #3. ANYWAY #4. BIRDS #5. WORM
Answer: SONGBIRD

102. **Jumbles:** #1. FAIR #2. MILD #3. FRONT #4. BREEZE #5. RAINBOW #6. FORECAST
Answer: TWISTER

103. **Jumbles:** #1. CITY #2. FARM #3. FABLE #4. PENNY #5. ENGINE #6. DOLLAR
Answer: COFFEE

104. **Jumbles:** #1. OBOE #2. CHORD #3. VIOLIN #4. GUITAR #5. MELODY
Answer: CLARINET

105. **Jumbles:** #1. SUNDAY #2. WEIGHT #3. CAPTAIN #4. PACKAGE #5. TUESDAY
Answer: AUGUST

106. **Jumbles:** #1. AUSTIN #2. PIERRE #3. HELENA #4. ALBANY #5. BOSTON #6. JACKSON
Answer: TOPEKA

107. **Jumbles:** #1. NICE #2. NAVY #3. NECK #4. NOUN #5. NIPPY #6. NOISY
Answer: NAPKIN

108. **Jumbles:** #1. LOPEZ #2. BENCH #3. WOODS #4. AUSTIN #5. AGASSI #6. GRETZKY
Answer: PAYTON

109. **Jumbles:** #1. HAIR #2. CHEST #3. TOOTH #4. BLOOD #5. MOUTH #6. ARTERY
Answer: STOMACH

110. **Jumbles:** #1. TOLL #2. MALL #3. FUNNY #4. CARRY #5. ARROW #6. COMMA
Answer: COMMON

111. **Jumbles:** #1. TAMPA #2. OMAHA #3. RALEIGH #4. JACKSON #5. RICHMOND
Answer: CHICAGO

112. **Jumbles:** #1. FAKE PHONY #2. FIND DETECT #3. TRIP JOURNEY #4. BLOCK HINDER #5. LAUGH GIGGLE
Answer: FAIL FLUNK

113. **Jumbles:** #1. CHILE #2. KENYA #3. JAPAN #4. TURKEY #5. FINLAND #6. PORTUGAL
Answer: THAILAND

114. **Jumbles:** #1. ROAD #2. ROOT #3. RIVER #4. RANCH #5. ROBOT #6. ROUND
Answer: RODENT

115. **Jumbles:** #1. GRAVY #2. BACON #3. TOMATO #4. LETTUCE #5. MUSTARD #6. SANDWICH
Answer: HAMBURGER

116. **Jumbles:** #1. PANDA #2. CAMEL #3. MOOSE #4. BEAVER #5. GOPHER #6. RACCOON
Answer: POLAR BEAR

117. **Jumbles:** #1. BOSTON #2. DETROIT #3. SEATTLE #4. ATLANTA #5. ORLANDO
Answer: DALLAS

118. **Jumbles:** #1. ISSUE #2. EGYPT #3. APRON #4. UNEVEN #5. AUGUST #6. OXYGEN
Answer: EXPRESS

119. **Jumbles:** #1. CROW #2. GOOSE #3. TURKEY #4. CANARY #5. OSTRICH #6. PEACOCK
Answer: PIGEON

120. **Jumbles:** #1. BIKE HIKE #2. BRICK TRICK #3. CHECK WRECK #4. CRIME PRIME #5. EAGLE BEAGLE
Answer: TRACK CRACK

121. **Jumbles:** #1. CASH #2. VALUE #3. PENNY #4. FRANC #5. COPPER #6. RECEIPT
Answer: CURRENCY

122. **Jumbles:** #1. SIX – SIX = ZERO
#2. TWO × FOUR = EIGHT
#3. EIGHT ÷ TWO = FOUR
#4. TEN × THREE = THIRTY
#5. FIFTY ÷ TEN = FIVE
Answer: EIGHT + EIGHT = SIXTEEN

123. **Jumbles:** #1. LUNAR #2. PLUTO #3. HUBBLE #4. GALAXY #5. ECLIPSE #6. NEPTUNE
Answer: SATURN

124. **Jumbles:** #1. MIAMI #2. BOSTON #3. PHOENIX #4. OAKLAND #5. PORTLAND #6. HARTFORD
Answer: DETROIT

125. **Jumbles:** #1. HARD #2. HUGE #3. LONG #4. SOFT #5. HAPPY #6. CLEVER
Answer: CLOUDY

126. **Jumbles:** #1. IODINE #2. COBALT #3. COPPER #4. RADIUM #5. SILICON
Answer: CALCIUM

127. **Jumbles:** #1. CHILE #2. EGYPT #3. BRAZIL #4. PANAMA #5. NORWAY #6. ENGLAND
Answer: NEW ZEALAND

128. **Jumbles:** #1. SAFE #2. SKULL #3. SALAD #4. SCARY #5. SMELL #6. SMOKE
Answer: SUMMER

129. **Jumbles:** #1. CRAB #2. CROW #3. HIPPO #4. PANDA #5. LIZARD #6. TURKEY
Answer: CHICKEN

130. **Jumbles:** #1. NEWTON #2. MOZART #3. GERMANY #4. EVEREST #5. AFRICA #6. KUWAIT
Answer: VIETNAM WAR

131. **Jumbles:** #1. OBOE #2. PIANO #3. CHORD #4. MUSIC #5. VIOLIN
Answer: PICCOLO

132. **Jumbles:** #1. BALL #2. PUCK #3. ALLEY #4. COACH #5. MATCH #6. TRIPLE
Answer: PRACTICE

133. **Jumbles:** #1. LAVA #2. SAND #3. GRASS #4. ISLAND #5. VALLEY #6. SURFACE
Answer: GLACIER

134. **Jumbles:** #1. FORD #2. NIXON #3. ARTHUR #4. WILSON #5. JACKSON #6. HARRISON
Answer: JOHNSON

135. **Jumbles:** #1. HAIR #2. BRAIN #3. BLOOD #4. MOUTH #5. KIDNEY #6. TONGUE
Answer: EARDRUM

136. **Jumbles:** #1. WILD #2. WELL #3. WALL #4. WANT #5. WARM #6. WHEEL
Answer: WAITER

137. **Jumbles:** #1. PASS #2. DRAFT #3. GUARD #4. BENCH #5. PRESS #6. CLOCK
Answer: BASKET

138. **Jumbles:** #1. IDAHO #2. MAINE #3. ALASKA #4. VERMONT #5. MICHIGAN #6. MARYLAND
Answer: VIRGINIA

139. **Jumbles:** #1. SICK #2. YOUR #3. DIGEST #4. HAIR #5. CHEST #6. COMMON
Answer: SAYINGS

140. **Jumbles:** #1. CHEF #2. JUDGE #3. COACH #4. WAITER #5. JANITOR #6. PLUMBER
Answer: MECHANIC

141. **Jumbles:** #1. MIAMI #2. SYDNEY #3. LONDON #4. WARSAW #5. CHICAGO #6. TORONTO
Answer: MOSCOW

142. **Jumbles:** #1. MITTEN #2. SLACKS #3. SHORTS #4. TUXEDO #5. UNIFORM #6. PAJAMAS
Answer: SHOELACE

143. **Jumbles:** #1. WEIGHT #2. TUESDAY #3. MANAGER #4. FEBRUARY #5. NOVEMBER
Answer: FRIDAY

144. **Jumbles:** #1. TYLER #2. HAYES #3. GRANT #4. HOOVER #5. LINCOLN #6. CLINTON
Answer: TAYLOR

145. **Jumbles:** #1. TINY #2. WARM #3. TOXIC #4. SHORT #5. ACTIVE #6. RANDOM
Answer: COMMON

146. **Jumbles:** #1. MOLE #2. OTTER #3. STORK #4. BEAVER #5. GORILLA #6.BUFFALO
Answer: MUSKRAT

147. **Jumbles:** #1. BOISE #2. TOPEKA #3. LANSING #4. AUGUST #5. TRENTON #6. CONCORD
Answer: AUSTIN

148. **Jumbles:** #1. MITT #2. SEASON #3. PITCHER #4. DEFENSE #5. UNIFORM #6. MANAGER
Answer: INNING

149. **Jumbles:** #1. CUBA #2. SYRIA #3. JORDAN #4. JAMAICA #5. ECUADOR #6. COLUMBIA
Answer: CAMBODIA

150. **Jumbles:** #1. SUNNY #2. DEGREE #3. CLIMATE #4. DROUGHT #5. BLIZZARD #6. MOISTURE
Answer: LIGHTNING

151. **Jumbles:** #1. DALLAS #2. MOBILE #3. SEATTLE #4. BUFFALO #5. MEMPHIS #6. PORTLAND
Answer: HOUSTON

152. **Jumbles:** #1. RIVER #2. GRASS #3. GLOBE #4. VALLEY #5. JUNGLE #6. SEASON
Answer: GEYSER

153. **Jumbles:** #1. YELL #2. YOLK #3. YOGA #4. YAWN #5. YIELD #6. YOUTH
Answer: YELLOW

154. **Jumbles:** #1. AMAZON #2. PACIFIC #3. BOLIVIA #4. CARACAS #5. ECUADOR #6. ATLANTIC
Answer: RAIN FOREST

155. **Jumbles:** #1. TELL #2. BALL #3. BERRY #4. WORRY #5. KITTEN #6. STRESS
Answer: BETTER

156. **Jumbles:** #1. PIZZA #2. SALAD #3. BACON #4. PICKLE #5. SHRIMP #6. WAFFLE
Answer: SANDWICH

157. **Jumbles:** #1. PACIFIC #2. URANUS #3. RUSSIA #4. ZEALAND #5. ATLANTIC #6. COMPACT
Answer: PANAMA CANAL

158. **Jumbles:** #1. OREGON #2. FLORIDA #3. GEORGIA #4. WYOMING #5. VIRGINIA #6. COLORADO
Answer: DELAWARE

159. **Jumbles:** #1. HEAD #2. BRAIN #3. GLAND #4. KIDNEY #5. THROAT #6. ENAMEL
Answer: ABDOMEN

160. **Jumbles:** #1. LIBYA #2. CHILE #3. MEXICO #4. NORWAY #5. BELGIUM #6. GERMANY
Answer: COLOMBIA

161. **Jumbles:** #1. PLUS MINUS #2. LOUD HUSHED #3. VANISH APPEAR #4. REJECT ACCEPT #5. FORMAL CASUAL
Answer: LOSS PROFIT

162. **Jumbles:** #1. FRANCE #2. GREECE #3. POLAND #4. SWEDEN #5. HUNGARY #6. GERMANY
Answer: ENGLAND

163. **Jumbles:** #1. HUSKY #2. BOXER #3. SPANIEL #4. BULLDOG #5. SHEPHERD
Answer: HOUND

164. **Jumbles:** #1. BERLIN #2. DALLAS #3. HAVANA #4. DENVER #5. WARSAW #6. MOSCOW
Answer: MADRID

165. **Jumbles:** #1. LIGHT #2. ORBIT #3. COMET #4. URANUS #5. GRAVITY #6. MERCURY
Answer: UNIVERSE

166. **Jumbles:** #1. KENYA #2. EGYPT #3. FRANCE #4. ECUADOR #5. VIETNAM #6. MOROCCO
Answer: DENMARK

167. **Jumbles:** #1. HUGE GRAND #2. CHILD YOUTH #3. DIRTY GRIMY #4. JOLLY HAPPY #5. BOTCH FUMBLE
Answer: HIGH LOFTY

168. **Jumbles:** #1. BASE #2. WALK #3. DRIVER #4. BOXING #5. PUTTER #6. LEAGUE
Answer: WRESTLING

169. **Jumbles:** #1. OVEN #2. EIGHT #3. APPLE #4. INNING #5. UNFAIR #6. AMAZON
Answer: IMPROVE

170. **Jumbles:** #1. FINCH #2. STORK #3. MACAW #4. PIGEON #5. VULTURE #6. CARDINAL
Answer: FLAMINGO

171. **Jumbles:** #1. GLADLY #2. SOFTLY #3. WEEKLY #4. PROUDLY #5. BRIGHTLY
Answer: BOLDLY

172. **Jumbles:** #1. IODINE #2. SULFUR #3. OXYGEN #4. HELIUM #5. MERCURY #6. NITROGEN
Answer: SODIUM

173. **Jumbles:** #1. TAFT #2. FORD #3. GRANT #4. HOOVER #5. KENNEDY #6. JACKSON
Answer: REAGAN

174. **Jumbles:** #1. SECOND #2. CAPTAIN #3. JANUARY #4. FREEWAY #5. DECEMBER
Answer: AFRICA

175. **Jumbles:** #1. PLUTO #2. SATURN #3. GALAXY #4. ECLIPSE #5. MERCURY #6. ASTEROID
Answer: SOLAR SYSTEM

176. **Jumbles:** #1. CAIRO #2. LISBON #3. SYDNEY #4. MADRID #5. BOMBAY #6. DETROIT
Answer: MONTREAL

177. **Jumbles:** #1. SIX – SIX = ZERO
#2. SEVEN – ZERO = SEVEN
#3. EIGHT ÷ EIGHT = ONE
#4. EIGHT × TWO = SIXTEEN
#5. FIFTY + FIFTY = ONE HUNDRED
Answer: SIX + SIX = ONE DOZEN

178. **Jumbles:** #1. CHILE #2. RUSSIA #3. JORDAN #4. URUGUAY #5. ANDORRA #6. PAKISTAN
Answer: HONDURAS

★★★★ JUMBLE® NEWS ★★★★

JUMBLE® is now available as an all new family game!

For two or more players ages eight to adult, JUMBLE® contains a game board, 70 letter tiles, 50 token clues, 600 JUMBLE® puzzles, four playing pieces, one special color-coded die, a one-minute timer, and a letter storage tray.

The scoop on the new game.

It's scrambled. It's surprising. It's JUMBLE®, the most recognized scrambled word game to millions of players . . . and it's now a fast paced, brainteasing family board game from Cadaco!

Educational and fun, the JUMBLE® game requires the same mind-stretching thought as the ever popular newspaper puzzles. With three levels of difficulty, JUMBLE® is perfect for adults and kids to play together. Each JUMBLE® puzzle has three clues to help players solve it . . . but they have to be quick or time will run out! Two-sided, color-coded JUMBLE® cards make play easy to follow.

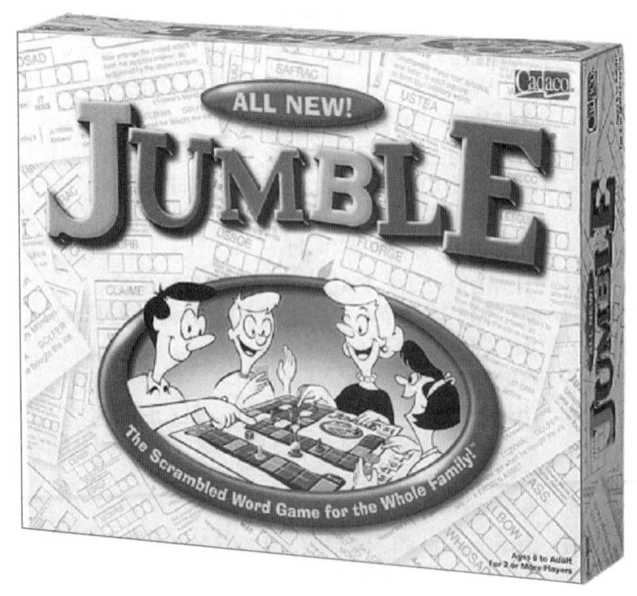

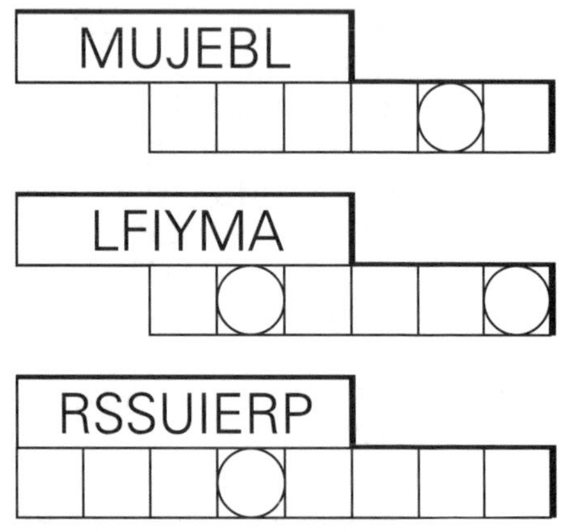

To get the all-new Jumble® game for your family, visit a local game retailer or contact Cadaco customer service at 1-800-621-5426 for a location near you.
(You can also order on-line at www.jumble.com.)